ROUTLEDGE HANDBOOK OF FREEDOM OF RELIGION OR BELIEF

Freedom of religion is an issue of universal interest and scope. However, in the last two centuries at least, the philosophical, religious and legal terms of the question have been largely defined in the West. In an increasingly global world, widening our knowledge of this right's roots in different cultural and legal systems becomes a priority. This Handbook seeks to attain this goal through a better understanding of the historical roots and expressions of the right to freedom of religion on the one hand and, on the other, of its theological background in different religious traditions. History and theology provide the setting for the analysis of the politics of freedom of religion, that is, how this right is used in the context of the dialogue/confrontation between countries placed in different cultural regions of the world, and of the legal strategies and tools that have been developed and are employed to protect and foster the right to freedom of religion. Behind these legal and political strategies, there is an ongoing debate about the nature of this right, whose main features are explored in the final section.

Global, historical and interdisciplinary in approach, this book studies the new relevance of freedom of religion worldwide and develops suitable categories to analyze and understand the role that freedom of religion can play in managing religious and cultural diversity in our societies. Authored by experts, through the contributions collected in these chapters, scholars and students will be able to broaden and deepen their knowledge of the right to freedom of religion and to develop the ability to go beyond the borders of the different cultural environments in which this right took shape and developed.

Silvio Ferrari is Professor of Law at the University of Milan, Italy.

Mark Hill QC is Associate Professor at the Centre for Law and Religion, Cardiff University; University of Pretoria; Notre Dame University Law School, Sydney; and King's College, London. He lectures in law at the Open University.

Arif A. Jamal is Associate Professor and Deputy Director of the Centre for Asian Legal Studies at the Faculty of Law, National University of Singapore.

Rossella Bottoni is Associate Professor of Law and Religion at the Faculty of Law of the University of Trento, Italy.

ROUTLEDGE HANDBOOK OF FREEDOM OF RELIGION OR BELIEF

Edited by
Silvio Ferrari, Mark Hill QC,
Arif A. Jamal, and Rossella Bottoni

Routledge
Taylor & Francis Group
LONDON AND NEW YORK

First published 2021
by Routledge
2 Park Square, Milton Park, Abingdon, Oxon OX14 4RN

and by Routledge
52 Vanderbilt Avenue, New York, NY 10017

Routledge is an imprint of the Taylor & Francis Group, an informa business.

British Library Cataloguing-in-Publication Data
A catalogue record for this book is available from the British Library.

Library of Congress Cataloging-in-Publication Data
Names: Ferrari, Silvio, editor. | Hill, Mark, 1965- editor. | Jamal, Arif A., editor. | Bottoni, Rossella, editor.
Title: Routledge handbook of freedom of religion or belief / edited by Silvio Ferrari, Mark Hill, Arif A Jamal, and Rossella Bottoni.
Description: Milton Park, Abingdon, Oxon ; New York, NY : Routledge, 2021. | Includes bibliographical references and index.
Identifiers: LCCN 2020027646 (print) | LCCN 2020027647 (ebook) | ISBN 9781138301290 (hardback) | ISBN 9780203732625 (ebook)
Subjects: LCSH: Freedom of religion (International law) | Freedom of religion. | Religious tolerance. | Religion and law.
Classification: LCC K3258 .R68 2021 (print) | LCC K3258 (ebook) | DDC 342.08/52--dc23
LC record available at https://lccn.loc.gov/2020027646
LC ebook record available at https://lccn.loc.gov/2020027647

ISBN: 978-1-138-30129-0 (hbk)
ISBN: 978-0-203-73262-5 (ebk)

Typeset in Bembo
by MPS Limited, Dehradun

TABLE OF CONTENTS

LIST OF CONTRIBUTORS

Idowu A. Akinloye is a Postdoctoral Fellow, Faculty of Law, Rhodes University, Grahamstown, South Africa.

Rossella Bottoni is Associate Professor of Law and Religion at the Faculty of Law of the University of Trento, Italy.

Eva Brems is Senior Full Professor of Human Rights Law and Head of the Human Rights Centre at Ghent University.

Patrice Brodeur is Associate Professor, Institute of Religious Studies, University of Montreal, Canada.

Peter G. Danchin is Professor of Law and Director of the International and Comparative Law Program, University of Maryland School of Law, USA.

Norman Doe is Professor of Law at the School of Law and Politics and Director of the Centre for Law and Religion at Cardiff University, UK.

Laura Dudley Jenkins is Professor and Graduate Director of Political Science, University of Cincinnati, USA.

Silvio Ferrari is Professor of Law at the University of Milan, Italy.

Mark Hill QC is Associate Professor at the Centre for Law and Religion, Cardiff University; University of Pretoria; Notre Dame University Law School, Sydney; and King's College, London. He lectures in Law at the Open University.

Arif A. Jamal is Associate Professor and Deputy Director of the Centre for Asian Legal Studies at the Faculty of Law, National University of Singapore.

Matthew LaGrone is Assistant Program Head at the University of Guelph-Humber, Toronto, Canada.

Laurens Lavrysen is a postdoctoral research fellow at the Human Rights Centre of Ghent University, Belgium.

David Little is a Research Fellow at the Berkley Center for Religion, Peace & World Affairs, Georgetown University, USA.

Jaclyn L. Neo is Associate Professor and Director of the Centre for Asian Legal Studies at the Faculty of Law, National University of Singapore.

Martin Ramstedt is Scientific Director of the International Institute for the Sociology of Law, in Oñati, Basque Country, Spain, and Fellow of Ikerbasque/Basque Foundation for Science.

Gerhard Robbers is Professor Emeritus of Public Law, University of Trier, Germany.

Caroline Sägesser is Researcher at the Centre de recherche et d'information socio-politiques and at the Centre interdisciplinaire d'étude des religions et de la laïcité, Université Libre de Bruxelles, Brussels, Belgium.

Wael Saleh is Associate Professor, Institute of International Studies of Montreal, University of Quebec, Canada.

Ahmed Salisu Garba is Dean of the Faculty of Law at Bauchi State University, Gadau, Nigeria.

Benjamin Schonthal is Associate Professor of Buddhism and Asian Religions, University of Otago, New Zealand.

Arvind Sharma is Birks Professor in Comparative Religion at the School of Religious Studies, McGill University, Canada.

Kevin YL Tan is Adjunct Professor at the Faculty of Law, National University of Singapore and at the S Rajaratnam School of International Studies, Nanyang Technological University, Singapore.

Kristina M. Teater is Adjunct Assistant Professor of Political Science at the University of Cincinnati, USA.

Johan D. van der Vyver is I. T. Cohen Professor of International Law and Human Rights at Emory University, USA.

John Witte Jr. is Robert W. Woodruff Professor of Law, McDonald Distinguished Professor of Religion, and director of the Center for the Study of Law and Religion at Emory University, USA.

Introduction

1

Locating the right to freedom of religion or belief across time and territory

Mark Hill QC

A generation ago, the concept of a handbook was virtually unknown in the academy. Published scholarship came in the form of textbooks, innovative monographs, and introductory works for students, or casebooks of materials with commentary.[1] The term 'handbook' was generally reserved for dull and anodyne publications, such as the owner's manual for a car or electric appliance or a turgid reference work containing nothing more than lists of data. But the handbook has gradually earned its place in the teaching environment of the twenty-first century as a repository for authoritative and original thinking on subjects of pressing social concern, on which differing views can be espoused with integrity.[2] To date, however, there has been no handbook published specifically addressing the right to freedom of religion or belief. This volume aims to be comprehensive but not necessarily exhaustive; authoritative but never polemical; and accessible but not simplistic. Traditionally, studies of religious freedom have tended to be law-focused, and many scholars and practitioners ignore the historical and theological foundations of the idea of religious liberty, as well as the existence of different histories and theologies. The innovative profile of this unique *Handbook* is its global, historical and interdisciplinary (law, theology, political science, etc.) approach. The *Handbook* aims to stimulate creative and refreshing ways to (re)think the role of religious freedom in the contemporary world.

Likewise, the topic of freedom of religion or belief has gained a currency in the political and social discourse of the current age which was far less visible in the past. While some see the concept of human rights as having its *fons et origo* in the doctrine and practices of the Judeo-Christian tradition, others see them firmly in the post-war rise of secularism, articulated in international instruments such as the Universal Declaration of Human Rights. This *Handbook* considers the history of the right to freedom of religion or belief, but not from exclusively Western and largely Christian perspectives epitomised by such scholarship in the past. Instead, the voices of distinguished contributors are heard in the context of globalisation which has become the hallmark of academic study today. We live in an increasingly multipolar world, where different cultural and religious traditions are re-emerging as reference points and

1 Multi-authored works arising from symposia have also been published. These include: Witte and van der Vyver (2001); Bielefeldt et al. (2016); Lindholm et al. (2004).

2 See, by way of example, Ahdar (2013).

providing a framework for global projects of living together. Due to migration and the globalisation of mass media, the clash of different traditions takes place within the borders of national and regional societies that previously were relatively homogeneous, heightening the level of religious and cultural diversity and conflict. In many parts of the world, this transformation is quite recent and the debate on how to manage it is still ongoing. While opinions about the best strategies and tools to help attain this goal vary widely, there is a growing consensus about the need for a better knowledge of the cultural sensibilities which are rooted in different religious traditions and macro-regional areas.

This *Handbook* aims at answering this perceived need through the exploration of the different facets of freedom of religion (theological, historical, political and legal) with reference to various religious traditions (Judaism, Christianity, Islam, Buddhism and Hinduism) and to the cultures within which they developed. Global, historical and interdisciplinary are the three words that define the approach adopted in this book to study the new relevance of freedom of religion worldwide and to understand the role that freedom of religion can play in managing religious and cultural diversity in our societies. The *Handbook* reveals the lived reality of the right to freedom of religion and belief from different viewpoints and trajectories: those of religious people and entities; and those of the government and the state in overtly political terms, from constitutional, international and non-State positions, and within the context of human rights more generally.

It will be immediately apparent that this *Handbook* represents a range of opinions from scholars dispersed throughout the globe, and from different religious traditions and none. Some are well-established experts in their field, for whom no introduction is needed and whose reputations precede them. Others are younger scholars, a fresh generation equipped and empowered not only to challenge the accepted truths and received wisdom of the past, but to carry forward the torch of freedom of religion with enhanced enthusiasm and clarity. And just as differing views are expressed by the contributors, so the quartet of editors have brought their own particular understandings to the venture. Whilst this Introduction travels under my name, it represents the product of a constructive, and occasionally combative dialogue, which has informed this project in its conception, development and delivery. All four of us have contributed to its content, and I am indebted to Rossella, Arif and Silvio for their comprehensive and thoughtful input and their characteristically robust criticism of successive drafts.

Having established our reasoning for the adoption of the handbook format, the obvious questions are why has the right to freedom of religion or belief been so little discussed in the academic world until the second half of the twentieth century? And why has the literature on the subject exploded in the past decade or so with textbooks, monographs, edited volumes and journals, together with blogs, chatrooms and every other form of the all-pervasive social media? And most pressing, why has there been a discernible shift from narrow national studies towards global and comparative research?

Freedom of religion or belief lies at a triangulation point where the individual, the faith community and the State converge. The paradigm, in the present age, is a peaceful and mutually affirming convergence where the rights (and duties) of all three players are at least recognised and, where possible, maximised. But this halcyon world, if it exists, would make for a rather dull book. The citizen, the religious organisation and the State are all somewhat angular, and there is bound to be friction when they rub up against each other. This can be problematic and destructive or, as with the editorship of this volume, it can foster a creative dynamism which is rich and fulfilling, leading to a whole which is greater than the sum of its parts.

In recent years, however, this triangulation point has become a much more contentious area – the level of friction has substantially increased. Individuals have become more assertive in expressing their rights against the State and – if they belong to one – their faith community. The age of deference has passed. Populism is in the ascendant with elite governing classes on the retreat. This seems to be happening globally. However, as I write, an unprecedented global phenomenon is causing us to rethink and recalibrate, namely the Covid-19 pandemic. It has led to a resurgence of authoritarianism, particularly in Western democracies, with towns, cities and entire countries being placed into lockdown and places of worship closed, with the active concurrence, or passive acceptance, of religious leaders. Civil rights, including freedom to manifest religion and belief, have effectively been suspended as a consequence of a global health emergency. Severe limitations on personal and associational autonomy – unthinkable in normal times – have been imposed, in circumstances in which most major faith groups have been complicit and supportive. It will be interesting to see how the landscape will have changed after the current public health emergency has passed. We are likely to see three forces at work, each exerting pressure in different directions: globalisation, securitisation and pandemic. But that is speculation for the future: let us return to the present.

One aspect of the current debate about freedom of religion or belief concerns whether there is an ongoing need to have protection for such freedom or whether this right, though historical, is something that can – and indeed should – be dispensed with, at least in its protection of religious beliefs because religion, it is suggested, is not something that should be protected. Academics such as Leiter (2013) and Sullivan (2018) point, respectively, to a philosophically or sociologically suspicious basis for protecting religion. The contributors to this volume suggest ways in which the promotion of freedom of religion remains worthy of support – globally, nationally and within communities.

Freedom of religion and belief necessitates, at its core, two negotiations: the first is bilateral, between the individual and the particular faith community. The second is more complex and has three distinct players: the citizen, the religious organisation and the State. In the first, the assumption of membership of a religious organisation carries with it the partial surrender of personal autonomy in the acceptance of the doctrines and instruments of governance as a matter of consensual compact or *quasi*-contract as with any other unincorporated association, or not-for-profit organisation. Sometimes the surrender is express in the sense of a rite of initiation, sometimes it is effected vicariously as with infant baptism, and sometimes social or cultural convention compels membership.

The second surrender of autonomy, also partial, relates to the manner in which the State grants freedoms – expressly or by implication – to religious organisations collectively, and to their adherents individually. The citizen enjoys freedom of religion and belief (in both its personal and associational guises) only to the extent permitted by the law of the sovereign state. The negotiation of this relationship is less susceptible to the individual conscience and more a matter of *realpolitik*. There is a *leit motif* throughout this volume concerning this surrender of autonomy: historically in the increasing readiness of States to promote pluralism by creating within the public square mechanisms and opportunities for faith organisations to flourish; geographically in the notably different ways in which States promote or tolerate both majority and minority religions; and doctrinally in the extent to which faith communities are prepared – as a tenet of their belief system – to collaborate with increasingly secular civic authorities. And inevitably, though rarely articulated, freedom of religion and belief intersects with other areas of law, such as international law or indigenous law.

But these negotiations did not exist independently of one another. As is explored in various chapters of this *Handbook*, the manner in which the relationship between the individual and the faith community develops has an impact on the tripartite relationship between citizen, state and religious institution (and probably vice versa). The different forms in which religious pluralism manifests itself in India or the United States of America may be related to the way in which, in these two countries, the relationship between the individual and the religious community has developed: with a stronger emphasis on the individual in the United States and on the community in India. These negotiations take place in parallel and overlap considerably: each has an impact on the other.

Before turning to the architecture of this *Handbook*, it is helpful to say a word about definitions and abbreviations. I have a long-standing visceral dislike for the acronym FoRB, which is ugly and suggestive of a chemical formula. Of course, in any informed discussion, the use of shorthand is desirable. However, its usage is becoming more commonplace and, like the King Canute of legend, I may not be able to hold back the rising tide. As we shall see, freedom of religion or belief is a complex and elusive matter, hard to pin down and understood in subtly different and increasingly nuanced ways. Sometimes, in the academic literature, authors appear to have deployed the acronym as a means of avoiding more meaningful engagement with the concept. The contributors to this volume tackle the topic head-on and in depth, so this intrusive and inadequate abbreviation is otiose and unnecessary. To avoid unnecessary repetition, the convention we have adopted throughout this volume is that unless the context indicates otherwise, the reader should assume that all references to 'freedom of religion' are to be read expansively as encompassing freedom of thought, conscience, religion or belief as framed in international human rights instruments but with particular reference to religion in its institutional sense, and the wider generality of belief systems, whether spiritual or humanist in their nature.

It is intended that this *Handbook* will prove to be an invaluable teaching aid for the burgeoning number of undergraduate and graduate courses in law and religion, 'church and state' and comparative religious laws.[3] At its core is the right to freedom of religion or belief, but this is examined from five discrete planes, aimed at informing enquiring students of emergent strains of thought and equipping them for more penetrating and informed analysis. The particular feature of this volume, however, is its global reach. Unlike previous works which have largely been tethered to Europe or North America, this volume paints on a broader canvass featuring particular contributions from Asia and Africa. These both complement and challenge the traditional understandings of the West. The intersection of freedom of religion with indigenous laws and practices, for example, is ripe for further study. This *Handbook* aims to bring perspectives derived from different religious traditions as well as from different places, to bear on discussion about the place and role – past, present and future – of freedom of religion or belief, revealing the various contexts in which it is being thought about.

Part I is overtly historical, looking as how understandings of freedom of religion and belief have evolved over centuries. John Witte examines the traditional perspective from the West but with an energy and insight that is often missing. Fresh and fascinating perspectives from Asia are the subject of Kevin Tan's chapter, and Ahmed Garba writes on Africa, whilst Caroline Sägesser gives an overview from the vantage point of secular humanism.

The focus changes in Part II to an evaluation of the right to freedom of religion and belief as understood and deployed by the major religious traditions. Buddhist perspectives are examined by Benjamin Schonthal, Christian understandings by Norman Doe, with a Hindu viewpoint presented by Laura Dudley Jenkins and Kristina Teater. An Islamic overview is provided by Wael Saleh with Patrice Brodeur, while Matthew LaGrone's focus is Jewish perspectives.

3 For example, it will be the core text for my forthcoming course at the University of Notre Dame, London Global Gateway, on international religious liberty.

This part concludes with an ambitious evaluation of an interreligious notion of the right to freedom of religion by Arvind Sharma.

Part III is rooted in the triangulation point identified above and comprises an exploration of the geopolitics of the right to freedom of religion, broadly interpreted, with chapters on the West, by Gerhard Robbers, on Asia, from Arif Jamal and Jaclyn Neo, and on sub-Saharan Africa, from Idowu Akinloye.

In Part IV, specialist authors map the right to freedom of religion, with Johan van der Vyver looking at various constitutional patterns of protection in domestic legislation, and Eva Brems and Laurens Lavrysen evaluating the right to freedom of religion in international law. Martin Ramstedt examines the right to freedom of religion in non-State legal orders.

The concluding pair of chapters which comprise Part V revisit some of the themes of the earlier chapters but broaden the ambit of investigation. David Little seeks to relate the particular right to freedom of religion to other human rights, both in national systems and as part of the global legal order, and the complex relationship between the universal and particular elements of the right; and Peter Danchin helpfully considers the dialectics between the universal and particular dimensions of the right to freedom of religion.

This *Handbook* ambitiously includes contributions that introduce new elements to the emergent discipline of freedom of religion and belief: traditional religions in Africa, Asian values, indigenous religions in Latin America, etc. These pose new questions that have a direct impact on the debate about the universality of the right to religious freedom to which the last section is dedicated. This *Handbook* is intended to be a bridge between the traditional debate on religious freedom and the new perspectives opened up by globalisation and the progressive shift of the world's centre of gravity eastwards. Whether this eastward shift has been accelerated by the Covid-19 pandemic and the resulting economic and social lockdown, only time will tell. But the need for students of freedom of religion actively to engage with these new perspectives and to question, or depart from, hard-wired traditional Western understandings has never been more urgent. It is hoped that this *Handbook* will expose students to new ways of thinking which may stimulate civic and religious leaders to new ways of action.

References

Ahdar, R. (Ed.), 2013. *Research Handbook on Law and Religion*. Edward Elgar.

Bielefeldt, H., Ghanea, N., Wiener, M. (Eds.), 2016. *Freedom of Religion or Belief: An International Law Commentary*. Oxford University Press.

Leiter, B., 2013. *Why Tolerate Religion?* Princeton University Press.

Lindholm,T.S., Durham, W.C., Tahzib-Lie, B.G., Sewell, E.A., Larsen, L. (Eds.), 2004. *Facilitating Freedom of Religion or Belief: A Deskbook*. Springer.

Sullivan, W.F., 2018. *The Impossibility of Religion*. Princeton University Press.

Witte, J., van der Vyver, J. (Eds.), 2001. *Religious Human Rights in Global Perspective: Pt 1 Religious Perspectives; Pt Legal Perspectives 2*. Eerdmans.

PART I

History of the right to freedom of religion or belief

2

The right to freedom of religion: An historical perspective from the West

John Witte, Jr.[1]

In its most basic sense, the right to religious freedom is the freedom of individuals and groups to make their own determinations about religious beliefs and to act upon those beliefs peaceably without incurring civil or criminal liabilities. More fully conceived, freedom of religion embraces a number of fundamental principles of individual religious liberty – freedom of conscience, exercise, speech, association, worship, diet, dress and evangelism; freedom from religious discrimination, coercion and unequal treatment; freedom of religious and moral education; and freedom of religious travel, pilgrimage and association with coreligionists abroad. It also involves a number of fundamental principles of corporate religious liberty – freedom of religious groups to organize their own polity and leadership; to hold and use corporate property; to define their own creed, cult, confessional community and code of conduct; to establish institutions of worship, education, charity and outreach; and to set standards of admission, participation and discipline for their members and leaders. These are now standard terms of religious freedom in modern international human rights instruments and many national constitutions (Durham and Scharffs, 2019).

The Western legal tradition came to this fuller understanding of 'the right to freedom of religion' only after many centuries of hard and cruel experience to the contrary. The phrase 'freedom of religion' (*libertas religionis*) emerged in the early third century; the phrase 'right to freedom' (*ius libertatis*) emerged in the twelfth. But it took five centuries more for 'the right to religious freedom' (*ius libertatis religionis*) to become a common phrase in religious and legal circles and for the abridgement of this right to trigger a cause of action in court, rather than a reason to flee or revolt. While religious freedom guarantees became more common in treaties and constitutions after the seventeenth century, they were still often honored in the breach by leaders of religious establishments and secular states alike. And while the twentieth century brought powerful major new guarantees of religious freedom in both national and international human rights instruments, vicious religious persecution remains commonplace in modern life around the globe today, including in many Western lands (Philpott and Shaw, 2018). This chapter highlights a few of the decisive steps in the development of religious freedom and religion–state relations in the Christian West.

1 This chapter is adapted in part from Witte and Nichols (2016: 7–23, 249–275). I am grateful to Dr. Justin Latterell for his research assistance and to Oxford University Press for permission to use this material herein.

First millennium

In the first three centuries of its existence, the Christian church separated itself from official Roman society and soon became a persecuted minority. Christians refused to acknowledge the divinity of the emperor, as required by Roman law, or to swear oaths or to join the pagan rituals necessary for participation in Roman civic, political or military life. Early Christians taught obedience to the political authorities but only up to the limits of Christian conscience, following Jesus's call to 'render to Caesar the things that are Caesar's, and to God the things that are God's' (Matt. 22:21). They also sought to expand their faith and reform society, following Jesus's command to 'make disciples of all nations, teaching them to observe all that I have commanded you' (Matt. 28:19–20). Both this nonconformity and agitation for reform by Christians brought reprisal from the Roman authorities. By the mid-first century, the Roman authorities began to repress Christians as well as Jews, departing from Rome's usual policy of indifferently tolerating all faiths that remained politically subservient and religiously sequestered. By the end of the first century, Rome declared Christianity to be an 'illicit faction' and outlawed Christian worship, charity and education, triggering intermittent waves of brutal persecution (Wilken, 2003: 22–23, 31–67, 156–163).

Several early Church leaders protested this oppression. Among the earliest was Tertullian of Carthage (ca. 160–220), a theologian with legal training. He was the first to introduce the term 'religious freedom' (*libertas religionis*) into Western Christian thought – in part as a gloss on the repeated New Testament statements on Christian freedom: 'For freedom [*libertas*], Christ has set us free' (Gal. 5:1) and 'Where the Spirit of the Lord is, there is freedom' (2 Cor. 3:17). You have all been given 'the glorious freedom of the children of God' (Rom. 8:21). After decrying Roman persecution of Christians, Tertullian wrote famously: 'It is only just and a privilege inherent in human nature that every person should be able to worship according to his own convictions; the religious practice of one person neither harms nor helps another. It is not part of religion to coerce religious practice, for it is by choice not coercion that we should be led to religion' and 'To take away freedom of religion [*libertas religionis*] and forbid free choice with respect to divine matters [only] fosters irreligion' (Wilken, 2019: 1, 11–13). Leading Church Father Lactantius (220–340) wrote similarly to the emperor: '[I]f you wish to defend religion by bloodshed, and by tortures, and by guilt, it will no longer be defended, but will be polluted and profaned. For nothing is so much a matter of free-will as religion; in which, if the mind of the worshiper is disinclined to it, religion is at once taken away and ceases to exist. The right method is that you defend religion with patience' (Lactantius and Fletcher, 1875, bk. v.20: 340).

With the Christian conversion of Constantine in 312, Christians came to enjoy a new measure of religious toleration under Roman law. The so-called 'Edict of Milan' (313) for the first time guaranteed to Christians alongside all other faiths 'a public and free liberty to practice their religion or cult' and 'free permission to follow their own religion and worship as befits the peacefulness of our times'. The Edict also recognized the rights of Christian groups to property and places of worship, 'which belonged by right to their body – that is, to the churches not to individuals,' and the right to restitution of properties confiscated in earlier times of persecution. Such guarantees of individual and group religious rights were granted, the Edict provided, 'so that the supreme Divinity, whose religion we obey with free minds, may be able to show in all matters His accustomed favor and benevolence towards us' (Ehler and Morrall, 1954: 3–6).

Had these provisions of the Edict of Milan been fully implemented for Christians *and* all other faiths, Rome would have instituted a regime of religious toleration that the Western tradition would not see again for more than a millennium. Even in Constantine's reign, however, and increasingly thereafter, the Roman emperors moved from a policy of open religious toleration of most peaceable faiths to a policy of increasing preference for Trinitarian Christianity. They also began to persecute 'Jews, pagans, apostates, and heretics' who opposed the Church's orthodox teachings, subjecting them to the same repressive and bloody measures that Christians had faced before the fourth century. An imperial edict in 380 sealed this shift in policy by legally establishing Trinitarian Christianity as the official state religion and declaring all other forms of faith as heresies that deserved punishment:

> [T]here is one Godhead, Father, Son, and Holy Spirit, in an equal Majesty and Holy Trinity. We order that those who follow this doctrine receive the title of Catholic Christians, but others we judge to be mad and raving and worthy of incurring the disgrace of heretical teaching, nor are their assemblies to receive the name of churches. They are to be punished not only by Divine retribution but also by our own measures.
>
> *(Ehler and Morrall, 1954: 7)*

This formal state establishment of Trinitarian Christianity brought the Christian Church under both the support and control of Roman political authorities. On the one hand, Christian clergy and monastics were given special criminal law protections, legal privileges and financial support to spread the faith, to educate the young, to care for the poor and to build new churches, monasteries, schools and charities. Heretics, pagans and Jews, in turn, were subject to severe repression and legal disability, and even matyrdom at times, which Christian bishops and clergy sometimes led at the behest of the emperor. On the other hand, the Roman emperors declared themselves to be the supreme rulers of both civil and religious affairs in the Empire. They convened the major ecumenical church councils, appointed and removed bishops and other clergy, and chartered and administered churches and monasteries. Numerous imperial laws regulated the internal activities of the church, the lives of its clerics and monks, the acquisition and disposition of church property and the definition of church doctrine and liturgy. The great compilations of Roman law, the *Theodosian Code* (438), the *Corpus Iuris Civilis* (529–533) and *Novels* (ca. 565), were filled with new imperial laws that governed the doctrine, liturgy, polity and property of the established church (Maas, 2005: 161–214).

This new form of church–state relations drew to itself a variety of new theories. The most famous was developed by St. Augustine (354–430), who contrasted the 'city of God' with the 'city of man' that coexist in earthly life. The city of God consists of all those who are predestined to salvation, bound by the love of God, and devoted to a life of Christian piety, morality and worship led by the Christian clergy. The city of man consists of all the things of this sinful world and the political and social institutions that God had created to maintain a modicum of order and peace on the earth. Augustine sometimes depicted this dualism as two walled cities separated from each other. But his more dominant teaching was that, in the Christianized Roman empire, these two cities overlapped in responsibility and membership. Christians would remain dual citizens until these two cities were fully and finally separated on the Return of Christ and at the Last Judgment of God. They remained bound by the sinful habits of the world, even if they aspired to greater purity of the Gospel. Christians remained subject to the power of both cities, even if they aspired to be a citizen of the city of God alone. If the rulers of the city of man favored and protected orthodox Christians, rather than persecuting them, so much the better. And it was better still if the civil authorities would 'compel' recalcitrant and destructive heretics 'to come in' (Luke 14:23) and join the true church (Augustine, 1958: bks. 4: 19–21).

It was crucial, however, that the spiritual and temporal powers that prevailed in these two cities remain separate in their core functions. Even though Christianity became the one established religion of the Roman Empire, patronized and protected by the political authorities, Augustine and other Church Fathers insisted that political authorities not intrude upon core spiritual functions. Even the Roman emperors were not ordained clergy but laity. They had no power to administer the sacraments or to mete out religious discipline. They were bound by the teachings of the Bible, the decrees of the ecumenical councils, and the traditions of their predecessors. They also had to accept the church's instruction, judgment and spiritual discipline. Thus, for example, Ambrose, Bishop of Milan (d. 397), excommunicated the powerful Emperor Theodosius (347–395) for massacring the people of Thessalonica and readmitted him to communion only after he had done public penance for his immoral act. Pope Gelasius I (r. 492–496) put the matter famously in 494 in a letter rebuking Emperor Anastasius (430–518):

> There are, indeed, most august Emperor, two powers by which the world is chiefly ruled: the sacred authority of the Popes and the royal power. Of these the priestly power is the more important, because it has to render account for kings of men themselves at [the Last Judgment]. For you know, our clement son, that although you have the chief place in dignity over the human race, yet you must submit yourself faithfully to those who have charge of Divine things, and look to them for the means of your salvation.
>
> *(Ehler and Morrall, 1954: 10–11)*

This 'two powers' passage became a *locus classicus* for many later theories of religion and state.

This system of tempered imperial or royal rule within the church largely continued in the West after the fall of the Roman Empire in the fifth century. Before their conversion, many of the pagan Germanic rulers were considered to be divine and were cult leaders as well as military leaders of their people. Upon their conversion to Christianity, they lost their divinity, yet continued as sacral rulers of the church within their territories. They found in Christianity an important source of authority in their efforts to extend their rule over the diverse peoples that made up their regimes. The clergy not only supported the Germanic Christian kings in the suppression of tribal religions but also looked upon such leaders as the Frankish Emperor Charlemagne (r. 768–814) and the Anglo-Saxon King Alfred (r. 871–899) as their spiritual leaders. Those Germanic rulers who converted to Christianity, in turn, supported the clergy in their struggle against heresies and gave them military protection, political patronage and material support. Feudal lords within these Germanic domains further patronized the church by donating lands and other properties to the church in return for the power to appoint and control the priests, abbots and abbesses who occupied these lands (Morrison, 2016: 26–67, 136–164).

The papal revolution

This first millennium model of church–state relations was turned upside down in the Papal Revolution. In the name of 'freedom of the church' (*libertas ecclesiae*), Pope Gregory VII (r. 1073–1085) and his successors threw off their political and feudal patrons and declared the Catholic Church itself to be an independent and superior legal and political authority of Western Christendom. In his revolutionary manifesto, *The Dictates of the Pope* (1075), Gregory proclaimed that emperors and kings had no authority over the church, or over its clergy and polity. Only the pope, Gregory declared, had authority to ordain, discipline, depose and reinstate bishops; to convoke and control church councils; and to establish and administer abbeys and bishoprics. Only the pope had authority 'to enact new laws according to the needs of the time' that were universally binding. Only the papal court was 'the court of the whole of Christendom' open and available to all Christians. The pope 'may depose emperors,' and 'the pope is the only one whose feet are to be kissed by all princes' (Berman, 1983: 85–119). Such a bold proclamation did not go unchallenged. For more than three generations thereafter, a good deal of Europe was locked in bitter religious and civil war, with the papacy and its supporters ultimately prevailing.

In the twelfth and thirteenth centuries, the church made good on a number of these claims. The papacy and clergy now claimed a vast new jurisdiction, an authority to 'declare the law' (*jus dicere*) for Christendom, based on the church's preeminent authority over spiritual and sacramental life. They claimed exclusive personal jurisdiction over clerics, pilgrims, students, heretics, Jews and Muslims. They claimed subject matter jurisdiction over doctrine, liturgy, patronage, education, charity, inheritance, marriage, oaths, oral promises and moral crimes. And they claimed concurrent jurisdiction with political authorities over secular subjects that required the church's special forms of Christian equity. A vast body of new church laws, called canon laws, issued by popes, bishops and church councils came to govern Western Christendom. A vast network of church courts and officials, centralized in Rome, enforced these laws throughout the West. From 1150 to 1350, the Catholic Church, ironically, was 'the first modern state' in the West, and its canon law was the first modern international law (Berman, 1983: 205–254; Tierney, 1982: 30–39).

The medieval canon law developed a refined jurisprudence of rights (*iura*) and liberties (*libertates*), including the right to religious freedom for individuals and groups. The canonists grounded these rights and liberties in natural law and associated them variously with the capacity (*facultas*) of rational human nature and with the property (*dominium*) of a person or the power (*potestas*) of an office of authority (*officium*). They repeated and expanded the subjective rights and liberties set out already in the texts of Roman law – especially the private rights and liberties of property, and what Gratian's *Decretum* (ca. 1140) called the 'rights of liberty' (*iura libertatis*) enjoyed by persons of various stations in life and offices of authority. The canonists also began to weave these early Roman law texts into a whole complex latticework of what we now call rights, freedoms, powers, immunities, protections and capacities for different groups and persons (Tierney, 1997: 56–69).

Corporate and individual rights to religious freedom figured prominently in this new legal system. The canon law defined the rights of the clergy to their liturgical offices and ecclesiastical benefices, their exemptions from civil taxes and duties and their immunities from civil prosecution and compulsory testimony. It defined the rights of ecclesiastical organizations like parishes, monasteries, charities and guilds to form and dissolve; to accept and reject members; to establish order and discipline and to acquire, use and alienate property. It defined the rights of church councils and synods to participate in the election and discipline of bishops, abbots and other clergy. It defined the rights of the laity to worship, evangelize, maintain religious symbols, participate in the sacraments, travel on religious pilgrimages and educate their children. It defined the rights of the poor, widows and needy to seek solace, succor and sanctuary within the church. A good deal of the rich latticework of medieval canon law was cast, substantively and procedurally, in the form and language of rights (Tierney, 1997: 43–92; Reid, 1995). These canonical rights formulations had parallels in medieval common law and civil law texts, too. Among sundry other medieval charters of rights, the English Magna Carta of 1215 set out a whole panoply of rights, starting with 'the Church of England shall be free [*libera*] and shall have all her whole rights [*iura*] and liberties [*libertates*] inviolable' (Stephenson and Marcham, 1972:

115–127). These medieval charters of rights later became important prototypes for early modern constitutional architects who crafted bills of rights and religious freedom provisions for European and American lands (Griffith-Jones and Hill, 2015: 81–156).

To be sure, medieval rights were not unguided by duties, nor were they available to all parties. Only the Catholic faithful – and, notoriously, not heretics, Jews, Muslims or Orthodox Christians – had full rights and protection under medieval law, and all rights were to be exercised with appropriate moral and sacramental constraints. But Tertullian's opening admonition against religious coercion was oft repeated by medieval writers, even if this ideal was also oft betrayed, especially during the brutality of the crusades, pogroms,and inquisitions. And these canonical rights formulations sparked a whole industry of sophisticated rights talk that would become axiomatic for the Western legal tradition. This included the work of nominalist philosophers like John Duns Scotus (1266–1308) and William of Ockham (1285–1307); political thinkers like Marsilius of Padua (1275–1342), Jean Gerson (1363–1429) and Conrad Summenhart (1455–1502); and sundry Spanish sages gathered at the University of Salamanca (Tierney, 1997: 93–206). This latter group included Francisco de Vitoria (1483–1546) and Bartolomé de las Casas (d. 1566) who made path-breaking advances in defending what they called the universal 'natural right of freedom of religion' (*naturale ius libertatis religionis*). Both of them decried the forced baptisms and conversions of Latin American natives and slaves and risked much to urge religious and political authorities to guarantee missionaries the freedom to preach the Gospel and natives the freedom to accept or reject that preaching without reprisal (Vitoria, 1991: 231–292, 339–352; Lantigua, 2016: 41–59).

In the fourteenth and fifteenth centuries, however, this medieval system of church–state relations and religious freedom began to crumble. Strong monarchs began to increase their control over the church, and clerical authority and religious freedom began to wane – in part because of widespread corruption and division even at the highest levels of church government. In response, the German Emperor Sigismund convoked a series of great church councils that declared their authority over Church polity and canon law, despite papal disapproval. In the Pragmatic Sanction of Bourges (1438) and again in the Concordat of Bologna (1516), French kings banned various papal taxes, limited appeals to Rome, required French bishops to be elected by church councils called by the king, subjected the clergy in France to royal discipline and increased royal control over church property. In Germany, strong princes and city councils began to pass what they called 'legal reformations' that placed limits on church property and taxation; disciplined wayward clergy; and curtailed the jurisdiction of church courts over crime, family, inheritance and contracts. Fifteenth-century Spanish monarchs subordinated church courts in Spain to the civil courts and took control of the prosecution and execution of heretics, Jews and Muslims, unleashing the terrifying Spanish Inquisition, which operated in Europe and later in Latin American colonies as well (Witte, 2002: 33–52).

The protestant reformation

These late medieval reforms helped fuel the Protestant Reformation. Inaugurated by Martin Luther (1483–1546) in 1517, the Reformation began as a call for 'freedom of the Christian' – freedom of the individual conscience from intrusive canon laws and clerical controls, freedom of political officials from ecclesiastical power and privileges and freedom of the local clergy from central papal rule and taxation. The Reformation soon split into Lutheran, Anabaptist, Calvinist, and Anglican groups living tenuously alongside each other and their Catholic neighbors. Peace treaties like the Peace of Augsburg (1555), Union of Utrecht (1579), Edict of Nantes (1598) and Peace of Westphalia (1648) provided measures of religious toleration for religious minorities. But religious persecution and religious warfare were tragically regular events in early modern Europe, and several Protestant lands created their own harsh religious establishments, despite the Reformation's opening calls for religious freedom.

The Lutheran reformers of Germany and Scandinavia gave the local Christian magistrate ample new political power over civil and spiritual affairs. Echoing the imperalist ideas of Christianzed Rome, Luther described the magistrate as God's vice-regent in the earthly kingdom, called to elaborate and enforce God's law and to reflect God's justice and judgment for earthly citizens. The Christian magistrate is 'a voice of the Ten Commandments,' wrote Luther's colleague Philip Melanchthon (1509–1560), 'a man holding in one hand the tables of the Ten Commandments and holding in the other a sword'. As custodians of the Decalogue, the magistrate must not only pass laws against idolatry, blasphemy and violations of the Sabbath that violate the Decalogue on its face, but he must also 'establish pure doctrine' and right liturgy, 'prohibit all wrong doctrine,' 'punish the obstinate' and root out the heathen and the heterodox (Witte, 2002: 110–113, 130–134).

This was the theoretical basis for the wave of new state establishment laws in Lutheran lands that copiously regulated spiritual life as well as the clergy, polity, property and finances of the established church. The Peace of Augsburg (1555) and the Peace of Westphalia (1648) confirmed the constitutional principle that each civil ruler was free to establish the religion of his of her own local polity (*cuius regio eius religio*). The Peace of Westphalia, however, which finally ended the bloody Thirty Years War of religion (1618–1648), also guaranteed 'the freedom of religious exercise' to all peaceable Catholic, Lutheran and Calvinists dissenters within these established religious communities. These religious dissenters were to be free from all violence and from coerced participation in the established forms of faith and were guaranteed 'a free conscience to frequent privately their place of worship' and to educate their children in their own private schools or homes. Over time, they also gained the right to establish their own charities, foundations and businesses within their neighborhoods, and to get professional licenses for trade, banking, navigation, legal and medical practice and more. All religious dissenters were also guaranteed the right to move (*ius emigrandi*) across state lines if they could no longer abide the religion or policies of their home territory (Ehler and Morrall, 1954: 164–172, 189–192).

By marked contrast to established Lutheranism, early modern Anabaptists called for the separation of church and state and for religious freedom for all peaceable believers. Echoing apostolic church ideals, various Anabaptists groups – Amish, Brethren, Hutterites, Mennonites, Baptists and Free Churches – ascetically withdrew from civil and political life into small, self-sufficient, open democratic communities. These communities were governed internally by biblical principles of discipleship, simplicity, charity and non-resistance. They set their own internal standards of worship, liturgy, diet, discipline, dress and education. They handled their own internal affairs of property, contracts, commerce, marriage and inheritance – so far as possible by appeal to biblical laws and practices, not those of the state. Recalcitrant sinners and community members who grew violent, destructive or persistently betrayed the community's ideals were shunned and if necessary banned from the community. Moreover, when Anabaptist communities grew too large or too internally divided, they deliberately colonized themselves, eventually spreading Anabaptists from Russia to Ireland to the furthest frontiers of North America.

The state and its law, most Anabaptists believed, were part of the fallen world, which was to be avoided so far as possible in accordance with biblical injunctions that Christians should not be 'of the world' or 'conformed' to it (John 15:19; Rom. 12:2). God had built a 'wall of separation' (*paries maceriae*) between the redeemed church and the fallen world, leading theologian Menno Simons (1496–1561) wrote, quoting Ephesians 2:14. God had allowed the world to survive by ordaining magistrates and their positive laws who are empowered to use coercion and violence to maintain a modicum of order and peace. Christians should obey the laws of political authorities, so far as the Bible commanded – paying their taxes, registering their properties, avoiding theft and homicide, keeping their promises and testifying truthfully. But Christians should avoid active participation in and unnecessary interaction with the world and the state – avoiding litigation, oath swearing, state education, banking, large-scale commerce, trade fairs, public festivals, drinking houses, theaters, games, political office, policing or military service. Most early modern Anabaptists were pacifists, preferring derision, exile or death to active participation in war or violence. This aversion to common political and civic activities often earned Anabaptists scorn, reprisal and repression by Catholics and Protestants alike and even violent martyrdom in many instances (Klaassen, 1981: 247–257; Estep, 1996).

While unpopular in its genesis, Anabaptism ultimately proved to be a vital source for Western legal arguments regarding the separation of church and state and the protection of civil and religious liberties of a plurality of peaceable faiths. The Anabaptist doctrine of adult, rather than infant, baptism underscored the teaching that each adult was called to make a free conscientious choice to accept the faith – metaphorically, to scale the wall of separation between the fallen world and the realm of religion to come within the perfect realm of Christ. This metaphor provided a powerful platform for claims of freedom of conscience and free exercise of religion. Diverse leaders within and beyond the Anabaptist world – John Smyth (d. 1612), Roger Williams (ca. 1604–1684), William Penn (1644–1718), Isaac Backus (1724–1806) and others – pressed hard for the absolute religious freedom of the individual to choose, change or reject religion. State coercion or control of this choice, either directly through persecution and repression or indirectly through withholding civil rights and benefits from those who made unpopular choices, was an offense against God and the individual. A plurality of religions should coexist in the community, and it was for God, not the state or the church, to decide which religion should flourish and which should fade (McLoughlin, 1971).

Calvinists scattered throughout Europe, and its colonies built on the teachings of Genevan reformer John Calvin (1509–1564) to chart a course between Lutherans and Anglicans. Like Anabaptists, Calvinists insisted on a basic separation of the offices and operations of church and state, leaving the church to govern its own doctrine and liturgy, polity and property, without interference from the state. Like Lutherans, Calvinists insisted that each local polity be an overtly Christian commonwealth that adhered to the general principles of natural law and translated them into detailed new positive laws for public, private and spiritual life. Unlike both groups, however, Calvinists stressed that both church and state officials were to play complementary roles in the creation of the local Christian commonwealth and in the cultivation of the Christian citizen. It was the church's responsibility to teach aspirational spiritual norms, using the tools of spiritual discipline alone. It was the state's responsibility to enforce mandatory civil norms, using criminal punishment if necessary in dealing with dangerous immorality or recalcitrant heresy (Witte, 2007: 56–80). This latter position led to the infamous execution of Michael Servetus in Geneva in 1553 for publicly critizing the doctrine of the Trinity and refusing to stay away from the city. Calvin and his followers defended the execution as necessary to maintain the morality and integrity of the local Christian republic of Geneva. His critics, notably Sebastian Castellio (1515–1563), decried it. 'To kill a man is not to defend a doctrine. It is to kill a man,' Castellio charged (Bainton, 1951: 75).

While some early modern Calvinists continued to persecute religious dissenters on both sides of the Atlantic, other Calvinists laid new foundations for Western theories of religious freedom and human rights for all, as they responded to vicious religious persecution that was killing their own coreligionists by the tens of thousands. Christopher Goodman (ca. 1530–1603), Theodore Beza (1519–1605), Johannes Althusius (1557–1638) and several others argued that humans have fundamental rights rooted in the Decalogue and other biblical commands. The Decalogue set out not only the natural duties of love owed to God and to neighbors, they argued, but also the complimentary natural rights to discharge these fundamental duties. A person's First Table duties toward God thus supported the rights to the free exercise of religion: the right to honor God and God's name, the right to rest and worship on one's Sabbath and the right to be free from false gods and false oaths. A person's Second Table duties towards others supported the neighbor's fundamental right to have those duties discharged. One person's duties not to kill, to commit adultery, to steal, to bear false witness or to covet their neighbor's household thus gives rise to another person's rights to life, property, fidelity, reputation and privacy. Goodman called these 'unalienable rights,' and Althusius pressed for written constitutions that enumerated these rights and provided procedures for their vindication. John Knox (ca. 1514–1572) and others argued further that the persistent and pervasive breach of these 'unalienable rights' by a tyrant triggered a further 'fundamental right' to resistance and rebellion, even revolution and regicide (Witte, 2007: 102–142).

Such ideas helped to drive the Protestant revolutions against political tyranny and religious persecution in early modern England, Scotland, France, and the Netherlands. These revolutionaries included strong protection of religious freedom in their demands for the full and free exercise of fundamental rights. A 1584 Dutch pampleteer, for example, wrote presciently: 'How is it possible to grant freedom of conscience without exercise of religion? ... There is no difference between so-called freedom of conscience without public worship, and the old rigour of the edicts and inquisition of Spain'. In England, John Lilburne (1614–1657) and John Milton (1608–1674) advocated liberty of conscience, free exercise of religion, religious pluralism and equality, basic separation of the offices and operations of church and state and the disestablishment of religion. New England jurist and theologian Nathaniel Ward (1578–1652) issued a 25-page 'Body of Liberties' in 1641, including detailed religious freedom provisions, drawing on these Calvinist teachings as well as the Magna Carta and the later common laws it had inspired (Witte, 2007: 143–150, 226–248, 279–288).

Religious establishment and religious freedom in Europe

These revolutionary ideas and actions in favor of fundamental religious and civil rights brought heavy reprisal from the establishment regimes in early modern England and France, among others. The English establishment went back to the sixteenth century, when King Henry VIII (r. 1509–1547) and early Anglican reformers like Thomas Cranmer (1489–1556) and Thomas Cromwell (1485–1540) severed England's ties with Rome and rapidly established the Church of England as the state established religion. The Supremacy Act (1534) declared the monarch to be the 'Supreme Head' of the Church and Commonwealth of England, with final authority to appoint, discipline and dismiss Anglican clergy; to call church councils and synods; to reform the church's doctrine, liturgy and canon law; to register church properties and personnel; and to collect church tithes and taxes. The state further orchestrated the massive seizure and dissolution of monasteries, schools and other church properties and claimed jurisdiction over charity, social welfare, education and the arts. Queen Mary (r. 1553–1558) sought forcibly to return England to Catholicism, executing and exiling hundreds of Anglicans and others who resisted. Queen Elizabeth I (r. 1558–1603) and her parliaments, however, reestablished a uniform Anglican liturgy and doctrine through *The Book of Common Prayer* (1559), *The Thirty-Nine Articles of Religion* (1571) and, later, the Authorized Version of the Bible (1611). Communicant status in the Church of England was a condition for citizenship status and various civil benefits in the Commonwealth of England. Contraventions of royal religious policy were punishable as both heresy and treason. Catholics and dissenting Protestants were subjected to growing repression during Elizabeth's later years and even more under her Stuart successors King James I (r. 1603–1625) and King Charles I (r. 1625–1649). Hundreds of Protestant and Catholic dissenters were martyred, and untold thousands were exiled to the continent of North America (Haigh, 1993: 105–284).

As repression continued, English Protestant dissenters together with Scottish Presbyterians led a violent civil war in the 1640s and 1650s, drawing on Calvinist ideas of rights, resistance and revolution. Led by Oliver Cromwell (1599–1658), the revolutionaries deposed and later executed King Charles I in 1649, outlawed the Anglican establishment and granted religious toleration to all Protestants – though not to Catholics or to Jews. In 1660, however, royal rule was restored, Anglicanism was forcibly reestablished and dissenters were again violently repressed. But when the dissenters again rose up in revolt and threatened a new civil war, Parliament passed the Toleration Act and Bill of Rights in 1689 that guaranteed limited freedoms of association, speech and worship to all Protestants. Many of the remaining legal restrictions on Protestants fell aside in the following decades. Catholics and Jews, however, remained formally banned from England until the Catholic and Jewish Emancipation Acts of 1829 and 1833 (Stephenson and Marcham, 1972: 607–679).

As part and product of this revolutionary struggle, English philosopher John Locke (1632–1704) and others encouraged more robust religious freedom. The church must be 'absolutely separate and distinct from the commonwealth,' Locke wrote, and must be free to determine its own worship, order, organization, membership, and discipline. But the church must also use 'no force' against its members, for 'true and saving religion consists in the inward persuasion of the mind' which only God can touch and tend. The state, in turn, must exercise no coercion over consciences either through 'confiscation of estate, imprisonments, [or] torments' or through mandatory compliance with 'articles of faith or forms of worship' established by law. Every person 'has the supreme and absolute authority of judging for himself' in matters of faith. Locke still presupposed a magistracy and community committed to a common Christianity. He also called for exclusion of Catholics and Muslims 'who deliver themselves up to the service and protection of another prince' as well as those 'who deny the being of a God' altogether, since 'promises, covenants, and oaths which are the bonds of human society, can have no hold upon an atheist' (Locke, 1824: vol. 5, 9–47).

In France, the monarchy gradually abandoned its earlier policies of religious toleration – particularly as they had been set out in the Edict of Nantes (1598) which had granted modest toleration to Protestant nonconformists. Supported by the antipapalism of the revived Gallican party in France, and by the new theories of absolute monarchy earlier expounded by Jean Bodin (1530–1596) and others, the French monarchs consolidated their control over a national Catholic Church. They also sharply curtailed remaining papal power over church property, ecclesiastical courts and clerical nomination. King Louis XIV (r. 1643–1715) passed more than 100 acts against Catholic and Protestant critics and dissenters, gradually restricting their freedoms and imposing crushing taxes upon them. Finally, in the Edict of Fontainebleau (1685), Louis XIV revoked the toleration policies of the Edict of Nantes and ordered all Protestant churches and schools destroyed, proscribed all liturgies and theologies that deviated from officially sanctioned Gallicanism and banished all dissenting clerics from France. Protestants fled from France by the tens of thousands, many making their way to Belgium, the Netherlands, Switzerland and Germany – and eventually to distant colonies in North America and Southern Africa (Ehler and Morrall 1954: 205–213). French Protestant Pierre Bayle (1647–1706) and others offered strong biblical and philosophical arguments for religious freedom for all and against religious coercion by the state, but these writings largely fell on deaf ears as the royal authorities destroyed most French Protestant communities and strengthened their hold on the Gallican Catholic establishment (Zagorin, 2003: 167–183).

In the eighteenth century, however, French political authorities turned on the Catholic establishment, too. Growing numbers of French Enlightenment writers – Voltaire (1694–1778), Jean Jacques Rousseau (1712–1778), Marquis de Condorcet (1743–1794) and many others – pressed liberal philosophical arguments not only for stronger religious freedom for individuals but also for stronger separation of church and state and reduction of Catholic privileges and prerogatives in French law and society. Condorcet, for example, urged the authorities 'to separate religion from the State'. Though priests should 'have the freedom of sacraments, censures, [and] ecclesiastical functions' within their own churches, he allowed, the state was 'not to give any civil effect to any of their decisions; not to give any influence over marriages or over birth or death certificates; not to allow them to intervene in any civil or political act; and to judge the lawsuits which would arise, between them and their citizens ... or between this association and private individuals' (Hamburger, 2002: 60).

In the French Revolution (1789), these Enlightenment liberal ideas about religion came to vivid and eventually violent expression. The French Declaration of the Rights of Man and Citizen (1789) provided that 'No one ought to be disturbed for his opinions, even religious ones, provided that their manifestation does not trouble the public order established by the law'. The 1790 Constitution further guaranteed 'the freedom of every man ... to exercise the religion to which he is attached'. But, in the 1790s, the French political authorities unleashed their fury against Catholicism, exiling some 30,000 priests, imprisoning and killing several hundred more, and killing tens of thousands of Catholic men, women and children in bloody battles and executions. The government closed all monasteries and convents, looted or destroyed much priceless religious art and converted numerous churches into sites for state-designed rites. An 1801 Concordat restored a measure of peace, order and restitution, but the Catholic Church and French state remained in perennial conflict for the next century and more. French authorities gained control over much remaining church property, education, charity and polity and then severed the state's financial support for the church in the 1905 Law of Separation of Church and State. The papacy condemned liberalism, human rights, religious freedom and separation of church of state – most notably in Mirari Vos (1832) and The Syllabus of Errors (1864) – a position that largely remained canonical until the sweeping reforms and embrace of religious freedom for all by the Second Vatican Council (1962–1965) (Maclear, 1995: 75–118; Ehler and Morrall, 1954: 201–213, 234–249, 355–371).

Religious establishment and religious freedom in the new world

This checkerboard of rival religious and political groups in early modern Europe was duplicated, in part, in the New World. Spanish and Portuguese Catholic rulers from the later fifteenth century onward extended their regimes through much of Latin America, the Caribbean, Mexico, Florida and far into the American southwest reaching to California. These Spanish regimes featured strong Catholic establishments and powerful church–state alliances that remained in place in many Central and Latin American countries until the twentieth century and still shape the culture of many Latin American lands to this day (Domingo and Mirow, 2020).

French Catholics established strong colonies and churches in Quebec and the Canadian Maritimes, and down the midwest corridor to Louisiana. Although the English later conquered Quebec, Parliament's Quebec Act (1774) guaranteed the 'free exercise of the religion of the Church of Rome, subject to the king's Supremacy' (Ehler and Morrall, 1954: 324). Dutch Protestant authorities chartered Dutch Calvinist companies to New York and the middle colonies, whose populations were bolstered by later waves of Calvinist colonists fleeing European persecution. Scandanavian Lutheran monarchs and merchants sponsored scattered colonial companies throughout North and Central America. The British colonized the entire Atlantic seaboard up to Canada and down to the Caribbean. By the time of the American Revolution of 1776, there were established Anglican churches in every American colony and part of the Diocese of London (Gaustad and Barlow, 2001: 1–54).

Colonial America was also a haven for European dissenters, many of whom introduced their new experiments in religious liberty. Colonial Rhode Island was established by Roger Williams in 1636 as 'a lively experiment [for] full liberty in religious concernments' and guaranteed members 'liberty of conscience' and 'the free exercise and enjoyment of all their civil and religious rights'. Pennsylvania Quaker leader William Penn (1644–1718) instituted a 'holy experiment' in religious liberty in Pennsylvania, guranteeing that no peaceable theist would 'be molested or prejudiced for his or her conscientious persuasion or practice. Nor shall he or she at any time be compelled to frequent or maintain any religious worship, place, or ministry whatever contrary to his or her mind, but shall freely and fully enjoy his, or her, christian liberty in that respect, without any interruption or reflection' (Witte and Nichols, 2016: 20–23).

These early colonial experiments helped inspire the new American constitutional experiment in religious freedom after the American Revolution of 1776. Particularly Enlightenment, Quaker and Baptist writers attacked the millennium-old Western idea that one form of Christianity must be established in a community and that the state must protect and support it against all other forms of faith. America would no longer suffer such governmental prescriptions and proscriptions of religion. All forms of Christianity had to stand on their own feet and on an equal footing with all other religions. Their survival and growth had to turn on the cogency of their word, not the coercion of the sword, on the faith of their members, not the force of the law. American Enlightenment writers such as Thomas Paine (1737–1809), Thomas Jefferson (1743–1826), and James Madison (1751–1836) argued strongly that the state should not offer the church any special tax exemptions, property donations, or criminal protections, nor predicate its laws on explicitly religious premises. The state should not fund or support religious schools or other religious causes or enlist the services of religious officials. Nor should the state interfere in the order, organization, or orthodoxy of religious bodies or abridge the peaceable religious choices and activities of any subjects. There must be a 'wall of separation between church and state,' Jefferson wrote; a 'clear line of division between religion and government,' Madison added (Witte and Nichols, 2016: 32–36). These new views were reflected in the new Amercan state constitutions and in the First Amendment to the United States Constitution that outlawed religious test oaths for political office and guaranteed that 'Congress shall make no law respecting an establishment of religion or prohibiting the free exercise thereof' (Witte and Nichols, 2016: 64–116). These federal and state guarantees have produced more than 250 United States Supreme Court cases and thousands of lower federal and state court cases vindicating the rights of religious freedom.

Modern religious freedom in the West and Beyond

Other Western nations gradually adopted comparable constitutional provisions, statutes and judicial opinons for the protections for the right of religious freedom for all peaceable faiths.

An influential early example was the Belgian Constitution of 1831 that included provisions for 'freedom of religions and their public worship;' 'no one can be compelled to join in any manner whatever in the rites and ceremonies of any religion, nor to observe its days of rest;' and 'the State shall have no right to interfere either in the nomination or in the installation of ministers of any religious denomination whatever' (Ehler and Morrall, 1954: 270–272). While the totalitarian regimes of Italy, Germany, Spain and the Soviet Union crushed religious freedom for many subjects, several European nations after World War II ratified strong new religious liberty protections, even while sometimes retaining their Christian establishments. The Italian Constitution of 1947 celebrated Italy's Catholic heritage but insisted that 'the State and the Catholic Church are independent and sovereign, each within its own sphere'. Morever, 'all religious denominations are equally free before the law' with 'the right to self-organisation according to their own statutes, provided these do not conflict with Italian law'. The Basic Law of the Federal Republic of Germany (1949) makes these provisions: 'Freedom of faith and conscience and freedom of religious and ideological profession shall be inviolable. Undisturbed practice of religion shall be guaranteed. No one may be compelled against his conscience to perform war service as a combatant'. The Spanish Constitution of 1978 has comparable provisions: 'Freedom of ideology, religion and worship of individuals and communities is guaranteed, with no other restriction on their expression than may be necessary to maintain public order as protected by law. No one may be compelled to make statements regarding his or her ideology, religion or beliefs. No religion shall have a state character. The public authorities shall take into account the religious beliefs of Spanish society and shall consequently maintain appropriate cooperation relations with the Catholic Church and other confessions'. Many other European nations combined generous religious freedom gurantees for all peaceable religions with constitutional provisions and concordats that privileged Catholic, Anglican, Lutheran, Reformed, or Greek Orthodox Christian churches. The Vatican led the way in forging concordats with a dozen Western countries (Maclear, 1995; Doe, 2012).

Strong religious freedom provisions also were woven into modern international human rights instruments. The Universal Declaration of Human Rights (1948), passed in response to the devastation of World War II, stated famously: 'All human beings are born free and equal in dignity and rights. They are endowed with reason and conscience and should act towards one another in a spirit of brotherhood'. The Declaration banned discrimination on religion and other grounds and provided that 'Everyone has the right to freedom of thought, conscience and religion; this right includes freedom to change his religion or belief, and freedom, either alone or in community with others and in public or private, to manifest his religion or belief in teaching, practice, worship and observance'. The 1966 International Covenant on Civil and Political Rights, a binding treaty ratified by 165 countries, provided further that 'No one shall be subject to coercion which would impair his freedom to have or to adopt a religion or belief of his choice. Freedom to manifest one's religion or beliefs may be subject only to such limitations as are prescribed by law and are necessary to protect public safety, order, health, or morals or the fundamental rights and freedoms of others'. The same Covenant also urged States Parties 'to have respect for the liberty of parents and, when applicable, legal guardians to ensure the religious and moral education of their children in conformity with their own convictions'. In 1993, the United Nations Human Rights Committee issued a lengthy 'General Comment' on the 1966 Covenant making clear that 'freedom of thought and the freedom of conscience are protected equally with the freedom of religion and belief,' and it includes 'theistic, non-theistic and atheistic beliefs,' whether traditional or new, whether held by a majority or minority. 'These freedoms are protected unconditionally; ... no one can be compelled to reveal his thoughts or adherence to a religion or belief'. Protected religious practices include 'ritual and ceremonial acts, the building of places of worship, the use of ritual formulae and objects, the display of symbols, and the observance of holidays and days of rest'. They also include 'observance of dietary regulations, the wearing of distinctive clothing or headcoverings, participation in rituals associated with certain stages of life, and the use of a particular language'. And they include, still further, 'freedom to choose their religious leaders, priests and teachers, the freedom to establish seminaries or religious schools and the freedom to prepare and distribute religious texts or publications' (Stahnke and Martin, 1998: 57–96). Comparably expansive religious freedom provisions appear in several other United Nations documents – most notably the Declaration on the Elimination of All Forms of Intolerance and Discrimination Based on Religion or Belief (1981) as well as in regional instruments like the European Convention on Human Rights (1950), the American Convention on Human Rights (1969), and the African Charter on Human and People's Rights (1981) (Stahnke and Martin, 1998: 101–160).

Modern religious communities within and beyond the West have become important advocates for religious freedom and other fundamental rights. Protestants, Catholics, Jews, Muslims, Buddhists and various ecumenical and interreligious groups proved critical to the early development of the international bill of rights, including its provisions on religious freedom (Morsink, 2017). The Second Vatican Council (1962–1965) transformed the Catholic Church into a powerful religious freedom advocate as well. Every person, the church now taught, is created by God 'with intelligence and free will' and has rights 'flowing directly and simultaneously from his very nature'. The church emphasized the religious rights of conscience, worship, assembly, and education, calling them the 'first rights' of any civic order. The church also stressed the need to balance individual and associational rights, particularly those involving the church, family and school. Governments everywhere were encouraged to create conditions conducive to the realization and protection of these 'inviolable rights' and encouraged to root out every type of discrimination, including notably religious discrimination. The Catholic Church also now advocated limited constitutional government, disestablishment of religion, and the separation of church and state (Gremillion, 1976: 203–218; Abbott and Gallagher, 1967: 675–696).

Orthodox Christian churches, too, rose in partial support of religious freedom and human rights, as they faced oppressive rule in the Soviet bloc and in various totalitarian regimes in the Middle East and northern Africa. The World Congress of Orthodox Bishops (1978), for example, called for 'prayers for those whose human rights are being denied and/or violated; for those who are harassed and persecuted because of their religious beliefs, Orthodox and non-Orthodox alike, in many parts of the world; for those whose rightful demands and persistence are met with greater oppression and ignominy; and for those whose agony for justice, food, shelter, health care and education is accelerated with each passing day'. A 1980 Orthodox Congress implored 'totalitarian and oppressive regimes to restore respect for the rights and dignity of the individual and to insure the free and unhindered exercise of these vital rights by all citizens, regardless of racial and ethnic origin, or political or religious espousal' (Harakas, 1982: 21–28). Other Orthodox theologians and church leaders, however, also warned the West about abandoning its faith in the name of freedom. Bartholomew, Orthodox Ecumenical Patriarch of Constantinople, put it provocatively: 'Faith is not a garment to be slipped on and off; it is a quality of the human spirit, from which it is inseparable'. 'There are a few things [the West] can learn from the Orthodox Church,' the Patriarch declared. Foremost is the lesson 'that, paradoxically, faith can endure without freedom, but freedom cannot long abide without faith' (Witte and Bourdeaux, 1999: 19–22).

Further reading

Helmholz, R., 2010. *The Spirit of the Classical Canon Law*. University of Georgia Press.
King, N., 1961. *The Emperor Theodosius and the Establishment of Christianity*. SCM Press.
Little, D., 2015. *Essays on Religion and Human Rights: Grounds to Stand On*. Cambridge University Press.
Kossman, E.H., Mellink, A. (Eds.), 1974. *Texts Concerning the Revolt of the Netherlands*. Cambridge University Press.
Morgan, E., 2003. *Puritan Political Ideas 1558–1794*. Liberty Fund.

References

Abbott, W., Gallagher, J. (Eds.), 1967. *The Documents of Vatican II*. Guild Press.
Augustine,1958. *City of God* (G. G. Walsh, Trans. and V. J. Bourke. Ed.). Image Books.
Bainton, R., 1951. *Sebastian Castellio: Champion of Religious Liberty*. Brill.
Berman, H., 1983. *Law and Revolution: The Formation of the Western Legal Tradition*. Harvard University Press.
Doe, N., 2012. *Law and Religion in Europe: A Comparative Introduction*. Oxford University Press.
Domingo, R., Mirow, M., 2020. *Great Christian Jurists in Latin American History*. Cambridge University Press.
Durham, W., Scharffs, B., 2019. *Law and Religion: National, International, and Comparative Perspectives*. Aspen Publishers.
Ehler, S., Morrall, J.B., 1954. *Church and State Through the Centuries: A Collection of Historic Documents with Commentaries*. Newman Press.
Estep, W., 1996. *The Anabaptist Story: An Introduction to Sixteenth-Century Anabaptism*. William B. Eerdmans.
Gaustad, E., Barlow, P., 2001. *New Historical Atlas of Religion in America*. Oxford University Press.
Gremillion, J. (Ed.), 1976. *The Gospel of Peace and Justice: Catholic Social Teaching Since Pope John*. Orbis Books.
Griffith-Jones, R., Hill, M. (Eds.), 2015. *Magna Carta, Religion, and the Rule of Law*. Cambridge University Press.
Haigh, C., 1993. *English Reformations: Religion, Society, and Politics Under the Tudors*. Clarendon Press.
Hamburger, P., 2002. *Separation of Church and State*. Harvard University Press.
Harakas, S., 1982. Human rights: an Eastern orthodox perspective *Journal of Ecumenical Studies*. 19, 13.
Klaassen, W., 1981. *Anabaptism in Outline: Selected Primary Sources*. Herald Press.
Lactantius, 1875. *The Works of Lactantius* vol. 2. (W. Fletcher, Trans.). T & T Clark.
Lantigua, D., 2016. The image of god, Christian rights talk, and the school of Salamanca. *Journal of Ecumenical Studies*. 31, 19.
Locke, J., 1824. *The Works of John Locke,* vol. 9. Rivington.
Maas, M. (Ed.), 2005. *Cambridge Companion to the Age of Justinian*. Cambridge University Press.
Maclear, J. F., 1995. *Church and State in the Modern Age: A Documentary History*. Oxford University Press.
McLoughlin, W., 1971. *New England Dissent, 1630–1833: The Baptists and the Separation of Church and State,* vol. 2. Harvard University Press.
Morrison, K., 2016. *Two Kingdoms: Ecclesiology in Carolingian Political Thought*. Princeton University Press.
Morsink, J., 2017. *The Universal Declaration of Human Rights and the Challenge of Religion*. University of Missouri Press.
Philpott, D., Shaw, T., 2018. *Under Caesar's Sword: How Christians Respond to Persecution*. Cambridge University Press.
Reid, C., 1995. *Rights in Thirteenth-Century Canon Law: An Historical Investigation*. PhD Dissertation. Cornell.
Stahnke, T. A., Martin, J. P., 1998. *Basic Religion and Human Rights Documents*. Center for the Study of Human Rights. Columbia University.
Stephenson, C., Marcham, S., 1972. *Sources of English Constitutional History*. Harper & Row.
Tierney, B., 1982. *Religion, Law, and the Growth of Constitutional Thought, 1150–1650*. Cambridge University Press.
Tierney, B., 1997. *The Idea of Natural Rights: Studies on Natural Rights, Natural Law, and Church Law, 1150–1625*. William B. Eerdmans.
Vitoria, F., 1991. *Vitoria: Political Writings*. (A. Pagden and J. Lawrance, Ed.). Cambridge University Press.

Wilken, R., 2003. *The Christians as the Romans Saw Them*. Yale University Press.
Wilken, R., 2019. *Liberty in the Things of God: The Christian Origins of Religious Freedom*. Yale University Press.
Witte, J., 2002. *Law and Protestantism: The Legal Teachings of the Lutheran Reformation*. Cambridge University Press.
Witte, J., 2007. *The Reformation of Rights: Law, Religion, and Human Rights in Early Modern Calvinism*. Cambridge University Press.
Witte, J., Bourdeaux, M. (Eds.), 1999. *Proselytism and Orthodoxy in Russia: A New War for Souls*. Orbis Books.
Witte, J., Nichols, J., 2016. *Religion and the American Constitutional Experiment*. Oxford University Press.
Zagorin, P., 2003. *How the Idea of Religious Toleration Came to the West*. Princeton University Press.

3

The right to freedom of religion: An historical perspective from Asia

Kevin YL Tan

Introduction

Asia is one of the world's most religiously diverse regions. It was the spawning ground for two of the world's major religions – Hinduism and Buddhism – as well as other home-grown beliefs and religions like Sikhism, Jainism, Daoism, Confucianism and Shintoism. European colonialism introduced Catholicism and other Christian denominations to the region, and trade and commerce brought Islam. Today, Asia is home to the largest number of Muslims in the world.

Until the advent of modern constitutions and constitutional guarantees, it makes little sense to talk about the 'right' to freedom of religion in Asia. For the masses, the mere 'freedom' to practise their religion without discrimination or persecution was as much a 'right' as could be imagined. That is not to say that there were no official positions taken on religious freedoms or practices prior to the modern period. Indeed, one of earliest and most accommodative official proclamations on religion and religious tolerance is found in the *Edicts* (Cunningham, 1877; Wheeler, 1877) of Ashoka (268–232 BCE), third Mauryan emperor of India. Although himself a devout Buddhist, Ashoka desired that 'all unbelievers may everywhere dwell (unmolested)' since 'they also wish for moral restraint and purity of disposition.'[1] Just as accommodative, but perhaps more programmatic in its privileging of the Buddhist faith was Article 2 of Prince Shotoku's Seventeen-Article Constitution (*Jushichijo Kenpo*) which dates from 604 CE[2] and states:

> Sincerely reverence [*sic*] the three treasures. The three treasures, viz. Buddha, the Law and the Priesthood, are the final refuge of the four generated beings, and are the supreme objects of faith in all countries. What man in what age can fail to reverence this law? Few men are utterly bad. They may be taught to follow it. But if they do not betake them to the three treasures, wherewithal shall their crookedness be made straight?
>
> *(Aston, 1956: 129)*

1 Rock Edict No 7, in Cunningham (1877: 121).

2 See Lu (1997: 22–26), where a translation of the 17 Articles is presented.

But much less tolerant was the Great Ming Code of Zhu Yuanzhang (1328–1398 CE), founder of China's Ming Dynasty who tried to completely reorder and remould China through a series of pronouncements, codes and regulations.[3] Chief among these documents were the *Ancestral Injunctions* or *Huang Ming Zu Xun* (皇明祖训)[4] and the Great Ming Code or *Da Ming Lu* (大明律; see The Great Ming Code, 2005) which, taken together, form the basis for the operation of Ming government (Wu and Jiang, 2007). The Ming state promoted Confucianism and ancestral worship and was highly suspicious of religion and 'sought to control religion by limiting the formation of religious sects, the spread of religious ideas and particular religious practices' (Peerenboom, 2002: 91–92). There were, for instance, rules 'against magical practices, prophecies and predictions; there were limits on heterodoxy; and private persons were prohibited from performing state religious rituals.'[5]

Asia's religious landscape in the precolonial period

The inclusivist religions of Asia

In a fascinating 2014 study, political scientist David C. Kang noted that there were no religious wars in premodern East Asia:

> in premodern East Asia, Korea, Japan, Vietnam, and China rarely experienced anything like the type of religious violence that existed for centuries in historical Europe, despite having vibrant religious traditions such as Confucianism, Buddhism, Daoism, and numerous folk religions. Given the abundant religious wars, crusades, pogroms, and witch-hunts that occurred in Europe throughout the centuries, the lack of religious wars in East Asian history is a puzzle.
>
> *(Kang, 2014: 966)*

After analysing 950 incidents of conflict over a 473-year period, Kang argues that the main reason for this was because most of the dominant religions in East Asia were 'inclusive and syncretic' rather than 'exclusive.' Inclusivist religions like Buddhism, Confucianism, Daoism and various folk religions 'do not have clearly delineated boundaries,' 'comprise numerous different deities and perhaps even many different types of deities, have no clear institutionalised hierarchy, leaders, or texts, and no fixed membership' (Kang, 2014: 966). As such, they 'did not easily lend themselves to appropriation by political leaders as a means of differentiating groups or justifying wars' (Kang, 2014: 966).

While Kang confined his observations to the dominant religions of East Asia, his argument might well apply to Hinduism and early Islamic practices as well (Brakel, 2004; Burman, 1996; Ghoshal, 2010). Another of Kang's observations might well be more universally applied. The more inclusive and syncretic a religion is, the less likely it is to precipitate confrontation and conflict. There is a further dimension to this observation. Because state power and legitimacy in East Asia did not depend on the imprimatur of any of these religions, it served little purpose to appropriate religion for political purposes. The converse is also true. If and when a particular religion becomes a legitimising (or delegitimising) tool for a political group or order, it will accordingly be appropriated and made a point of separation and, consequentially, of confrontation

3 On Zhu's attitude towards religion, see DuBois (2011: 15–52).

4 An English translation of the Huang Ming Zu Xun, see Farmer, 1995: Appendix I.

5 Peerenboom, 2002: 92; see also 'Laws on Rituals' in *The Great Ming Code*, 2005: chapter 4.

and discrimination. The observations above may equally apply to many other parts of Asia, such as the Indian subcontinent and Southeast Asia which included Buddhists, Hindus and Muslims.[6]

Religious domination, discrimination and persecution

The dominance of syncretic faiths in Asia did not, however, mean the absence of religious discrimination and persecution. Notable among these were the early persecutions against 'foreign religions' – including Buddhism and Christianity in China (De Groot, 1903–1904) and Hinduism and Buddhism in India by Muslim rulers.

The Tang emperor Wuzong (814–846 CE) was reputedly a zealous Daoist and was deeply concerned with the rise of Buddhism as a major religious, economic and political force (Smith, 1994). In 842 CE, he issued an edict[7] to weed out sorcerers and convicts from among the Buddhist monks and nuns and return them to lay life. By 845 CE, 4,600 'gaudy, useless' temples had been demolished and 26,500 monks and nuns and over '100,000 idle and unproductive Buddhist followers' had been returned to lay life. In addition, 40,000 privately established temples were demolished to release valuable land for cultivation. A further 2,000 Christians and Zoroastrians were also ordered to 'return to lay life and to cease polluting the customs of China' (de Bary and Bloom, 1999: 585–586).

In the eighth century, when Umayyad Muslim armies under Muhammad Qasim invaded the Sindh in northwest India, Buddhists and Hindu temples were desecrated (Eaton, 2000) and Buddhists and Hindus were enslaved and even forced to convert to Islam (Elliot and Dowson, 1867–1877: 140–211). Records of Muslim persecutions of Buddhists and Hindus in India can be found from the thirteenth century to the arrival of the British in the seventeenth century although several Muslim monarchs – such as Alauddin Khalji (1296–1316), Sikandar (1399–1416) and Aurangzeb (1658–1707) – were known to be rather less tolerant than others.

One group that suffered religious discrimination throughout Asia from the earliest times were the Christians – both Catholics and Protestants – who first came as missionaries, and then as conquerors. Missionaries and early converts – as adherents of strange and 'foreign' religions – were at times favoured in the royal courts of Asia, but more often discriminated against. For example, Christians or 'Nestorians' (as they were commonly referred to) thrived briefly at the beginning of the Tang dynasty (618–907 CE) as there was then a 'great openness to things foreign,' leading to 'a remarkable degree of tolerance of other religions,' but this gave way to 'proscriptions, persecutions and the confiscation of churches and monasteries in the middle of the ninth century' (Giullman and Klimkeit, 1999: 268). Christianity then flourished again during the Mongol Yuan Dynasty (1271–1368 CE), and many prominent figures in early Mongol history were Nestorians (Giullman and Klimkeit, 1999: 287). Several Mongolian princesses, including the mother of Kublai Khan, were Nestorians as well (Giullman and Klimkeit, 1999: 289). However, Christians – along with Buddhists – were once again persecuted during the Ming period (1368–1644) by emperors who were highly suspicious of 'foreign religions' and who promoted ancestor worship and Confucianism as state ideology. Emperor Yongzheng (1678–1735) formally withdrew the Chinese state's tolerance of Christians and of Catholics in particular, and this led to the closure of Catholic churches (Rausch, n.d.). It was only after China's defeat in the First Opium War that things began to change. The Treaties of Tientsin (Tianjin) opened up more Chinese ports to foreign trade, permitted the establishment of foreign

6 On the spread of Asian religions in Southeast Asia, see de Casparis and Mabbett (1992), Andaya and Ishii (1992).
7 Emperor Wuzong, 'Edict of the Eight Month,' in de Bary and Bloom (1999: 585–586).

legations in the capital, Beijing, legalised the importation of opium and allowed Christian missionary activity throughout the Treaty Ports. Article 8 of the Treaty of Tientsin 1858 provided:

> The Christian religion, as professed by Protestants or Roman Catholics, inculcates the practice of virtue, and teaches man to do as like would be done by Persons teaching or professing it, therefore, shall all alike be entitled to the protection of the Chinese authorities, nor shall and such, peaceably pursuing their calling and not offending against the laws, be persecuted or interfered with.

The treatment of Christians in India was rather less discriminatory but was still nonetheless restrictive. India's Hindu rulers were generally tolerant of Christians and their proselytising activities, and even under the Muslim Mughal rulers, they were – at least initially – relatively free to own property, build churches and bury their dead, as well as to convert others to their faith and hold services publicly (Roy-Chowdhury, 1941: 348). The Emperor Akbar (1542–1605) even issued a *farman* (royal order) in 1594, stating that 'if any of the infidels wishes to build a church or synagogue, or idol temple, none were to prevent them' (Roy-Chowdhury, 1941: 348). Akbar's successor, Jahangir (1569–1627), was equally accommodating but not Jahangir's son, Shah Jahan (1592–1666), who forbade Christians to convert Muslims. Aurangzeb (1618–1707), however, forbade Hindus from changing their religion except to Islam (Roy-Chowdhury, 1941: 349). Christians also did not have to pay Jeziah (or Jizya) the annual tax historically levied on non-Muslims permanently residing in Muslim lands during the reigns of Akbar, Jahangir and Shah Jahan. However, Aurangzeb reimposed this tax in 1569 (Roy-Chowdhury, 1941: 350).

Anti-Catholic violence was also recorded in Japan and Korea, especially in the sixteenth century shortly after the first Jesuits arrived for slightly different reasons. In Japan, the Jesuits found favour with the ruling elite by facilitating trade and the sale of firearms and even succeeded in converting some of them. However, this strategy backfired as they grew in power and influence. For example, in 1586, Toyotomi Hideyoshi (1537–1598), Japan's preeminent *daimyo* (feudal lord) requested and secured the assistance of Gaspar Coelho, the Jesuit Vice-Provincial, to garner Christian support in his invasion of Kyushu (where most of the Catholics were located). And while Hideyoshi was happy to have the support of the Catholics, he turned on them after his successful conquest of Kyushu. In 1587, he ordered the expulsion of foreign missionaries, the apostasy of Japanese Catholics under the pain of exile or death and seized and destroyed their property, on the grounds that 'Catholic attacks on other religions threatened public order and stability' (Rausch, n.d.). Catholics suffered government-sponsored violence almost as soon as the first Catholic community took root in 1784 (Rausch, n.d.). Rausch argues that this violence was the result of the weakness of the Chosun kings, who lacked the power to contain the violence. Catholicism and Catholics were perceived as dangerous and evil by the elite scholars of Korea and by the common folk and this allowed rulers to use Catholics as a convenient scapegoat to help unite their nobles and supporters.

The colonial period and attitudes toward religion

European colonialism

After Portuguese explorer Bartholomew Dias rounded the Cape of Good Hope in 1488, the Europeans began sailing to Asia and thus began a period of colonisation that ended almost 500 years later. The first were the Portuguese and the Spanish, who were followed by the Dutch and the English and later by the French and Germans (see generally Cotterell, 2010; von Albertini and Wirz, 1982). With the traders came missionaries and Christianity; first the Catholics, and then the Protestants (see generally Moffett, 2005). And while Christians continued to be discriminated against in some Asian states such as China and Japan, they gained the upper hand in territories which came under the colonial yoke. However, nowhere in Asia, save for the Philippines did Christianity supplant the dominant local religion.[8] By the seventeenth century, when the European powers began their colonising enterprise, the religious landscape of Asia had attained a pattern instantly recognisable by a modern-day observer. Islam and Hinduism were dominant on the Indian subcontinent, while Theravada Buddhism thrived in Ceylon and what is today Burma, Thailand, Laos and Cambodia. Islam was the dominant religion of Southeast Asia, while what is today Vietnam saw a flourishing mix of Mahayana Buddhism and Daoism. In China, Daoism and Confucianism dominated, while Buddhism remained in the background.

By the end of the nineteenth century, all of Asia, save for China, Japan and Siam, had been colonised. The Portuguese, who were the first to arrive, continued to occupy Macau and Timor till the late twentieth century, while the Dutch ruled the Netherlands East Indies or what is now Indonesia till 1945. Britain ruled over the largest swathe of territories which included British India (modern-day India, Pakistan and Bangladesh), Ceylon (modern-day Sri Lanka), Burma (Myanmar), Malaya, Singapore, North Borneo and Hong Kong; and the French were lords of Indochina (present-day Vietnam, Cambodia and Laos).

The Portuguese attitude

Because a Portuguese explorer first rounded the Cape of Good Hope, it seems inevitable that the first European power to venture across the Indian Ocean and establish colonies in Asia was Portugal. Alfonso de Albuquerque, the ambitious, expansionist Portuguese admiral, became Viceroy of the Portuguese in India in 1509 and then proceeded to conquer Goa (in 1510) and then Malacca (in 1511). The main motivation for this expansion was, of course, trade and the desire to break the Ottoman-Arab stranglehold on the trade routes in the Indian Ocean. As Desai noted, the three G's – God, Gold and Glory – which were said to be the prime motivations for colonial expansion should be discarded as, with the Crusades, 'service to Mammon early took precedence over service to God' (Desai, 1969: 501–502). Insofar as administration was concerned, the Portuguese adopted a system of indirect rule and, for the most part, left the local population to its own devices. The Portuguese did not actively persecute the Muslims or Hindus but had no compunction using the 'religious factor' to punish those who opposed them commercially or politically. Indeed, Albuquerque even introduced the *Politica dos Casamentos* (Inter-Marriage Policy) which encouraged Portuguese men to marry local women (da Silva Gracias, 1997). It was hoped that with this assimilation, the local population would also imbibe Portuguese language, culture and Catholicism as well. At the same time, the lack of a competent cohort of Portuguese administrators meant that capable locals of every religious persuasion were employed by the Portuguese establishment and held their offices by dint of their ability. As such, non-Christians were free to practise their religion in relative peace and without overt persecution.

The Dutch approach

Dutch rule in the East Indies may be divided into two periods. The first period, starting from the 1600s to about 1800, was a period of monopolistic mercantilism that coincided with the

8 On the conversion of the Filipinos to Catholicism, see Sitoy Jr (1985).

life of the *Vereenigde Oostindische Compagnie* (VOC or Dutch East India Company) which was founded in 1602 and became defunct in 1799. The second period – which coincided with the Dutch government's direct involvement in the East Indies – was a period of political domination. In the first period, the VOC forced local leaders to accept their monopolistic trade practices by the threat or use of armed force. The main concern for the VOC officials was trade rather than control over the population, and Dutch attitudes toward Islam were 'shaped by a contradictory combination of exaggerated fears and hopes' due to their total ignorance of that faith (Benda, 1958: 338; see also Steenbrink, 2006). Throughout this period, the VOC met with Muslim hostility, but the Dutch made no attempt to subjugate them and suppressed attacks only insofar as they affected trade. However, local resistance hardened toward the late eighteenth century, fuelled by the large numbers of Muslims who, returning from their pilgrimage to Mecca, brought back 'orthodox teachings which were gradually displacing the mysticism and syncretism formerly prevalent in Indonesian Islam' (Benda, 1958: 338). In 1825, Prince Diponegoro (1785–1855), a Javanese prince, and son of the Sultan of Yogyakarta, led a revolt against the 'infidel' Dutch, precipitating what has been called the Java War. The revolt lasted till 1830 when the Dutch suppressed the locals, captured Diponegoro and exiled him to Makassar (Carey, 2007: 505–656). Even more serious than the Java War was the violence that broke out in Aceh in 1873 after the Dutch tried to bring the region within its control. The series of conflicts, which formally lasted till 1904, was known to the Dutch as the Aceh War but to the Acehnese as the Dutch War. In 1883, as a result of yet another conflict, and this time with the Acehnese military dominated by religious *ulama* who preached the concept of a 'holy war,' the conflict came to be known as the Infidel War (Taslim, 2013).

Bleeding from the human and economic cost of both the Java and Aceh wars, the Dutch began formulating a more conciliatory policy toward the Indonesians. The principal architect of this new approach was Christiaan Snouk Hurgroje, a Dutch scholar of Arab studies and Islam, who was appointed to the newly-created office of Advisor on Arabian and Native Affairs in 1889 (Benda, 1958: 340). Snouk Hurgronje divided Indonesian Islam into two parts: one religious and the other political. He argued for toleration and religious neutrality not only to convince 'the majority of religious officials but also most, if not all *ulama* of the Dutch administration's honest intentions and would persuade them that they had nothing to fear from the colonial government as long as they abstained from political propaganda' (Benda, 1958: 342).

Thereafter, even as missionaries continued to try to convert the denizens, the Dutch colonial authorities adopted a separatist approach to religion and the state. As historian David Bentley-Taylor noted, 'it was their deliberate plan to keep Christianity to themselves and to withhold it from the peoples of the land they had conquered' (Bentley-Taylor, 1967: 16). The Dutch policy was that of 'absolute impartiality, in the granting of complete religious liberty as long as the freedom of the other people or public morality is not thereby affected' (de Kat Angelino, 1931: 336–337). This was specifically stipulated in the *Indische Staatsregeling* (Constitution of the Netherlands East Indies) of 1925.[9] Article 173 guaranteed every person the right to 'confess their religious opinions with complete freedom' save where public interests need to be protected. However, this freedom did not apply uniformly throughout the Indies as 'Christian teachers, priests and missionaries' needed the Governor-General's special permission to operate in 'certain parts of the Dutch East Indies' [Art 177(1)]. Non-Christian priests or preachers were, at the same time 'placed under the supervision' of local princes and

9 See The Ninth Chapter of the Indische Staatsregeling 1925, 'Of Religion' in Engelbrecht (1933: 86–87).

rulers insofar as they fell within the religious jurisdictions of such rulers (Art 178). In any case, the exercise of this freedom was subject to 'general ordinances' for the protection of the public (Arts 173–175).

The Dutch approach had two key characteristics. The first was to ensure that the public is protected from harm, and the second was non-interference in the personal law of individuals:

> The authorities have in this field no duties apart from a certain supervision so as to make sure that the population suffers no harm. With this aim in view they see to it that it is not compelled to deliver materials and money for the building of mosques, while a certain amount of control of the finances of the mosques is also exercised. The collection of religious contributions (*djakat* and *pitrah*) takes place without any administrative intervention, but care is taken that no pressure should be exercised. It is furthermore the wish of the Government that official account should be taken of the celebration of Moslim [sic] festal days in so far as the interests of the service will allows this. ... The pilgrimage to Mecca is also neither hampered nor encouraged by the Government.
>
> *(Engelbrecht, 1933: 337)*

This policy continued right up till the Dutch were driven out of Indonesia in 1945.

The Spanish

The Spanish were the first to circumnavigate the globe and settle in the Philippines. Over the next few hundred years, the Spanish Empire in the East included the Philippines, Formosa (modern-day Taiwan), Sulawesi (Celebes) and Moluccas (Maluku). Like the other European powers, the Spanish were out to stake their claim on a slice of the lucrative spice trade and, less urgently, to maintain the spirit of the *Reconquista* – the movement to destroy Muslim power and influence in the Iberian Peninsula and beyond. A striking feature of Spanish colonialism was the *Patronato Real* (Royal Patronage system) which bound the church and state inextricably to each other. Thus, Spanish monarchs had tremendous power over the church's administration, revenue and selection of church personnel. At the same time, the church enjoyed the backing of the Spanish state in all its activities and actions, including its efforts to convert the native inhabitants.

In 1594, the Philippines was partitioned into different spheres of operation by the various Spanish missionary orders: Augustinians in Cebu, Panay and the Tagalog and Pampango regions in Luzon; Franciscans in the Bicol Peninsula and Laguna de Bay; the Dominicans in Bataan, Pangasinan, Zambales and northern Luzon; and the Jesuits on the islands of Bohol, Leyte, Samar and parts of Mindanao (Sitoy Jr, 2001: 654–655). The Spanish missionaries were extremely successful in their conversion efforts, and by the first decade of the seventeenth century, Catholic missions could credibly claim that 'almost all Filipinos in territory under Spanish control professed the Catholic faith' (Moffett, 2005: 156). According to Sitoy, this success was largely due to the fact that

> Christianity in its Catholic form was congenial with traditional Filipino animistic religion. Indeed, the structure and the worldview of pre-Christian Filipino religion dovetailed with those of Catholicism. Moreover, the healing powers attributed to baptism and the belief that Christian ceremonials and symbols were effective against the dreaded evil spirits drew masses of Filipinos to the new faith.
>
> *(Sitoy Sunquist 2001: 655)*

The only region the missions failed to penetrate was Moro, in the south, which remained resolutely Muslim. But in the areas under Spanish control, the authorities maintained order and kept their converts, often resorting to the use of force to do so. The story is told of Bankaw, a chief who was among the earliest to convert. In 1621, in old age, Bankaw apostatised and joined another traditional priest to return to the faith of his fathers. The Spanish sent a flotilla of 40 armed ships to defeat Bankaw. They beheaded him and posted his head on a stake to warn others who might consider apostasizing (Moffett, 2005: 158). By the nineteenth century, Catholicism was so dominant that it was the only form of Christianity allowed in the Philippines. It was only 1898 when the United States gained control of the islands that Protestants were free to enter. The Philippines and Vietnam were the last Asian states to be opened to Protestant missions (Sitoy Jr, 2001: 656).

The French in Indochina

The French were latecomers to Asia, settling in what was to become the Indochinese Union only in 1887. The environment they entered was hostile to the French and their Catholic missions. The Union consisted of three separate and distinct areas – Tonkin (in the north), Annam (centre) and Cochinchina (south) – which were conquered at different times. After the Sino-French War of 1884–1885, France gained control of the northern part of modern-day Vietnam and then subsequently took control of what is now Vietnam and Cambodia. After the Franco-Siamese War of 1893, what is now Laos was added to the empire.

Religious freedom of the Catholics, or rather the lack of it was France's main excuse for intervening militarily in Vietnam. The first Catholic missions arrived in Vietnam in the first decades of the sixteenth century. Despite persecution from the Vietnamese rulers – who saw Christianity as a threat to Confucian order and harmony (Tucker, 1999: 26; see also McLeod, 1992) – Catholic churches expanded rapidly (Pan and James, 2001: 877; see also Goscha, 2017: 186). Some 90,000 Catholics were killed during the seventeenth and eighteenth centuries, and another 40,000 were killed during the reign of three Vietnamese emperors between 1820 and 1883 (Pan and James, 2001: 877). The Vietnamese rulers also persecuted Buddhists and Taoists, but not with the same intensity as they did the Catholics. It was the mistreatment of Catholic missionaries that provided the French with an excuse for intervening in Vietnam (Tucker, 1999: 27). In 1857, the French navy attacked Danang harbour and by 1859 seized Saigon. Admiral François Page, who led the French, was instructed to sign a treaty that would guarantee religious liberties and French consuls in the major Vietnamese ports (Tucker, 1999: 29). This came to pass when, in 1862, Emperor Tu Duc signed the Saigon Treaty ceding the three Cochinchina territories – Bien Hoa, Gia Dinh (Saigon) and My Tho (Truong Dinh) – to France (Goscha, 2017: 60 and 71). The Treaty included a range of protections for Catholics and, thereafter, the Nguyen court ceased its persecution of Catholics (Keith, 2012: 49). By 1883, all of Vietnam fell to the French who continued to enforce the protections from discrimination against the Catholics.

British approaches to religious management

The first of Britain's eastern colonies was India where the East India Company established a trading post at Surat in 1612, and then later Presidency towns in Madras (1640), Bombay (1648) and Calcutta (1690). Later, it acquired Penang (1786), Malacca and Singapore (1824), Burma (1824–1885), Hong Kong (1897), North Borneo (1888) and Brunei (1906). The period of British colonisation in the East was during the reign of Queen Victoria

(1837–1901) which was also a time when Christian missionary activity was at its height. And while the overriding motivations were 'commerce and Christianity,' the British took a very practical approach to evangelism and the management of natives and their customs and beliefs. This was to be done through an enlightened approach in the application of English law to the colonised territories and to the administration of justice in these territories.

The British acquired their possessions either through discovery, conquest or cession. Such territories are usually governed under a constitutional framework set out in an Order in Council. And in territories that accepted British Advisors, their relationship with the metropolis was set out through bilateral treaties. However, none of these instruments accord any constitutional rights to British subjects. Rights of individuals were safeguarded through the application of the common law, and it is to the courts that we need to turn to see how religious liberties were administered. In India, the British East India Company first introduced and enforced an English-style legal and judicial system through the establishment of a court system modelled on that of England (see generally Fawcett, 1934; Lindsay, 1936). The first such court was established in 1687 by the Company itself through a Charter that constituted Madras as a municipality with a Mayor, and established the Mayor's Court with civil and criminal jurisdiction over all inhabitants of Madras.

Later, in 1726, a Royal Charter formally established Mayor's Courts in all three Presidency Towns. The Mayor's Courts consisted of a mayor and nine aldermen (at least seven of whom were to be 'natural born' British subjects). At the same time, the presidents and councils of these settlements were designated Justices of the Peace and were empowered to hold criminal quarter sessions. These early courts suffered from two main flaws. The first was that they sat side-by-side with traditional judicial bodies in India, such as the Zamindar's Court and did not have jurisdiction over all persons within their territory, especially the native inhabitants. Second, members of the Mayor's Court were subordinate to the East India Company and were liable to be dismissed by the Company's governor and councils. As such, they did not have judicial independence. This fact was duly noted by Lord North in 1772 when he was appointed by the Secret Committee of the House of Commons to enquire into Indian affairs. North, who was also Britain's Prime Minister at the time, further noted that the judges administering justice in the Mayor's Courts were generally ignorant of English law.

That said, the Charter of 1726 was important in two ways. First, because the Mayor's Courts were established by the grant of a Royal Charter, these courts were technically part of the system of the King's courts and were not those of the Company alone. Second, the Charter enjoined the Court to 'give Judgment and Sentence according to Justice and Right' to try persons 'accused of any Crimes or Offences … in the same, or the like Manner and Form will admit of' as in England. At the same time, the Court was instructed to inflict punishment in a manner such that it 'shall not be repugnant to the religious Customs or Manners of the Person on whom it is to be inflicted.' This is highly significant since it effectively imported the whole of the English common law into India and required judgement to be on the same basis and on the same standards as English law. At the same time, it afforded local courts sufficient latitude to apply the law in a way that took into account local circumstances, including the religious sensitivities of the local inhabitants. This was thus the established template for the export of British justice and colonial courts to other territories.

The main defects of the 1726 Charter were rectified by the passage of the East India Company Act (better known as the Regulating Act) which Lord North presented to Parliament in 1773. Section 13 of the Act specifically provided for the establishment of a Supreme Court of Judicature in Fort William in Bengal, consisting of a Chief Justice and three other Judges 'being Barristers in England or Ireland, of not less than five years' standing' to be appointed by the King.

This ensured that judges administering justice were familiar with English law. Courts of civil, criminal and ecclesiastical jurisdiction were also established in all three Presidency towns. To further safeguard judicial independence, the Regulating Act forbade the Governor-General and Judges from accepting any presents and engaging in any commerce. Section 36 required all rules, ordinances and regulations passed by the Governor-General in Council to be 'just and reasonable' and not 'repugnant to the laws of the realm' and registered and published in the Supreme Court Registry.

Following the Regulating Act, a Royal Charter establishing the Supreme Court of Judicature at Fort William in Calcutta was issued in March 1774. The Court was to have both common law and equity jurisdictions, and criminal justice was to be administered in exactly the manner as the central criminal courts in England. The Court of Judicature had admiralty jurisdiction, and appeals of its decisions were to be made to the King in Council (Privy Council). In addition, the Charter empowered the Court to approve, admit and enrol lawyers to appear before the Court as well as to regulate the legal profession generally.

The use of courts to substantively regulate rights was a distinctly British innovation which impacted religious freedom in several ways. First, because all courts established in the British territories formed part of a single network of courts that applied the same rules, there was no discrimination in application of the law. Second, all locally constituted courts were enjoined to take into account local circumstances, including the religion of the local inhabitants in the application of English law. Third, the judicial branch of colonial government acted independently from the executive branch and was often staffed by much more highly qualified individuals than ordinary colonial servants. All judges were, for example, persons who were legally qualified – oftentimes from top universities such as Oxford or Cambridge – and who had attained a knighthood before they were posted to the colonies.

This is not to say that Christian missionaries from Britain and other European countries, such as France and Portugal, did not flourish (see generally Carey, 2011). The colonial government offered them many facilities – such as choice sites for churches and schools – to enable them to carry out their missions, but were careful not to be seen as forcing Christianity down the throats of the local population.

The Japanese as colonisers

Among the states in Asia, the Japanese were the first to constitutionalise the right to the freedom of religion. The Meiji Constitution of 1889 provides that all Japanese subjects 'shall, within limits not prejudicial to peace and order, and not antagonistic to their duties as subjects, enjoy freedom of religious belief.' This constitutional guarantee did not, however, apply to states which the Japanese colonised – notably Taiwan and Korea.

Taiwan – or Formosa, as the Portuguese sailors called the island – was first colonised by the Spanish and then the Dutch in the seventeenth century and was annexed as part of the Qing empire in 1683. Since many of its inhabitants were immigrants from China and of Han Chinese extraction, they practised Taoism, Confucianism and other Chinese folk religions (see Jones, 2003: 15–16). The brief Spanish occupation introduced Catholicism to the island, and later on, Dutch missionaries introduced Presbyterianism as well. Japan occupied Taiwan in 1895, following China's defeat in the Sino-Japanese War, and ruled the island till 1945. Japanese policy toward religion evolved over three distinct periods. In the first period, from about 1895 to 1915, Japan adopted a 'laissez-faire attitude toward native religion.' This gave way to a second period, from 1915 to 1937, when the Japanese 'tried more vigorously to investigate and regulate local religious institutions and practices.' In the final period, which coincided with

Japanese hostilities against mainland China, the Japanese tried to 'Japanise' the local population (Jones, 2003: 19). The 'Japanization Movement' attempted to 'turn the Han people of Taiwan into ethnic Japanese' by imposing

> a ban on any Chinese dialect in print or public discourse, the enforcement of Japanese-style dress, pressure to renovate homes in accordance with customary Japanese design, inviting loyal families to apply for new Japanese names, and a ban on Chinese cultural activities. ... In the religious sphere, this involved efforts to wean people away from traditional Chinese religion and into the nexus of State Shinto.
>
> *(Jones, 2003: 24)*

This strategy was known as *Kominka*, or 'total assimilation,' a 'union with the Emperor's people' or 'changing into Imperial subjects' (Meltzer, 2017: 15). Among other things, the racial discrimination against the Taiwanese was 'legally scrapped and mixed marriages and social integration were allowed.' At the same time, 'each home was required to have a Shinto shrine altar on which to honour the Sun Goddess and the Emperor Hirohito' (Meltzer, 2017: 15).

The story was much the same in Korea, a state made up of three earlier kingdoms – Goguryeo, Baekje and Silla. The Goryeo or 'Koryo' period (918–1392) is considered the 'golden age of Buddhism' as it became the national religion, displacing traditional folk religion and shamanism. Later, Buddhism was supplanted by Confucianism as a state ideology at the end of the fourteenth century, and Buddhists were persecuted, as in China. Christianity arrived on Korean shores towards the end of the eighteenth century, and Christians were almost immediately persecuted on the grounds that their religion abolished the traditional Confucian practice of ancestor worship (Suh and Kim, 2001). The Japanese, who had begun exerting influence in Korea in 1871, annexed the state in 1910. In the 15 years leading up to its annexation, the Japanese promoted Buddhism as they saw it as 'a highly useful way of winning the Korean population over to their cause' and abolished the anti-Buddhist laws of the Confucian-dominated Korean government (Sorensen, 1993: 51). The Japanese Resident-General in Korea, Ito Hirobumi, also promoted Christianity because he felt that religion must be 'tolerated and encouraged' as civilisation depended on morality and there was no higher morality than religion (Sorensen, 1993: 58). However, when the Koreans began asserting their right to self-determination with the launch of the Independence Movement in 1919, the Japanese turned on Christianity, which they saw as a major anti-colonial force (Sorensen, 1993: 61). Many churches were closed, and practically all Christian pastors in Seoul were arrested and imprisoned (Kang, 1967: 129). On the other hand, the Japanese found Confucianism useful for controlling the Korean population and encouraged classical learning and education (Sorensen, 1993: 62). By 1931, at the start of Japan's militarist period, it attempted to make Koreans loyal citizens by urging all Koreans to participate in Shinto ceremonies and building more new Shinto shrines throughout Korea (Kang, 2014: 146). This urging turned to compulsion after 1937 when Japan invaded Manchuria following the Marco Polo Bridge Incident (Kang, 2014: 153–155). And in 1940, in celebration of the 2600th anniversary of Japan's founding, all Koreans were ordered to abandon their traditional family names and adopt Japanese names. At the same time, the names of all missionary institutions and churches were also ordered to be changed. For example, the Salvation Army became the Salvation Society, while the Methodist Church became the Methodist Society (Kang, 2014: 156).

Japan's expansionist campaigns into China precipitated the Pacific War, with attacks on Pearl Harbour in Hawaii, and the conquest of Burma, Malaya, Singapore, Borneo and the Philippines. As in Korea and Taiwan, the Japanese took a hard-line stance against the local population and ruled by decree. The Japanese attitude toward religion was largely political rather than spiritual. In some colonies, there was an attempt – as in Korea and Taiwan – to *Nipponise* the population by forcing the conquered peoples to learn Japanese, sing *Kimigayo*, the Japanese national anthem, bow in the direction of Japan and in many cases, restrict the practice of certain religions, especially, Christianity. Restrictions on religious freedoms were more drastic if the religion or its congregation was seen as a threat to the Japanese power or authority. But to the many colonised territories in Asia, the Japanese painted themselves as fellow Asian liberators and decolonisers. They were thus anxious to woo the local populations to their cause and not unnecessarily upset the local rulers and their people by taking too hard a line on religion. This was particularly so in Malaya, Indonesia and Brunei where the Japanese 'adopted a policy of non-interference in local cultural practices, giving due respect to Islamic and Malay customs' (Abu Talib Ahmad, 2002: 107; see also Akashi, 1969). This policy was unevenly administered and had the tendency to incense, rather inspire, the locals. As Kratoska noted, in relation to Malaya:

> the Japanese lacked a coherent policy toward the Malay community, and their insistence that people bow in the direction of the Imperial Palace, their use of religious occasions to deliver propaganda, the inclusion of prayers to the Emperor and to Japanese soldiers killed during the war in mosque services, and the promotion of lotteries and other forms of gambling offended many Muslims. Moreover, for want of active support from the administration, officials concerned with religious affairs found it difficult to carry out their duties, and the observance of religious obligations became noticeably lax. It was, of course, impossible for Muslims in Malaya to make the pilgrimage to Mecca for the duration of the occupation.
>
> *(Kratoska, 1998: 111)*

In the Philippines, the Japanese Military Administration (JMA) promised not to interfere in the affairs of the Catholic Church which also tried to cooperate with the Japanese forces. However, given the Japanese record of brutality in Korea and Manchuria, the Filipinos never really trusted the Japanese. Again, religious liberty was accommodated and tolerated only insofar as it did not trump Japanese military expediency. Priests were murdered, churches and their valuables were seized, and the former turned into dance halls by soldiers or used as warehouses by the JMA who sought to pulverise the Church into total submission (Parpan, 1969: 463–464). In Burma, the influential Buddhist monks mistakenly assumed that Japan, being a Buddhist country, 'would see that religion was accorded its rightful place once the British were thrown out' but were quickly disabused of this notion when 'the occupying Japanese proved to be even less considerate of the monks than the civilian population' (Cady, 1953: 155).

Decolonisation and the making of modern states and constitutions

The Pacific War came to an abrupt end with Japan's unconditional surrender to the Allied Forces in August 1945. The British returned to their former territories in Southeast Asia and Hong Kong, while the French resumed control of Indochina. The Dutch would spend the next four years fighting nationalist forces in the Dutch East Indies in a war of independence that ended with the Dutch recognising Indonesian independence in December 1949. The end of World War II brought on the age of decolonisation. In Asia, the old British, French, Portuguese and Dutch powers would soon be forced to divest themselves of their former colonies, either by force (as in the case of the French and Dutch) or by negotiation (as in much of the former British territories). Accompanying the birth of these new states was a flurry of constitution-making activity which, among other things, constitutionalised the right to the freedom of religion by embedding it in the constitution.

When the United Nations was established in 1945, one of the first things the General Assembly did was to appoint a Human Rights Commission under the chairmanship of Eleanor Roosevelt. The Commission lost no time in working on a charter of human rights that would eventually become the Universal Declaration of Human Rights (see Glendon, 2001). One of the key provisions the Commission wrestled with was Article 18, regarding the freedom of religion, which states (see Lindvist, 2017):

> Everyone has the right to freedom of thought, conscience and religion; this right includes freedom to change his religion or belief, and freedom, either alone or in community with others and in public or private, to manifest his religion or belief in teaching, practice, worship and observance.

While the general principles underlying Article 18 were uncontroversial, several Muslim-majority states – Afghanistan, Egypt, Iraq, Saudi Arabia and Syria – objected to the inclusion of the right to change one's religion on the grounds that Islam forbade a Muslim from changing or abandoning his or her religion. However, Pakistan's Zafrullah Khan – a distinguished Islamic scholar and diplomat – argued that the Quran did in fact support the freedom of religion (Lindvist, 2017: 95–96). When put before the General Assembly, no Muslim country objected to Article 18. This clause was eventually fleshed out in more concrete form in the International Covenant of Civil and Political Rights (ICCPR), also in Article 18, as follows:

> 18(1) Everyone shall have the right to freedom of thought, conscience and religion. This right shall include freedom to have or to adopt a religion or belief of his choice, and freedom, either individually or in community with others and in public or private, to manifest his religion or belief in worship, observance, practice and teaching.
>
> (2) No one shall be subject to coercion which would impair his freedom to have or to adopt a religion or belief of his choice.
>
> (3) Freedom to manifest one's religion or beliefs may be subject only to such limitations as are prescribed by law and are necessary to protect public safety, order, health, or morals or the fundamental rights and freedoms of others.
>
> (4) The States Parties to the present Covenant undertake to have respect for the liberty of parents and, when applicable, legal guardians to ensure the religious and moral education of their children in conformity with their own convictions.

What is notable in the ICCPR version of Article 18 is the characterisation of this as a derogable right where limitations may be imposed on grounds of public safety, order, health and morality. Article 18 of the ICCPR is significant in offering itself as a template for adoption and adaptation by several Asian states, such as India, Pakistan, Malaysia and Singapore, where the grounds of derogation were included in extenso.

We noted earlier that the first constitutional guarantee of the freedom of religion in Asia was found in Article 28 of the Meiji Constitution of 1889 which provides that all Japanese subjects 'shall, within limits not prejudicial to peace and order, and not antagonistic to their duties as subjects, enjoy freedom of religious belief.' The Provisional Constitution of the Republic of

China 1912, drafted after the 1911 Revolution that ended imperial rule in China, provides that citizens 'shall have the freedom of religion.'[10] However, these early efforts in constitutionalising the freedom of religion were exceptions rather than the norm. It was only after the end of World War II that serious efforts were made to infuse constitutional documents with rights, including that of religious freedom.

The flurry of constitution-making activity in the immediate post-War period saw inclusion of religious freedom clauses in almost all constitutions. These clauses came in two forms: (1) a direct clause guaranteeing freedom of religion to all persons and (2) a supplementary anti-discrimination clause as part of the general provisions on equality. The Constitution of India of 1950, provides, for example, that among other things, no citizen may be discriminated against 'on grounds only of religion, race, caste, sex, place or birth or any of them' [Art. 15(1)]. At the same time, it provides that subject to 'public order, morality and health ... all person are equally entitled to the freedom of conscience and the right to freely profess, practise and propagate religion' [Art. 25(1)].

However, beyond these generalities, constitutional arrangements and guarantees regarding religious freedom varied greatly throughout Asia. Neo, studying contemporary constitutions in Asia, provides a useful tripartite map to locate the approach adopted by the Asian states. The first category of states explicitly privileges a particular religion; the second subordinates religion to state interests; and the third steadfastly maintains the separation between state and religion (Neo, forthcoming). Historically, the first states in Asia to privilege religion – either by proclaiming 'state' or 'official' religions – were Indonesia (1945),[11] Cambodia (1947)[12] and Laos (1947).[13] These states were later joined by Pakistan (1956),[14] Malaysia (1957),[15] Sri Lanka (1978),[16] Bangladesh (1988),[17] Myanmar (2008),[18] and Maldives (2008).[19] In most of these cases, the various constitutions simultaneously recognise the right of individuals to profess a faith of their choice. For example, Article 3 of the Federal Constitution of Malaysia proclaims Islam as the 'religion of the Federation,' while Article 11 of the same constitution guarantees every person 'the right to profess and practice his religion.' We should note that in some states, the privileging of religion came later in their constitutional lives. For example, the Ceylon Constitution of 1948 provided that there be no law enacted that would 'prohibit or restrict the free exercise of religion' [Art. 29(2)(a)], but this was changed 30 years later in 1978 when a new constitution was adopted that required Sri Lanka to 'give to Buddhism the foremost place' and to 'protect

10 Article 6(7) of the 1912 Provisional Constitution of the Republic of China, in 6(3) *American Journal of International Law, Supplement: Official Documents*, 1912: 149–154.

11 Article 29(1) of the Constitution of the Republic of Indonesia, 1945, provides that 'The State shall be based upon One and Only God.'

12 Article 8 of the Constitution of the Kingdom of Cambodia, 1947, proclaims Buddhism to be the state religion.

13 Article 7 of the Constitution of the Kingdom of Laos, 1947, proclaims Buddhism as the religion of the state and the King as its 'High Protector.'

14 The Preamble of the 1956 Pakistan Constitution states that Pakistan shall be 'a democratic State based on Islamic principles of social justice,' while Article 1 proclaims it to be a federal state known as the Islamic Republic of Pakistan.

15 Article 3 of the Federal Constitution of Malaysia proclaims Islam as the 'religion of the Federation.'

16 Article 9 of the Constitution of Sri Lanka, 1978, requires the state to 'give to Buddhism the foremost place' and places a duty on the state to 'protect and foster the Buddha Sasana.'

17 Article 2A of the Constitution of Bangladesh declares Islam to be the 'state religion.'

18 Section 361 of the Constitution of the Republic of the Union of Myanmar, 2008, recognises the 'special position of Buddhism.'

19 Article 10(a) of the Maldives Constitution, 2008, proclaims Islam to be the religion of the state.

and foster the Buddha Sasana.' Similarly, when the state of Bangladesh was established in 1971, a strictly secular constitution was drafted. However, this was jettisoned in 1988 when Islam was proclaimed the state religion.

States that subordinate religion to state interests are statist or communitarian states 'that do not adopt a particular religious commitment but see religion as a subject of state control' (Neo, forthcoming). Among these are the communist states of China, Vietnam, North Korea and Laos as well as states such as India and Singapore. In these countries, state interests trump those of any religion or religious group. Finally, Neo lists three states that maintain a strict separation between state and religion: Philippines, South Korea and Japan. Two of these – Philippines and South Korea – have constitutions that contain anti-establishment clauses, while the Japanese Supreme Court has ruled that the constitutional guarantee of the freedom of religion requires the state to be religiously neutral (Neo, forthcoming).

Conclusion

Useful as the above three categories are, they do not paint a sufficient picture of the state of religious freedom in Asia. Except for Brunei and the Maldives, all states in Asia have constitutions with a bill of rights that embed the right to religious freedom in one form or another. Yet this right is often ignored or negated, or worse still, actively suppressed by the very states that are constitutionally obliged to protect it (see for example Bouma et al., 2010).

The history of religions and their practice in Asia is a long one. In contrast, the history of the right to religious freedom is much shorter and problematic. Asian states and societies did not value individuals in the same way states steeped in the Judeo-Christian tradition do. As a result, there was little attempt to transform religious choice and practice into rights that individuals could use against the state. In most cases, the best that could be hoped for is the absence of persecution or discrimination. For many Asian states, religion was both a unifier and destroyer because of the power of religious belief to mobilise the masses. States and rulers who profess or closely identify with a particular religion might use it to galvanise the people or to destroy its opponents. Even in the age of constitutional guarantees, religion is used in many cases to dominate and oppress.

References

Abu Talib Ahmad, 2002. Japanese policy towards Islam in Malaya during the occupation: a reassessment. *Journal of Southeast Asian Studies*. 33(1), 107.

Akashi, Y., 1969. Japanese military administration in Malaya – its formation and evolution in reference to Sultans, the Islamic Religion, and the Moslem-Malays, 1941–1945. *Asian Studies*. 7(1), 81.

Andaya, B.W., Ishii, Y., 1992. Religious developments in Southeast Asia c1500–1800. In: N. Tarling (Ed.), *The Cambridge History of Southeast Asia*, vol. 1. Cambridge University Press. 508.

Aston, W.G., 1956. *Nihongi: Chronicles of Japan from the Earliest Times to AD 697*. George Allen & Unwin.

Benda, H.J., 1958. Christiaan Snouck Hurgronje and the foundations of Dutch Islamic Policy in Indonesia. *Journal of Modern History*. 30(4), 338.

Bentley-Taylor, D., 1967. *The Weathercock's Reward: Christian Progress in Muslim Java*. Overseas Missionary Fellowship.

Bouma, G.D., Ling, R., Pratt, D., 2010. *Religious Diversity in Southeast Asia and the Pacific: National Case Studies*. Springer.

Brakel, L.F., 2004. 'Islam and local traditions: syncretic ideas and practices'. *Indonesia Malay World*. 32(92), 5.

Burman, J.J.R., 1996. Hindu-Muslim syncretism in India. *Economic and Political Weekly*. 31(20), 1211.

Cady, J.F., 1953. Religion and politics in modern Burma. *The Far Eastern Quarterly*. 12(2), 149.

Carey, H.M., 2011. *God's Empire: Religion and Colonialism in the British World, c 1801–1908.* Cambridge University Press.
Carey, P., 2007. *The Power of Prophecy: Prince Dipanagara and the End of an Old Order in Java, 1785–1855.* KITLV Press.
Cotterell, A., 2010. *Western Power in Asia: Its Slow Rise and Swift Fall, 1415–1999.* John Wiley & Sons.
Cunningham, A., 1877. *Corpus Inscriptionum Indicarum: Inscriptions of Asoka*, vol. 1. Office of the Superintendent of Government Printing.
da Silva, G.F., 1997. The impact of Portuguese culture on Goa: a myth or a reality? In: C.J. Borges and H. Feldmann (Eds.), *Goa and Portugal: Their Cultural Links.* Concept Publishing. 41.
de Bary, W.M.T., Bloom, I. (Eds. and Trans.), 1999. *Sources of Chinese Tradition*, vol. 1. Columbia University Press. 585.
de Casparis, J.G., Mabbett, I.W., 1992. Religion and popular beliefs of Southeast Asia before c1500. In: N. Tarling (Ed.), *The Cambridge History of Southeast Asia*, vol. 1. Cambridge University Press. 276.
De Groot, J.J.M., 1903-1904. *Sectarianism and Religious Persecution in China: A Page in the History of Religions.* 2 vols. J Muller.
de Kat Angelino, A.D.A., 1931. *Colonial Policy – Volume 2: The Dutch East Indies.* (G.J. Renier, Trans.). Martinus Nijhoff. 336.
Desai, D.R.S., 1969. The Portuguese administration in Malacca, 1511–1641. *Journal of Southeast Asian History.* 10(3), 501.
DuBois, T.D., 2011. *Religion and the Making of Modern East Asia.* Cambridge University Press.
Eaton, R.M., 2000. Temple desecration and Indo-Muslim states. *Journal of Islamic Studies.* 11(3), 283.
Elliot, H.M., Dowson, J. (ed. and transl.), 1867-1877. *The History of India as Told by Its Own Historians*, vol. 1. Kitab Mahaal. 140.
Engelbrecht, E.M.L. (ed.), 1933. *De Nederlandsch-Indische Wetboeken Benevens de Grondwet Voor Het Koninkrijk der Nederlanden [The Dutch Indies Code and the Constitution for the Kingdom of the Netherlands].* AW Sijthoff's Uitgenersmij NV. 86.
Farmer, E.L., 1995. *Zhu Yuanzhang & Early Ming Legislation: The Reordering of Chinese Society following the End of Mongol Rule.* Brill.
Fawcett, C., 1934. *The First Century of British Justice in India: An Account of the Court of Judicature of Bombay, Established in 1672, and of Other Courts of Justice in Madras, Calcutta and Bombay, from 1661 to the Latter Part of the Eighteenth Century.* Clarendon Press.
Ghoshal, B., 2010. Arabization: the changing face of Islam in Asia. *India Quart.* 66(1), 69.
Giullman, I., Klimkeit, H.-J., 1999. *Christians in Asia Before 1500.* Curzon Press.
Glendon, M.A., 2001. *A World Made New: Eleanor Roosevelt and the Universal Declaration of Human Rights.* Random House.
Goscha, C., 2017. *The Penguin History of Modern Vietnam.* Penguin Books.
Jones, C.B., 2003. Religion in Taiwan at the end of the Japanese colonial period. In: P. Clart and C.B. Jones (Eds.), *Religion in Modern Taiwan: Tradition and Innovation in a Changing Society.* University of Hawaii Press. 10.
Kang, D.C., 2014. Why was there no religious war in premodern East Asia?. *European Journal of International Relations.* 20(4), 965.
Kang, W.J., 1967. *The Japanese Government and Religions in Korea, 1910–1945.* PhD dissertation. University of Chicago.
Keith, C., 2012. *Catholic Vietnam: A Church from Empire to Nation.* University of California Press.
Kratoska, P., 1998. *The Japanese Occupation of Malaya 1941–1945.* Allen & Unwin.
Lindsay, B., 1936. British justice in India. *University of Toronto Law Journal.* 1(2), 343.
Lindvist, L., 2017. *Religious Freedom and the University Declaration of Human Rights.*Cambridge University Press.
Lu, D.J., 1997. *Japan: A Documentary History.* ME Sharpe.
McLeod, M.W., 1992. Nationalism and religion in Vietnam: Phan Boi Chau and the catholic question. *The International History Review.* 14(4), 661.
Meltzer, J.J., 2017. *Taiwan's Transformation: 1895 to the Present.* Palgrave Macmillan.
Moffett, S.H., 2005. *A History of Christianity in Asia, Volume II: 1500 to 1900.* Orbis Books.
Neo, J.L. (forthcoming). State religion arrangements and religious freedom in Asia. In: Law D.S., Lau, H., Schwartz, A. (Eds.), *Oxford Handbook of Comparative Constitutional Law.* Oxford University Press.
Pan, P.C., James, V., 2001. Vietnam. In S.W. Sunquist (Ed.), *A Dictionary of Asian Christianity.* William B Eerdmans Publishing Co. 876.

Parpan sj A.G., 1969. The Japanese and the Philippine church, 1942–45. *Philip. Stud.* 37, 451.
Peerenboom, R., 2002. Law and religion in early China. In A. Huxley (Ed.), *Religion, Law and Tradition: Comparative Studies in Religious Law*. Routledge. 84.
Rausch, F., n.d. Violence against catholics in East Asia: Japan, China and Korea from the late sixteenth century to the early twentieth century. In *Oxford Handbooks Online*. Oxford University Press.
Roy-Chowdhury, M.L., 1941. Position of Christians in the Mughal Empire. Proceedings of the Indian History Congress. 5, 347.
Sitoy Jr, T.V., 1985. *A History of Christianity in the Philippines, Vol 1: The Initial Encounter*. New Day Publishers.
Sitoy Jr, T.V., 2001. Philippines. In S.W. Sunquist (Ed.), *A Dictionary of Asian Christianity*. William B Eerdmans Publishing Co. 654.
Smith, R.J., 1994. Buddhism and the great persecution in China. In K. Keulman (Ed.), *Critical Moments in Religious History*. Mercer University Press. 59.
Sorensen, H.H., 1993. The attitude of the Japanese colonial government towards religion in Korea (1910–1919). *Copenhagen Journal of Asian Studies*. 8, 49.
Steenbrink, K., 2006. *Dutch Colonialism and Indonesian Islam* (J. Steenbrink and H. Janesen, Trans.). Rodopi.
Suh, D., Kim, H.S., 2001. Korea, freedom of religion in. In: S.W. Sunquist (Ed.), *A Dictionary of Asian Christianity*. William B Eerdmans Publishing Co. 449.
Taslim, N., 2013. Narratives of war: Achenese perceptions of the *Prang Kaphe* in the 19th/20th century colonial era. *Malay Literat.* 26(2), 139.
The Great Ming Code: Da Ming Lü, 2005. Translated and introduced by J. Yonglin. University of Washington Press.
Tucker, S.C., 1999. *Vietnam*. University Press of Kentucky.
von Albertini R., Wirz, A., 1982. *European Colonial Rule, 1880–1940: The Impact of the West on India, Southeast Asia and Africa* (J. G. Williamson, Trans.). Greenwood Press.
Wheeler, J.T., 1877. *History of India: Hindu, Buddhist and Brahmanical*. Trübner & Co.
Wu, Y., Jiang, Y., 2007. The Emperor's four bodies: embodied rulership and legal culture in early Ming China. *Frontiers of History in China*. 2(1), 25.

4

The right to freedom of religion: An historical perspective from Africa

Ahmed Salisu Garba[1]

Introduction

It is far from easy to discuss the right to freedom of religion in Africa from an historical perspective. This is because Africa is a conglomeration of over 50 countries, each with its own history and politics, and each consisting of numerous ethnic groups with a wide-ranging mixture of cultures, languages and religions. This raises two challenges concerning the sources and limitations of the existing studies (An-Na'im, 2012).

As far as sources are concerned, it should be noted that debates among scholars on freedom of religion or belief in Africa are mainly focused on the universality of the concept as a component of human rights and the regulation of religion. These works do not address the history and perception of the concept of freedom of religion in Africa. Nevertheless, there are works on the general history of religion in Africa from which conclusions on the history and perception of this concept can be derived. This chapter therefore draws on the general literature on the history of religion to explore and explain the historic trajectory of freedom of religion in Africa. It grapples with the challenges involved in analyzing the interactions of the three major religions: African Traditional Religion (ATR), Islam and Christianity. Conventional historical methods of research are not easy to apply to issues of religion in Africa because scholars have not focused on ATR from an historical perspective due to the absence of sufficient material (Westerlund, 1991; Ikenga-Metuh, 1987; Ray, 1976: 11; see also Ikenga-Metuh, 1985). In addition, as regards African history in places such as central Sudan, the Kano and Borno chronicles are important documents but little of them survived. The second challenge regards the apparent bias of some early missionaries, travelers and colonial officers who studied the history of ATR in the eighteenth and nineteenth centuries (Ochonu, 2014), such as Sir Samuel Baker and Sir Richard Burton, who described ATR as fetishistic, cannibalistic, animistic, complicated, bizarre, savage and primitive beliefs and practices (Evans-Pritchard, 1965: 231).

Moreover, Trimingham (1962: 3) notes that Muslim and early European travelers 'help us to penetrate the veil a little, but only a little' because frequently they did not fully understand what they saw. He gives the example of Ibn Battuta, who lived among his own people in the

1 I am grateful to Professor Mark Hill QC and Professor Silvio Ferrari for their assistance in the preparation of this chapter.

merchant quarters of the capital of Mali and other towns, but could not get below the surface (1962: 3). Trimingham's legitimate concern is that with such limited material available, historians have tended falsely to regard states as fully organized Muslim Kingdoms, whereas in truth they were pagan in essence, with only the immediate court entourage and largely foreign trading communities making a profession of Islam.

This chapter starts with a discussion of Africa, its people and religion, before the coming of Islam and Christianity. Thereafter comes a discussion of the emergence of Islam in North Africa, Sudan and the Sahara and its lasting impact for the present day. The manner in which Africans accommodated the mode of propagation of Islam and Christianity in their domains is illustrative of how Africans understood the concept of freedom of religion. The remainder of the chapter is devoted to the emergence and spread of Christianity in Africa and the interaction of Christians with practitioners of ATR.

The chapter argues that Africans have a unique perception of the concept of freedom of religion and belief which exists in the form of live and let live without any condition. This African perception was not due to any conscious knowledge of what freedom of religion and belief means in modern times. Rather, this perception was formed by the influence of features of African Traditional Religion: in particular ATR is not a revealed religion, it has no founder, it is accommodating in its nature, and it is non-proselyting. Thus, the concept of freedom of religion may have originated in Africa but without Africans and the world at large being aware of it.

The continent of Africa

Africa is the second largest and second most populous continent in the world, after Asia. It covers 6% of the earth's total surface area which equates to about 11.7 million square miles and 20.4% of the total land area of the globe (Sayre, 2009). With an excess of a billion people in more than 50 countries including the Sahrawi Arab Democratic Republic,[2] this represents about 14.72% of the world's population (Sayre, 2009).

Precolonial Africa comprised a conglomeration of close to 10,000 different states and societies with various political systems (Meredith, 2006). These consisted of small family groups of hunter-gatherers such as the San people of Southern Africa, the large Sahelian Kingdoms, autonomous city-states and kingdoms such as those of the Yoruba and Igbo people in West Africa, and the Swahili coastal trading towns of East Africa (Mokhtar, 1990).

By the ninth century, a series of dynastic states, including the earliest of the Hausa,[3] stretched across the sub-Saharan savannah from the western regions to central Sudan. The most powerful of these were Ghana, Gao and the Kanem-Bornu empire which embraced Islam in the eleventh century (O'Brien, 2005). Ghana fell in the eleventh century but was succeeded by the Mali empire which consolidated much of western Sudan in the thirteenth century. In the forested regions of the West African coast, independent kingdoms grew up which were little influenced by the Muslim north. The Kingdom of Nri – a city-state of the Igbo people[4] – was among the first to be established sometime in the ninth century. It is also one of the oldest kingdoms in modern-day Nigeria and was ruled by the Eze Nri. It is famous for its elaborate bronzes found at the town of Igbo Ukwu (Oliver and Atmore, 1994).

---

2 Asante (2007). Note that Sahrawi is a member state of the African Union whose statehood is disputed by Morocco.

3 They were a group of neighboring states in what is today northern Nigeria. The Hausa people are the largest ethnic group of the area.

4 The Igbo people are an ethnic group living in south central and southeastern Nigeria. Nri was a medieval kingdom of the Igbo people.

The continent today is generally spoken of regionally as West Africa, North Africa, East Africa, and Southern Africa. West Africa stretches from Senegal along the Atlantic coast, all the way to Nigeria, and down to the Gulf of Guinea. This part of Africa experienced trade with Europeans and Muslims from North Africa for a long time. East Africa comprises modern Sudan, Ethiopia, Eritrea, Djibouti, Somalia, Kenya, Uganda and Tanzania. There are more than 200 distinct indigenous societies, all with different languages, economic systems and cultures which traded with the Arabs along the coast of East Africa. Southern Africa consists of Botswana, Zimbabwe, Mozambique, Swaziland, Lesotho, Namibia and the Republic of South Africa.

African traditional religion, Islam and Christianity

African Traditional Religion (ATR) is a belief system that originated in Africa and is practiced by generations of Africans (Egonu, 1988). It was the dominant religion in Africa for centuries and continues to exist in many forms (Ibenwa, 2014: 149–150). It is regarded as tolerant in form, with a deep-seated ethnic and cultural underlay and a culture in which generosity and hospitality might be recognized as particular virtues.[5] Holding or maintaining to a uniform doctrine is not the essence of indigenous African religions (Robinson, 2004: 141; see also Bewaji, 2004). An important feature is that it is not proselytizing nor oppositional to other belief systems (Onyeidu, 1999). There are no recorded instances of religious bigotry (Onyeidu, 1999), and in contrast to Islam and Christianity, it has no recognized founder, no scripture and no creeds (Ibenwa, 2014: 149). There is little in the way of written literature, yet it is ubiquitous in Africa and the wider world (Awolalu and Dopamu, 1979). Its doctrines are largely in the oral tradition of myth and folklore (Awolalu and Dopamu, 1979). Ekwunife (1990) states that it has been 'transmitted to the present generation by successive African forebears mainly through oral traditions (myths and folktales, songs and dances, liturgies, rituals, proverbs, pithy sayings and names).'

ATR shares common features with Islam and Christianity such as belief in God or gods (theism), a system of worship (cult) prayer, sacrifices and a distinct differentiation between the holy (sacred) and unholy (profane) (Ibenwa, 2014: 149–150). Ibenwa (2014: 149–150) is of the opinion that these are features which might have prepared the mind of Africans for the acceptance of Islam and Christianity. In addition, ATR has its own social control system in the form of taboos, swearing of oaths, making of blood pacts, trial by ordeal, oracles, vows, secret societies and the observance of custom and tradition (Jordan, 1948).

A dominant academic argument regarding ATR concerns its homogeneity or heterogeneity. Arguing for heterogeneity, Booth (1977: 3) and Mbiti both maintain that ATR is diverse and must be spoken of in the plural sense. Mbiti stated, 'we speak of African Traditional Religions in the plural because there are one thousand African Peoples (tribes) and each has its religious system' (1969; see also 1970). But the tide has shifted in favor of homogeneity, backed by leading scholars such as Magesa (1997), Idowu (1973), Maquet (1972) and Parrinder (1962). Even Mbiti, who had argued against the homogeneity of ATR in his previous works moved to support it, proposing five interrelated elements which together constitute ATR (1991a: 11–13; see also 1991b). Stammer, a proponent of the homogeneity school, described ATR, despite its diverse forms of expression, as:

5 See, by way of analogy, Izutsu (1966).

> a global framework of life, encompassing every human situation and governing the whole of society. It is closely linked to the ancestral soil and places each African both in the succession of the generations (the ancestors), in his relationship with his fellow creatures and in his productive activities. Everything is religious!
>
> *(Stammer, 1995: 121–125)*

Professor Jacob Olupona commented on the dynamism, inclusiveness and flexibility of ATR in the following terms:

> African spirituality has always been able to adapt to change and allow itself to absorb the wisdom and views of other religions, much more than, for example, Christianity and Islam. While Islam and Christianity tend to be overtly resistant to adopting traditional African religious ideas or practices, indigenous African religions have always accommodated other beliefs. For example, an African amulet might have inside of it a written verse from either the Koran or Christian Bible. The idea is that the traditional African practitioner who constructed that amulet believes in the efficacy of other faiths and religions; there is no conflict in his mind between his traditional African spirituality and another faith. They are not mutually exclusive. He sees the 'other faith' as complementing and even adding spiritual potency to his own spiritual practice of constructing effective amulets. Indigenous African religions are pragmatic.
>
> *(Chiorazzi, 2015)*

Islam in North Africa

Against this understanding of ATR, we turn to the propagation of Islam in North Africa, home to Berbers and many other African tribes, the Sahara and the Sudan. Christians and pagans (including Muslims who accommodated pagan practices in their Islamic practices) were subjugated by Muslim Arabs in the name of jihad. In some instances, the subjugated communities were forced to accept Islam, while others were forced to pay *jizya*[6] but allowed to continue to practice their religion and remained independent for a long time. For example, according to Trimingham, during an expedition in the Byzantine area (AH 27),[7] Abdullah Ibn Sa'd did not force the inhabitants to accept Islam, even though he had the opportunity to do so. Instead, he entered into a treaty with them in return for a large tribute on the orders of Caliph Uthman. In contrast, when he first came to power (AH 41–51), Caliph Mu'awiya, the founder of the Umayyad Caliphate, ordered the invasion of North Africa. His men subjugated the region of Ifriqiya and founded Qairawan.

Trimingham observes that the religious conversion of Christians living in North African towns and the mainly pagan Berbers of the hills and plains happened in the second century of the *hijra* because Islam enjoyed a more advantageous position than Christianity due to being the religion of the ruling minority. And Muslim rulers used their privileged position to impose a tax on Christians in the form of *jizya* which encouraged rapid conversion of Christians to Islam. A second reason was the inability of Christian missionaries to protect the Christian Berbers

6 A capitation tax formerly levied on non-Muslims by an Islamic state.

7 The Hijri era is calculated according to the Islamic lunar calendar and not the Julian or Gregorian solar ones. Thus, it does not begin on 1 January in 1 CE, but on the first day of the month of Muharram, which occurred in 622 CE. Its Julian equivalent was 19 April.

by paying the tax imposed on them so that they could keep their religion. The Christian missionaries could not do so because of the acrimonious competition among themselves which was a major distraction (Trimingham, 1962: 17). They became more interested in their internal sectarian conflicts and paid less attention to their followers, ultimately losing them to Islam.

As for the Berber pagans, they became Muslim by 'contagion and association.' Their conversion was gradual because of the conflict with their Muslim Arab masters. The latter considered them inferiors even though they formed the main body of the Muslim Arab armies that had conquered the Maghrib and Spain. The Berber pagans defeated the Arabs but could not sustain their victory because of internal divisions and persistent tribal conflicts among themselves. The Muslim Arabs returned a few years later, defeated the Berbers and reasserted their rule over eastern but not western Maghrib (Trimingham, 1962: 17). It took a lot of time and effort before the Muslim Arabs brought the whole areas occupied by the Berbers under their control. Ibn Khaldun, a Muslim Arab scholar, summarized the experience as follows:

> After the formation of the Islamic community, the Arabs burst out to propagate their religion among other nations. Their armies penetrated into the Maghrib and captured all its cantonment and cities. They endured a great deal in their struggles with the Berbers who, as Ibn Abi Yazid has told us apostatized twelve times before Islam gained a firm hold over them.

What is revealed is two different scenarios. The first one shows Muslim Arabs peacefully co-existing with the African population who payed *jizya* and continued to practice their religion. The second one shows the use of force in the name of jihad to advance Islam.

The Moors and the Tuareg of Central Sahara

The Berber merchants are widely regarded as being responsible for the Islamization of the pagans without the involvement of the Muslim Arabs even though they, as Muslims, mixed their Islam with pagan practices. The Moors and the Tuareg of central Sudan were descendants of the Sanhaja, a Berber clan. They occupied large parts of the Sahara from Mauritania to Ahaggar as far as South Sudan. They were Muslims, but with pagan practices woven into their Islamic way of life. They worshiped the sun and ate unclean meat (Trimingham, 1962: 17). They emerged in the ninth century, grouped into three tribes consisting of Lamtuna (Saharan Berbers), Masufa and Godala. The dominant strain was the Lamtuna who arrived in the Mauritania town of Adrar in the second half of the eighth century and then moved to the south to gain control of the caravan center of Awdaghast. They displaced many of the pagans then residing in the region and forced them to embrace Islam. They had a nomadic existence and wandered in search of greener pasture but were also engaged in jihad. In the process, they took over places occupied by native pagans. Some of the pagans agreed to remain and pay taxes (*jizya*), while others simply left. Ibn Khaldun writes:

> They subdued those desert regions and waged the jihad against the Negro peoples who lived in them to constrain them to adopt Islam. Many complied but others elected to pay the Jizya. Under Talagagin, (Tiklan) and especially his successor, Tilutan (d. AH 222) (AD 836–7), they imposed their authority over both Berber and Negro groups in Mauritania, with the exception of Gana, and it was some time before the two powers came into decisive conflict.
>
> *(quoted by Trimingham, 1962: 21)*

Their leader Tarsina, a Lamtuni, may have been the first important Muslim Sanhaja ruler. He undertook the pilgrimage to Mecca and in the process learned about jihad which he deployed to justify his campaigns against pagans. However, he was killed fighting them in 1023 and his son-in-law, Yahaya Ibn Ibrahim, a Godala, succeeded him. Yahaya went on pilgrimage with other Sanhaja chiefs in 1035 AD and on his return journey approached a famous jurist of Qairawan, Abu Imran Musa Ibn Isa (d. 1038 AD), asking him to teach his semi-pagan tribesmen the Islamic faith. Abu Imran instead referred him to Wajjaj ibn Zalwi, head of a school of religion in the town of Naffis called *dar al-murabitin*, who persuaded one of his disciples, Abdallah ibn Yasin, to go. Ibn Yasin did not succeed in his mission among the Godala, and they turned against him after the death of Yahaya because of what they perceived as an attempt to reform their customs. He withdrew from the town and moved to somewhere on the Atlantic coast of Mauritania along with eight companions, including Yahaya ibn Umar and his brother Abu Bakr, who were Lamtunis. He established a *ribat* center (a place designed for proselytism). The center became a recruitment place for a jihad and when members of the group reached 1,000, ibn Yasin decided to initiate it. He first directed his disciples to return to their own people as missionaries (Trimingham, 1962: 23).

> Go under the protection of God and warn your fellow tribesmen. Teach them the law of God, and threaten them with His chastisement. If they repent and return to the truth and amend their ways, then leave them in peace; but if they refuse and persist in their errors and infidelity, let us invoke the aid of God against them and make war upon them until God decides the issue between us.

Ibn Yasin and his disciples successfully waged the first war against the pagan Godala. They defeated one tribe after another and compelled the people to accept Islam. Research, however, indicates that the group's inclination was Sufi Islam and that was what they forced people to accept (Trimingham, 1962: 24). This was the beginning of the Murabit dynasty which was short-lived because the transplanted nomads later renounced orthodoxy by their conduct to the extent that a Masmuda called Ibn Tumart proclaimed himself the Mahdi in AH 515 (1121/1122 AD) and founded the 'Unitarians' (*al-Muwahhidun*). He denounced the Murabitun as infidels and declared jihad against them to be a religious obligation. Ibn Tumart's successor, Abd al-Mu'min ibn Ali, AH 527–558 (1133–1163 AD) of the Kumya tribe,[8] destroyed the Sanhaja dynasty and established the rule of the *Muwahhidun* throughout North Africa from Syrte to the Atlantic. This lasted up until the thirteenth century when it broke up (Trimingham, 1962: 25).

In some parts of central Sudan however, contrary to the narrative summarized above, some Jihadists showed respect for the pagans' right to freedom of religion. For example, when jihad became successful in some Hausa states, the pagans were not forced to accept Islam as had happened within the old territories of the Byzantine Empire. Instead, they were allowed to practice their religion and were required to pay *jizya*. Trimingham noted that:

> By 1810, Fulbe [an ethnic group of Sahel and West Africa] had full control over Hausa states. Those Hausa who kept Islamic feasts and at the same time indulged in pagan rites were asked to destroy their shrines, although it is said that the Fulbe could not get rid of the famous gidan tsafi [the house of spirits] called choka in Kano city and that

8 Member of the Zanata Berber confederation.

> the new chiefs fulfilled their inherited communal obligation of providing *sadakan iskoki*, animals for sacrifice to the spirits of the locality. The free pagan Hausa or maguzawa were not forced to join Islam but left as tribute-paying cultivators, and at the time of British occupation half were still pagans whom the Fulbe regarded as legitimate prey.
>
> *(Trimingham, 1962: 200)*

The above treatment is more consistent with the provisions of Islamic law as Imam Malik explained. He said the following on the subjugation of the Fezzan people (which probably took place during his lifetime):

> They question Malik concerning the Fezzanis (al-Fazazina) who are a race of Ethiopians (*jinsun min al-Habasha*). He replied: 'I am not of the opinion that one should fight them before having invited them to embrace Islam .... If they do not accept, one should invite them to pay the Jizya, at the same time keeping to their religion; if they respond favorably one should accept it of them.'
>
> *(quoted by Trimingham, 1962: 16)*

Sudan

Islam came to Sudan through commerce with traders exchanging manufactured goods from Mediterranean lands and salt of the Sahara for slaves and raw materials from the Sudan: gold, ivory and gum (Trimingham, 1962: 26). The Islamic faith passed through the western trade routes among the Saharan Soninke[9] and the ancestors of the Tokolor[10] and then eastward up to the valley of Senegal. In this part of Africa, the practice of Islam had spread among the native Africans, long before its adoption by coercion.

The first attempt in the Sudan to propagate Islam by force came through the Berbers of western Sahara who had joined the *Murabitun* movement, a secondary aspect of this movement being Berber reaction against Soninke supremacy over Awdaghast[11] and the trade routes. When Abd Allah ibn Yasin left his *ribat* in 1042 AD and his agents began to preach his militant religious ideology as the gospel of truth among the Berbers of the Adrar and Tagant,[12] they had contacts with the African natives of Takrur (Futa Toro)[13] and Silla[14] who were in active opposition to the Soninkes of Gana (Trimingham, 1962: 28).

The *Murabitun* under Abu Bakr Ibn Umar (d. 1078 AD) occupied Awdaghast in AH 446 (1054–1055 AD) and later Gana (1076). The fall of Gana brought victory to Islam throughout the Sahil region between Senegal and Niger. The Soninke of Gana were compelled to accept Islam. Not only did they do so in large numbers, but they also propagated it amongst the many peoples over whom they ruled (Trimingham, 1962: 30). It should be remembered that the peaceful penetration of Islam along trade routes into borderland towns had begun before the *Murabitun* movement was born. Native African rulers were tolerant and allowed traders to conduct their commercial business with full liberty and at the same time practice their Muslim

9 A people located in Senegal.
10 A Muslim people living in Senegal and Mali.
11 Former Berber town, located north west of Timbuktu.
12 Plateaus of Mauritania.
13 A region situated in the middle valley of the Senegal River.
14 A city along the Senegal River.

faith (Trimingham, 1962: 31). A possible explanation for this degree of accommodation by the Africans might be the pragmatic benefits deriving from trade. It could also be that the Arab Muslims were less interested in promoting Islam than in achieving success through business. Gana and other towns contained Muslim districts, whilst the rulers of Takrur and other states had converted to Islam. Therefore, the role played by the *Murabitun* was simply to accelerate a process that had already begun.

In summary, pagan rulers were tolerant of Muslims and welcomed their thriving businesses in their midst. This accounts for the peaceful spread of Islam. The objective was not persecution but neutralization (Trimingham, 1962: 142). A possible explanation for this tolerant behavior might be that the Arab Muslim traders living within their domain were accommodating and integrated themselves into society. They felt at home living among pagan communities and were not regarded by the pagans as a threat.

It was against this backdrop of accommodation that the reformers of the nineteenth century embarked on jihad throughout Africa (Trimingham, 1962: 143). This is evidenced in the encounter between Borno and the Sokoto Caliphate in central Sudan. Borno was a known Muslim state, yet Muhammad Bello justified the Fulani[15] jihad against it on the ground that they mixed their Islamic lifestyle with pagan practices. He wrote:

> But we have been told that their rulers and chiefs today have places to which they rife where they offer sacrifices and then pour the blood on the gates of their towns. They have great houses containing snakes and other things to which they offer sacrifices. They performed rites to the river just as the Copts used to do to the Nile in Time of Ignorance. We heard that they keep such festivals in which they, their Qur'an-reciters, their rulers and the populace participated, but no one else, which they designate 'the custom of the country ...'
>
> *(Trimingham, 1962: 153)*

In fact, the Fulbe and Borno had to sit down and agree on their respective spheres of influence during the jihad. Al-Kanami wrote to Muhammad Bello:

> We profess the same religion, and it is not fitting that our subjects should make war on each other. Between our two Kingdoms are the pagan Bedde tribes, on whom it is permissible to levy contribution: let us respect this limit: what lies to the east of their country shall be ours: what lies to the west shall be yours.
>
> *(Trimingham, 1962: 209)*

Despite this encounter, historical facts have shown that non-Muslims under the Sokoto Caliphate enjoyed the right to practice the religion of their choice. The leadership of the Caliphate adopted rules governing the treatment of non-Muslims under an Islamic State (Bunza, 2007: 7–8). Even in matters of litigation, non-Muslims were allowed to choose either to go to a Sharia court or invoke customary laws (Naniya, 1994: 164–165). In addition, Shehu Usmanu Danfodiyo declared throughout the Caliphate that to make war, enslave or seize the property of the heathen to whom peace had been granted was unlawful (Bunza, 2007: 9). The level of freedom and liberty granted to non-Muslims in the Sokoto Caliphate is

15 A people scattered in western Africa, who created an empire through a series of holy wars (1804–1810). The Fulani empire – a sort of Muslim theocracy – flourished in the nineteenth century in western Sudan.

demonstrated by the pockets of untouched Maguzawa (non-Muslim) elements in the midst of the powerful Caliphate in areas such as Tsafe and Kotorkoshi in the present-day Zamfara State (Bunza, 2007: 9). Indeed, it has been argued that there is no clear evidence of forceful conversion to Islam in the Caliphate. E. A. Ayandele stated:

> There is no record that captured slaves were being converted to Islam. In Zaria and Kano emirates, there were the maguzawa, indigenous and pure Hausa people who up to now have refused to embrace Islam. They were left alone as freemen, both in Habe and Fulani Zazzau. It may be noted that in Zazzau the Fulani appointed an official to be in charge of their affairs (non-Muslims) administratively. Surely if the Fulani Jihadists had wished, the Magazuwa could have been compelled to become at least nominally Muslims.
>
> *(Ayandele, 1979: 71–72)*

Some other emirs even protected non-Muslims living under their jurisdiction in places such as Muri Emirate (Makar, 1979: 452).

Zimbabwe

This African sense of accommodation is further illustrated by the conversion of the Shona people of Zimbabwe by Christian missionaries. Historically, Portuguese Catholics were the first missionaries to enter Zimbabwe through the efforts of Gonzalo da Silveira accompanied by Brother Andre da Costa and Father Andre Fernandes (Jankins and Stebbing, 1966: 2). Research shows that the Portuguese missionary authorities first sent him to Mozambique in response to a request for missionaries to be sent to his people from a Mozambican chief called Gamba.

While doing his evangelism in Gamba's domain, Gonzalo got to know about the kingdom of the Monomotapa (Zimbabwe), and he concluded that they also needed to be evangelized. He arrived in Zimbabwe on Christmas Eve, 1560, and recorded considerable success in his evangelization. The people received and accommodated him, offering him valuable presents such as gold, cattle and slaves which he respectfully declined. His conduct drew attention from their chief, Chisamharu, who allowed Gonzalo to build his own house. Gonzalo propagated Christianity among the Zimbabweans through an interpreter; within a month, the chief and his mother were baptized along with 300 councilors and attendants (Baxter and Turner, 1966: 34).

However, trouble soon started. Some of the Arab Muslim traders became disturbed by the sudden and unexpected growth of Christianity at Monomutapa. Specifically, one of their leaders, Mingane, poisoned the mind of Chief Chisambaru against Gonzalo through allegations that he was a sorcerer who, if not sent away, would bring drought and famine on the country, kill the chief and set his subjects at war with one another (Jankins and Stebbing, 1966: 5). On 15 March 1561, the Zimbabweans killed Gonzalo (Du Plessis, 1911: 10; see also Jankins and Stebbing, 1966: 5–6).

Subsequently, no other missionary activity took place in Zimbabwe until the nineteenth century. Robert Moffat, a member of the London Missionary Society, spent most of his life at the station of Kuruman, in what later became known as the British Bechuanaland, which is now Botswana. From Kuruman, he courageously visited the Ndebele[16] king, Mzilikazi, who was

16 A people speaking Bantu and living in what is today southwest Zimbabwe.

alleged to be 'thirsting for the blood of the first white person to fall into his hands' (Jankins and Stebbing, 1966: 12). The king received him politely but rejected any suggestion of missionary activity in order to protect his Ndebele people from outside forces. In 1857, Moffat visited the king with Sam Edward and won the trust of Mzilikazi's son Lobengula. This opened up the country of Zimbabwe to the British (Jankins and Stebbing, 1966: 12). Moffat visited Matabeleland again in 1859 along with his son, John Smith Moffat, William Sykes and Morgan Thomas and established his missionary station at Inyati with the permission of the king (Wallis, 1945: 3–31; see also Jankins and Stebbing, 1966: 12). It took a long time to evangelize the Ndebele people because of the refusal of their king to allow conversion. It reached the point where the missionaries themselves called for the dismantling of the Ndebele Kingdom in order to allow for full proselytization of the people (Fripp and Hiller, 1949: 201–202).

It is difficult to extrapolate conclusions on freedom of religion from King Mzilikazi's refusal to allow missionary activity in his domain, which was probably just a display of protectionism by the king of the traditional beliefs of his people based on fear of displacement by the newly and more powerful religion of Christianity in his domain.

Conclusion

From what we know of their pre-jihad interactions with Islam and Christianity, Africans were undoubtedly tolerant of other religions and allowed Muslim Arab and Christian missionaries to operate freely in their midst. This African sense of toleration allowed Arab Muslim traders and Christian missionaries to integrate themselves into the society of pagans who did not perceive the presence of different religious practices to constitute a threat to their society. It could be argued that this sense of toleration from Africans was exhibited in order to enjoy commercial benefits because of trading activities (particularly with Muslims). However, Africans were influenced by features of ATR which (1) was non-proselytizing, (2) did not oppose other belief systems and (3) lacked any element of bigotry. Herein lies the African perception of what the concept of freedom of religion and belief means, which, as explored in this chapter, takes the form of live and let live without any condition.

Muslim Arabs and Christian missionaries that engaged in religious propagation in Africa showed little or no understanding of the concept of freedom of religion or belief as the concept is understood today. For instance, missionaries called for the dismantling of the Ndebele Kingdom in order to allow for full proselytization instead of allowing the king and his people to continue with their traditional religion and decide on their own whether to accept Christianity or not. Arab Muslim traders on the other hand became disturbed by the abrupt and unanticipated growth of Christianity at Monomutapa so they poisoned the mind of Chief Chisambaru against missionaries to limit their religious activities. Why did they discourage people from deciding whether or not to accept another religion? Why were they worried because somebody exercised the same right they were exercising to propagate their own religion? This is in contrast to the live and let live principle that forms the basis of the African understanding of the concept of freedom of religion.

This principle as it relates to freedom of religion and belief is more conducive to peaceful coexistence of people. The expedition of Abdullah Ibn Sa'd and Caliph Mu'awiya in the Byzantine area in AH 27 supports this assertion. Abdullah Ibn Sa'd's approach on the orders of Caliph Uthman yielded a more positive result than the forceful strategy of Caliph Mu'awiya which did not allow him to capture any region permanently (and in the process lose one of his commanders at the hands of the Berber chief Kasila). This is an example of the unsettled question, still discussed among Muslims and Christians today, about the legitimacy of forceful conversion of people without regard for the right of those people to adopt the religious belief of their choice. However, it should be noted that, concerning Muslims, the reaction of Imam Malik to questions about the Fazazina of southern Libya clearly demonstrated the position of Islam on forceful conversion. According to Malik, one should not fight non-Muslims before inviting them to convert to Islam. If they accept, fine; otherwise, they should pay the *jizya* and be free to practice their religion. As far as freedom of religion is concerned, Islam recognizes the live and let live principle but not in the African way, because Islam imposes conditions.

Freedom of religion or belief as understood in the world today might have historical roots in Africa, though on a different foundation. The tolerant behavior of Africans toward other belief systems is due to the live and let live principle which is a consequence of the non-proselytizing nature of the ATR. First, in contrast to Islam and Christianity, nothing in the ATR urges its followers to seek out converts. Second, ATRs are inextricably connected with ethnic groups' practices. As religion is seen as part of the traditional practice or custom of ethnic groups, inviting some people to adopt it is akin to calling people to abandon their own traditional practices and adopt the practices of another ethnic group, which is not an easy thing. These reasons are some way distant from any conscious perception of freedom of religion and belief as understood in modern times. However, the same thing cannot be said of Christian missionaries and Arab Muslims. They were driven by the impulse to convert Africans to the true religion and, to achieve this goal, resorted sometimes to persuasion and sometimes to force, largely negating the concept of freedom of religion as understood in modern times.

This chapter demonstrates that a unique perception of the meaning of freedom of religion and belief existed in the pre-jihad period of African interaction with Islam and Christianity. This perception was not based on any conscious recognition of the concept of freedom of religion as it exists today but was one of the intrinsic features of ATR. In addition, the existence of this unique African perception of the meaning of freedom of religion and belief shows that the foundation of this concept as it is construed today had been in existence for a long time in Africa. The modern concept of freedom of religion and belief might have originated from within Africa but without Africans themselves or the world at large being aware of it.

References

An-Na'im, A.A., 2012. Experiences in freedom of religion in the African context. In: M.A. Glendon and H.F. Zacher (Eds.), *Universal Rights in a World of Diversity. The Case of Religious Freedom*. The Pontifical Academy of Social Sciences, 193.

Asante, M., 2007. *The History of Africa*. Routledge.

Awolalu, J.O., Dopamu, P. A., 1979. *West African Traditional Religion*. Onibonoje Press Ltd.

Ayandele, E.A., 1979. *Nigeria Historical Studies*. Frank Cass.

Baxter, T.W., Turner, R.W.S., 1966. *Rhodesia Epic*. Citadel Press.

Bewaji, J.A.I., 2004. Ethics and morality in Yoruba culture. In: K. Wiredu (Ed.), *A Companion to African Philosophy*. Blackwell Publishing, 396.

Booth, J.S., 1977. An approach to African religions. In: Booth, J.S. (Ed.), *African Religions, A Symposium*. Nok Publishers, 1.

Bunza, M.U., 2007. *Christian Missions Among Muslims: Sokoto Province, Nigeria, 1935–1990*. Africa World Press.

Chiorazzi, A., 2015. The spirituality of Africa. *The Harvard Gazette*. Available from https://news.harvard.edu/gazette/story/2015/10/the-spirituality-of-africa.

Du Plessis, J., 1911. *A History of Christian Missions in South Africa*. Longmans, Green and Co.

Egonu, I.T.K. (Ed.), 1988. *Reading in African Humanities, African Perspective in World Culture*. Vivians Publishers.

Ekwunife, A.N.O., 1990. *Conservations in Igbo Traditional Religion*. Snaap Press Limited.
Evans-Pritchard, E.E., 1965. *Theories of Primitive Religions*. Clarendon Press.
Fripp, C.E., Hiller, V.W. (Eds.), 1949. *Gold and the Gospel in Mashonaland 1888*. Chatto & Windus.
Ibenwa, C.N., 2014. Influences of Christian religion on African traditional religion and value system. *Research on Humanities and Social Science* 4(9), 148.
Idowu, E.B., 1973. *African Traditional Religion: A Definition*. SCM Press LTD.
Ikenga-Metuh, E., 1985. *African Religions in Western Conceptual Schemes: The Problem of Interpretation*. IMICO Press.
Ikenga-Metuh, E., 1987. *Comparative Studies of African Traditional Religions*. IMICO Publishers.
Izutsu, T., 1966. *Ethico-Religious Concepts in the Quran*. McGill.
Jankins, D., Stebbing, D., 1966. *They Led the Way*. Oxford University Press.
Jordan, J.P., 1948. *Bishop Shanahan of Southern Nigeria*. Glonmore and Reynolds.
Magesa, L., 1997. *African Religion: The Moral Traditions of Abundant Life*. Orbis Books.
Makar, T., 1979. The relationship between the Sokoto Caliphate and the non-Muslim peoples of the middle Benue region. In: Y. B. Usman (Ed.), *Studies in the History of the Sokoto Caliphate*. Dept. of History, Ahmadu Bello University for The Sokoto State History Bureau. 450.
Maquet, J.J., 1972. The Kingdom of Ruanda. In: D. Ford (Ed.), *African Worlds*. London: Oxford University Press, 164.
Mbiti, J., 1969. *African Religions and Philosophy*. Heinemann.
Mbiti, J., 1970. *Concepts of God in Africa*. SPCK.
Mbiti, J., 1991a. *Introduction to African Traditional Religion*. Heinemann.
Mbiti, J., 1991b. Flowers in the garden: the role of women in African traditional religion. In: J. Olupona (Ed.), *African Traditional Religion in Contemporary Society*. Paragon House, 67.
Meredith, M., 2006. *The Fate of Africa-A Survey of Fifty Years of Independence*. Public Affairs.
Mokhtar, G. (Ed.), 1990. *UNESCO General History of Africa,* vol. 11. University of California Press.
Naniya, T.M., 1994. The British conquest of the Sokoto Caliphate and its impact on interpretation and application of the Shari'ah. *Paiduma* 40, 163.
O'Brien, P.K., 2005. *Oxford Atlas of World History*. Oxford University Press.
Ochonu, M.E., 2014. *Colonialism by Proxy: Hausa Imperial Agents and Middle Belt Consciousness in Nigeria*. Indiana University Press.
Oliver, R., Atmore, A., 1994. *Africa Since 1800*. Cambridge University Press.
Onyeidu, S.O., 1999. *African Traditional Religion: The Problem of Definition*. Easy Quality Press.
Parrinder, G., 1962. *African Traditional Religion*. Sheldon Press.
Ray, B.C., 1976. *African Religions: Symbol, Ritual and Community*. Prentice-Hall.
Robinson, D., 2004. *Muslim Societies in African History*. Cambridge University Press.
Sayre, A.P., 2009. *Africa*. Twenty-First Century Books.
Stammer, J., 1995. *Islam in Sub-Saharan Africa*. Estella.
Trimingham, J.S., 1962. *A History of Islam in West Africa*. Oxford University Press.
Wallis, J.P.R. (Ed.), 1945. *The Matabele Journals of Robert Moffat, 1829–1860,* vol. 1. Chatto & Windus, 3.
Westerlund, D., 1991. 'Insiders' and 'outsiders' in the study of African traditional religions. Notes on some problems of theory and method. In: J. K. Olupona (Ed.), *African Traditional Religion in Contemporary Society*. Paragon House, 15.

5

The right to freedom of belief: An historical perspective on secular humanism

Caroline Sägesser

Next to people who did not share the faith of the majority and who fought for their right to believe and to worship differently, there were people who did not believe at all: they didn't want freedom *of* religion, they wanted freedom *from* religion. This contribution reflects on the quest for equality of those who refused to have their identity shaped by their belonging to a religious group or who simply fought for the right to voice radical criticism of their faith. It also reflects on the development of secular humanism as a philosophy and a specific ethical choice.[1]

Freedom of consciousness, the freedom not to believe, deep in one's consciousness, is a natural human right that cannot be taken away. But to publicly express one's convictions, to try to convince others of their well-foundedness, to refuse to participate in religious rites, to choose to educate one's children outside of religious education or to organize oneself with others who have the same convictions, are actions that were generally banned in most states until the eighteenth century. Today, they remain impossible or dangerous in many parts of the world. Freethinkers were persecuted not for what they thought, but because of what they said or, in most cases, wrote. Freedom of (un)belief therefore largely encompasses freedom of expression, and to consider the history of secular humanism is also to study the development of free speech.

Scholars have long argued about whether the natural condition of humankind was to be religious or atheist. It was widely believed that man was naturally religious, being driven to believe in the existence of God(s) by unexplained natural phenomena, until anthropology and ethnology uncovered some humans and cultures who did not seem to have any sense of the divine in their lives. The debate remains open. But, as far as freedom of belief is concerned, the fight for the right to not believe, to be openly atheist and to be recognized as such, naturally appeared after religious beliefs had firmly established themselves. Far from being confined to a philosophical debate, the history of the establishment of secular humanism as a legitimate way of life is that of a political struggle. Because State and Church have often formed throughout

1 We will use the term 'secular humanism' to refer to a philosophy relying on reason and ethics, with no reference to God or religion, to foster the personal development of individuals and the improvement of society. We will use 'atheism' or 'atheists' to refer to those who do not believe in the existence of a God, with or without building an alternative philosophy.

history a very firm alliance to control society, to challenge the authority of the second was to run into trouble with the first. The history of atheism is inseparable from that of anticlericalism.

The precursors

Secularism did not appear in modern times. In antiquity already, philosophers contested the existence of the gods or the necessity to worship them. It is thought that the frequency of unbelief among Romans of the first centuries is one of the factors that facilitated the expansion of Christian monotheism. Casting doubt on prevalent beliefs has always been dangerous: those who deny divinity expose themselves to the ostracism of their peers. It is by his detractors that Theodorus of Cyrene (ca. 340–250 BC), whose treatise *On the Gods* has unfortunately not reached us, was nicknamed Theodorus the Atheist, after his disrespect for religion led him to be expelled from the Athenian school where he was teaching. The same misfortune had already befallen one of the greatest thinkers of antiquity, Socrates (ca. 470–399 BC): the Athenian philosopher was put on trial, found guilty of impiety ('not believing in the gods of the state') and sentenced to death. Out of caution, other great philosophers, such as Plato (ca. 428–348 BC), contented themselves with dismantling the pantheon of Greek gods while accepting the existence of the divine; Plato is still regarded as one of the precursors of Christianity. While not many ancient writings have been preserved – 'history is written by those who prevail, so the lively free-thinking voices of antiquity were mostly suppressed' (Whitmarsh, 2016) – atheism was a subject of debate in the ancient world.

In medieval Christian Europe, dissenting voices struggled to be heard: life evolved around Christianity, from baptism to the afterlife. The pope had become the leader of Western Christendom, the representative of Christ himself on Earth, with canonical authority. The prohibition of atheism throughout the Middle Ages was reinforced by the alliance of Church and State: having chosen to legitimize themselves on the basis of a supposed divine authority, one of the primary concerns of temporal authorities was to make sure that God was not called into question. The atheist denies the foundations of social cohesion: one had to submit to the religious order of society or risk being considered an *infidel*. Anyone who was not a devout Christian was labeled as such; in the thirteenth century, St Thomas Aquinas distinguished four types of infidels: pagans, heretics, Jews and apostates. In this period of a Christianity very sure of itself, there was no possible recognition of atheism as a coherent philosophical position. An infidel had either not (yet) met the Christian God, and he was a pagan or a Jew – a special distinction being made for the people of the Old Testament – or he had met God and rejected him and was, according to the case, a heretic or an apostate.

The crusades (1095–1270) reinforced papal authority and the persecution of non-Christians. After 1184, the Inquisition became the spearhead of the struggle against heretics. The archives of the Inquisition attest to the vigorous repression of heresy and blasphemy. So, too, does the high number of excommunications pronounced. The repression that struck the atheists throughout the old regime renders difficult any estimation of the frequency of unbelief. Yet some studies have convincingly demonstrated that next to the handful of scholars who questioned the attributes of the divine or the power of the clerical institutions in cautious terms, there was also widespread popular disbelief or at least disaffection with religious rites; Le Roy Ladurie (1975) showed examples of unbelief in the French countryside in the heart of the Middle Ages.

One prominent voice against religious orthodoxy, albeit from a different religious tradition, was that of Ibn Rushd (1126–1198), better known as Averroes. His writings emancipate philosophy from religion and defend the scholar's freedom of thought. He affirms the eternity of the material world and denies the resurrection of the body. Toward the end of his life, Ibn Rushd was condemned and sentenced to banishment by an Islamic court in Cordoba and his works were burned. His legacy survived in the Latin world, but in 1270 Averroism was condemned by the Catholic Church. Indeed, in the twelfth century, a form of skeptical thought spread in the confines of the Mediterranean, where the Muslim and Christian worlds met (Minois, 1998: 74–82). Freedom of speech and thought was encouraged at the court of Emperor Frederick II (1194–1250), a fact that attracted the wrath of Pope Gregory IX: the king of Sicily was excommunicated no less than four times.

With the Renaissance, new forms of free inquiry were born. Ancient writers were rediscovered; travels to new continents brought contact with 'pagan' people whose existence and ways of thinking challenged the generally accepted beliefs of the times; and scientific progress increasingly questioned the Church's ability to know and tell the truth. The European spirit began to become secularized in the sixteenth century; René Descartes (1596–1650) stopped short of questioning God's existence, but François Berriot has convincingly demonstrated that disbelief was widespread in France at the time (Berriot, 1984). With the Reformation came a radical questioning of the Church's authority. Martin Luther (1483–1546) established a new free examination, substituting a personal relation with God for the Revelation. However, in a Europe divided between Catholic states and Protestant states, people moved from one religion to another at the whim of their rulers under the principle *cujus regio, illius religio*. A Europe torn by the wars of religion did not offer a better freedom of conscience to its people.

The Church reacted, notably at the Council of Trent (1545–1563), in an attempt to curb the free examination and development of the critical exegesis of texts brought about by the development of Protestantism and the invention of printing. The Index was established in 1557, listing all the books that people were now prohibited from reading. Repression of heretical thought went on. In 1600, the philosopher and cosmologist Giordano Bruno (1548–1600) was burned in Rome, after eight years of trial for sustaining a heretical thesis. Whether or not he was an atheist, Bruno had been a direct opponent of the Church's authority (Ottaviani, 2013). In France, Jean Meslier (1664–1729) avoided a similar fate by not voicing his radical critique of religion before his death (Deruette, 2008). One of the most important figures of early modern science, Galileo Galilei (1564–1642) was investigated by the Inquisition in 1615; his demonstration of heliocentricism was found heretical, and he was forced to recant. But the Catholic Church was not alone in its condemnation of freethinking: Protestants and Catholics alike saw it as a danger to public order and morality. In Geneva, Jacques Gruet (?–1547) was executed in 1547, and Michel Servet (1511–1553) in 1553, both for challenging the Protestant doctrine of the Republic.

While religious authorities prosecuted all those who harbored ideas that might undermine their power, few of them openly declared themselves atheists. Indeed, the link between religion and morality was firmly established at the time. In Thomas More's *Utopia* we can see a ban on atheism as being destructive to morality: men will not hesitate to break the law and commit crimes if they don't fear or hope anything beyond the material life (1516). In Italy, Machiavelli (1469–1527) could not imagine a society where people are not kept in obedience by religion (Machiavelli, 1531).

Despite the rigid doctrinal position of its leaders, the Reformation was an encouragement to formulate questions that had been unspoken or unthought of until then. In the seventeenth century, England and the Netherlands harbored many freethinkers. Spinoza (1632–1677) is one of the most famous. He revolutionized the interpretation of the Scriptures and was one of the most eloquent critics of the clergy, which, he believed, prevented the exercise of critical thought. Spinoza was a true humanist. In his posthumous book, *Ethica*, he stated that virtuous behavior could be sustained by the use of reason only. In France, Pierre Bayle (1647–1706) also argued in favor of *the virtuous atheist*, quite a revolutionary idea at a time when virtue was necessarily religious. For Bayle, ethics and religion had to be separated.

The classic thinkers Thomas Hobbes (1588–1679) and John Locke (1632–1704) contributed to the deconstruction of religious dogmas. Published in the context of the English Civil War, Hobbes' *Leviathan* did not affirm that God did not exist but stated that his nature was beyond human understanding. Radically anticlerical, Hobbes laid the foundation for a new secular philosophy emancipated from theology, established the primacy of civil over Church authority and urged men to devote their efforts to building the best possible society. He offered a new moral doctrine, no longer based on divine commands but on man's best interest (Stauffer, 2010).

Such a concept is not exclusively European. Next to Ibn Rushd, already mentioned, who discussed Aristotelian ethics and was, as far as his cautious writings allow us to conclude, in favor of the existence of a natural moral order (Hourani, 1962), we can also say the Chinese Wang Yang (1472–1529), the leading figure in the neo-Confucian School of Heart, argued that every person knows from birth the difference between good and evil (Ivanhoe, 2002).

The enlightenment

Following in the footsteps of Hobbes and Locke, the philosophers of the eighteenth century continued to explore religion and to criticize the Church and clergy. It was often as much opposition to the clergy and its privileges as an affirmation of the inanity of the professed beliefs that occupied the philosophers of the Enlightenment. The vast majority of them remained deists, out of conviction or opportunism. Did Voltaire (1694–1778) himself not say that 'if religion did not exist, it would have to be invented?' (Voltaire, 1877–1885, 1768). The need for religion as keeper of social order was indeed thought crucial.

Born into a Catholic family, Baron d'Holbach (1723–1789) is the most anticlerical and the only explicitly materialistic atheist of the encyclopedists. An internationally recognized scholar and an intellectual in Paris, he nevertheless published his most challenging texts under a pseudonym. Like Diderot (1713–1784), Buffon (1707–1788) and Helvetius (1715–1771), d'Holbach abandoned the belief in a creative power in favor of materialism and the triumph of nature. In *Le Christianisme dévoilé* (1766), he is highly critical of the moral influence of the Christian religion. For him, Christianity has no monopoly on ethical values, and, far from reinforcing them, religion weakens their foundation by attributing them to an elusive God. Crime should not be prohibited by calling on God or by making people fear a divine punishment, but rather by evoking a natural morality which calls for the self-preservation of man. D'Holbach's views on religion, as having a negative influence on the evolution of society, would find an echo in Marxist philosophy a century later: 'Religion is the art of intoxicating men with enthusiasm, to prevent them from dealing with evils, of which those who govern them overwhelm them here below' (d'Holbach, 1766: 282). D'Holbach is one of the first philosophers who can be called a secular humanist and who insisted on ethics being among his reasons to abandon religious faith.

Moral issues, albeit of a different kind, are also at the root of the libertines' rejection of religion. They aimed to overcome the moral imperatives of religion, especially in sexual matters. Their ultimate representative is, without a doubt, the Marquis de Sade (1740–1814). Perhaps no one has been more violent toward God and religion than the Marquis, yet he seems to have recognized the social value of religion for some (Jeangene Vilmer, 2008).

If the eighteenth century saw free thought develop, the rules uniting a government to a Church and vice versa hardly changed. Timid reforms were put forward by enlightened despots toward the end of the century: edicts of toleration were issued by Russian Empress Catherine II in 1773 (religious tolerance in the Empire, except for Jews), by Austrian Emperor Joseph II in 1781 and 1782 (religious tolerance for Protestants and Jews) and in 1787 the Edict of Versailles, issued by Louis XVI, formally ended persecution of non-Catholics (Protestants and Jews) in France. However, although those texts allowed for alternative forms of worship, they did not make provisions for those who professed no religion at all.

In 1791, the American Bill of Rights inscribed religious freedom in the United States Constitution. The fathers of the new Republic, having witnessed the various religious conflicts to which the Old Continent had been subjected throughout the centuries, established a separation of Church and State in the new country. Nevertheless, religious faith – preferably Christian – remained a very important feature of American society. American sociologist Robert Bellah (1967) would use the concept of 'civil religion' to describe the special relationship enjoyed by faith and patriotism in the United States.

The triumph of anticlericalism?

What had remained largely theoretical in the eighteenth century, as an intellectual posture of many philosophers, was put into practice in the nineteenth century, after the French Revolution. Not only did the Revolution end the privileges of the Catholic Church in France and in the territories conquered by the French armies, but it also actively sponsored a secular vision of the world. Mistrustful of the void left by the departure of religion, the Revolution established the cult of the Supreme Being and with it a set of ethics based on natural law. Besides, as the greatest historian of the Revolution, Jules Michelet (1798–1874) would argue, the Revolution itself had been some kind of religious phenomenon: the Republic replaced the Church as the producer of purpose, values, laws and ethics. Indeed, while God and the fatherland would often be joined in invocation – notably on the battlefields – it could also be convincingly argued that the growth of the concept of the nation-state in the nineteenth century, which took place alongside dechristianization and secularization, indeed provided people with an alternative ideology, a form of civil religion.

For centuries, atheism, skepticism or the simple criticism of Church authorities had to be hidden in Europe; freethinkers fought for the right to express their beliefs and live accordingly. It is therefore not surprising that having obtained this freedom, they retained a combative attitude.

The nineteenth century would see the development of secularism in Europe along with a burst of anticlericalism. The promoters of materialism and rationalism – the great atheist philosophers Auguste Comte (1798–1857), Ludwig Feuerbach (1804–1872), Arthur Schopenhauer (1788–1860) and Friedrich Nietzsche (1844–1900) – would join the theorists of socialism and communism – Friedrich Engels (1820–1895), Karl Marx (1818–1883) and Mikhail Bakunin (1814–1876) – in denouncing religion as a source of oppression of the mind or the body, before Sigmund Freud (1856–1919) explored the unconscious, uncovering new explanations of religion that had no connection to the existence of any deity. Their intellectual posture was supported by the development of scientific knowledge, foremost among which is the elaboration of the theory of evolution by Charles Darwin (1809–1882). Simultaneously, the birth of the study of religion as a scientific discipline, along with new disciplines such as sociology and anthropology shifted uncomfortably the position of Churches.

But in this century of scientific and technological progress, and of misery for those exploited by the development of industry and capitalism, many more would rise against the power of the ruling classes served by that of the Church: anticlericalism became a powerful political motor. Not surprisingly, anticlericalism developed mostly in countries where the Catholic Church had been dominant: France, Belgium Italy, Spain, Latin America, etc. In the context of the encyclical *Quanta Cura* and the *Syllabus or Catalogue of the Main Errors of Time* (1864), in which pope Pius IX wiped out all modern liberties, anticlericalism became one of the most widely shared beliefs in the world. The founding Congress of the World Union of Free Thinkers was held in Brussels in 1880 (Witte, 1977).

In the French Third Republic, anticlericalism would eventually triumph: republican universalism imposed the secularization of public education and the law of separation of Church and State of 1905. Elsewhere, as in Italy, results were mitigated. While after 1861 the new Italian state experienced various forms of anticlericalism both to the left and right of the political spectrum – Italy, after all, was born out of a war against the pope – the conflict between Church and State ended up in a truce. The Lateran Treaty of 1929 and the Italian people remained largely Catholics well into the twentieth century.

Modern constitutions granted freedom of worship to all while often keeping a mention of God in their preambles. In some countries, a struggle between Catholics and Liberals occurred; in others Catholicism and Lutheranism competed for state favors. Despite the strength of anticlericalism in countries such as France, Belgium and Italy, European colonial states still relied on the collaboration of church missionaries in civilizing vast colonial empires. Now as before, religion was regarded as a useful tool to establish and maintain a peaceful society.

Secular humanism to the test of the twentieth century

The twentieth century would take Europe 'to hell and back' (Kershaw, 2015). Alone, the Great War of 1914–1918 claimed around 20 million lives, while armies on each side proclaimed to have God on their side. The Second World War would be worse, and the systematic destruction of European Jews by the Nazi regime would bring humankind to new lows. For some, Auschwitz illustrated the absence – or departure – of God from the world; after 1945, many found in these horrors an argument for their atheist philosophy (Jonas, 1994; Wiesel, 1995).

After the creation of the Soviet Union in 1922 and the extension of the communist system to all of Eastern Europe and beyond after 1945, atheism became the official dogma in many countries. The leader of the Bolshevik Revolution, Vladimir Lenin (1870–1924), had made his views on religion abundantly clear in 1909: "Fear made the gods' (...) Religion is the opium of the people – this dictum by Marx is the corner-stone of the whole Marxist outlook on religion. Marxism has always regarded all modern religions and Churches, and each and every religious organization, as instruments of bourgeois reaction that serve to defend exploitation and to befuddle the working class' (Lenin, 1973 (1909)). The Soviet concept of 'state atheism' had among its objectives the elimination of existing religion and the prevention of future religious belief. Religious property was confiscated and religious beliefs were ridiculed in schools and generally looked down upon in public. While religion was not banned, it became socially unacceptable to affirm one's faith or to participate in religious rites. Russia evolved from a bastion of conservative Orthodoxy in the nineteenth century into the world's leading promoter of atheism in the twentieth (Smolkin, 2018). While the communist regime may be regarded as the triumph of atheism, it proved to be short-lived: the religious revival that had been smoldering for some years flourished in most former communist countries after 1989. In Cuba, a 1992 reform abolished atheism as the state ideology, declaring the country to be secular instead. Few would agree today that communism provided good examples of humanist regimes. The contempt communists showed toward freedom of belief was just one of the many basic human rights they didn't respect. Indeed, the contrast between ideals and political practice, as far as human rights were concerned, and the revolt it inspired in people, contributed to the demise of the system (Thomas, 2005).

Some observers like to emphasize that neither Adolf Hitler nor Josef Stalin was religious, and they throw in the figure of Pol Pot for good measure in concluding that atheism was responsible for most twentieth-century atrocities. This is naturally a fallacious reasoning, for atheism was not at the core of the Nazi or communist ideologies. Similarly, crimes committed during the Crusades and the Wars of Religions do not permit one to conclude that Christianity is intrinsically violent, just as the atrocious record of ISIS does not allow one to draw conclusions about the evilness of Islam. History has made it abundantly clear that there is no connection between religion and morality, or between atheism and immorality: humanism is a value shared by people of all kinds of faiths, beliefs and unbelief.

This discussion on the vicissitudes of atheism in twentieth-century Europe should not offset the existence of secularism in other parts of the world, such as China and India. In India, the Constitution institutes a secular state, notably to accommodate the religious diversity of the peninsula, and there are several Indian rationalist organizations (Quack, 2012).

Freedom of belief in international instruments

The post-1945 period saw the triumph of human rights principles, first carried by the victors of Nazi Germany on both sides of the Atlantic and later enshrined among the founding principles of the United Nations. Among them are freedom of thought and religion, as stated in Article 18 of the Universal Declaration of Human Rights adopted in December 1948: 'Everyone has the right to freedom of thought, conscience and religion; this right includes freedom to change his religion or belief, and freedom, either alone or in community with others and in public or private, to manifest his religion or belief in teaching, practice, worship and observance.'

This article explicitly confers freedom to practice a religion and to change religion but does not explicitly grant the freedom to have no religion. Despite its symbolic weight, the UN Human Rights declaration is not a legally binding instrument. For this reason, the UN General Assembly adopted the *International Covenant on Civil and Political Rights* (ICCPR) in 1966. This multilateral treaty legally obliges the state which ratifies it. In 2019, the Covenant had been ratified by 171 member states, but some have reserved the right to interpret the treaty within the context of Islamic law. Some theocracies (among them Saudi Arabia and Vatican City) have not signed the Covenant. Again, Article 18 of the Covenant is more protective of religious freedom than freedom of unbelief: 'Everyone shall have the right to freedom of thought, conscience, and religion. This right shall include freedom to have or to adopt a religion or belief of his choice, and freedom, either individually or in community with others and in public or private, to manifest his religion or belief in worship, observance, practice, and teaching. Nevertheless, in recent times, it has become increasingly clear that the right to free exercise of religion implies the right to free exercise of non-religion' (Sullivan, 1992).

After 20 years of debate, on 25 November 1981, the General Assembly adopted the *Declaration on the Elimination of All Forms of Intolerance and of Discrimination Based on Religion or Belief.*[2] While the 1981 Declaration also lacks any enforcement procedures, it is the most

2 Declaration on the Elimination of All Forms of Intolerance and of Discrimination Based on Religion or Belief, G.A. res. 36/55, 36 U.N. GAOR Supp. (No. 51) at 171, U.N. Doc. A/36/684 (1981).

important contemporary codification of the principles of freedom of religion and belief. When the Declaration was adopted, the USSR and several other communist countries expressed reservations, finding that the Declaration did not take sufficient account of atheistic beliefs. Indeed, Article 1 of the 1981 Declaration, again, stipulates: 'Everyone shall have the right to freedom of thought, conscience and religion. This right shall include freedom to have a religion or whatever belief of his choice, and freedom, either individually or in community with others and in public or private, to manifest his religion or belief in worship, observance, practice and teaching'.

The question of the inclusion of atheism among the beliefs expressly protected by UN instruments was finally addressed in 1993, when the Human Rights Committee issued a comment on Article 18 of the 1948 Human Rights declaration, stipulating that "Article 18 protects theistic, non-theistic and atheistic beliefs, as well as the right not to profess any religion or belief. The terms 'belief' and 'religion' are to be broadly construed. Article 18 is not limited in its application to traditional religions or to religions and beliefs with institutional characteristics or practices analogous to those of traditional religions."[3]

In Europe, the main instrument protecting human rights is the Convention for the Protection of Human Rights and Fundamental Freedoms, signed in Rome in 1950. It was the first instrument to give effect to the rights stated in the Universal Declaration of Human Rights. Respect for the Convention is ensured by the European Court of Human Rights (ECHR). The Court has developed an extensive jurisprudence on Article 9 of the Convention which reads as follows: 'Everyone has the right to freedom of thought, conscience and religion; this right includes freedom to change his religion or belief and freedom, either alone or in community with others and in public or private, to manifest his religion or belief, in worship, teaching, practice and observance. Freedom to manifest one's religion or beliefs shall be subject only to such limitations as are prescribed by law and are necessary in a democratic society in the interests of public safety, for the protection of public order, health or morals, or for the protection of the rights and freedoms of others'. From the 1990s onward,[4] the ECHR has ruled that Article 9 also guaranteed the right not to belong to a religion and not to practice it, and that public authorities could not require a person to conduct an act which might be seen as swearing allegiance to a given religion, such as taking an oath on the Bible.[5]

Within international human rights protective instruments, the main controversial point for freethinkers probably concerns the education of children. The first protocol to the Convention for the Protection of Human Rights and Fundamental Freedoms, adopted in 1952, specifies: 'No person shall be denied the right to education. In the exercise of any functions which it assumes in relation to education and to teaching, the State shall respect the right of parents to ensure such education and teaching in conformity with their own religious and philosophical convictions'. Likewise, Article 14 of the UN Convention on the Rights of the Child (1989) states: '(1) States Parties shall respect the right of the child to freedom of thought, conscience and religion. (2) States Parties shall respect the rights and duties of the parents and, when applicable, legal guardians, to provide direction to the child in the exercise of his or her right in a manner consistent with the evolving capacities of the child'.

Many Freethinkers denounce a contradiction between the two paragraphs of the text and argue that a child should be brought up in a neutral way, while being introduced to every life

---

3 Human Rights Committee, General Comment 22, Article 18 (Forty-eighth session, 1993).

4 See ECtHR, *Kokkinakis v Greece*, application no. 14307/88, judgment of 25 May 1993.

5 Guide on Article 9 of the European Convention on Human Rights, last updated on 30 April 2019. Available at https://www.echr.coe.int/Documents/Guide_Art_9_ENG.pdf.

stance and philosophy. Article 5 of the 1981 UN Declaration mentioned above also offers similar guarantee of the parents' right to educate children according to their beliefs. This debate may evolve into a conflict between religious freedom on the one hand and the rights of children on the other. The debate over the advisability of banning circumcision for religious reasons, which has developed in some European countries, revolves around similar lines. Partisans of the ban invoke inter alia the freedom of choice of the child (Cohen, 2014).

The conflict is particularly apparent as far as religious education is organized in schools. In this matter, in addition to the dispensation of religious classes to children, there is the fact that in some countries, religious education is mandatory, even for children raised in non-believing families. The European Court of Human Rights has ruled that attendance may be compulsory only in case of nondenominational teaching; in cases of denominational teaching, the authorities must allow an exemption. Since 2002, the Parliamentary Assembly of the Council of Europe has formulated several recommendations in favor of adapting religious education to the twenty-first-century religious diversity of the continent and adopting comparative study of religions: 'the aim of this education should be to make pupils discover the religions practised in their own and neighboring countries, to make them perceive that everyone has the same right to believe that their religion is the "true faith" and that other people are not different human beings through having a different religion or not having a religion at all.'[6]

Another subject of concern for freethinkers is the existence of legislation criminalizing blasphemy. The eradication of blasphemy laws represents a major demand of secular movements. In Europe, such laws tend to disappear or have fallen into disuse. The blasphemy issue illustrates a difference between religion and atheism as far as enjoying public freedoms is concerned. Public freedom of worship has no exact equivalent for secular humanists – except maybe for some ceremonies such as baby naming. And, in fact, public displays of atheism often take the form of a critique of religion, or at least are regarded as such by believers.

In contrast to the development of religious freedom protection in international instruments, upheld by international courts, and first of all by the European Court of Strasbourg, state laws based upon Islamic law prohibiting apostasy prevent a similar development in the Muslim world (Saeed, 2004).

In 1986, the United Nations Commission on Human Rights appointed a 'Special Rapporteur on religious intolerance' whose mandate title was later (2000) changed to 'Special Rapporteur on freedom of religion or belief'. Ahmed Shaheed has occupied the position since 2016. The Special Rapporteur submits annual reports to the Human Rights Council, the Commission on Human Rights and the General Assembly.

In March 2017, the Office of the UN High Commissioner for Human Rights (OHCHR) launched the 'Faith for Rights' framework initiative. The Beirut Declaration on 'Faith for Rights' aimed to make faith and human rights mutually reinforcing spheres: 'we are convinced that our religious or belief convictions are one of the fundamental sources of protection for human dignity and freedoms of all individuals and communities with no distinction on any ground whatsoever. Religious, ethical and philosophical texts preceded international law in upholding the oneness of humankind, the sacredness of the right to life and the corresponding individual and collective duties that are grounded in the hearts of believers'.[7] In all but a few occurrences, the text calls for people belonging to religions *and beliefs* throughout the world to unite their effort, yet the primary purpose of the declaration is

6 Parliamentary Assembly of the Council of Europe. Recommendation 1720 (2005) *Education and religion.*

7 Available at https://www.ohchr.org/Documents/Press/21451/BeirutDeclarationonFaithforRights.pdf.

clearly to prevent interfaith conflicts: 'religious actors should be enabled, both nationally and internationally, to assume their responsibilities in defending our shared humanity against incitement to hatred'. The fact that the declaration is primarily aimed at believers is indicated by the quotation at the forefront: 'There are as many paths to God as there are souls on Earth,' attributed to the Sufi mystic Djalâl ad-Dîn Rûmî. This is an example of an effort made to include secular humanists – although they are not referred to by this name – into the various convictions that call for universal respect. Yet the specific stance of secularism, that flourished in taking a certain distance from religion, makes it difficult to transform it into just one of the components of the convictions landscape.

Secular humanism, a new religion?

The historical epicenter of Christianity, Western Europe, has been going through an accelerated secularization for about 50 years. Paradoxically, this situation has given secular humanism lots of room to develop, while rendering one of its main lines of development, anticlericalism, less important.

Nevertheless, in several countries, secular humanists have organized themselves to promote their vision of a secular state and their own ethical view, although the diversity of the movements does not make it possible to agree on very specific points but rather on common values, and in the first place, human rights. In Belgium, the Centre for Secular Action (Centre d'action laïque, CAL), founded in 1969, stated a twofold purpose: 'building a just, progressive and fraternal society, with impartial public institutions,' but also the development of a 'concept of life based on human experience, to the exclusion of any confessional, dogmatic or supernatural reference' (Sägesser, 2010). Fifty years later, the center is thriving and enjoys public recognition and state financing as a representative organization for secular humanists. Secular moral counseling is available to inmates in prisons, to patients in hospitals and elsewhere.

In recent years, a network of secular organizations has developed throughout Europe. On rare occasions, those organizations which defend a humanist philosophy of life with no reference whatsoever to transcendence receive public recognition and finance. In 1991, the European Humanist Federation (EHF) was set up in Prague by a dozen humanist associations from several European countries. One of the main goals of the EHF is 'the promotion of secularism throughout Europe and at EU level. It encompasses the protection of freedom of religion or belief, including the right not to believe and the right to change one's beliefs'.[8]

In the United States, the environment is less favorable to organized secularism. The American Humanist Association (AHA) ('Good without a God') was formed in 1941. Already in the early 1930s, humanist organizations had been set up in major cities such as Chicago and New York. They included prominent members such as Julian Huxley and Albert Einstein. *A Humanist Manifesto* was published in 1933. The AHA aimed to demonstrate compatibility between atheism and morality in a country where godless people were generally looked down on as people of weak morality. In *Humanism: A New Religion*, Charles Potter exposed a philosophy which openly rejected traditional Christian beliefs and replaced them with a humanism drawing on various aspects of naturalism, rationalism and socialism (Potter, 1930). Over the years, the AHA has fought for a deeper secularization of American society and institutions, opposing religious instruction in schools or supporting the pro-choice movement for the legality of abortion. In recent years, the AHA has launched more visible advertising campaigns,

8 See https://humanistfederation.eu/who-we-are/our-missio

on buses among other platforms, using slogans like 'Why Believe in a God? Just Be Good for Goodness' Sake'. The focus is still on making people understand that secular humanism is as respectable a life choice as any religion. It also organizes ceremonies with humanist celebrants such as weddings, memorials or baby namings. In most American states, humanist celebrants enjoy the same status as members of the clergy as far as performing ceremonies go.

Secular humanism in Europe developed as a by-product of secularization; it was constructed as a response to the global life interpretation of religions, and sometimes tried to imitate them by creating alternative rites. Humanist celebrants who perform child namings, coming-of-age ceremonies, weddings, funerals or other rituals enjoy legal status in some countries. This state recognition has often been obtained following a court decision in a lawsuit based on discrimination; this was the case in Scotland in 2005 and in Northern Ireland in 2017. That same year, the funeral of former First Minister of Wales Rhodri Morgan was the first national funeral in the UK to be led by a humanist celebrant. In Scotland, according to Humanist Society Scotland, it appears that humanist marriages have become the largest type of marriage outside civil registrations.[9]

The similarity between religious groups and secular humanist groups received a confirmation in Article 17 of the 2007 Lisbon Treaty on the European Union. It reads as follows:

1. The Union respects and does not prejudice the status under national law of churches and religious associations or communities in the Member States.
2. The Union equally respects the status under national law of philosophical and non-confessional organizations.
3. Recognizing their identity and their specific contribution, the Union shall maintain an open, transparent and regular dialogue with these churches and organizations.

While secular humanist associations opposed the institutionalization of religious dialog within the EU and regarded Article 17 as a defeat, they have become increasingly active in the framework of this dialog. In the setup of the official dialog with religious organizations, initially entrusted to the Bureau of European Policy Advisers (BEPA) of the European Commission, Christian churches were the best represented. Jewish and Islamic organizations had initially only little weight, and secular humanists had to battle to gain access to those meetings as well. Nowadays, two annual meetings take place: one with religious organizations and one with representatives of secular humanism, among which is the EHF mentioned above.

Beyond the Western World

Traditionally, Islamic societies tolerate groups from other religions: in a Muslim country such as Egypt, where several religions coexist, an individual is labeled as Muslim, Christian or Jewish. Religious identity tends to merge with a form of ethnic identity, leaving no room for nonbelievers. The only position nonbelievers can take is the uncomfortable one of apostate. Conflict-torn countries where religious dividing lines play a part, such as Lebanon or Israel, also apply a rigorous categorization of citizens along confessional lines. It is very difficult for those who wish to emancipate themselves from any religious faith to lead a public life.

9 See https://www.humanism.scot/what-we-do/news/humanist-society-scotland-named-biggest-marriage-ceremony-provider-in-scotland

Throughout the twentieth century, repression and opprobria touched those who dared to question the foundations of the faith. The Egyptian writer Ismail Adham (1911–1940), who in 1937 questioned the authenticity of the *hadiths* in his book *Why I Am an Atheist*, was driven to suicide. The cases of Salman Rushdie (b. 1947) and Taslima Nasreen (b. 1962), who were persecuted as a result of their so-called blasphemous writings, are better known. After the publication of his novel *The Satanic Verses* (1988), Ayatollah Khomeini, the Supreme Leader of Iran, issued a fatwa calling for the assassination of Rushdie who was placed under police protection. Taslima Nasreen, a native of Bangladesh, suffered a similar fate and was banned from her country for a strong defense of women's rights and hard criticism of religion throughout her award-winning literary production. In the twenty-first century, former Muslims, with the help of the Internet and social networks, started to organize themselves. In 2007, the Council of Ex-Muslims of Britain (CEMB) was created in London on the initiative of Maryam Namazie, an Iranian woman in exile.[10] The CEMB, whose manifesto calls for freedom of religion and atheism and freedom to criticize religion, publishes a report on the conditions faced by apostates in each Muslim country.[11] It reviews the multiple cases of freethinkers sentenced to imprisonment, fines or even death. In Germany, the ZDE or Zentralrat der Ex-Muslime (Central Council of Ex-Muslims) was also founded in 2007.[12] A similar initiative in the Netherlands, the Centraal Comité voor Ex-moslims (Central Committee for Ex-Muslims), was apparently short-lived due to lack of success. The Institute for the Secularization of Islamic Society produced in 2007 the St Petersburg Declaration, calling for the separation of mosque and state. The institute was founded in 1998 by Ibn Warraq, the pseudonym of a writer who has published extensively on Islam in a highly critical stance (Ibn Warraq, 1998, 2002). While his lack of expertise has been criticized by academics, Ibn Warraq enjoys some recognition in political circles. In many countries, atheists are still persecuted: according to the Freedom of Thought report published by Humanist International, in 13 countries people convicted of blasphemy or apostasy may face the death penalty and are submitted to torture. Afghanistan, Iran and Saudi Arabia are consistently the worst countries in regard to respect for free thought.

Conclusion

In many regions of the world, atheists and freethinkers in general still face legislation prohibiting apostasy. In Europe, the Americas and part of Asia, secular humanists are no longer ostracized. It is rather the most devout believers and the fundamentalists who may experience limitations to their freedom of worship. Nevertheless, and while a recent evolution tends to have public authorities consider secular humanism as just one philosophical choice among many, the very nature of atheism makes it difficult for atheists themselves to accept this position. Historically, secular humanism was built as a reaction to the power of religious institutions and the influence of religious doctrine on people's behavior. In the twenty-first century, opposition between secular humanists and religious groups has not vanished, as illustrated by the 2004 controversy surrounding the proposed preamble to the Treaty establishing a European Constitution: the possible inclusion of a reference to God or to the continent's Christian roots sparked vigorous opposition among secular organizations, mostly in France and Belgium. They were backed by their respective governments. The final wording of the preamble left God and Christianity out,

10 See https://www.ex-muslim.org.uk.

11 The 2017 report on *Political and Legal Status of Apostates in Islam* is https://muslim.org.uk/wp-content/uploads/2017/08/political-and-legal-staus-of-apostates-in-Islam-Final.pdf.

12 See https://exmuslime.com

reading as follows: 'Drawing inspiration from the cultural, religious and humanist inheritance of Europe, from which have developed the universal values of the inviolable and inalienable rights of the human person, freedom, democracy, equality and the rule of law'. The preamble was incorporated into the revised Treaty on European Union.

Over the centuries, the strength of the power, both spiritual and temporal, of religious institutions has led to the growth of a vigorous movement of opposition in Europe. Anticlerical freethinkers fought for their freedom of belief, but also to demonstrate that secular humanism promotes ethics that are just as valid as religious values. Nevertheless, the wide variety of secular humanists have not allowed them to define specific core values beyond respect for human rights; yet those are indeed the common and sufficient ethical base of believers and unbelievers.

Further reading

Edham, I.A., 1937. *Why Am I an Atheist? (Limadha ana mulhid?).* Cooperation Press.

Haffen, M., 1990. *L'athéisme.* Granger.

International Humanist and Ethical Union. 2018. The Freedom of Thought Report 2018: A Global Report on the Rights, Legal Status and Discrimination Against Humanists, Atheists and the Non-religious. Available from https://fot.humanists.international.

Staquet, A. (Ed.), 2013. *Athéisme dévoilé aux temps modernes.* Académie Royale de Belgique.

Bellah, R., 1967. Civil religion in America. *Daedelus* 96(1), 1.

Berriot, F., 1984. *Athéismes et athéistes en France au XVIème siècle.* Éditions du Cerf.

Cohen, M.-L. (Ed.), 2014. *La circoncision en question. Actes du colloque organisé à Toulouse le 24 janvier 2014.* Éditions Orizon.

Deruette, S., 2008. *Lire Jean Meslier, curé et athée révolutionnaire. Introduction au mesliérisme et extraits de son œuvre.* Aden.

d'Holbach, P., 1766. *Le christianisme dévoilé, ou examen des principes et des effets de la religion chrétienne: par feu M. Boulanger.* A Londres.

Hourani, G.F., 1962. Averroes on good and evil. *Studia Islamica.* 16, 13.

Ivanhoe, P.J., 2002. *Ethics in the Confucian Tradition: The Thought of Mengzi and Wang Yangming.* Hackett Publishing.

Jeangene Vilmer, J.-B., 2008. *La religion de Sade.* Editions de l'Atelier.

Jonas, H., 1994. *Le concept de Dieu après la Shoah.* Rivages Poche.

Kershaw, I., 2015. *To Hell and Back: Europe, 1914-1949.* Allen Lane.

Lenin, V. I., 1973 (1909). The attitude of the workers' party to religion. Reprinted in. *Lenin Collected Works* vol. 15. Moscow, 402.

Le Roy Ladurie, E., 1975. *Montaillou, Village Occitan de 1294 à 1324.* Gallimard.

Machiavelli, N., 1531. *Discorsi sopra la prima deca di Tito Livio.* Bernardo Giunti.

Minois, G., 1998. *Histoire de l'athéisme. Les incroyants dans le monde occidental des origins à nos jours.* Fayard.

Ottaviani, D., 2013. 'Giordano Bruno et l'athéisme' A. Stacquet (Ed.), *Athéisme voilé aux temps modernes.* Académie Royale de Belgique. 101.

Potter, C., 1930. *Humanism: A New Religion.* Simon and Schuster.

Quack, J., 2012. *Organized Rationalism and Criticism of Religion in India.* Oxford University Press.

Saeed, A., 2004. *Freedom of Religion, Apostasy and Islam.* Routledge.

Sägesser, C., 2010. La reconnaissance et le financement de la laïcité organisée. In: C. Sägesser and J. P. Schreiber (Eds.), *Le financement public des religions et de la laïcité en Belgique.* Academia Bruylant, 159.

Smolkin, V., 2018. *A Sacred Space Is Never Empty: A History of Soviet Atheism.* Princeton University Press.

Stauffer, D., 2010. 'Of religion' in Hobbes's *Leviathan*'. *J. Polit.* 72(3), 868.

Sullivan, K., 1992. Religion and liberal democracy. *Univ. Chicago Law Rev.* 59, 195.

Thomas, D., 2005. Human rights ideas, the demise of communism, and the end of the cold war. *Journal of Cold War Studies.* 7(2), 110.

Voltaire. 1877-1885 (1768). Epître à l'auteur du livre des trois imposteurs. In: *Oeuvres complètes de Voltaire*, vol. 10. Garnier, 402.
Warraq, I., 1998. *The Origins of the Koran*. Prometheus Books.
Warraq, I., 2002. *What the Koran Really Says: Language, Text, and Commentary*. Prometheus Books.
Whitmarsh, T., 2016. *Battling the Gods: Atheism in the ancient world*. Faber & Faber.
Wiesel, E., 1995. *The Trial of God*. Shocken Books.
Witte, E., 1977. De Belgische Vrijdenkersorganisaties (1854-1914). Onstaan, Ontwikkeling en Rol. *Tidschrift voor de Studie van de Verlichting* 5, 127.

PART II

The right of religious freedom from the religions' perspective

6

Buddhist perspectives on freedom of religion or belief

Benjamin Schonthal

> I always say that every person on this earth has the freedom or not to practice religion (Gyatso, 2005).
>
> – *The 14th Dalai Lama of Tibet*

> Buddhism is simply a way of mindfulness and peace. The presence of Buddhism does not mean having a lot of schools, hospitals, cultural institutions, and political parties run by Buddhists. Rather, the presence of Buddhism means that all these things are permeated and administered with humanism, love, tolerance, and enlightenment (Sivaraksa, 1992: 70).
>
> – *Thai Buddhist activist and founder of the International Network of Engaged Buddhists, Sulak Sivaraksa*

> Buddhists have always been tolerant. There is no other teaching (*dharmayak*) in the world that preaches more about the value of tolerance and about not being vengeful than the Buddha's dharma (All-Ceylon Buddhist Congress, 1956: 317).
>
> – *Passage from a Sinhala-language report written by the All-Ceylon Buddhist Congress*

At first glance, several principles of similarity link together the above quotes. Most obviously, each quote appears to endorse religious freedom, toleration and coexistence as important social ideals. Either directly or implicitly, the quotes also present those ideals as consistent with Buddhist teachings and institutions. Supporting this linkage are the authority and credentials of the authors: the first quote comes from the world's most prominent Tibetan Buddhist monk, the second from a famous Buddhist activist and social critic in Thailand and the third from a collective of eminent Buddhist monks and laypersons in Sri Lanka, who together represented the country's largest Buddhist nongovernmental organisation, the All-Ceylon Buddhist Congress.

Other similarities appear when one investigates further. Although all three quotes invoke ideas of toleration and freedom, each of the authors wrote at a time when their own freedoms seemed to be under threat. The Dalai Lama's sentiments came in a context (still ongoing) in which he and his co-religionists were facing severe restrictions from the Chinese government – which, incidentally, also claims to speak for Tibetan Buddhists (Powers,

2016). Sulak Sivaraksa, who authored the second quote, has been accused by certain government officials and senior monks of advancing heterodox conceptions of Buddhism that undermine the Thai state (Swearer, 1996). The statements given by the All-Ceylon Buddhist Congress are excerpted from a much longer report that, in part, accused the Buddhist-majority government of newly independent Ceylon of restricting Buddhists' religious freedom while covertly supporting Christian interests (Smith, 1966).

I start with these quotes – and their very brief analysis – because taken collectively they illustrate several challenges associated with investigating 'Buddhist perspectives on religious freedom.' Looking at these quotes, one sees clearly that Buddhists (and Buddhism) do not speak with a single voice. As with other religious communities, questions of authority and orthodoxy are heavily debated among Buddhists, making any claim to speak on behalf of the religion or all of its adherents contentious. Adding to this multiplicity of voices is the fact that there are multiple schools and sects within Buddhism, most of which are not centrally or hierarchically organised around a single pope-like leader. When it comes to speaking for Buddhists, even the Dalai Lama's authority has been challenged. Looking at these quotes, and the historical contexts surrounding them, also alerts one to the not-always-obvious presence of restrictive or exclusionary agendas among certain Buddhist organisations and actors. Similarly to the histories of Christianity, Islam, Hinduism and other traditions, the history of Buddhism is filled with stories of certain religious groups attempting to silence or marginalise others.[1] Finally, at the rhetorical level, these quotes highlight the simultaneous omnipresence and multivocality of 'freedom of religion' as a phrase invoked by Buddhists in different places and times: most Buddhists speak in support of religious freedom; at the same time, Buddhists' interpretations of religious freedom can vary widely and tend to reflect specific historical, social and political circumstances.

With these considerations in mind, this chapter offers not *the* Buddhist perspective on freedom of religion, but the perspectives of certain Buddhists living in specific places and times. In choosing which perspectives to include, I have taken seriously the mandate of this volume to investigate 'diversity' and 'difference' in interpretations of religious freedom. Thus, I focus especially on those perspectives that complicate dominant understandings of freedom of religion in international law, most of which draw upon understandings of religion and rights taken from Euro-American strains of liberal political theory (Danchin, 2008; Hurd, 2015). Using examples from Buddhist texts, epigraphy, history and legal traditions, this chapter helps to parochialise two key assumptions about religious freedom that undergird a great deal of religious freedom jurisprudence in international law: the assumption that religions are universal, comparable and to some degree isomorphic and the assumption that individuals and states should respect and tolerate equally the religions to which they do not adhere.

My goal in using this approach is neither to juxtapose fully nor to harmonise perfectly Buddhist philosophical principles with influential understandings of freedom of religion. Focussing entirely on juxtaposition would risk exoticising Buddhists as members of an epistemic community whose values and reasoning sit outside those of the Euro-American liberal tradition. Such a binary is neither historically nor analytically defensible, ignoring, as it does, the key roles played by Buddhists in shaping, interpreting and implementing principles of freedom of religion in both Asia and the North Atlantic – to say nothing of the important influence of Buddhists and other non-European thinkers on the development of liberal political philosophy (e.g., Mehta, 1999). Focussing entirely on harmonisation, on the other hand, would risk overlooking or trivialising the unique possibilities offered by Buddhist sources to reconsider,

1 On the association of Buddhism with ecumenism and pacifism, see (Frydenlund, 2017a).

reimagine or contest religious freedom as political principle. Taking this second approach runs the risk of reducing a chapter like this into a kind of conceptual concordance that simply adduces passages or ideas from Buddhist texts (which the author selects) as 'proof' of Buddhism's special affinity with the modern notion of religious freedom.

In choosing the examples below, I have other goals in mind. Rather than opposing Buddhism and religious freedom (in order to compare them as isolates), I want to show how Buddhists participate actively in the definition of religious freedom within specific jurisdictions and historical contexts. Similarly, rather than simply assume Buddhists' affirmation of religious freedom as a concept, I want to examine how specific Buddhist texts or ideas actually help individuals to question or reimagine religious freedom in both creative and instrumental ways. In pursuing these goals, I draw upon texts, epigraphy and histories from locations and modes of Buddhism with which I am most familiar, namely the Theravāda Buddhist traditions of Southern Asia, especially those of Sri Lanka.

Reconsidering religious freedom Part I: Is Buddhism a religion?

It's obvious, but bears repeating: the very idea of freedom of religion assumes the existence of an entity called 'religion.' It also assumes that religions, although they may be different in type, are analogous in kind. To use the biological metaphor, freedom of religion assumes that religions (Christianity, Buddhism, Islam, etc.) are separate species within a single genus. Indeed, the organisation of this volume operates according to this popular assumption, as do many other scholarly works and academic departments throughout the world.

Despite a growing scholarly literature that historicises and critiques this vision of religion, it is nevertheless the case that the most influential interpretations of freedom of religion in international law presume the commensurability of *religions* as entities within society. This situation is visible the fact that the vast majority of global constitutions and higher judiciary judgements disaggregate the right to religious freedom into two parallel sub-rights, which are thought to apply with equal fit to all religious traditions: an absolute right to freedom to believe one's religion and a right to manifest one's religion which is limitable under certain conditions (Danchin, 2008; Taylor, 2005).

This understanding of religions–as similarly structured and consisting of separable beliefs and practices, with the former being more important than the latter–is not universally accepted by Buddhists around the world. In fact, even the oldest Buddhist texts make a distinction between the dispensation of the Buddha, described as *sāsana*, and the teachings of other charismatic leaders and groups, for which a variety of other words tend to be used, including (in Pāli sources[2]) 'teaching' (*dhamma*), 'view' (*diṭṭhi*), or 'doctrine' (*vāda*) (see, e.g., Fuller, 2005).[3] Throughout Asia, but especially in South and Southeast Asia, when Buddhists speak in local vernaculars about protecting their distinctive rituals, beliefs and practices, they speak about protecting the *sāsana*.

Why is this distinction significant? For a start, the Pāli word *sāsana* – as well as the Sinhala, Burmese and Thai and other variants of the term that make up contemporary Asian vernaculars –

2 Unless otherwise specified, the terms I use in this chapter are given in the form in which they appear in the Pāli language, the dominant Buddhist liturgical language for Southern Asia. This chapter also draws upon numerous translations from Sinhala, the language spoken by most Buddhists in Sri Lanka. All translations are my own unless indicated otherwise.

3 This is not to say that the term sāsana is never applied to other groups in historical texts. Occasionally it is. But, in the contemporary public discourse in Southern Asia, sāsana tends to refer primarily to Buddhism.

tends to be a broader and more encompassing term than the English noun *religion*. *Sāsana* derives from a Sanskrit verbal root *śas*, meaning to instruct or command, and has come to refer, by extension, to the entire legacy of instruction and teaching that the Buddha set into motion. This legacy includes, on the one hand, the various rules and principles laid out by the Buddha: his soteriological and moral teachings (the *dhamma*), his disciplinary rules for monks (*vinaya*), his didactic stories (*suttas, jātakas*) and philosophical reflections (*abhidhamma*), all of which comprise the traditional three-part textual canon for Buddhists (*tipiṭaka*).

On the other hand, *sāsana* is not just a term that implicates ideas, doctrines or texts. It also implicates the broader material embodiments of the Buddha's legacy: the physical vestiges and human implications of the instructions that he gave. To this end, *sāsana* has been interpreted as including Buddhist holy sites and ceremonies, monks and laypersons, chants, relics, manuscripts and many other tokens of the Buddha's imprint in the world. For example, one Sri Lanka Supreme Court judge (Wanasundera J.) glossed *sāsana* in an opinion from 1987 as 'a compendious term encompassing all ancient, historic and sacred objects and places which have from ancient times been or are associated with the religious practices and worship of Sinhala Buddhists.'[4] More recently, a special Presidential Commission appointed in 2002 to investigate the condition of Buddhism in Sri Lanka offered an even more expansive Sinhala-language definition:

> the Buddha, the nine other-worldly truths (*dhamma*-s) discovered by the Buddha, the complete teaching of the Buddha (*dhamma*), the jewel of the monks, the limb of Buddhist temples together with forest hermitages and meditation centres, bodhi trees, stupas, image houses, relic palaces, monastic preaching books and [other] books, meeting houses for monks, fields and properties that belong to temples, Buddhist education, the shrines to important deities endowed by Buddhist kings (*devalaya*), female renunciants (*silmātā-s*) and their sanctuaries, the lay persons who have gone to the triple gem for refuge, Buddhist literature, culture and civilisation, Buddhist festivals, processions (*perahaera*), offerings and customs, virtuous conduct (*pratipatti*) and ethics (*ācāra dharma*), as well as those things like this that are basic to [the Sāsana's] cultivation.
>
> *(Government of Sri Lanka, 2002: 15)*

In both cases, one can immediately see striking differences between regnant definitions of religion in international law and the use of *sāsana* in Buddhist historical texts and modern Sri Lankan legal contexts. Where the term *religion*, in the first context, implies the presence of multiple, equal and isomorphic modes of human activity which, at their core, involve the dissemination, reflection and expression of particular beliefs concerning (to take one recent gloss from the UK Supreme Court) 'mankind's nature and relationship to the universe,'[5] *sāsana* implies a broader and more diverse array of things that extend well beyond beliefs: teachings, people, places, properties, ritual accoutrements, books, culture, civilisation, rituals, customs, ideas and ethics.

In parts of Southern Asia, this distinction between religion and *sāsana* has had major implications for the interpretation and implementation of religious freedom. Consider, for example, the drafting of Sri Lanka's post-independence constitutions. From 1970 to 1972, constitutional draftpersons aimed to accommodate, among other things, two strident demands

4 Dissenting opinion in: 1987 2 SLR 312, *Thirteenth Amendment to the Constitution and Provincial Councils Bill*. 364.

5 UKSC, 2013. *R (on the Application of Hodkin and Another) (Appellants) v. Registrar General of Births, Deaths and Marriages (Respondent)*. Paragraph 54.

regarding religion. On the one hand, they faced popular pressure to give the majority religion, Buddhism, special protections in the new republican constitution; on the other hand, key figures in the constitution-writing process wanted to ensure that all citizens of the island would be guaranteed fundamental rights to freedom of religion consistent with those contained in the Universal Declaration of Human Rights. The final balancing of these two demands can be seen in Chapter 2 of Sri Lanka's First Republican Constitution of 1972 which reads:

> The Republic of Sri Lanka shall give to Buddhism the foremost place and accordingly it shall be the duty of the state to protect and foster Buddhism, while assuring to all religions the rights [to freedom of 'though, conscience and religion, including the right to have or adopt a religion of his choice' and the freedom to 'manifest' one's religion alone or with others in 'worship, observance, practice or teaching'].[6]

At first glance, the English text seems unremarkable: it blends together special protections for the majority religion with fundamental rights to freedom of religion, in a manner similar to a great many of the world's constitutions. Why then was this formula ultimately rejected and replaced only six years later when the constitution was revised? The reasons come from popular and political reactions against the 1972 Constitution's rhetorical conflation of religion with *sāsana*. While not visible in the English-language version of the provision, the syntax of the Sinhala-language draft of Chapter 2 seems to imply that Buddhism (S: *buddhāgama*) is (simply) one type of religion (S: *āgama*) among many and is, therefore, analogous in form to Hinduism (S: *hindu-āgama*), Islam (S: *muslim-āgama*) or Christianity (S: *kristiyāni-āgama*). This was unacceptable to many Buddhist lobbyists and politicians. They worried that the rhetorical equation of Buddhism with other religions (as analogous types of *āgama*) would not only reduce the special status of the majority dispensation but might also limit the scope of government protections for it because the Sinhala term *āgama* has much more limited denotative scope than that of *sāsana*.

On both counts, the Buddhist lobbyists were probably correct and there is a longer history as to why. As in much of the colonial world, no perfect vernacular equivalent for religion existed in the local languages of Sri Lanka at the time of colonial occupation. Thus, missionaries, jurists, civil servants and others who wanted to translate European phrases – such as freedom of religion or, in the case of Christian missionaries, 'the true religion' – into local dialects needed to designate specific local terms as appropriate approximations for religion. *Āgama* was the term chosen for this particular back-translation in Ceylon. Prior to the nineteenth century, the term had been used by Saivite and Buddhist scribes to refer generally to an inherited philosophical tradition as well as to a particular genre of devotional texts. As adopted in the nineteenth century by missionaries and colonial officials, though, *āgama* came to blend those older associations with a more specific set of denotations drawn from European understandings of Christianity.[7] Specifically, *āgama* came to connote religion in a very specific sense: as a discrete set of propositional truths and related ritual practices adhered to by a single social group

---

6 *Constitution of Sri Lanka 1972, Chapter II.* The original text says 'rights granted by section 18(1)(d).' I have put the rights referred to in brackets here so as not to confuse the reader. In the 1978 Constitution, discussed below, *those* same rights are also referred to, but using their new section numbers [Articles 10, 14(i)(e)]; and in the forthcoming analysis, I will refer to those section numbers.

7 In fact, this intimate association with Christianity is still visible in the fact that the word, *āgama*, used alone can denote Catholicism. For example, one might hear the phrase '*eyā āgamek*' in contemporary vernacular Sinhala, meaning 'he is a Catholic.'

(Carter, 1977; Malalgoda, 1997; Scott, 1996).[8] Over time, from the early 1800s to the 1970s, the term was gradually popularised and came to be used both to translate religion into Sinhala as well as to designate, compare and distinguish major devotional traditions on the island along the lines of a 'world religions' model (Masuzawa, 2005). Today, *āgama* still retains its original, specific denotations as referring, somewhat narrowly, to isomorphic systems of belief and practice, rather than the broader range of material and institutional referents associated with *sāsana.*[9]

This semantic specificity of *āgama*, along with its suggestion of homology among the island's soteriological traditions, led drafters of the 1978 Constitution to insist that the government's duties to the majority dispensation should not be described as duties to 'Buddhism' (S: *buddhāgama*), but as duties to 'the Buddha *Sāsana'* (S: *buddha śāsanaya*) with the Sinhala term standing, unglossed, in all three official-language versions of the island's foundational law: English, Tamil and Sinhala. That is, rather than the state being obliged to 'protect and foster Buddhism,' the redrafted version of Chapter 2, which remains in place today, obliges the state to 'protect and foster the Buddha *Sāsana*.'[10] In making this change, legal draftpersons also affected legal and popular understandings of freedom of religion, adding in some uncertainty. What does it mean to balance government obligations to the *sāsana*, understood as the total historical, material and human legacy of the Buddha, with government assurances of religious freedom for all individuals? In rejecting the idea that Buddhism is, essentially, a form of religion, drafters have opened up the possibility of two different types, or levels, of protections for the various dispensations: those who adhere to the dispensation of the Buddha seem to be entitled to a set of rights and freedoms covering an ostensibly broader array of persons and things than the rights and freedoms available to non-Buddhists. Distinctions between religion and *sāsana*, in this case, do not undermine the freedom of religion in Sri Lanka, *per se*, but call into question its underlying assumption about the commensurability of faiths and therefore the ability to apply one standard of protection to all devotional groups.

Freedom of conscience, in two parts

The history of religious rights jurisprudence in Sri Lanka shows, at times, the powerful implications of this semantic-*cum*-legal distinction between *sāsana* and religion. Not only has the distinction (and the comparatively wider connotations of *sāsana*) permitted litigants, legal activists and judges to call upon the government to protect a variety of Buddhist spaces, artefacts and social practices that would fall outside of the purview of generic religious freedoms protections offered to adherents of other faiths (Schonthal, 2016: chapter 5), but it even allows

8 Evidence of this gradual semantic transformation can be seen in a 1895 Sinhala-English dictionary written by the Wesleyan missionary Rev. B. Clough, which rendered *āgama* as 'an approaching, coming; grammatical augment; science, a work of any of the sacred sciences; the word is universally used in colloquial intercourse to express religion' (Clough, 1892: 63).

9 A similar definitional history of the term *āgama* can be seen in other postcolonial contexts, although with differing political and legal implications. Consider, for example, Michel Picard's (2000, 2003) insightful work on the history of the term's use in Bali.

10 It should be noted that the phrase *buddhāgama* has not been eliminated completely from the constitution. The first half of the chapter still refers to *buddhāgama* as having the 'foremost place' (*pramukhasthānaya*). I suspect that *āgama* persisted there because in that section the suggestion of commensurability actually helps single out Buddhism as being more significant than other *āgama*. By contrast *śāsanaya* remained essential in the second part of the chapter because that is where the state's obligations to the privileged entity are mentioned, and that is where asserting the distinctiveness of sāsana (*vis-à-vis* religion) has a major impact.

judicially minded Buddhists to make more subtle claims about the distinct nature of Buddhists' 'conscience' and the conditions of its freedom.

One can see this process with special clarity in the legal archive of one of the most important religious rights' cases in Sri Lanka's modern history: a 2004 judicial review case heard by the Supreme Court regarding a Private Members Bill that aimed to criminalise 'forcible' conversions from one religion to another. A brief history of the case is helpful to know.[11] During the 1990s and early 2000s, many in Sri Lanka became alarmed by the idea that groups of foreign or foreign-funded Christian fundamentalists (S: *kristiyāni mūladharmavādayo*) were engaging in unethical (*sadācara virōdhī*) conversion practices. Stories circulated that Christian missionaries were specifically targeting the island's poorest and most vulnerable communities and were 'tricking' them into converting to Christianity by offering money, material assistance or by promising to would-be converts overseas visas and opportunities for employment.

In the middle of this panic about fundamentalist conversions, a political party led by Buddhist monks introduced into parliament a bill making it a custodial offence to 'convert or attempt to convert' another person through 'the use of force or by allurement or by any such fraudulent means.'[12] Definitions of these rubrics were vague and, for the bill's many critics, impermissibly broad. Following Sri Lanka's procedures of pre-enactment constitutional review of legislation, a number of petitioners challenged the bill before the island's Supreme Court. They implored, among other things, that, if ratified, the 'Anti-Conversion Bill' (as it came to be known in popular media) would violate citizens' constitutional rights to 'freedom of thought, conscience and religion, including the freedom to have or adopt a religion or belief of his choice.'[13]

Over the course of the Anti-Conversion Bill case, the distinction between religion and *sāsana* came to play an important role in the dispute, particularly as it related to the meaning of freedom of conscience, the more important of two fundamental rights relating to religious freedom in Sri Lanka's constitution (see above).[14] The petitioners who opposed the bill argued that restricting the abilities of religious groups to proselytise was tantamount to restricting religious freedom (*qua* freedom of conscience) because it curtailed citizens' opportunities to encounter other religious worldviews and thereby to 'adopt' another faith. They also insisted that the idea of 'forcible conversion' was self-contradictory because a citizen's conscience was within his/her control and could not be coerced into adopting a new set of beliefs involuntarily.

Rejecting the idea that conscience functioned similarly for all religious groups, Buddhist defenders of the bill offered an alternative, Buddhist narrative of induced conversion. Conversion, they insisted, need not be the voluntary adaptation of a new faith by an unswayed conscience; it could also be something coercive because Buddhists understood conscience as a highly fragile thing. Rather than a mental faculty that was resistant to outside influence, conscience could be easily manipulated and disrupted. Such an act of disruption, they argued, was itself an aggression against Buddhist piety because of the premium that Buddhists placed on cultivating a serene mind (Schonthal, 2016: 245–248). Following this line of reasoning,

11 The following section relies on Schonthal (2016: chapter 7).

12 *The Prohibition of Forcible Conversion of Religion Bill*, presented by Ven. Dr. Omalpe Sobhitha Thero. Gazette of the Democratic Socialist Republic of Sri Lanka, May 28, 2004, Pt. II.

13 *Constitution of Sri Lanka* 1978, Art. 10.

14 As in other jurisdictions, in Sri Lanka, freedom of conscience is legally more consequential than the freedom to manifest one's religion because it is not subject to the same range of limitations, e.g., in the interests of 'national security, public order and the protection of public health or morality, or for the purpose of securing due recognition and respect for the rights and freedoms of others, or of meeting the just requirements of the general welfare of a democratic society.' *Constitution of Sri Lanka* 1978, Art. 14(vii).

Buddhist lawyers who responded to the petition urged the Supreme Court to uphold the constitutionality of the Anti-Conversion Bill in order to protect Buddhists' freedom of religion (*qua* freedom of conscience) and to prevent aggressive and unwanted intrusions on their ability to cultivate mental calm, equanimity, 'sober reflection' and 'free thinking.'[15]

The Anti-Conversion Bill was ultimately deemed unconstitutional, mainly on account of the procedures it included for investigating, charging and sentencing those who engaged in (or even abetted) 'forcible conversion' (Schonthal, 2016: 251–260). However, the Anti-Conversion Bill case is not the only example of litigants invoking a distinction between Buddhism (or *sāsana*) and religion to challenge understandings of freedom of religion. There have been others in Sri Lanka as well as in other parts of Southern Asia (Frydenlund, 2017b, c; Schonthal, 2018). Distinguishing *sāsana* from religion has not destroyed the idea of religious freedom in these places. Instead, it has pluralised the category and rendered it more contentious. It has also made more transparent the politics, biases and material implications of defining religion in different ways.

Reconsidering religious freedom Part II: Buddhist tolerations?

By beginning my discussion of Buddhists' perspectives on religious freedom with a critique of the category of religion, I do not mean to suggest that the category of religion is problematic for Buddhists alone. Indeed, scholars, lawyers and judges who examine religious freedom cases are especially aware of the challenges associated with defining religion for the purposes of adjudicating disputes over asylum, legal recognition or tax immunity (Beaman, 2003; Gunn, 2003; Urban, 2011: 155–176). If nothing else, critical scholarship on religious freedom has, in recent years, established that religion is not a one-size-fits-all category that can accommodate all soteriological and ritual traditions (Sullivan, 2005; Sullivan et al., 2015). Many have taken this be a shortcoming of laws protecting freedom of religion: because those laws rely on a narrow, partial and non-universal understanding of religion, they unwittingly pressure subjects into reconceiving or altering their own devotional practices in order to make them legally legible; and that process harms the very freedom and independence promised by the right in the first place (Mahmood, 2006; Fernando, 2010; Moustafa, 2013).

From the perspective of classical liberal theory, any forced homogenisation of human lives is a bad thing because a key purpose of liberal rights, like the right to religious freedom, is to protect citizens from unwanted intrusions on their liberty or autonomy. Yet, from the perspectives of more communitarian types of political theory – and, perhaps, from the perspective of interventionist judiciaries or reform-minded governments – the socially transformative influence of legal categories like religion might not be entirely bad. This is because, from their perspectives, advancing particularistic understandings of religious freedom does have a positive purpose: helping recalibrate citizens' behaviours and attitudes in ways that conduce toward and cohere with a shared understanding of justice (Berlin, 1969).

What understandings of justice are advanced, then, by laws protecting freedom of religion? Among other things, policymakers who defend and advance protections for religious freedom tend to endorse strong ideas of toleration: the notion that a fair society is one in which citizens

15 Written Submissions, SC (SD) 4/2004, Intervenient Petitioner, Ven. Omalpe Sobhita Thero, p. 24. The submission makes a distinction between the Indian Constitution which guarantees the 'freedom of conscience' and the Sri Lankan Constitution which guarantees the 'freedom of thought,' insisting thought is much broader than conscience, and glossing it as 'the process or power or manner of thinking, faculty of reason, sober reflection, consideration etc.'

professing one religion (or no religion) ought not to interfere with the religious convictions of others, including those with which they disagree.[16] So intimate is the perceived link between religious freedom and toleration that the two are often invoked as part of a single conceptual complex in which one supports and indexes the presence of the other (Habermas, 2004; Stepan, 2000; Zagorin, 2005).

Buddhists, too, have strong perspectives on toleration for other religions. As seen in the quotes above, Buddhist leaders (from the Dalai Lama to the Vietnamese Zen monk Thich Nhát Hạnh) have acted as powerful defenders of the idea. Yet, Buddhist perspectives on toleration are more complicated than they first appear. Even within Theravāda Buddhism – to say nothing of the many variant schools of Mahāyāna Buddhism – one cannot find a single concept which might be considered a perfect analogue to toleration as it is deployed in post-Enlightenment political theory. Instead, one finds multiple ways in which Theravāda Buddhists imagine, justify and enact the core impulses of toleration, both in texts and in programmes of practice.

In previous work (2017a), I attempted to distil these toleration-like impulses into three major modes of 'Theravāda toleration,' each of which gains special prominence in a particular type of Buddhist literature and practice. In didactic stories about the Buddha's preaching (*suttas*), one finds many examples of (what I term) *philosophical toleration*, the idea that Buddhists ought to reject the beliefs and methods of spiritual leaders other than the Buddha, while not speaking or acting disparagingly toward those leaders or their followers in public. By contrast, in royal inscriptions and lineage texts (*vaṃsas*) in Southern Asia, one sees evidence of *imperial toleration*, a tendency toward accommodating the beliefs and practices of non-Buddhists within Buddhist-majority polities, but only on the condition that they are deemed nonthreatening to the *sāsana*. According to a third mode of Theravāda toleration, *cosmological toleration*, Buddhists accept religious differences by absorbing others' deities, myths and practices into their own system of beliefs and practices. Practices of cosmological toleration include the rewriting of myths to give the Buddha authority over local deities (Obeyesekere, 1972), the restructuring of rituals to include prayers to the Buddha at beginning and end (Carbine, 2000) and the broadening of temple compounds to include shrines and priests dedicated to new deities (Holt, 2004).

These modes of Buddhist toleration also have legal embodiments in contemporary Asia. For example, all Buddhist-majority countries in Southern Asia have constitutions that enshrine individual freedoms to believe and practice one's own religion (a legal elaboration consonant with philosophical toleration). At the same time, these freedoms are also conditioned by the fact that the same constitutions give to Buddhism special status and protections (an arrangement reminiscent of imperial toleration).[17] When one takes into account these multimodal understandings of Theravāda tolerations, contemporary legal arrangements look less like deficient forms of 'Western' toleration than legalistic embodiments of the multiple, sometimes competing, impulses present within Theravāda Buddhist traditions themselves. While these modulated forms of religious toleration might differ from the absolute vision of radically equal religions that is celebrated by most advocates of religious freedom (if not always realised in practice), they nevertheless cohere closely with the competing understandings of toleration visible in Buddhist texts.

16 I adopt this definition of *toleration* from (Spencer, 2017: x–xv).

17 Of the seven states in Southern Asia that have a majority Buddhist population, all but one (Vietnam) give to Buddhism special status in their constitutions. In their own ways, the constitutional texts of Myanmar, Thailand, Sri Lanka, Laos, Cambodia and Bhutan each single out Buddhism as deserving special attention, protection and/ or state patronage (Schonthal, 2017b).

Tolerating interventions

Yet, there is another idea that inheres in these Buddhist notions of toleration which also affects how religious freedom is deployed and understood: in the same way that public law in Southern Asia confers special legal status on Buddhism, it also confers on governments special powers to intervene in Buddhist institutions. Historically, the extra protections that governments have given to Buddhism have often been paired with extra powers of oversight over Buddhist monks, institutions and places of worship.

At first glance, this fact might seem contradictory to and erosive of the protections given both by special constitutional prerogatives for Buddhism and by the general rights to religious freedom. After all, as mentioned above, Euro-American perspectives on freedom and toleration tend to place a premium on the independence of individuals and groups. Governmental powers of supervision or oversight seem to cut against that value. Yet, here too, such classical liberal assumptions may be misleading. In many historical periods, Buddhist writers and jurists have insisted that government involvement in Buddhist institutions is a necessary condition for the freedom and independence of Buddha's dispensation.

If one looks at Theravāda Buddhism's textual corpus, one can find numerous examples in which monks and rulers assert that the health of the *sāsana* depends upon political (often royal) intervention (Baker and Phongpaichit, 2016; Mahānāma and Geiger, 1968; Ratnapala, 1971). Two overarching ideas justify this. The first idea is that the *sāsana,* unlike other religions, is something that is in a process of progressive deterioration. Therefore, it cannot simply be isolated *from* political involvement, but it must be actively supported *by* powerful laypersons, especially political elites. The second idea is that the clerical guardians of the *sāsana*, the Buddhist monks, because of their occasional penchant for schism or laxity, must be periodically 'purified' by kings and governments.

The idea that the *sāsana* requires active support to combat its decline stems from the doctrine, central to Buddhist philosophy, that everything in the world is impermanent. Thus, the *sāsana* is no different to anything else in the universe: it comes into being, grows, declines and disappears. Buddhists around the world hold different views about the length of the *sāsana*'s lifespan. In the Theravāda-majority countries of Southern Asia, the timespan most frequently cited is 5,000 years. Thus, the story goes, from the time of the final enlightenment (*parinibbāna*) of the Buddha, the *sāsana* will exist for five millennia and, toward the end of that period, its disappearance will progress in stages, with some parts of the Buddha's dispensation starting to disappear as early as the third millennium (Nattier, 1991: chapter 3; Turner, 2014: chapter 2).

This means that Buddhists are now living in a dangerous period of time for the *sāsana*, in which the dispensation is in the second half of its life. This fact confronts Buddhists not just in religious myths, but in their everyday lives. In many Buddhist-majority countries, including Thailand, Cambodia, Myanmar, Sri Lanka and Laos, important official dates are given not only using the Gregorian (or Julian) dating systems that calculate history from the time of Jesus (as BC and AD) but using a Buddhist calendar (or Buddhist Era calendar, sometimes abbreviated B.E.) which has as its year 0, the year of the Buddha's final enlightenment, dated usually around 544 BCE.[18] In looking at the Buddhist-era reckoning for 2019, then, Buddhists cannot but be aware that they are living roughly 2563 years after the Buddha's enlightenment and more than halfway through the life of the *sāsana*.

18 Scholars give a different time period for the probable death of the Buddha, based on manuscript and epigraph evidence, mostly placing it closer to 400 BCE (Drewes, 2017; Prebish, 2008).

This panic about the (relatively) immanent decline of the *sāsana* has, from early periods, motivated and justified state-led attempts to support the Buddha's dispensation. In the premodern periods, these anxieties stood behind a variety of royal projects across Asia to copy manuscripts, engrave Buddhist texts in stone, build and support Buddhist shrines and monasteries as well as issue edicts and decrees requiring that subjects protect the *sāsana* (Blackburn, 2017: 75–76; Blackburn, 2010: chapter 1; Leider, 2004). In more recent history, supporting a declining *sāsana* has been an important rationale used by twentieth-century governments to give special protections to Buddhism as part of a larger programme of protecting freedom of religion. Since independence, vast amounts of state funds have been spent in Sri Lanka, Myanmar, Thailand, Cambodia and other Buddhist-majority countries to fund projects specially designed to support the *sāsana*. These include the restoration of Buddhist holy sites and monasteries, the revitalisation of monastic education, the creation and consolidation of national and transnational Buddhist organisations, the spread of Buddhist meditation techniques and the critical editing, translating and publishing of important Buddhist texts. Some of the most focused and intense efforts were made around 1956, a date that many Buddhist leaders in Southern Asia declared to be 2500 years in the lifespan of the *sāsana* (Bond, 1988; Jordt, 2005; Smith, 1965).

For many, if not most, Buddhist political leaders in the region, these projects of state support for Buddhism remain consistent with, and even iterations of, government protection for freedom of religion. In a logic similar to that described above, defenders of these actions insist that guaranteeing religious freedom for Buddhism requires that Buddhist-majority polities don't merely 'stay out of the way' of the *sāsana*, but actively support it in a manner consistent with that of earlier Buddhist kings. This argument has a long history in Sri Lanka and other parts of Southern Asia. For example, Sri Lanka's leading Buddhist lay organisation wrote in a memorandum to the Prime Minister in 1951 that Buddhism, unlike other religions, required direct interventions by the state in order to thrive because it did not have clear institutional hierarchies or networks of international support (which the Christian churches enjoyed). In fact, they argued, the Buddha's dispensation was, itself, predicated on a politico-religious bargain between state and *sāsana*: 'Buddhism could not take a lasting hold on any soil,' the lay group wrote, 'not even on the hallowed soil of Lanka, without the active support of the State' (All-Ceylon Buddhist Congress, 1951: 3).

It is not just the *sāsana*'s vulnerability and its history of royal support that legitimates state interventions into Buddhist life under the sign of freedom of religion. Also permissible within (or alongside) constitutional mandates to protect religious freedom are systems of government oversight for Buddhist monks. This, too, is taken to be essential for protecting the *sāsana*. All of the Buddhist-majority states of Southern Asia have special laws authorising government departments to audit and oversee the conduct of Buddhist monks. Thailand's Sangha Act (1962, most recently amended 2018) gives the king and government ministers the right and obligation to help oversee the discipline and administration of Thai monks. Multiple statutes in Myanmar – among them, the Sangha Organization Basic Rules (1980, amended 1995) and the Sangha Lawsuit Resolution Procedures (1980) – provide similar mandates for a state-supervised system of sangha control. In Sri Lanka, the Buddhist Temporalities Ordinance (1931, most recently amended 2013) obliges the government to act as an auditor of monastic property and income. It also requires the government to maintain a national register of ordained monks.

Some may see an irony in these unique legal arrangements given to Buddhism in Southern Asia: the special prerogatives given to Buddhism under the guise of protecting the freedom and well-being of the *sāsana* also limit the autonomy of Buddhist monastic institutions and give added religious powers to the state – which, according to liberal political philosophy, is the primary entity against which religious rights are supposed to protect citizens. Yet, this arrangement has a long history in the Buddhist world, as intimated above. The most outstanding examples are the edicts issued by the Indic emperor Aśoka, who during his reign (268–232 BCE) brought much of the Indian subcontinent under his control and, in the process, became a powerful patron of Buddhism. As described in hagiographies, Aśoka's support for Buddhism also involved his 'cleansing' the monkhood of lax, undisciplined and heterodox clerics. In addition to giving food, materials and financial support to the *sāsana*, therefore, he also acted as a reformer, auditor and administrator of Buddhist clerics (Strong, 1983). From the turn of the common era, Buddhist texts and rulers have cited Aśoka's actions as paradigmatic precedents for the periodic need (and ongoing prerogative) of rulers to act as arbiters and enforcers of monastic purity (Gunawardana, 1979; Tambiah, 1976). This so-called Aśokan paradigm also stands behind contemporary arguments for legislation that permit state intervention in the sangha as a necessary part of maintaining Buddhists' freedom of religion (Bartholomeusz, 2000; De Silva Wijeyeratne 2007).

Conclusion

Rather than offering a single Buddhist perspective on freedom of religion, this chapter has examined a variety of views given by Buddhist actors, texts, practices and epigraphy. These perspectives not only shed new light on the category of religious freedom itself, they also help to expose the particularity certain key ideas that undergird a great deal of thinking about religious freedom by scholars, jurists and public lawyers: the idea that religions are commensurable and structurally similar and the idea that a just society is one in which all religious dispensations should be granted equal toleration and independence by citizens and the state. In various places and times (from contemporary courtrooms to ancient Buddhist polities) and in various forms (from didactic Buddhist texts to constitutional law), Buddhists have argued in ways that challenge these regnant assumptions. Buddhists have refuted the idea that the Buddha's dispensation is isomorphic with that of other religious leaders, and they have challenged the categorisation of Buddhism as a religion. In certain cases, they have even called into question the universality of religious conscience as something that functions identically for Buddhists and Christians. When it comes to notions of toleration, one finds among Buddhists political attitudes and dispositions that echo certain features of classical liberal thought while contesting others. In some cases, Buddhist thinkers have supported the position that, in order to protect Buddhism, governing regimes must interfere with its institutions.

If some Buddhists hold different views about the universality of religion or toleration, does that mean that Buddhism, as a tradition, is not supportive of religious freedom? I hope that this chapter has helped answer this question, in part, by calling attention to the limitations built into the query itself. Rather than accept or reject the idea of freedom of religion, Buddhists in different places and times have advanced arguments that both endorse and challenge particular features of religious freedom jurisprudence as it has developed in international law and liberal political theory. This process, I would suggest, has not been zero-sum, but additive. Whether one considers the interpretations of religious freedom by contemporary Buddhist lawyers or the modalities of toleration in ancient Buddhist texts, thinking about religious freedom from the perspectives of specific Buddhist actors and texts has the potential to multiply perspectives and add to the connotative diversity of freedom of religion as a conceptual or legal rubric. Such an effort exposes the (historical, linguistic, geographic and/or cultural) specificity of now-dominant interpretations in international law. It also calls attention to the ways in which particular glosses or uses of the phrase *freedom of religion* can come to serve particular (political, social or even religious) purposes. Having traversed this terrain, it is now possible to see that even the title of this chapter – 'Buddhist perspectives on freedom of religion and belief' – can serve a variety of discursive agendas. Some might see the phrase as entrenching a Eurocentric legal paradigm, others as universalising international human rights categories and yet others as distinguishing Buddhist traditions and viewpoints from all others. Which of these agendas or purposes prevails at any one moment depends less on the category of freedom of religion and more on the actors that invoke it.

References

All-Ceylon Buddhist Congress, 1951. *Buddhism and the State: Resolutions and Memorandum of the All Ceylon Buddhist Congress*. Oriental Press.

All-Ceylon Buddhist Congress, 1956. *bauddha toraturu parīkṣaka sabhāvē vārtāva [Report from the Committee Investigating Buddhist Matters*. Visidunu Prakāśanayaki Colombo.

Baker, C., Phongpaichit, P., 2016. *The Palace Law of Ayutthaya and the Thammasat: Law and Kingship in Siam*. Cornell University Press.

Bartholomeusz, T., 2000. First among equals: Buddhism and the Sri Lankan state. In: I. Harris (Ed.), *Buddhism and Politics in Twentieth Century Asia*. Continuum Press, 173.

Beaman, L.G., 2003. The myth of pluralism, diversity, and vigor: the constitutional privilege of protestantism in the United States and Canada. *J. Sci. Stud. Religion* 42, 311.

Berlin, I., 1969. Two concepts of liberty. In: I. Berlin (Ed.), *Four Essays on Liberty*. Oxford University Press, 118.

Blackburn, A.M., 2010. *Locations of Buddhism: Colonialism and Modernity in Sri Lanka*. University of Chicago Press.

Blackburn, A.M., 2017. Buddhist technologies of Statecraft and Millennial moments. *History and Theor* 56, 71.

Bond, G., 1988. *The Buddhist Revival in Sri Lanka*. University of South Carolina Press.

Carbine, J.A., 2000. Yaktovil: the role of the Buddha and Dhamma. In: F. Reynolds, J. Carbine (Eds.), *The Life of Buddhism*. University of California Press, 162.

Carter, J.R., 1977. A history of early Buddhism. *Religious Studies*. 13, 263.

Clough, R.B., 1892. *Clough's Sinhala-English Dictionary*. Wesleyan Mission Press.

Danchin, P., 2008. The emergence and structure of religious freedom in International Law Reconsidered. *Journal of Law and Religion*. 23, 455.

De Silva Wijeyeratne, R. 2007. Buddhism, the Asokan Persona, and the galactic polity: rethinking Sri Lanka's constitutional present. *Journal of Social and Cultural Practice*. 51, 156

Drewes, D., 2017. The idea of the historical Buddha. *Journal of the International Association of Buddhist Studies*. 40, 1.

Fernando, M., 2010. Reconfiguring freedom: Muslim piety and the limits of secular law and public discourse in France. *American Ethnologis*. 37, 19.

Frydenlund, I., 2017a. Buddhism has made Asia Mild. In: H. Havnevik, U. Hüsken, M. Teeuwen, V. Tikhonov, K. Wellens (Eds.), *Buddhist Modernities: Re-Inventing Tradition in the Globalizing Modern World*. Routledge, 204.

Frydenlund, I., 2017b. Religious liberty for whom? The Buddhist politics of religious freedom during Myanmar's transition to democracy. *Nordic Journal of Human Rights* 35, 55.

Frydenlund, I., 2017c. The birth of Buddhist politics of religious freedom in Myanmar. *Journal of Religious and Political Practice*. 4, 1.

Fuller, P., 2005. *The Notion of Diṭṭhi in Theravada Buddhism*. Routledge.

Government of Sri Lanka, 2002. *Buddha śāsana janādhipati komiśan vārtāva [Presidential Commission Report on the Buddha Sasana]*. Ministry of Buddha Sasana.

Gunawardana, R.A.L.H., 1979. *Robe and Plough: Monasticism and Economic Interest in Early Medieval Sri Lanka*. University of Arizona Press.

Gunn, T.J., 2003. The complexity of religion and the definition of religion in International Law. *Harvard Human Rights Journal*. 16, 189.

Gyatso, T. (14th Dalai Lama). 2005. A biased mind cannot grasp reality. Available at: https://www.dalailama.com/messages/religious-harmony-1/religious-harmony.

Habermas, J., 2004. Religious tolerance: the pacemaker for cultural rights. *Philosophy* 79, 5.
Holt, J., 2004. *The Buddhist Visnu*. Columbia University Press.
Hurd, E.S., 2015. *Beyond Religious Freedom*. Princeton University Press.
Jordt, I., 2005. Women's practices of renunciation in the age of *Sāsana* Revival. In: M. Skidmore (Ed.), *Burma at the Turn of the Twenty-First Century*. University of Hawai'i Press, 41.
Leider, J.P., 2004. Text, lineage, and tradition in Burma: the struggle for norms and religious legitimacy under King Bodawphaya (1782–1819). *Journal of Burma Studies*. 9, 82.
Mahānāma, V. and Geiger, W. (Trans.), 1968. *The Mahāvamsa (The Great Lineage)*. Asian Educational Services.
Mahmood, S., 2006. Secularism, hermeneutics, and empire: the politics of Islamic reformation. *Public Culture*. 18, 323.
Malalgoda, K., 1997. Concepts and confrontations: a case study of Agama. In: M. Roberts (Ed.), *Collective Identities Revisited* (vol. 1). Marga Institute Press, 55.
Masuzawa, T., 2005. *The Invention of World Religions: or, How European Universalism was Preserved in the Language of Pluralism*. University of Chicago Press.
Mehta, U.S., 1999. *Liberalism and Empire: A Study in Nineteenth-Century British Liberal Thought*. University of Chicago Press.
Moustafa, T., 2013. Liberal rights versus Islamic Law? The construction of a binary in Malaysian politics. *Law Soc. Rev.* 47, 771.
Nattier, J., 1991. *Once Upon a Future Time: Studies in a Buddhist Prophecy of Decline*. Asian Humanities Press.
Obeyesekere, G., 1972. Religious symbolism and political change in Sri Lanka. In: B. Smith, F. Reynolds, G. Obeyesekere (Eds.), *The Two Wheels of Dhamma*American Academy of Religion, 58.
Picard, M., 2000. Agama, Adat, Budaya: the dialogic construction of 'Kebalian'. *Dialog* 1, 85.
Picard, M., 2003. What is in a name: Agama Hindu Bali. In: M. Ramstedt (Ed.), *Hinduism in Modern Indonesia*. Routledge, 56.
Powers, J., 2016. *The Buddha Party: How the People's Republic of China Works to Define and Control Tibetan Buddhism*. Oxford University Press.
Prebish, C.S., 2008. Cooking the Buddhist books: the implications of the new dating of the Buddha for the history of early Indian Buddhism. *Journal of Buddhist Ethics*. 15, 1.
Ratnapala, N., 1971. *The Katikāvatas: Laws of the Buddhist Order of Ceylon From the 12th to the (Critically Edited, Translated and Annotated) 18th Century*. Münchener Studien zur Sprachwissenschaft Beiheft N. R. Kitzinger.
Schonthal, B., 2016. *Buddhism, Politics and Limits of Law: The Pyrrhic Constitutionalism of Sri Lanka*. Cambridge University Press.
Schonthal, B., 2017a. The tolerations of Theravāda Buddhism. In: V.A. Spencer (Ed.), *Toleration in Comparative Perspective*. Lexington Books, 179.
Schonthal, B., 2017b. Formations of Buddhist constitutionalism in South and Southeast Asia. *International Journal of Constitutional Law* 15, 705.
Schonthal, B., 2018. Economies of expert religion in Sri Lanka. *Journal of Religious and Political Practice*. 4, 27.
Scott, D., 1996. Religion in colonial civil society: Buddhism and modernity in 19th-century Sri Lanka. *Cultural Dynamics*. 8, 7.
Sivaraksa, S., 1992. Buddhism with a small 'b'. In: S. Sivaraksa (Ed.), *Seeds of Peace: A Buddhist Vision for Renewing Society*. Parallax Press, 62.
Smith, D.E., 1965. *Religion and Politics in Burma*. Princeton University Press.
Smith, D.E., 1966. The sinhalese Buddhist revolution. In: D.E. Smith (Ed.), *South Asian Politics and Religion*. Princeton University Press, 453.
Spencer, V.A., 2017. *Toleration in Comparative Perspective*. Lexington Books.
Stepan, A., 2000. Religion, democracy, and the 'twin tolerations'. *Journal of Democracy* 11, 37.
Strong, J.S., 1983. *The Legend of King Aśoka: A Study and Translation of the Aśokāvadāna*. Princeton University Press.
Sullivan, W.F., 2005. *The Impossibility of Religious Freedom*. Princeton University Press.
Sullivan, W.F. Shakman Hurd, E., Mahmood, S., Danchin, P.G. (Eds.), 2015. *Politics of Religious Freedom*. University of Chicago Press.
Swearer, D., 1996. Sulak Sivaraksa's vision for renewing society. In: C.S. Queen, S.B. King (Eds.), *Engaged Buddhism: Buddhist Liberation Movements in Asia*. SUNY Press, 195.

Tambiah, S.J., 1976. *World Conqueror and World Renouncer: A Study of Buddhism and Polity in Thailand Against a Historical Background*. Cambridge University Press.

Taylor, P.M., 2005. *Freedom of Religion: UN and European Human Rights Law and practice*. Cambridge University Press.

Turner, A.M., 2014. *Saving Buddhism: The Impermanence of Religion in Colonial Burma*. University of Hawai'i Press.

Urban, H.B., 2011. *The Church of Scientology: A History of a New Religion*. Princeton University Press.

Zagorin, P., 2005. *How the Idea of Religious Toleration Came to the West*. Princeton University Press.

7

Religious freedom: Christian perspectives

Norman Doe

In the past 50 or so years, Christians' discussions of civil concepts of human rights in general and of religious freedom in particular are to be found mainly in the scholarship of theologians (often around the specific official teaching of particular churches), not in that of lawyers. It is only very recently that legal scholars have begun to address human rights and religious freedom from Christian perspectives – and sometimes (as in theology) this is done on the basis of moral or natural law thinking about conceptual correlatives of civil law human rights in the form of universal ethical *duties* incumbent on all humans. However, to date, neither theologians nor legal scholars have examined in a comparative way the idea of religious freedom as it is treated in and across the *laws* of Christians in their various institutional churches.[1] Significantly, the ecumenical Christian Law Panel does not deal with the issues treated in this chapter in its Statement of Principles of Christian Law (2016). Formed in Rome in 2013 with members from eight different historic church traditions worldwide, the Panel established in 2017 an informal partnership with the Faith and Order Commission of the World Council of Churches (see Hill and Doe, 2017). This represents a serious gap which this study seeks to remedy. As such, the chapter explores religious freedom from contemporary perspectives of Christians as developed in the regulatory and other normative instruments of international Christian communities and alliances, their member churches (mainly those in the United Kingdom, though reference is also made to churches globally), and, ecumenically, the World Council of Churches. What follows suggests a typology to address the issues: (1) churches' understandings of religious freedom; (2) churches as advocates of religious freedom in wider civil society; (3) churches' use of religious freedom as an instrument of ecumenism; (4) churches as beneficiaries of religious freedom under civil law *and* as guardians of their own religious freedom under their internal church laws; and (5) churches' regulation/limitation of their own collective religious freedom, and the individual religious freedom of the faithful, by means of church law, but also their use of rights of conscience. The chapter, therefore, connects thinking about religious freedom with church law. The laws and other regulatory norms of churches provide a key expression of Christian thinking about religious freedom as it is translated into action

1 For human rights as prefigured and inspired by churches' historic defence of human dignity, see, e.g., Ruston (2004), Moyn (2015); see also Witte (2010); for the suggestion that church law on human rights should be studied, see Doe (2013). For historic Christian approaches to religious liberty, see, e.g., Taliaferro (2014): the legal texts included are from civil law, not laws of churches.

through their own internal norms of conduct. The chapter evaluates Christian approaches and proposes the reform of church law in this field.

The Churches' understandings of religious freedom

The churches' understandings of religious freedom mirror secular ideas in international law; however, the churches' reasons for religious freedom differ from those of international law and the churches' understandings are found and elaborated on in church teaching not church law. For Christians, *freedom* is an essential for *faith*. For the World Council of Churches: 'God's redemptive dealing with men is not coercive;' thus, 'human attempts by a legal enactment or by pressure of social custom to coerce or eliminate faith are violations of the fundamental ways of God with men. The freedom which God has given ... implies free response to God's love.'[2]

The Roman Catholic Church has a rich concept of religious liberty. *Dignitatis humanae*, the Second Vatican Council Declaration on Religious Liberty, 1965, places religious freedom within traditional church teaching on human dignity. Religious freedom is the cornerstone of a society that promotes human dignity. It is a fundamental human right. It follows on the duty and right of all people to seek the truth about God. It includes freedom *from* and *for* religion. It requires a society *both* to refrain from preventing people from living out their religion *and* to help create conditions for religion to flourish. A free society is one in which people actively seek religious truth and fully live it out in public and private. Moreover, as humans are social, it belongs to groups, not just individuals. So, 'religious communities' may govern themselves; worship publicly; teach and witness to the faith; instruct members; promote institutions to act in accordance with religious principles; appoint ministers; and acquire and administer property and funds. But there are limits: these rights are exercisable 'provided the just demands of public order are observed' and 'subject to certain regulatory norms.' These include the requirement of 'the moral law to have respect both for the rights of others and for their own duties toward others and for the common welfare;' the right of society 'to defend itself against possible abuses committed on the pretext of freedom of religion;' the 'adequate care of genuine public peace;' and 'a proper guardianship of public morality.' Therefore, 'religious freedom [should] be everywhere provided with an effective [civil] constitutional guarantee and respect be shown for the high duty and right of man freely to lead his religious life in society.'[3]

The worldwide Anglican Communion has a somewhat less sophisticated account. The Lambeth Conference simply endorses the United Nations Declaration of Human Rights, and, rather crudely, it sees 'each person's freedom of thought, conscience and religion' as an 'absolute right.'[4] The laws of churches do not directly address the nature of religious freedom. However, the Principles of Canon Law Common to the Churches of the Anglican Communion (2008) recognise two types of right – inherent and acquired: 'all persons, equal in dignity before God, have inherent rights and duties inseparable from their dignity as human beings created in the image and likeness of God and called to salvation through Jesus Christ.'[5] Also, all the faithful, ordained and lay, enjoy such rights to government, ministry, teaching, worship, sacraments, rites,

2 'Statement on Religious Liberty,' New Delhi Report: The Third Assembly of the World Council of Churches 1961 (New York: WCC, 1962) 159.

3 *Dignitatis humanae*: 4–5, 15. These ideas are repeated in numerous other church teaching documents. See also Grasso and Hunt (2006).

4 For Lambeth Conference 1998 statements, see Doe (2002: 185).

5 Principles of Canon Law Common to the Churches of the Anglican Communion (2008), hereafter PCLCCAC, Principle 26.1-4. See, e.g., Anglican Church of (the Province of) Papua New Guinea: Constitution, Art. 3.

and property as may flow from their human dignity, baptism, the duties of others, 'and the law of that church;' indeed, 'in a church there is to be no unlawful denial of equal rights, status or access to the life, membership, government, ministry, worship, rites and property of that church on grounds of' *inter alia*, race, colour, sex, sexual orientation, disability, or age.[6]

Lutheran ideas on religious freedom also mirror international law, and they place the primary duty to protect it on the State. For example, the Council of the Lutheran World Federation in 2013 issued a Statement on Religious Freedom or Belief which it 'believes' is a 'right given by God' to all. The Council also affirmed Federation support for United Nations' work to protect religious liberty.[7] At the national level, the Lutheran Church in Australia has a particularly full treatment of human rights, but religious freedom is not specified: 'The concept of human rights is based on two convictions: that certain actions against other human beings are wrong no matter what; and that in all circumstances all people are entitled to respect and proper treatment as human beings.' Preserving society belongs to the earthly kingdom in which God rules through the law: governments, as 'ministers of God,' must preserve citizens' liberties. Christian citizens have the *duty* to urge their governments to honour human rights – and investigate, protest, and agitate for reform where they are ignored or violated. The foundation for this is the dignity of all as creatures of God and the divine command to love our neighbour.[8]

By way of contrast, United Methodist Church *law* acknowledges 'all persons as equally valuable in the sight of God' each with 'inherent dignity;' and it asserts 'the right of all religions and their adherents to freedom from legal, economic, and social discrimination.'[9] For the United Reformed Church in Great Britain, too, 'civil authorities, being always subject to the rule of God, ought to respect the rights of conscience and of religious belief and to serve God's will of justice and peace for all humankind.'[10] And the law of the Presbyterian Church in Ireland states: 'although civil rulers are bound to render obedience to Christ in their own province, yet they ought not … to constrain anyone's religious beliefs, or invade the rights of conscience.'[11]

With the long Baptist tradition on religious liberty, the General Council of the World Baptist Alliance in 2017 understood that religious freedom is 'a gift of God to all people,' regardless of denomination or religion; and it committed itself to the understanding of it enshrined in the United Nations Declaration of Human Rights, Article 18.[12] Likewise at the national level: the Baptist Union of Southern Africa accepts 'The principle of religious liberty, namely, that no individual should be coerced either by the State or by any secular, ecclesiastical or religious group in matters of faith;' in turn, as such: 'The right of private conscience is to be respected.'[13]

In short, the churches' understandings of religious freedom mirror those in international law; but their reasons for religious freedom differ from those in international law – religious freedom is the will of God (its theocratic element); churches' understandings of it are found usually in church teaching not in church law; and the primary duty to protect religious freedom rests on the State. Official church teaching adds little to civil concepts of religious liberty. There has also

---

6 PCLCCAC, Principle 26.7-8. See, e.g., the Episcopal Church USA: Canons I.17.5: nondiscrimination.
7 See: https://www.lutheranworld.org/news/lwf-council-statement-religious-freedom.
8 Commission on Theology and Inter-Church Relations, *Human Rights* (1994, edited 2001).
9 United Methodist Church in Northern Europe and Eurasia: Book of Discipline, pars. 103, 121, 161, 162, 164.
10 Manual, Basis of Union A, Schedule D, Version I, 8.
11 Code, I.III.13.
12 Bangkok, Thailand, July 5–7, 2017; see also: http://bwanet.org/resources/bwa-currentresolutions.
13 Bylaws, 4.2.7.

been no attempt by churches, in teaching or law (with the exception of the Roman Catholic Church) to root Christian ideas about religious liberty in universal duties; this matter is ripe for consideration by the Panel engaged in developing Principles of Christian Law (see below).[14]

The Churches as advocates of religious freedom in civil society

Churches are advocates of religious freedom in civil society. International church communities may assert for themselves a corporate *right* or *duty* to advocate it, or they *exhort* advocacy by member churches. They assert the right/duty, or issue an exhortation, in their legal instruments. They also have institutions to promote in civil society human rights in general or religious freedom in particular. These legal arrangements are mirrored at the national level of churches.

Canon law of the Roman Catholic Church asserts its *right* to advocate: 'The Church has the *right* always and everywhere to proclaim moral principles, even in respect of the social order, and to make judgments about any human matter in so far as this is required by fundamental human rights or the salvation of souls;'[15] but there is no specific canonical duty to advocate for religious liberty in society. By way of contrast, the Anglican Lambeth Conference, 1998, speaks of a *responsibility* to advocate religious liberty: it calls on 'all faith communities, especially the Christian Church, to acknowledge our responsibility to mobilise our spiritual, moral and material resources' to promote it; and it calls on 'governments of all the nations our Churches represent to strive for creation of just and free conditions for people of all religions' to practise their beliefs freely (Doe, 2002: 187). But Conference resolutions are not laws; they do not bind the autonomous member churches of the Anglican Communion: the 1998 resolution is a moral *exhortation*. Moreover, no church specifically obliges itself canonically to promote religious freedom: there is an implicit *right* to do so. However, the churches do engage in religious freedom advocacy through their own commissions (some mandated by law, others permissive) on human rights (Doe, 1996: 58).

Protestant churches are different. The *constitution* of the Lutheran World Federation imposes a duty on the Federation to promote 'peace and human rights.'[16] Its Council Statement on Religious Freedom, 2013, calls upon its member churches *and* the ecumenical community to strengthen their commitment to freedom of religion; to cooperate in promoting and defending it in their own societies and internationally; and for its churches 'to intercede with both state and religious authorities for the defence of individuals or groups' whose religious freedoms are being curtailed.[17] The World Communion of Reformed Churches also has a constitutional duty to engage in 'promoting and defending religious, civil, and all other human rights wherever threatened throughout the world.'[18] And one of the constitutional objects of the Baptist World Alliance is to defend human rights at the global level, 'including full religious liberty.'[19] It has a Commission on Religious Freedom,[20] and it is active in religious liberty advocacy globally.[21]

---

14 For Christian approaches to universal ethical duties, see, e.g., Doe (2017): especially, on natural law in ecumenical dialogue, 164–176.

15 *Codex Iuris Canonici* (Code of Canon Law 1983), hereafter CIC: c. 747.2.

16 Constitution, Art. III.

17 See n. 8 above.

18 Constitution, Art. V; see also Art. IV: its values include 'the dignity of every person.'

19 Constitution, Art. II.

20 See: http://www.bwanet.org/programs/14-programs/mej/65-religious-freedom.

21 See n. 7 above.

Similar advocacy duties appear in some Methodist laws at the national level. For example, the law of the United Methodist Church requires itself to 'defend religious freedom;' to combat acts of hate or violence based on 'religious affiliation;' to support 'policies and practices that ensure the right of every religious group to exercise its faith free from legal, political, or economic restrictions;' and to condemn 'all overt and covert forms of religious intolerance.'[22] The Baptist Union of Southern Africa, too, has a constitutional duty to 'maintain religious liberty.'[23]

The Principles of Christian Law (2016) state: 'All humans, having been created in the image of God, share an equality of dignity and fundamental human rights;' and 'A church should protect and defend human rights in society for all people.'[24] The statement, however, does not deal specifically with religious freedom advocacy in society – it could have, but it did not.[25]

In sum, while the primary duty to protect religious liberty is on the State (see the section above), churches assume for themselves either a *right* or else a *duty* to engage in religious freedom advocacy. Episcopal churches tend to use a right of advocacy (express/implied) and Protestant churches to assume a duty of advocacy. In some churches, the duty is imposed by teaching, in others by church law or soft law, and in some by both. One challenge for churches is to assess whether these mechanisms are sufficient to enable them to engage effectively in religious freedom advocacy. After all, the churches have elaborate norms on more mundane matters. When churches have a duty to advocate religious freedom, the public has a correlative right to this (or at least a legitimate expectation) – when they do not, the public has no such right.

The Church uses religious freedom as an ecumenical instrument

The ecumenical movement seeks greater visible unity between churches. The laws of most churches carry a duty to engage in ecumenism on the basis of assertions of their own belonging to the church universal (Doe, 2016: 279–284). However, to what extent do the movement and churches party to it *require* ecumenical collaboration on religious liberty in civil society? The World Council of Churches has a major role here.[26] It has issued a number of soft law documents on religious freedom.[27] These show how religious freedom may also serve as an instrument of ecumenism.

The Declaration on Religious Liberty was adopted at the First Assembly of the World Council of Churches held in Amsterdam in 1948. First, religious freedom is a key Christian issue:

> An essential element in a good international order is freedom of religion. This is an implication of the Christian faith and of the world-wide nature of Christianity. Christians, therefore, view ...religious freedom as an international problem. They are concerned that [it] be everywhere secured. In pleading for [it], they do not ask for any privilege to be granted to Christians that is denied to others. While the liberty with

22 United Methodist Church in Northern Europe and Eurasia: Book of Discipline, pars. 103, 121, 161–164.

23 Constitution, Art. 5.3.

24 Principles of Christian Law (2016): X.2.

25 An obvious candidate would be: 'The State should recognise, promote and protect the religious freedom of churches corporately and of the faithful individually, as well as their freedom of conscience' (Doe, 2013: 397).

26 The WCC Constitution does not list promoting human rights or religious liberty as a WCC object.

27 For human rights ecumenical statements, see Koffeman (2017).

which Christ has set men free can neither be given nor destroyed by any Government, Christians, because of that inner freedom, are both jealous of its outward expression and solicitous that all men should have freedom in religious life. The nature and destiny of man by virtue of his creation, redemption and calling, and man's activities in family, state and culture establish limits beyond which the government cannot with impunity go. The rights which Christian discipleship demands are such as are good for all men, and no nation has ever suffered by reason of granting such liberties (Preamble).

Second, therefore, the rights declared in the instrument 'shall be recognized and observed for all persons without distinctions as to race, colour, sex, language, or religion, and without imposition of disabilities by virtue of legal provision or administrative acts' (Preamble). Third, the Declaration enumerates four rights in ways which elaborate on international law:

1. *Freedom to determine belief*: 'Every person has the right to determine his own faith and creed' – this includes adhering to or changing belief; instruction and education; and access to information to allow personal religious decision and belief. But there are limits; for example, all ought to take into account their higher self-interests and belief implications for others' well-being.[28]
2. *Freedom of religious expression*: 'Every person has the right to express his religious beliefs in worship, teaching and practice and proclaim the implications of his beliefs for relationships in a social or political community' – this includes teaching, preaching, persuasion, and activities dictated by conscience. But its use is limited by parental rights to determine religious points of view to which their children are exposed; limitations prescribed by law necessary to protect order, welfare, morals, and others' rights; and the duty 'to respect authority at all times,' even when conscience requires taking issue with those in authority or the position they advocate.[29]
3. *Freedom of association*: 'Every person has a right to associate with others and to organize with them for religious purposes' – this includes freedom to form religious organisations, to seek membership in them, and to sever relationships with them. However, its exercise is subject to the same limits imposed on all associations by way of nondiscriminatory laws.[30]
4. *Freedom of institutional autonomy*: 'Every religious organization, formed or maintained by action in accordance with the rights of individual persons, has the right to determine its policies and practices for the accomplishment of its chosen purposes' – because 'rights of the individual to religious liberty ... become the rights of the religious organization.' This includes its right to determine its faith and creed; to engage in worship, public and private; to teach, educate, preach, and persuade; to express implications of belief for society/ government; and to govern itself. So that 'these rights may be realized in social experience,' the State has correlative duties to respect religious autonomy.[31] Yet, the (wider) community has the right to require obedience to nondiscriminatory laws passed in the interest of the public order and well-being. 'In the exercise of its rights, a religious organization must respect the rights of other religious organizations and must safeguard corporate and individual rights of the entire community.'[32]

28 Declaration Art. 1.
29 Declaration Art. 2.
30 Declaration Art. 3.
31 Declaration Art. 4.
32 See: http://www.religlaw.org/content/religlaw/documents/wccdecreliglib1948.htm.

Next, 'On Religious Liberty' was adopted by the Third Assembly, New Delhi, in 1961.[33] This embellishes the terms of the Declaration of 1948. First, the mischief: because humankind is 'threatened by many forces which curtail or deny freedom,' there is 'urgent need to reinvigorate efforts to ensure that every person has opportunity for the responsible exercise of religious freedom.'[34] Second, on a theological basis, 'religious liberty [is] a consequence of God's creative work, of his redemption of man in Christ and his calling of men to his service.' Accordingly, the freedom God has given 'implies a free response to God's love, and the responsibility to serve fellow-men at the point of deepest need.' This represents 'a distinctive Christian basis' for religious liberty.[35] Third, religious liberty is 'a distinctive human right' based on 'the inherent dignity and inalienable rights of all members of the human family.'[36] The instrument then defines the right in much the same way as the WCC Declaration of 1948.[37] Fourth, duties attend the right: 'The freedom with which Christ has set us free calls forth responsibility for the rights of others. The civil freedom which we claim in the name of Christ must be freely available for all to exercise responsibly.' Fifth, '[i]t is the corresponding obligation of governments and of society to ensure the exercise of these civil rights without discrimination. It is for the churches in their own life and witness recognizing their own past failures in this regard to play their indispensable role in promoting the realization of religious freedom for all.'[38] However, the 1961 text does not require churches to cooperate in this ecumenically.

Finally, the World Council of Churches has a Commission on International Affairs.[39] It has a working group on 'human rights and freedom of religion or belief.'[40] In 2003, the Commission offered its 'Religious Freedom and Liberty in the Emerging Context' which sees protecting religious freedom as a 'shared obligation: between State and Church, between the churches themselves, between individual Christians and the churches themselves, [and] between Christians and people of other faiths.'[41] However, the Commission also recognises the need 'to review and revisit the definition' of religious liberty 'in light of the experience of churches,' because (1) 'religion has emerged as a key factor in the civil and political life of nations;' (2) religion is now seen variously as theology, ethics and values, and a bearer of culture[42]; (3) 'official state religion' with 'constitutional and legislative powers and privileges' may jeopardise 'the freedom of citizens to choose and practice the belief of their choice;' (4) 'the secular and plural basis of the state is under widespread assault and religious extremism and intolerance is on the rise;' and (5) 'difficult questions arise for the ecumenical movement which has declared opposition to proselytism.'[43] In 2013, the Faith and Order Commission saw 'religious freedom

33 On Religious Liberty. (1963). *J. Church State* 5(2), 243–245.

34 On Religious Liberty 1.

35 On Religious Liberty 2 and 3.

36 On Religious Liberty 4 and 5: the latter repeats terms of the UN Declaration Article 18.

37 On Religious Liberty 7: the 'inner freedom' (e.g., to information); 8: the right to manifest (worship, teaching, practice, and observance); 9: the right to change religion; 10: associated human rights (e.g., assembly).

38 On Religious Liberty 11.

39 Set up in 1946, in 2006 it merged with the Commission on Diakonia and Development, Commission on Justice, Peace and the Integrity of Creation, and Reference Group on Inter-Religious Relations and Dialogue.

40 WCC: https://www.oikoumene.org/en/what-we-do/ccia.

41 CCIA: Religious Freedom and Liberty in the Emerging Context (18 December 2003).

42 See: https://www.oikoumene.org/en/resources/documents/commissions/international-affairs/freedom-of-religion-documents-of-the-ccia.

43 See: https://www.oikoumene.org/en/resources/documents/commissions/international-affairs/human-rights-and-impunity/religious-freedom-and-liberty-in-the-emerging-context.

as one of the fundamental dimensions of human dignity,'[44] and the World Council of Churches called for greater religious freedom literacy in international diplomacy.[45]

While the legal systems of most churches contain a duty to engage in ecumenism, the evidence suggests that it is *not* a principle of Christian law that churches must collaborate with ecumenical partners in promoting religious freedom in civil society; the law of no church seems to specify such an ecumenical duty.[46] While they may have an obligation to *promote* religious freedom, they have no *legal* duty to *cooperate* with ecumenical partners in discharging that duty. However, the World Council of Churches does assume for itself a duty to engage in promoting religious freedom in civil society – but the responsibility which it recognises for the churches to *collaborate* with each other to do so is an *aspirational norm* only. It is not a legal duty – the member churches are autonomous, and the World Council of Churches has no competence to force them to do so. There can only be a legal duty on a church to collaborate with ecumenical partners in promoting religious freedom in civil society if the church, in an exercise of its own autonomy, imposes such a duty upon itself. And whether the churches should impose upon themselves a legal duty to collaborate should be a matter for debate.

The Church must safeguard its own civil religious freedom

Needless to say, as a matter of formal secular constitutional law,[47] churches are beneficiaries of religious freedom under civil law – and they assert their autonomy in their own church law. Church and State are independent but potentially cooperative guardians of the religious liberty of churches. The most common legal justifications offered for the State to respect religious autonomy are the collective right to manifest religious belief in the external forum; the institutional separation or mutual independence of churches and the State; and the churches are essentially private bodies – therefore, the State should play no part in their internal affairs (see, e.g., Doe, 2011: 117–119).

From the perspective of churches, the Principles of Christian Law (2016) provide that a church is 'autonomous' in its system of government to carry out the mission of Christ (which includes proclaiming the Gospel, administering sacraments, and serving the wider community).[48] Thus, for example, a church has the right to acquire, administer, and dispose of property; to seek legal personality under civil law to do so; to receive funds; and to make rules for the administration and control of its finances (but civil law on financial accountability must be complied with).[49] However, the Principles, in the section on Church and State Relations, provide that '[a] church should cooperate with the State in matters of common concern, but each is independent in its own sphere; the faithful may participate in politics save to the extent prohibited by church law; and cooperation between a church and the State may be exercised on the basis of, for instance, the establishment of a church by the State; an agreement or civil legislation negotiated freely with the State; and the fundamental institutional autonomy of a

44 *The Church: Towards a Common Vision* (Geneva: WCC, 2013) par. 60.

45 See: https://www.oikoumene.org/en/press-centre/news/wcc-holds-discussion-on-religious-freedom-literacy-and-diplomacy.

46 However, the Roman Catholic Church requires itself to collaborate ecumenically on *human rights: Directory for the Application of Norms and Principles of Ecumenism* (Vatican: 1993) par. 64.

47 For churches as victims of religious liberty violations, see, e.g., United Nations Special Rapporteur on Freedom of Religion or Belief Annual Reports to the Human Rights Council, Commission on Human Rights and General Assembly: https://www.ohchr.org/en/issues/freedomreligion/pages/annual.aspx.

48 Principles of Christian Law (2016) I.1.4-5.

49 Principles of Christian Law (2016) IX.1.1-3, 3.1 and 4.1.

church in carrying out its lawful objects and its freedom in these areas from intervention by the State.'[50] These principles are derived in part from the laws of institutional churches in the United Kingdom and elsewhere.

For the Roman Catholic Church, there is no authority but from God; the 'political community and public authority are based on human nature and therefore ... belong to an order established by God;' political authority must be exercised within the limits of the moral order; and it is 'the role of the State to defend and promote the common good of civil society' (i.e. 'the sum total of social conditions which allow people ... to reach their fulfilment).' However, 'in their own domain, the political community and the church are independent from one another and autonomous' but should develop a 'mutual cooperation' in favour of the welfare of all.[51] Nevertheless, canon law itself recognises the qualified applicability of State law to the church: 'When the law of the Church remits some issue to the civil law, the latter is to be observed with the same effects in canon law, in so far as it is not contrary to divine law, and provided it is not otherwise stipulated in canon law.'[52] In turn, for the faithful, 'unjust laws ... would not be binding in conscience.'[53] Moreover, canon law regulates appointing papal legates to States, forbids clerics to hold public office if this means sharing in civil power, asserts church rights to appoint bishops are not conceded to civil authorities, and enables church tribunals not to impose a penalty if the faithful have been/will be 'sufficiently punished by the civil authority.'[54]

Lutherans have the doctrine of the 'two kingdoms' – earthly and heavenly. This 'does not call for a separation of church and state but for a proper distinction between them;' God rules 'all people ... in his earthly kingdom through the agency of secular government' and 'he rules all Christians in his spiritual kingdom ... through the gospel [and] grace.' Christians are 'citizens' of both 'mutually dependent' kingdoms: the church needs the State for religious liberty and the State needs 'the prayers and intercessions of the church.' Moreover, the church has 'every right' to be 'the conscience of society' and 'hold governments ... accountable to the public, and ultimately to God.' Thus, the State must not interfere with proclaiming the gospel, and 'the church must not use the agency of the state ... to promote the gospel or Christianise society' or 'interfere ... in the affairs of the State: but it must bear witness to the truth ... and may ... for the instruction of its members and as a public testimony, have to condemn or approve acts of the State' even if 'oppression and persecution' follow. While Lutherans are subject to 'the laws of the land,' '[o]bedience to all forms of human government is never absolute but always limited and conditional. If it means disobedience to God, our allegiance to God must come first.'[55]

United Methodist Church law is similar: (1) 'civil government derives its just powers from the sovereign God;' (2) '[s]eparation of church and state means no organic union of the two, but it does permit interaction;' (3) the church 'should exert a strong ethical influence upon the state, supporting policies and programs deemed to be just and opposing [those] that are unjust;' (4) '[i]t is the duty of all Christians, and especially ... ministers, to observe and obey the laws ... of the country of which they are citizens;' but (5) 'governments, no less than individuals, are subject to the judgment of God;' and so the church recognises 'the right of

50 Principles of Christian Law (2016) X.

51 Catechism of the Catholic Church (1994) pars. 1918–1924, 1927; *Guadium et spes* (1966) S 26, 74, 76.

52 CIC: c. 22; see, e.g., cc. 98 and 110: guardians/adoption; 1284: property; 1290: secular contract law.

53 Catechism of the Catholic Church (1994) pars. 1897–1942; GS 29–31.

54 CIC: cc. 285, 362–367, 377, and 1344.2.

55 Statement on the Two Kingdoms, 3; and Theses on the Church, par. 16; scripture is cited.

individuals to dissent when acting under the constraint of conscience and, after having exhausted all legal recourse, to resist or disobey laws that they deem to be unjust or that are discriminately enforced' – but without violence and 'being willing to accept the costs of disobedience.'[56] Moreover, the Methodist Church in Great Britain has State law devoted especially to it.[57] In the Methodist Church in Ireland, '[n]o lawsuit ... shall be commenced without the consent of the General Committee ... except by direction of the Conference;' otherwise, parties pay the costs incurred.[58]

The (Presbyterian) Church of Scotland is a national church, and its autonomy is protected by the civil Church of Scotland Act of 1921. The Presbyterian Church of Ireland has State law devoted exclusively to it,[59] and members of the United Free Church of Scotland should not approach the courts of the 'civil power' to resolve their disputes.[60] In the United Reformed Church, 'Christ, the only ruler and head of the Church, has therein appointed a government distinct from civil government and in things spiritual not subordinate thereto,' and 'civil authorities, being always subject to the rule of God, ought to respect the rights of conscience and of religious belief and to serve God's will of justice and peace for all humankind.'[61] Yet, again, the church has State law devoted exclusively to it, as does the Baptist Union of Great Britain.[62]

Generally, the churches themselves, in their postures on their own religious liberty, agree with and benefit from religious freedom regimes in civil law. Whether any civil regime, in which churches participate and acquiesce, should be reformed is a different issue – and many churches may, and sometimes do, litigate the application of this regime to them if the State limits their use of religious freedom. Certainly, churches assert their own freedom and their institutional autonomy and separation from the State – but by and large, churches cooperate with it, often have tailor-made State legislation to protect their own interests, and obey its laws, unless the faith itself is threatened.

The Church regulates/limits its own internal religious freedom

Christians understand that the church was born free but with responsibilities fixed by divine law: to proclaim the Gospel; to worship; and to provide care for people. To what extent, then, do churches permit internal religious freedom? The pattern which emerges is that churches *reverse* the image of religious liberty appearing in civil law and which they advocate when it comes to the regulation of their own internal affairs. Civil law begins with the *right* to religious liberty and moves to limits on its exercise. Church law begins with *duties* on the faithful and moves to freedoms found in exceptions to rules, norms to relax law, and rights of conscience (see, e.g., Doe, 2011: 122).

Religious freedom *within* a church – and the extent it is enjoyed by the faithful – is defined by the law of that church (alongside its belief and doctrine). Theology articulates Christian belief (the primary stimulus for law), it proposes values (the primary source of law), it contemplates action (the primary focus of law), and it animates these values in norms of conduct

56 United Methodist Church in Northern Europe and Eurasia: Book of Discipline, pars. 103, 164; Articles of Religion, Art. XXVI.
57 Constitutional Practice and Discipline, Bk. I, Methodist Church Act 1976.
58 Regulations, Discipline and Government, 29.20.
59 Irish Presbyterian Church Act 1871.
60 Constitution, Art. V.II.8.
61 Manual: Basis of Union, A, Sch. D, Version I, 8.
62 United Reformed Church Acts 1972, 1981 and 2000; and Baptist and Congregational Trusts Act 1961.

(the primary character of law) (Doe, 2013: 29–41). Many of the Principles of Christian Law (2016), induced from their laws, indicate how laws of the historic churches have a profound effect on religious freedom within those churches, arising not least from the very nature of church law. They illustrate well the delicate balance between ecclesial *freedom* and permissible *limitations* on its proper exercise.

First, as to *purposes of church law as servant*, church law exists to serve a church in its mission and witness to the salvific work of Christ; laws constitute the institutional organisation of a church and facilitate and order its activities. Second, as to *structure, effect, and relaxation*, church laws principally deal with ministry, government, doctrine, worship, rites, discipline, and property. They consist of various juridical formulae, such as precepts, prohibitions, and permissions, and may be cast as principles and rules, rights and duties, and functions and powers. Laws may be binding or exhortatory. All members of a church are subject to its laws as are its institutions, to the extent that the law provides. A church may have in place a mechanism to enforce and vindicate the rights and duties of the faithful.[63] Third, there *is the rule of law*: an ecclesial institution must comply with church law and may be subject in exercising its functions to substantive and procedural limitations prescribed by law; and a local church, its assembly, and other institutions, such as a council, have such authority and functions as are lawfully inherent to it or conferred on it by institutions of the wider ecclesial entity to which it belongs.[64]

Fourth, *duties and rights*: All the faithful should be equal in dignity. Baptism generates duties and rights for the faithful. The law of a church should set out the basic rights and duties of all its members. A layperson should engage in the collective ecclesial life, in proclaiming the Word of God, participating in worship, and receiving sacraments; maintain Christian standards in their private lives; bring the teaching of Christ into every-day life; and be of service to the church and the wider community.[65] Ordained ministers must be authorised by their church to exercise ministry, namely preach the Word of God, teach the faith, administer the sacraments, and provide pastoral care; and they must account for their ministry to the competent authority in the manner prescribed by church law.[66] The same notions of freedom and its limited and responsible exercise are found throughout the Statement of Principles of Christian Law (2016),[67] and they are induced from laws, across traditions, as they apply to 'duties and rights' within the church (see generally Doe, 2013).

On the other hand, there are facilities to enable freedom in the form of the relaxation of law, limited doctrinal dissent, and conscientious objection – but the use of the facility is not unrestricted. First, dispensation: for instance, Roman Catholic canon law defines *dispensation* as 'the relaxation of a merely ecclesiastical law in a particular case.' Dispensation may be granted, 'within the limits of their competence, by those who have executive power', and by others 'whether by virtue of the law itself or by lawful delegation.' However, it must not be granted without 'a just and reasonable cause' or to relax laws constituting juridical institutions or acts. A bishop may dispense for the good of the faithful, but cannot dispense from procedural or penal laws, or in cases reserved to the Apostolic See. The Pontiff has wide dispensing powers, but there is no appeal/recourse against a judgement or decree of the Roman Pontiff.[68]

63 Principles of Christian Law (2016): I.3-4.
64 Principles of Christian Law (2016) IV.5.
65 Principles of Christian Law (2016) II.1-3.
66 Principles of Christian Law (2016) III.3.
67 Principles of Christian Law (2016): IV: governance; V: discipline; VI: doctrine and worship; VII: rites of passage; VIII: ecumenism; IX: church property.
68 CIC: cc. 87–93; c. 333: pontiff. See also Principles of Christian Law (2016): I.4: a law may be relaxed by means of dispensation, economy, or other form of equity for the good of the individual and ecclesial community.

Second, doctrinal dissent: again, regulation of doctrine illustrates the reversal by church law of the image of religious liberty in civil law.[69] For instance, Lutheran ministers must uphold church doctrine[70]; and members' must 'ensure faithful adherence to the Confession' and 'apply discipline when departure from the doctrine of the Church is evident' – but 'differences of opinion ... should not be held to in a way which hinders friendly discussion, and makes submission to the Scriptures difficult or ... impossible.' Indeed, 'pious opinions can enrich the church [and] have often stimulated thinking and discussion on central matters of faith.'[71] Likewise, in British Methodist churches, '[n]o person shall be appointed to office in the Church who teaches doctrines contrary to those of the Church, or who holds doctrines likely to injure the peace and welfare of the Church;'[72] but ministers may resign if unable to accept doctrine.[73]

Third, provision for conscience: for instance, in the case of remarriage after divorce in Anglicanism, a minister may refuse to solemnise the marriage of a divorced person on grounds of conscientious objection.[74] In Lutheranism, a remarriage may occur if, *inter alia*, 'the pastor can officiate with a good conscience.'[75] In Methodism, '[u]nder no circumstances does the Conference require any person authorised to conduct marriages who is subject to the discipline of the Church ... to officiate at the marriage of a particular couple should it be contrary to the dictates of his/her conscience to do so.'[76] Presbyterianism is similar: 'the Connexion does not lay on any minister the duty of officiating at the marriage of a divorced person if, in so doing, he would be acting against his own conscience and judgment, and that of the elders.'[77]

Conclusion

While at one level there is very little difference between understandings of religious freedom in secular laws and those of Christians, a key distinguishing feature is that, for Christians, religious freedom is a gift from God. The historic churches assume for themselves a duty to engage in advocacy for religious freedom in civil society. In some, the duty is imposed by church teaching, in others by church law or soft law, and in some by both. While the World Council of Churches assumes for itself a duty to promote civil religious freedom, the churches impose on themselves no *legal* duty to *cooperate* with ecumenical partners in discharging that duty. As they may be beneficiaries of collective religious liberty under civil law, churches have robust assertions in their laws of their own religious freedom in the form of institutional autonomy, but they also provide for cooperation with the State and general compliance with civil law. Nevertheless, churches regulate and limit the exercise of religious freedom by the faithful within the church. This is inherent to their use of laws to facilitate and order ecclesial life, the nature and binding effect of church law, the rule of law in church, and processes for church discipline. However, churches *reverse* the image of religious liberty in civil law (which they themselves advocate) when it comes to the regulation of their own internal affairs. Civil law

69 Principles of Christian Law (2016) VI.3: Doctrinal Discipline.
70 Lutheran Church in Great Britain: Rules and Regulations, Responsibilities and Duties of Pastors, 1–24.
71 Lutheran Church of Australia: Constitution, Art. VI.7; Public Doctrine and Pious Opinion, 1984, ed. 2001.
72 Methodist Church in Great Britain: Constitutional Practice and Discipline, Deed of Union 7; Standing Orders 010(1).
73 Methodist Church in Ireland: Regulations, Discipline and Government, 4E.07.
74 PCLCCAC, Principle 71.
75 Lutheran Church of Australia: Marriage, Divorce and Re-Marriage, III.1–3.
76 Methodist Church in Great Britain: Constitutional Practice and Discipline, Standing Order 011A; and VI.2.15.
77 Presbyterian Church of Wales: Handbook of Rules, 9.4.

begins with the *right* and moves to limits on its exercise. Church law begins with *duties* on the faithful and moves to freedoms found in exceptions to rules, norms to relax church law, and rights of conscience (in areas such as church doctrine and rites).

In light of these findings, there is a strong case for the Christian Law Panel, in its partnership with the Faith and Order Commission of the World Council of Churches, to debate: (1) whether it is already possible to induce from the laws of the historic churches principles of Christian law with regard to religious freedom on the basis of juridical assumptions, related to church teaching, about religious freedom; and (2) if such principles cannot be found, to debate whether the historic churches should create new laws about their commitment to religious freedom. There are five reasons to do so: (1) the legislative process within churches would necessitate the development of a more fulsome Christian understanding of religious freedom which may relate religious liberty to the theology of duties deducible from universal moral or ethical principles about the human pursuit of religious truth; (2) the existence of law in a church would oblige that church to engage in religious liberty advocacy and so translate any existing church teaching on this into enforceable duties; (3) the development of church law to oblige inter-Christian collaboration over religious freedom would invigorate the general ecumenical duty; (4) the creation of these legal duties would not threaten but strengthen the collective religious freedom of churches under civil law; and (5) creating such laws would enable articulation of principles of Christian law in the matter of religious liberty which individual churches may pray in aid when involved in collective religious freedom claims in the wider environment of the civil law.

As a result, the following are offered as a basis for these debates. First, religious freedom is a necessary element of the Christian faith, a gift of God, and part of the divine plan for all humankind. The State should recognise, promote, and protect the religious freedom of churches corporately and of the faithful individually. The free pursuit of religious truth is a universal value, and the State should respect and facilitate this. Second, churches should be advocates of religious liberty for all in civil society – each church should have institutions dedicated to its promotion in the public sphere. Third, the churches should cooperate in the promotion of religious freedom in civil society as part of the ecumenical enterprise for greater visible Christian unity. Fourth, each should act as a guardian of its own religious freedom and institutional autonomy in civil society in order to promote its divinely given mission and witness. Fifth, on the basis that all the faithful in a church are equal in dignity by virtue of their baptism, a church should in its laws clearly define the limits on the exercise of its own religious freedom by ecclesial institutions within it and by the faithful who are members of it. However, the extent to which a church through its law provides for conscientious objection and the appropriate relaxation of its norms on grounds of individual conscience is a matter for that church in an exercise of its own autonomy, notably with regard to matters of doctrine and faith.

References

Doe, N., 1996. *Canon Law in the Anglican Communion*. Oxford University Press.

Doe, N., 2002. Canonical approaches to human rights in Anglican churches. In: M. Hill (Ed.), *Religious Liberty and Human Rights*. University of Wales Press.

Doe, N., 2011. *Law and Religion in Europe*. Oxford University Press.

Doe, N., 2013. *Christian Law*. Cambridge University Press.

Doe, N. (Ed.), 2017. *Christianity and Natural Law*. Cambridge University Press.

Grasso, K.L., Hunt, R.P. (Eds.), 2006. *Catholicism and Religious Freedom*. Rowman and Littlefield.

Hill, M., Doe, N., 2017. Principles of Christian law. *Ecclesiastical Law Journal* 19, 138.

Koffeman, L.J., 2017. Natural law in the ecumenical movement. In: N. Doe (Ed.), *Christianity and Natural Law*. Cambridge University Press. 162.
Moyn, S., 2015. *Christian Human Rights*. University of Pennsylvania Press.
Ruston, R., 2004. *Human Rights and the Image of God*. SCM Press.
Taliaferro, K. (Ed.), 2014. *Religious Freedom: Sourcebook of Scriptural, Theological and Legal Texts*. Georgetown University Press.
Witte, J. (Ed.), 2010. *Christianity and Human Rights: An Introduction*. Cambridge University Press.

8
Hindu perspectives on the right to religious freedom

Laura Dudley Jenkins and Kristina M. Teater

This chapter places the issue of freedom of religion in today's India in the context of Hindu legal, religious, and political traditions. Drawing on a sample of key individuals writing on this topic, the chapter includes a diverse range of perspectives and reflects on the links between contemporary problems and their cultural and historical backgrounds.

After an overview of the origins of Hinduism and the contemporary diversity of Hindus, we discuss the global geographical distribution of Hindu populations and the possible implications of majority or minority status for their perspectives on religious freedom. We introduce the constitutional protections of religious freedom in India, the home of the majority of Hindus in the world. These legal protections of religious freedom and subsequent applications of these principles relate to Indian conceptions of and debates over secularism and tolerance.

We then turn to examples of individual Hindus who have articulated different perspectives on religious freedom in three prominent but contested issue areas: caste, religious minorities, and women. While geographically focused on the perspectives of Hindus in India, our examples range from late colonial to contemporary controversies. Our conclusion stresses the impossibility of defining a single Hindu perspective on religious freedom, while recognizing the contributions of a variety of Hindu perspectives to the complication, expansion, contraction, and rearticulation of this idea. Reflections on continuing tensions between religious freedom and equality reveal the need for further comparative study of the idea of religious freedom and its applications and consequences around the world.

Hinduisms

Hinduism is simultaneously one of the oldest and youngest religions in the world. Although some of the plethora of practices, deities, and texts associated with Hinduism today have been around for thousands of years, such as key legal and religious texts known as the Vedas, the words Hindu and Hinduism and the conceptualization of these varied practices, deities, and texts as constituting one religion developed later. By the mid-1600s, the word Hindu, or Hindoo, became the term used in Persian and English to refer to people living around the Indus River (known in Sanskrit as Sindhu) (Jeffrey and Harriss, 2014: 89). The region became Industan, then Hindustan, and still later India – although the Indus River at the beginning of this linguistic genealogy is now in Pakistan. At first, Hindu was a geographic term, so one could be a 'Hindoo Muslim' or 'Hindoo Christian,' but this geographic descriptor eventually became a religious one, as it began to mean people in India who had not become Muslim, and eventually people who embraced 'Hinduism' (Jeffrey and Harriss, 2014: 89).

'Hinduism' as a singular, but polytheistic, religion emerged in the early nineteenth century, appearing in the *Oxford English Dictionary* in 1829 and at the World's Parliament of Religions in 1893 (Jeffrey and Harriss, 2014: 90–91). It was an agglomeration of local and regional religious elements, with varied deities, religious leaders, texts, and traditions, drawn together by a colonial government seeking coherence and order in pursuit of control and by Indian religious reformers keen to achieve recognition of Hinduism as a world religion, or even the universal religion (Jeffrey and Harriss, 2014: 91). One such reformer, Swami Vivekananda (1863–1902), appeared at the World's Parliament of Religions in 1893 and advocated for Hindu tolerance and universality. Vivekananda highlighted the Vedas as the central scriptures of Hinduism, akin to the Bible or the Koran.

The growing emphasis on a central text represented an attempt to bring Hinduism into conformity with predominant (western) conceptions of religion centered on one holy book. This development, however, downplayed the variety of Hindu textual and oral traditions. The attention to the Vedas reinforced the supremacy and perspectives of the highest castes, or Brahmins. Hinduism, like other religions, cannot be understood via texts alone or without also examining the many popular Hindu practices and beliefs across different times, spaces, and peoples, including a variety of castes and communities outside India. For instance, indentured laborers from India who ended up in the British Caribbean colony of Trinidad in the nineteenth century also came to think of themselves as Hindus and developed Hinduism through complex social, cultural, and political interactions (Rocklin, 2019).

Alexander Rocklin argues that it was in part the British colonial ideology of 'religious freedom' that inspired efforts to fit rituals and practices into the category of 'religion.' Organizing these into Hinduism was in part an endeavor by inhabitants of Trinidad to benefit from religious freedom. In effect, religious freedom helped constitute Hinduism. Several other scholars have analyzed religious freedom as a system of modern governance, which shapes religions, peoples, practices, and power relationships (Hurd, 2015: 15; Sullivan et al., 2015; Jenkins, 2019: 3; Mahmood and Danchin, 2014: 1–8, 5). This is a valuable counterpoint to the assumption that religious freedom is an empty space in which religions and people freely roam. As a practical matter, if religions do not conform to dominant (often colonial, or Western) notions of what a religion should be, adherents of that religion are not eligible for religious freedom. Those who do conform may benefit, but the standardization of Hinduism (partly in pursuit of 'freedom') has consequences that can also restrict religious freedom, by sidelining the interpretations, rituals, and priorities of marginalized groups, such as lower castes, sexual minorities, syncretic communities, or Hindus outside of India. Hinduism*s* may be more accurate sociologically, but Hinduism is a useful construct for making religious freedom claims.

The absence of a single authoritative text, the polytheistic nature, and the myriad differences in practice across caste, place, and gender contribute to Hinduism's complexity. Many Hindus view their religious beliefs and practices as *sanatana dharma*. Translated as eternal religion or eternal way of life, this interpretation prompts some adherents to consider Hinduism not as one of many religious traditions, but rather an eternal way of life that encompasses all other faiths (Jeffrey and Harriss, 2014: 90). This view has the potential to either support or undermine the religious freedoms of subgroups within Hinduism or of other religious communities. Sociopolitical mobilization of Hindus, specifically the rise of Hindu majoritarianism in India, has undermined the freedoms of minorities there and further complicated opinions and perspectives on religious freedom. For example, Hindu nationalists sometimes use the rhetoric of

Hindu religious universalism, while promoting the political singularism of the Hindu nationalist Bharatiya Janata Party (BJP) and related Hindu nationalist organizations.

In India, the BJP has significantly increased in political relevance since the 1990s. Rina Verma Williams and Nandini Deo make an important distinction between the BJP's 'politicized Hinduism' and Hinduism as a religion. They define politicized religion as 'the mobilization of religious symbols, discourses, and narratives for political gain' (2018: 549). The BJP taps into majoritarian sentiments and enacts laws and regulations that stifle the religious rights of the adherents of non-Hindu faiths. Religious conversion from Hinduism to other religions, deeply contested in India, also faces challenges in Hindu majority Nepal. Before the abolishment of the monarchy in 2007, Nepal was 'officially' a Hindu state. Although Nepal is now a secular democratic republic, religious conversion is contested and prohibited by law (Williams and Moktan, 2019). Mauritius, where Hindus are also a majority, however, does not exhibit the same contestation over religious conversion. Thus, Hindu perspectives on religious freedom emerge from a variety of religious and geographic contexts.

Varied contexts of Hindus' religious freedom

Fifteen percent, or one billion people, of the world's population are Hindus, and 95% of them live in India, making Hinduism one of the most geographically concentrated religions in the world. Moreover, 97% of Hindus live in countries where Hinduism is the majority religion, including India (80% Hindu), Nepal (81%), and Mauritius (56%) (Pew Research Center, 2012). Despite their majority status in India, Hindu nationalist groups portray themselves politically as being under attack from other religions, especially Islam and Christianity, which, although in the minority, have significant populations in other countries (Williams and Jenkins, 2015: 20). These conservative Hindus' concern over the vast global footprint of Islam and Christianity 'plays out as ongoing struggles over religious rights and freedoms' both in South Asia and among Hindus living in the diaspora (Williams and Jenkins, 2015: 19).

Hindus have migrated from South Asia all over the world, a process that occurred in three major phases. Precolonial migration to Southeast Asia served as a predecessor to colonial migration of laborers from India to other British colonies. Migration during colonialism initially involved Hindus serving as servants to people in British colonies including Malaysia, Burma, and Sri Lanka, followed by Hindus serving as indentured servants and laborers in countries such as Mauritius, Fiji, and South Africa. After World War II and following the end of colonialism, Hindus migrated first to Britain and then to the United States and the Arab states of the Persian Gulf (Warrier, 2008: 87–88; Jacobs, 2010: 108). As such, Hindu migration resulted in a very diverse diaspora, and, even today, their experiences and the way they choose to organize and represent themselves varies according to their origin, including region, language, sect, caste, migration route, and the country in which they reside (Warrier, 2008: 86).

Hindu perspectives and issues related to religious freedom differ according to the country in which Hindus reside and specifically whether they constitute the majority or minority population. Hindus, who represent the majority of citizens in India and Nepal, have a notable but minority presence in North America, the Middle East, Australia, Africa, Fiji, Singapore, and the Caribbean Islands (Warrier, 2008: 86). The religious freedom issues they face in each of these places vary according to sociopolitical factors. For example, in Malaysia, where Hindus constitute 6% of the population, government regulations on religion restrict the belief and practices of adherents of non-Islamic faiths. Article 3(1) of the constitution of Malaysia, which states, 'Islam is the religion of the Federation; but other religions may be practiced in peace and harmony in any part of the Federation', complicates the religious practice of non-Muslims

(Constitution of Malaysia). In this multiethnic and multireligious society, constitutional protections for both religious and liberal rights, as well as parallel legal regimes, both civil and religious, impact how Hindus navigate a broad range of issues ranging from conversion to burial rites (Teater, 2019; Moustafa, 2018).

Religious freedom, secularism, and tolerance in India

Hindu perspectives on religious freedom are closely linked with the ideas of secularism and religious tolerance. These three concepts have been the focus of constitutional deliberations, political debates, and philosophical ruminations, particularly in the context of establishing independent India, and continue to this day. Religious freedom in the largest Hindu majority country, India, is protected by Article 25 of the Constitution, in effect since 1950. The key sections of the Article assert that:

> 1. Subject to public order, morality and health and to the other provisions of this Part, all persons are equally entitled to freedom of conscience and the right to freely profess, practise and propagate religion.
> 2. Nothing in this article shall affect the operation of any existing law or prevent the state from making any law –
>
>   a. regulating or restricting any economic, financial, political or other secular activity which may be associated with religious practice;
>   b. providing for social welfare and reform or the throwing open of Hindu religious institutions of a public character to all classes and sections of Hindus.
>
> *Explanation I.* – The wearing and carrying of kirpans shall be deemed to be included in the profession of the Sikh religion.
> *Explanation II.* – In sub-clause (b) of clause (2), the reference to Hindus shall be construed as including a reference to persons professing the Sikh, Jaina or Buddhist religion, and the reference to Hindu religious institutions shall be construed accordingly.

India's Constituent Assembly worked on drafting a constitution beginning in 1946 until 1949. This is the same era as the Universal Declaration of Human Rights, adopted in 1948, so religious freedom discussions were happening all over the world. India's religious freedom clause has several caveats, which allow restrictions on religious freedom for reasons of public order, morality, and health, but its protections are quite wide ranging. Notably, in addition to professing and practicing a religion, religious freedom in the Indian Constitution includes the right to propagate (which was less popular among some Hindu members of the Constituent Assembly, who thought that propagation was a Muslim or Christian practice). The caveats provide legitimate reasons to restrict freedom, while the list of protected activities is quite broad, setting the stage for future tensions. For instance, there have been frequent challenges to religious propagation in order to preserve public order (Jenkins, 2019: 12–16, chapter 4).

Clause 2b and Explanation II within Article 25 are particularly relevant to our consideration of religious freedom in the context of Hinduism. Clause 2b means that religious freedom should not prevent the state from interfering in religious matters for purposes of social reform or to open up Hindu temples to all classes of Hindus. In this way, the writers of the Constitution endeavored to prevent the use of religious freedom to perpetuate caste discrimination. Although caste is not unique to Hindu communities – it exists in many Christian and Muslim communities in South Asia as well – it has been a persistent problem in Hindu societies (Jenkins, 2019: chapter 5). Clause 2b means that the state can put in place social reform or welfare legislation in order to uplift lower castes and can override religious leaders who try to keep lower castes out of temples.

Explanation II states 'the reference to Hindus shall be construed as including a reference to persons professing the Sikh, Jaina or Buddhist religion' – a constitutional definition of Hindus that might puzzle religious studies scholars or even members of these communities themselves. Although these are commonly considered distinct religions, this expansive constitutional definition of Hinduism continues to have an impact in the area of personal laws, one of the ways India puts religious freedom into practice. While criminal laws and many civil laws in India are uniform, personal laws are distinct sets of religious civil laws, particularly family laws relating to marriage, divorce, inheritance, and adoption, for different religious communities, including Hindus, Muslims, and Christians. The Hindu personal law continues to encompass Sikh, Jain and Buddhist religious communities (Teater and Jenkins, 2019; Williams, 2006).

Debates in the Constituent Assembly over religious freedom included articulations of the idea of Hindu tolerance, to be discussed in more detail below. In the words of Constituent Assembly member Lokanath Misra, 'Vedic culture excludes nothing,' so he expressed concern that including the freedom to propagate would pave the way 'for the complete annihilation of Hindu culture, the Hindu way of life and manners.' He argued, 'Justice demands that the ancient faith and culture of the land should be given a fair deal' (Constituent Assembly Debates, 6 December 1948, Part I). This perspective from 1948 foreshadows growing anxiety among some Hindus in the postcolonial era over secularism in India (Williams and Jenkins, 2015).

The word 'secular' was not in the original Indian Constitution. It was added to the preamble of the Constitution in 1976, in the Emergency period during which Prime Minister Indira Gandhi suspended many democratic rights. This preamble now describes India as 'a Sovereign Secular Socialist Democratic Republic.' In their constitutional deliberations, some Constituent Assembly members argued for a distinctive Indian version of secularism. For example, K. M. Munshi argued that United States style secularism, with its emphasis on non-establishment and a line between church and state, was 'inappropriate for Indian conditions.' In pursuit of a 'characteristically India secularism,' Munshi pointed to India's 'deeply religious moorings' but also its 'tradition of religious tolerance' and the 'broad outlook of Hinduism,' advocating a form of secularism premised on 'equal respect' for each different religion (Jha, 2002: 3176; see also Williams and Jenkins, 2015: 23–26).

This was not the only view on secularism, even in the Constituent Assembly debates. Scholars have identified several different types of secularism in these debates alone, and the larger debate over how to actually implement secularism continues (Williams and Jenkins, 2015: 26; Jha, 2002: 3176; Chiriyankandath, 2000: 9). India's first Prime Minister Jawaharlal Nehru pondered the meaning of secularism and its relationship to freedom. Nehru posited that Indian secularism 'does not obviously mean a state where religion is discouraged. It means freedom of religions and conscience, including freedom for those who have no religions … [and] the idea of social and political equality' (quoted in Bhatt, 1992: 263). Notably, Nehru saw a necessary linkage between freedom and equality in this articulation of Indian secularism.

Indian secularism as 'equidistance' is a term attributed to Dr. S. Radhakrishnan, the second president of India. An example of equidistance is state funding on an equal basis for private religious institutions of higher education, including historically Muslim universities (such as Aligarh Muslim University) and historically Hindu universities (such as Benares Hindu University). 'Of course, this formulation leaves dangling the question of what constitutes equal treatment: proportional to population? Absolute equality? Based on need? Defined how?' (Williams and Jenkins, 2015: 21–22). More recently Amartya Sen has characterized Indian secularism in a related but slightly different way as 'a basic symmetry of treatment,' in contrast to strict separation or the idea that 'the state must stay clear of any association with any religious matter whatsoever' (Sen, 2005: 269).

Many of these ideas about Indian secularism counter the notion of religious freedom as an unencumbered space, free from government interference, within which religious communities and individuals operate. Hindu intellectuals theorizing about secularism vary in their terminology, but many recognize the role of the government in enabling religious communities and practices to continue, such as by adjudicating religious personal laws in Indian courts or funding religious educational institutions. Many, like Nehru, also emphasize religious equality, not just religious freedom, in their conceptions of Indian secularism. How to operationalize equality is complicated – is it symmetry, equidistance, or equal respect? And how should the state interact with society to achieve this? These questions are still being debated, but Indian secularism adds to global discussions of religious freedom in important ways: Proponents of Indian secularism may disagree on the details but largely recognize that, first, state action (and not just separation) constitutes religious freedom and, second, equality is an important aspect of religious freedom.

Hindu perspectives on religious freedom are often put in terms of Hinduism's unique tolerance for other religions. At the above-mentioned 1893 World's Parliament of Religion in Chicago, Swami Vivekananda spoke of being proud of belonging to a religion that has 'taught the world both tolerance and universal acceptance. We believe not only in universal tolerance, but we accept all religions as true' (quoted in Davis, 2008: 360). Vivekananda's speech helped bring attention to the idea of Hindu tolerance and is often viewed as a moment when the world recognized it as such. Despite Vivekananda's claim, critics argue that the Hindu theory of tolerance does have limitations. They point out that the acceptance of other religions does not mean the absence of hierarchy and that 'inclusivity is not the same as qualified tolerance' (Davis, 2008: 361).

According to Bhikhu Parekh, a 'Hindu theory of tolerance' finds its foundation in four beliefs: the primacy of conduct, moral duties, individual uniqueness, and religious pluralism (Parekh, 2003: 48). The emphasis on the primacy of conduct implies that for Hindus, the ethical quality of life is more important than religious dogma, and moral duties or dharma guide an ethical life. Individual uniqueness means that religions should allow adherents to adapt religious teaching according to their needs, and religious pluralism implies equal respect for all religions and peaceful coexistence (Parekh, 2003: 48–53).

Hindu tolerance, therefore, is different from Western liberal Protestant conceptions of tolerance in the following principal respects. Hindus have much latitude to borrow from other faiths while continuing to remain Hindu. The emphasis on morality rather than religious beliefs means that Hindus can hold any form of beliefs as long as they lead a good life. According to its proponents, the Hindu theory of tolerance places itself at the intersection of religion and morality and, in doing so, stays away from disputes over which religious path is more favorable and should be spread to others (Parekh, 2019: 276). As such, advocates of the theory of Hindu tolerance contrast Hinduism with religions that more openly prioritize proselytization, including Islam and Christianity. Their critique of the latter religions, however, belies their purported religious toleration. Is a competition over which religion is most tolerant a form of intolerance? In Hindu majority countries such as India and Nepal, this tension at times manifests itself through legislative measures that regulate religious freedom, including placing limits on religious conversion. In India, anti-conversion laws, widely supported by Hindu nationalists, are in place in several states, and conversions to Hinduism are outside the scope of many of these laws. Likewise, Nepal's 2015 constitution prohibits any attempt to convert an individual from one religion to another. Hindu tolerance and religious freedom arguments have been used to rationalize these restrictions on the religious freedom to convert, particularly to minority religions in these Hindu majority countries (Jenkins, 2019: chapter 4).

Critics of the idea that Hinduism is exceptionally conducive to tolerance draw attention to the distinction between tolerance within Hinduism and Hindu tolerance toward other religions. These critics point to Hinduism's social practices as examples of the unfair and inequitable treatment that erodes the liberty of some of its constituents. Hindu tolerance of other religions, they argue, has done little to alleviate the struggles of Dalits, women, and Hindus from lower castes (Spinner-Halev, 2005: 37). Ongoing debates about caste-based discrimination and about women's temple access, to which we now turn, are examples of how the rhetoric of Hindu tolerance may disguise ongoing oppressions within Hindu communities. The diversity of Hindus and Hinduisms creates opportunities for religious tolerance unmatched by other religions, but it also creates scope for disagreements. The religious freedoms of lower castes, non-Hindus, and women are three areas in which different Hindus have come to opposing conclusions.

Religious freedom and caste

Mohandas Gandhi (1869–1948) and Dr. B. R. Ambedkar (1891–1956) both became known for their critiques of caste discrimination but via decidedly different views on Hinduism and its implications for freedom. Both men were born Hindus. Gandhi remained a Hindu throughout his life, while arguing for reforms to make it more equitable. He wrote, 'My religion is Hinduism which, for me, is the religion of humanity and includes the best of all the religions known to me' (Brown, 2008: 64). Gandhi had an open attitude toward other religions and drew inspiration from many of their teachings. Ambedkar also studied many different religions but, in contrast to Gandhi, declared in 1936, 'I will not die a Hindu, for this is within my power' (quoted in Jenkins, 2019: 65). Ambedkar rejected Hinduism, largely due to caste and gender inequalities. Two decades after his announcement and shortly before his death, he converted to Buddhism, along with hundreds of thousands of his followers. Gandhi and Ambedkar's disputes over Hinduism and its implications for freedom in the context of caste discrimination played out in the late colonial and early independence period, when the framework for religious freedom in India was forged.

Gandhi came from a middle caste background, whereas Ambedkar was from the very lowest status group sometimes referred to as untouchables, Depressed Classes, Scheduled Castes, or Dalits (the latter literally meaning oppressed or crushed). Both studied abroad: Gandhi studied in London followed by several years practicing law and spearheading protests on behalf of the Indian community in South Africa, and Ambedkar studied at Columbia University in New York and in London. Each returned to India in the midst of the late colonial agitations and demands for independence from Britain. In their own ways, they both took religion and freedom very seriously in their intellectual and political lives. They opposed discrimination and violence against the lowest castes, known as untouchability, although they disagreed over strategies to combat it (Jenkins, 2003: chapter 7). They also disagreed on another aspect of caste, specifically *varna,* a four-fold division of the hundreds of Indian castes into an occupation-based hierarchy (see Williams and Moktan, 2019). Although he fought against the most egregious forms of caste discrimination, namely untouchability, Gandhi continued to stand up for the idea of *varna:*

> the law of *varna* means that everyone shall follow as a matter of *dharma* – duty – the hereditary calling of his forefathers, in so far as it is not inconsistent with fundamental ethics. He will earn his livelihood by following that calling. He may not hoard riches, but devote the balance for the good of the people.

> The four *varnas* have been compared in the Vedas to the four members of the body, and no simile could be happier. If they are members of one body, how can one be superior or inferior to another?
>
> *(quoted in Mukherjee, 1996: 219)*

Gandhi rejected hierarchy, while defending the hereditary occupational categories associated with varna. By saying that even the menial laboring castes should be considered equal to the scholarly or warrior castes, Gandhi maintained his defense of *varna* as a social and religious ordering principle, while advocating for equality (Sharma, 2004: 54–55). Since even the higher status varnas should not 'hoard riches,' Gandhi assumed this religiously sanctioned order could prevent ambition, conflict, and excessive materialism, as people, whatever their occupation, would receive a basic livelihood and devote the rest of their resources for the 'good of the people.'

Gandhi advocated for freedom – both religious freedom and freedom from the British – but not a free-for-all. 'Anticolonial intellectuals like Gandhi thus found themselves in something of a double bind. They wanted to lay claim to liberty but needed to do so in terms that did not reinforce the hegemony of liberalism, with its valorization of the free individual ... Accordingly, anticolonial thinkers sought to pry the ideal of freedom away from England and Englishness' (Scott, 2019: 49). As a Hindu social structure in a chaotic time of upheaval, *varna* could provide a social and religious framework for freedoms. This may have been *varna*'s continuing appeal for Gandhi, even as he challenged untouchability and caste discrimination.

In contrast, Ambedkar opposed all aspects of the caste system. This became a source of disagreement between them that highlights their differing takes on religious freedom. Ambedkar rejected Gandhi's incremental, reformist stances. In his most scathing critique of caste, *The Annihilation of Caste,* Ambedkar argued that lower castes could not be truly free unless they changed their religion:

> You must give a new doctrinal basis to your religion – a basis that will be in consonance with liberty, equality, and fraternity, in short, with democracy. ... This means a complete change in the fundamental notions of life. It means a complete change in the values of life. It means a complete change in outlook and in attitude towards men and things. It means conversion ... it means a new life.
>
> *(quoted in Jenkins, 2019: 64)*

Ambedkar wrote this address at the invitation of a group of Hindus interested in caste-related reforms. He was uninvited when they saw an advance copy, but he published it anyway.

Ambedkar developed his view of freedom, or liberty, in other writings, in which he noted the dangers of neglecting fraternity, which he felt was sorely missing in India's caste-ridden society. 'Without Fraternity Liberty would destroy equality and equality would destroy liberty' (quoted in Jaffrelot and Kumar, 2018: 248). Considering both Indian and Western ideas, Ambedkar even argued that certain philosophical strands within Hindu traditions 'had greater potentialities for producing social democracy *than* the idea of fraternity' but that these became marginalized as the Hindu social system was increasingly 'designed to be undemocratic. Its division of society into *varnas* and castes, and of castes and outcastes ... are all barricades raised against democracy' (quoted in Jaffrelot and Kumar, 2018: 248).

Gandhi's view that *varna* could organize society without hierarchy remains unfulfilled, and Ambedkar's critiques remain salient. For example, a recent study showed the prevalence of Brahmins in India's elite science institutes and the pervasiveness of these professors' Brahminical ideologies to justify their supposedly natural dominance of these fields (Thomas, 2020). Thus, although *varna* is seen as an important part of Hinduism to many, it remains an impediment to the freedoms of many lower caste Hindus.

Religious freedom and religious minorities

Perspectives regarding religious minorities range from an emphasis on the exclusivity of Hinduism to the accommodation of minority beliefs and practices and a more inclusive stance. The rise of Hindu nationalism, especially in Hindu majority contexts, contributed to religious minorities being considered as the 'threatening other' (Jaffrelot, 1996: 6). Hindu nationalism, in its organized form, emerged in the 1920s. In Hindu majority India, anxiety over the Muslim population's perceived level of cohesion, militancy, and organization facilitated the making of a Hindu consciousness (Jaffrelot, 1996: 25). The goal of Hindu nationalists was to form a Hindu identity that not only glorified the 'golden age' of the past but also used Hindu traditions to guide the future. As such, 'Indian culture was to be defined as Hindu culture, and the minorities were to be assimilated by their paying allegiance to symbols and mainstays of the majority as those of the nation' (Jaffrelot, 2007: 5).

One of the elites instrumental to the early Hindu nationalist movement was Vinayak Damodar Savarkar (1883–1966). Savarkar, an extremist, who penned his most influential work, *Hindutva: Who is a Hindu,* while in jail, would later become president of the Hindu Mahasabha or Hindu Grand Assembly (1937–1942). *Hindutva,* first published in 1923, still impacts contemporary Hindu nationalist thought. Savarkar's emphasis on a common culture, territorial unity, and racial criteria in an effort to create a Hindu identity places a qualifier on the rights of religious minorities and devalues difference. Referencing Christians and Muslims, Savarkar questions the loyalty of religious minorities whose holy land is outside of India when he writes:

> For though Hindustan is to them a Fatherland as to any other Hindu, yet it is not to them a Holyland too. Their Holyland is far off in Arabia and Palestine. Their mythology and godmen, ideas and heroes are not children of this soil. Consequently, their names and their outlook smack of a foreign origin. Their love is divided.
>
> *(Savarkar, 1969: 113)*

Savarkar links religion to nationality again in *Six Glorious Epochs of Indian History* when he argues that a religion that proselytizes with persuasion or force resulting in conversion 'causes a change of nationality in those converted' (Savarkar, 1985). But Savarkar and Hindu nationalist views are not the only Hindu perspectives concerning religious minorities. Other approaches emphasize the importance of unity and inclusivity, and among those voices was Sarojini Naidu.

A contemporary of Savarkar, Sarojini Naidu (1879–1949) was one of the most prominent women leaders of the Indian Independence movement. A renowned poet and the first woman to hold the Office of Governor in Independent India, Naidu repeatedly spoke about the appeal and necessity for unity among the adherents of Hinduism and the followers of minority religions. Her speeches, letters, and poems offer a contrary view to Savarkar's intertwining of national identity with Hindu identity. Naidu argued that religious difference must not be devalued but instead should be recognized, especially to achieve the higher purpose of national unity. In a speech at the Madras Special Provincial Conference in December 1917, Naidu stated:

> If you truly wish India to be united and not divided, even as you value your religious beliefs, even as you cherish your religious faiths and your prejudices, if they ask that as a token of the gifts of your love, you will not object to the little thing they demand that when our Hindu procession pass the Moslem mosques, they should not violate

> one of the primary mandates of Islam that there should not be sound to break the silence of the mosque.
>
> *(Naidu, 1925: 140–141)*

For Naidu, the Hindu majority needed to recognize and accommodate the religious beliefs and practices of minorities, and in this case, Muslims. As such, Naidu's argument is a counterpoint to some Hindu nationalists who argue that Muslims and other minorities must accept the centrality of Hinduism to Indian civilization, acknowledge central Hindu figures as civilizational heroes, accept the historical narrative that Muslim rulers destroyed parts of Hindu civilization including Hindu temples, and eschew claims to special privileges, including religious personal laws (Varshney, 1993: 231). Unlike Savarkar, for whom 'a benchmark of Indian identity is refusing to follow foreign gods,' Naidu's focus is on recognition and accommodation (Mehta, 2004: 118). In doing so, Naidu's conceptualization of religious freedom goes beyond tolerance.

Akin to Savarkar and Naidu, dueling perspectives on religious freedom are evident in contemporary debates between Hindu nationalists and their Hindu critics, and even in countries where Hinduism is a minority religion. Currently, in the United States, the Hindu American Foundation (HAF), the most established organization of Hindu interests with headquarters in Washington DC, actively engages with U.S. policymakers on a range of issues, including international religious freedom, from a Hindu nationalist perspective. According to the Hindu American Foundation, the organization supports religious freedom based on the Universal Declaration of Human Rights and 'what it has failed to include, [such] as the right to retain one's tradition and be free from religious intrusion, harassment, intimidation, and exploitative and predatory proselytization' (Hindu American Foundation, 2020).

Other Hindu organizations, however, highlight inclusion and support multireligious pluralism. Hindus for Human Rights, a smaller advocacy organization, also based in the United States, calls for 'the dissolution of the historical oppressive structure of caste' and engages in calls for peace, justice, and human rights 'of all communities from a Hindu perspective' (Hindus for Human Rights, n.d.). Thus, adherents and organizations that represent Hindu interests offer a wide range of views in relation to religious minorities. Regardless of the majority–minority contexts, some hold to a more exclusivist view of Hinduism and emphasize an actual or perceived threat to Hinduism, whereas others have a more open perspective, conducive to the religious freedoms of all communities.

Religious freedom and gender

At many Hindu temples, women and girls are expected to refrain from entering when they are menstruating. This is 'not new,' and there is a long history of formally and informally banning certain people deemed impure (including lower castes and menstruating women of any caste) to preserve the purity of temples and their devotees (Kumar, 2016: 1). Both Gandhi and Ambedkar were involved in temple entry movements, which were nonviolent protests by lower castes to gain access to Hindu temples beginning in the early 1900s (Jeffrey, 1976: 13–17). Demands for women to gain access are a more recent development, culminating in a contemporary dispute over whether women should be allowed to enter the Sabarimala Temple in the Indian state of Kerala. This conflict features opposing Hindu perspectives on the application of the principle of religious freedom.

The Sabarimala temple case went to the Indian Supreme Court. Some Hindus argued that the temple's rule excluding women of childbearing age (defined as women between the ages of

10 and 50) must be respected to protect the religious freedom of the devotees of the temple deity, Lord Ayyappa, by preserving the celibacy of the deity and the purity of the temple. Other Hindus viewed the exclusion of women from the temple as a violation of both gender equality and Hindu women's religious freedom. The High Court of Kerala upheld the temple rule excluding women from 10 to 50 years of age, but the Supreme Court of India overruled it, allowing women to enter the temple.

To articulate opposing viewpoints on this issue, we feature two responses by prominent Hindu women. The first is the dissenting opinion opposing the Supreme Court's 2018 judgment that the Sabarimala temple should be opened to all women. The dissent was written by Supreme Court Justice Indu Malhotra. She was the second woman to be named a Senior Advocate by the Supreme Court in 2007 and is an expert in commercial arbitration. Malhotra was appointed to be a Supreme Court Justice in 2018 and was the only woman on the bench that decided the Sabarimala case. The second perspective is from an interview with writer K. R. Meera in the newspaper *The Hindu*. Meera, the first woman reporter at the *Malayala Manorama* newspaper in Kerala, became renowned for her literary writing, including the 2012 novel *Arachaar* (Hangwoman). She has won the Sahitya Akademi literary award, a prestigious national honor, several times (Sudhish, 2018).

Malhotra's dissenting opinion in the Supreme Court ruling in *Indian Young Lawyers Association & Others v. The State of Kerala & Others* (2018) includes the following articulation of the meaning of India's religious freedom clause:

> Article 25(1) confers on every individual the right to freely profess, practise and propagate his or her religion. The right of an individual to worship a specific manifestation of the deity, in accordance with the tenets of that faith or shrine, is protected by Article 25(1) of the Constitution. If a person claims to have faith in a certain deity, the same has to be articulated in accordance with the tenets of that faith.
>
> In the present case, the worshippers of this Temple believe in the manifestation of the deity as a '*Naishtik Brahmachari*' [one who has taken a vow of celibacy]. The devotees of this Temple have not challenged the practises followed by this Temple, based on the essential characteristics of the deity.

Malhotra argues that 'Courts normally do not delve into issues of religious practises, especially in the absence of an aggrieved person from that particular religious faith, or sect.' But who is a 'person from that particular religious faith, or sect?' In her view, the women who want to enter the temple and brought this claim are not members of that particular sect, because if they were members of that sect, they would believe that they should not enter, so there is no basis to protect their freedom to enter. Malhotra argues that a person who 'claims to have faith' in a certain deity must do so 'in accordance with the tenets of that faith' to be eligible for religious freedom.

In contrast, novelist K. R. Meera reflected on how banning women from temples violates the Constitution and democratic principles:

> I grew up a believer and temple visits were a part of everyday life. But now I realise how even such a harmless routine can be a potential stimulus for toxic ideologies. … In an earlier devaprasanam [a type of temple ceremony focused on problems and solutions], a tantri [the temple authority, usually a hereditary position] made a dramatic declaration that a woman had entered the shrine much to the wrath of its celibate deity. Then a woman came forward and confessed to entering the temple a couple of years ago leading

> to an elaborate purification ritual. Does that mean that Ayyappa wasn't celibate during this interval? Is celibacy something that can be retrieved every now and then? ... We should not promote any customs that negate the basic principles of the constitution and democracy. When your faith lacks the backing of law, it becomes mere superstition.
>
> *(quoted in Sudhish, 2018)*

At the heart of the Sabarimala debate are key questions about religious freedom, which are not unique to Hinduism, but certainly complicated by its tremendous diversity: Who has the authority to define which religious practices, rules, or beliefs are part of a religion? Which individuals can legitimately claim religious freedom as members of a religion? What is religion? In the Sabarimala case, as in others, the Indian Supreme Court has delved into the 'essential religious practice test' to determine which practices should receive constitutional protection and, in doing so, has also assumed the role of theological interpreter. Ronojoy Sen argues that 'the Court's use of the essential practices doctrine has served as a vehicle for legitimizing a rationalized form of high Hinduism, and delegitimizing usages of popular Hinduism as superstition' (Sen, 2019).

Malhotra's logic is that women who want to enter are not truly devotees by definition because devotees of that temple and deity would believe in and follow the temple rules. But this implies that the Supreme Court should defer to temple priests (who are traditionally, and still predominantly, upper caste men) and their rules as the ultimate arbiters of Hindu essential practices and religious freedom, a problematic assumption. In contrast to Malhotra, Meera questions whether 'customs' that contradict democratic constitutional principles should be considered religion at all, or merely 'superstition.' Who gets to decide when certain aspects of religions, or entire religions, can be downgraded to mere customs or superstitions, outside of the purview of religious freedom protections?

On top of these competing claims about religious freedom in the context of women's rights, religious authority in the Sabarimala case became further complicated by tribal rights claims. The Mala Arya community, an Adivasi (also known as 'Scheduled Tribe') group in the area, argued that the 'deity Ayyappan is their ancestral god and it was Brahminism that, with the help of state institutions, forcefully appropriated their god and the rights over the temple' along with their land in the early nineteenth century (Thadathil, 2019). Oral histories of this community suggest that excluding women on the basis of 'age and bodily condition' is a more recent development that may have occurred along with the transformation of Ayyappan into a 'hypermasculine deity' in the 1950s (Thadathil, 2019). Religious authority and religious freedom are neither stable nor clear-cut.

Conclusion

The wide variety of Hindu perspectives on religious freedom enrich discussions of this concept, even while at times competing and conflicting with each other. In the colonial era, Hindu traditions in India and other British colonies became more standardized, in part to be recognized as a 'world religion' and to facilitate religious freedom claims. But more recently, the Sabarimala case shows how standardization is not essential to Hindu religious freedom claims; even very distinctive sects or particular temple rules have become the basis for religious freedom claims and can be influential, especially if they reinforce the authority of dominant groups. Around the world, religious freedom advocacy often elevates the perspectives of religious authority figures, at the expense of lived religion in all its multiplicity and the freedoms of marginalized groups (Hurd, 2015). The Sabarimala decision shows that robust constitutional protections of equality can sometimes offset this tendency to prioritize the authority of male, higher status, and/or religiously conservative individuals in religious freedom cases. Nevertheless, religious freedom cases in the context of Hinduism, like other religions, raise difficult questions: Who gets to decide what is a religion; which rules, practices, or beliefs constitute it; and who are its members?

Disagreement over the proper application of the idea of religious freedom in disputes over caste, religious minorities, and women reveal tensions between the goals of religious freedom and equality – tensions that are not unique to Hinduism or India. Indeed, these examples from India highlight one of the most pressing questions in religious freedom debates around the world today: To what extent should we be religiously free to discriminate? Upper caste, majoritarian, and patriarchal Hindu perspectives on religious freedom, the ideological offshoots of Savarkar, are on the rise, to the detriment of lower castes, minorities, and women (Nussbaum, 2007; Mishra, 2017: 253–255, 271–272). Thus, the rich tradition of countervailing views on Hinduism and religious freedom requires amplification. These include Sarojini Naidu's insight that you can cherish your own religion while accommodating and respecting other religions and B. R. Ambedkar's recognition that freedom without equality and fraternity is not truly democracy. In such articulations, religious equality and freedom are indivisible and mutually reinforcing.

In addition to noting that equal access to religious freedom is key, Indian intellectuals writing on secularism have also been more willing than many of their Western counterparts to recognize that state action, and not just separation, constitutes religious freedom. These intellectuals, discussed above, range from early national leaders Jawaharlal Nehru and S. Radhakrishnan to contemporary scholar Amartya Sen. The Indian Constitution's religious freedom clause does not prevent state action for social reform. Indeed, many aspects of religious freedom necessitate state action, including administering religious personal laws, state funding for religious educational institutions, and various religious regulations to achieve a form of secularism variously described as equal respect, equidistance, or basic symmetry (Teater and Jenkins, 2019).

The strength of the political clash between religious freedom and antidiscrimination principles and the power of state action in this area is epitomized by a recent development in India. Religious freedom is the purported justification for a discriminatory law, the Citizenship Amendment Act of 2019, which allows all who fled religious persecution in neighboring countries to have a track to citizenship in India – except for Muslims. Minority Muslim sects face religious persecution throughout South Asia and thus also flee for that reason. Moreover, the religious distinction in the Citizenship Amendment Act is a disturbing precedent that undermines religious freedom, secularism, and tolerance in India. Further comparative work on the politics of religious freedom is essential to understand such impasses and reveal alternatives that would better protect the freedoms of all.

Reference

Bhatt, S.R., 1992. Secularism and pluralism. In: M.M. Sankhdher (Ed.), *Secularism in India: Dilemmas and Challenges*. Deep & Deep. 261.

Brown, J. (Ed.), 2008. *Mahatma Gandhi: The Essential Writings*. Oxford University Press.

Chiriyankandath, J., 2000. Creating a secular state in a religious country: the debate in the Indian Constituent Assembly. *Commonwealth and Comparative Politics* 38, 1.

Davis, R., 2008. Tolerance and hierarchy: accommodating multiple religious paths in Hinduism. In: B. Chilton, J. Neusner (Eds.), *Religious Tolerance in World Religions*. Templeton. 360.

Hindu American Foundation, 2020. Where We Stand. Available at https://www.hafsite.org/about-us/where-we-stand#international-religious.
Hindus for Human Rights, n.d. Our Vision. Available at https://www.hindusforhumanrights.org/our-vision.
Hurd, E.S., 2015. *Beyond Religious Freedom: The New Global Politics of Religion*. Princeton University Press.
Jacobs, S., 2010. *Hinduism Today: An Introduction*. Bloomsbury Publishing.
Jaffrelot, C., 1996. *The Hindu Nationalist Movement in India*. Columbia University Press.
Jaffrelot, C. (Ed.), 2007. Introduction: the invention of an ethnic nationalism. In: C. Jaffrelot (Ed.), *Hindu Nationalism: A Reader*. Princeton University Press. 1.
Jaffrelot, C. and Kumar, N., 2018. *Dr Ambedkar and Democracy: An Anthology*. Oxford University Press.
Jeffrey, C. and Harriss, J., 2014. *Keywords for Modern India*. Oxford University Press.
Jeffrey, R., 1976. Temple-entry movement in Travancore, 1860–1940. *Social Scientist* 4, 3.
Jenkins, L.D., 2003. *Identity and Identification in India: Defining the Disadvantaged*. Routledge.
Jenkins, L.D., 2019. *Religious Freedom and Mass Conversion in India*. University of Pennsylvania Press.
Jha, S., 2002. Secularism in the constituent assembly debates, 1946–1950. *Economic and Political Weekly*. 47, 3175.
Kumar, A., 2016. Menstruation, purity and right to worship. *Economic and Political Weekly*. 51(9). Available at https://www.epw.in/journal/2016/9/web-exclusives/menstruation-purity-and-right-worship.html.
Mahmood, S. and Danchin, P., 2014. Politics of religious freedom: contested genealogies. *South Atlantic Quarterly*. 113(1), 1.
Mehta, P.B., 2004. World religions and democracy: Hinduism and self-rule. *Journal of Democracy*. 15, 108.
Mishra, P., 2017. *Age of Anger: A History of the Present*. Farrar, Straus and Giroux.
Moustafa, T., 2018. *Constituting Religion: Islam, Liberal Rights, and the Malaysian State*. Cambridge University Press.
Mukherjee, R. (Ed.), 1996. *The Penguin Gandhi Reader*. Penguin.
Naidu, S., 1925. *Speeches and Writings of Sarojini Naidu*. GA Natesan & Company.
Nussbaum, M., 2007. *The Clash Within: Democracy, Religious Violence, and India's Future*. The Belknap Press of Harvard University Press.
Parekh, B., 2003. Some reflections on the Hindu theory of tolerance. *Seminar*. 521 48.
Parekh, B., 2019. *Ethnocentric Political Theory: The Pursuit of Flawed Universals*. Springer.
Pew Research Center, 2012. The Global Religious Landscape. Available at https://www.pewforum.org/2012/12/18/global-religious-landscape-exec.
Rocklin, A., 2019. *The Regulation of Religion and the Making of Hinduism in Colonial Trinidad*. University of North Carolina Press.
Savarkar, V.D., 1969. *Hindutva: Who Is a Hindu*. Veer Savarkar Prakashan.
Savarkar, V.D., 1985. *Six Glorious Epochs of Indian History* (S. T. Godbole, Trans. and Ed.). Veer Savarkar Prakashan.
Scott, J.B., 2019. Only connect: three reflections on the sociality of secularism. *Cambridge Journal of Postcolonial Literary Inquiry*. 6, 48.
Sen, A., 2005. *The Argumentative Indian: Writings on Indian History, Culture and Identity*. Allen Lane.
Sen, R., 2019. *Articles of Faith: Religion, Secularism, and the Indian Supreme Court*. Oxford University Press.
Sharma, A., 2004. *Hinduism and Human Rights: A Conceptual Approach*. Oxford University Press.
Spinner-Halev, J., 2005. Hinduism, Christianity, and liberal religious toleration. *Political Theory*. 33 28.
Sudhish, N., 2018. Allow women into Sabarimala. Ban the men: K. R. Meera. *The Hindu*, 10 November. Available at https://www.thehindu.com/society/allow-women-into-sabarimala-ban-the-men-says-writer-kr-meera/article25452875.ece.
Sullivan, W.F., Shakman Hurd, E., Mahmood, S., Danchin, P.G. (Eds.), 2015. *Politics of Religious Freedom*. University of Chicago Press.
Teater, K.M., 2019. *Using Transnational Advocacy Networks to Challenge Restrictions on Religion: Christian Minorities in Malaysia and India*. PhD dissertation. University of Cincinnati.
Teater, K.M., Jenkins, L.D., 2019. Religious regulation in India. In: *Oxford Research Encyclopedia of Politics*. Oxford University Press.
Thadathil, A., 2019. Adivasi claims over Sabarimala highlight the importance of counter-narratives of tradition. *Economic and Political Weekly* 54(1). Available at https://www.epw.in/engage/article/adivasi-claims-over-sabarimala-highlight-the-importance-of-counter-narratives-of-tradition.
Thomas, R., 2020. Brahmins as scientists and science as Brahmins' calling: caste in an Indian Scientific Research Institute. *Public Understanding of Science*. 29(3), 306.

Varshney, A., 1993. Contested meanings: India's national identity, Hindu nationalism, and the politics of anxiety. *Daedalus* 122, 227.
Warrier, M., 2008. Diaspora. In: S. Mittal and G.R. Thursby (Eds.), *Studying Hinduism: Key Concepts and Methods*. Routledge. 86.
Williams, R.V., 2006. *Postcolonial Politics and Personal Laws: Colonial Legal Legacies and the Indian State*. Oxford University Press.
Williams, R.V., Deo, N., 2018. Hinduism and democracy: religion and politicized religion in India. In: S. Hua (Ed.), *Routledge Handbook of Politics in Asia*. Routledge. 548.
Williams, R.V., Jenkins, L.D., 2015. Secular anxieties and transnational engagements in India. In: M. Wohlrab-Sahr, M. Burchardt, M. Middell (Eds.), *Multiple Secularities Beyond the West: Religion and Modernity in the Global Age*. De Gruyter. 19.
Williams, R.V., Moktan, S., 2019. Hinduism: India, Nepal, and Beyond. In: *Oxford Research Encyclopedia of Politics*. Oxford University Press.

9

The right of religious freedom in contemporary Islamic thought

Wael Saleh and Patrice Brodeur

Introduction

What are the dominant types of religiosity (way of living a religion) in contemporary Islamic thought? What is the impact of these religiosities on the notion of the right of religious freedom? How do these different religiosities address issues such as the violation of human rights in the name of religion? These issues are intrinsically linked to the theoretical religious, philosophical, political and moral models that these religiosities offer to today's Muslims in majority Muslim countries as well as in their countries of emigration where their minority diasporic experiences influence the production of knowledge in their countries of birth. This research seeks to provide answers to these questions based on transnational perspectives on the right of religious freedom in contemporary Islamic thought.

Contemporary Muslim intellectuals relate to human rights in general and to individual freedoms in particular, especially that of conscience and of religion, along three different directions within and across Sunni and Shia thought, and sometimes even within the same school of jurisprudence (*fiqh*) in relation to certain specific legal opinions: (1) the exclusivist pole, where these rights are understood to be foreign to the Islamic tradition; (2) the inclusivist pole, where these rights are understood to be rooted in an old, pre-modern Islamic tradition that Western European philosophers or jurists of the sixteenth to eighteenth centuries 'borrowed' from the Islamic tradition (Afifi, 1994; Wafa, 1998); and (3) the in-between pole, which sways between the two previous poles, where these rights are understood to be in part rooted in pre-modern Islam, including scriptural references, and in part the result of modern thinking on human rights that emerged initially in Western legal and political philosophy especially over the last century. Scholars of Islam, whether Muslim or not, generally fall into one of these three positions, too (see Saddigh, 1979; Mayer, 2007; Diop, 1994; Pansier and Guellaty, 2000; Baderin, 2003; Baber, 2004; Waltz, 2004; Saeed and Hassan, 2016; Şentürk, 2005).

Muslim thinkers have developed different responses that can be generally categorized under one of three main types of religiosity (*tadayyun*): reformist Muslim, holistic activist

Muslim and liberal humanist Muslim.[1] The first part of this chapter gives concrete examples of from these three kinds of Muslim discourses with their respective conceptions of human rights associated with religious freedom. The second part focuses on two very specific concepts at the root of tensions within contemporary Islamic thought on the divisive notion of the right of religious freedom: apostasy (*ridda*) and heresy (*zandaqa*). Both concepts go back to the first century emergence of Islam.

Examples from three Muslim religiosities that demonstrate their respective conceptions about the right of religious freedom

Below we provide recent examples of the three above categories of religiosity. The main criterion used for their selection is the degree of autonomy (or not) given to human beings. In the first section, four examples from holistic activist islamism are given: Abu'l-A'la Mawdudi, Sayyid Qutb, Muhammad 'Abd al-Salam Faraj and The World Islamic Front's *Declaration of Jihad* signed by Osama bin Laden, Ayman al-Zawahiri, Abu Yasir Rif'ai Ahmad Taha, Sheikh Mir Hamza and Fazlur Rahman [Bangladeshi].[2] In the second section, five examples from Muslim reformism are provided: Muhammad Husayn al-Tabataba'i, Mohammad Hashim Kamali, Muhammad Sai'd al-'Ashmawy, Abdullahi A. An-Na'im and *The Charter of Makkah*, signed on 28 May 2019, by more than 1,200 muftis and scholars from 139 countries around the world.[3] In the third section, five examples from Muslim humanism are presented: Fatḥī al-Maskīnī, Abdurrahman Wahid, Fazlur Rahman [Pakistani], Sa'd al-Dīn al-Hilālī and 'Abd al-Ğawwād Yāsīn.[4]

Examples from Holistic Activist Islamism

The textual sources from the formative period of Islam often indicate that, while Muslims believed that every human being must enjoy the freedom of belief, including the freedom not to enter Islam, based on the well-known verse 'There is no compulsion in religion' (Qur'an 2:256), Muslims ought not to have the freedom to exit Islam. This comes from the argument that this verse was abrogated by the following verse revealed later: '[Believers], fight them until there is no more persecution, and all worship is devoted to God alone' (Qur'an 8:39-4). This issue of leaving Islam or apostasy (*ridda*) remains a matter of controversy and negotiation in Islam, as do many other contemporary facets of religious freedom. Although no temporal punishment for apostasy is prescribed in the Qur'an, and though the Prophet appears to have allowed some converts to Islam to leave the faith,

1 Based on the degree of autonomy or heteronomy of politics as well as on the place given to religion, current Arab-Muslim thought can be subdivided into three broad categories (all of which do not dispute their belonging to Islam as a religion): 1. heteronomous thought (activist holistic islamism); 2. compromise thought (Muslim reformism); 3. autonomous thought (Muslim humanist liberalism). See also Gauchet (1998: 14). We agree with Ṣalāḥ Sālim (2014: 17), who believes that the nuances between the different ways of thinking and the different political behaviors of these movements (jihadists, radicals, or moderates) can be explained only if one analyzes the phenomenon of political Islam as if it is static (horizontally and flatly). With a dynamic look (vertically and historically), we discover that these nuances are temporal and related to the phases that the phenomenon goes through. These nuances are the phenomenon itself but in different phases of its evolution. This phenomenon is based on the same logic that the divine directly supervises the temporal or the terrestrial.

2 These examples are cited in Anderson and Taliaferro (2014).

3 The first three examples are cited in Anderson and Taliaferro (2014).

4 The first two examples are cited in Anderson and Taliaferro (2014).

advocates of the death penalty for apostasy rely on citing the canonical *hadith*, 'Whoever changes his religion, kill him.'[5]

Abu'l-A'la Mawdudi (1903–1979), a Pakistani philosopher and founder of the *Jamaat-i-Islami*, a religious and political movement that aimed to promote Islamic values and practices, writes:

> as regards Muslims, none of them will be allowed to change creed. In case any Muslim is inclined to do so, it will be he who will be taken to task for such conduct, and not the non-Muslim individual or organization whose influence might have brought about this change of mind. The dhimmis will never be compelled to adopt a belief contrary to their conscience, and it will be perfectly within their constitutional rights if they refuse to act against their conscience or creed, so long as they do not violate the laws of the land.
>
> *(Mawdudi, 1955, 178–192)*

Mawdudi goes on to say:

> To everyone acquainted with Islamic law it is no secret that according to Islam the punishment for a Muslim who turns to kufr (infidelity, blasphemy) is execution. [...] All these collectively will assure you that from the time of the Prophet to the present day one injunction only has been continuously and uninterruptedly operative and that no room whatever remains to suggest that perhaps the punishment of the apostate is not execution.
>
> *(Mawdudi, 1994)*

Sayyid Qutb (1906–1966), a prolific writer and influential voice in the field of Islamic political philosophy, was a member of the Muslim Brotherhood. Convicted of planning to assassinate Egyptian president Gamal Abdel Nasser, he was executed in 1966. In his work *On the Nature of Jihad*, he theorizes that:

> according to the explanation of Imam Ibn Qayyim, first of all, Muslims were restrained from fighting against the polytheists and unbelievers, then permission was accorded them to fight, then they were commanded to fight against the aggressors and ultimately they were commanded to fight all the polytheists and the unbelievers. These clear verses of the Holy Quran, the traditions of the Holy Prophet prompting and inciting to Jihad, the Islamic wars of the early period, rather the entire Islamic history replete with the description of Jihad – are such eloquent testimonies in the presence of which every Muslim's heart will abhor to accept the commentary about Jihad conceived by minds having been defeated by the pressure of unfavorable conditions and treacherous propaganda of the Orientalists.
>
> *(Qutb, 1981)*

Muhammad 'Abd al-Salam Faraj (1954–1982) was a radical Egyptian thinker who wrote about jihad and was executed in 1982 for his involvement in the assassination of Egyptian president Anwar Sadat. He argues:

5 Sahih Al-Bukhari, Volume 9, Book 84, Number 57.

> It is a well-established rule of Islamic Law that the punishment of an apostate will be heavier than the punishment of someone who is by origin an infidel (and has never been a Muslim), and this in many respects. [...] Hence, it is the view of the majority (of jurists) than an apostate has to be killed, and this is in accordance with (the opinions held in) the Schools of Law of Malik, Al-Shafi'i and Ahmad (ibn Hanbal).
>
> *(Faraj, 1986)*

In the *Declaration of Jihad* by The World Islamic Front, Osama bin Laden (1957–2011), Ayman al-Zawahiri (b. 1951), Abu Yasir Rif'ai Ahmad Taha (1954–2016), Sheikh Mir Hamza and Fazlur Rahman theorize that:

> Praise be to God, revealer of the Book, controller of the clouds, defeater of factionalism, who says in His Book: 'When the forbidden months are over, wherever you find the polytheists, kill them, seize them, besiege them, ambush them.' Prayers and peace be upon our Prophet Muhammad bin Abdallah, who said, 'I have been sent with a sword in my hands so that only God may be worshipped, God who placed my livelihood under the shadow of my spear and who condemns those who disobey my orders to servility and humiliation.'
>
> *(bin Laden et al., 2005)*

Examples from Muslim Reformism

Mohammad Hashim Kamali (b. 1944) is an Afghan Islamic scholar, a former professor of law at the International Islamic University of Malaysia and the author of some influential books and articles on shari'a and Islamic jurisprudence. He thinks that:

> this discussion has emphasized the fact that the Qur'an explicitly declares freedom of religion to be one of the principles of Islam. The Qur'anic declaration to this effect, found in Sura al-Baqarah 2:256, is consistently endorsed and substantiated in numerous other contexts in the Holy Book. Unfortunately, there are those who have promoted a misleading and politically motivated discourse, which declares that Islam denies the freedom of religion, and that the Qur'anic passages which advocate this freedom were subsequently abrogated and overruled by its other provisions on the subject of jihad. The proponents of this view have used abrogation, itself a highly controversial issue, as their primary tool in an attempt to whittle away at one of the cardinal principles in the Qur'an. [...] This school of thought lacks sound reasoning and has been less than convincing in its attempt to overshadow the essence of the Qur'anic message concerning the freedom of the conscience. The unequivocal recognition of this freedom in the constitutions of the present day Muslim nations bears testimony to a decisive movement in favor of the basic rights of the individual, including the freedom to follow the religion of his or her choice.
>
> *(Kamali, 1992: 80–81)*

Muhammad Husayn al-Tabataba'i (1903–1981), an Iranian philosopher who wrote some of the most important contributions in the field of the doctrines and history of Shia Islam, argues that:

> 'There is no compulsion in the religion' negates and disapproves compulsion and coercion in religion. Religion is a set of truths which are believed in, and some of

> them are then acted upon. In short, religion is belief and faith, it is a matter of conscience, and such a thing cannot be created by coercion and compulsion. One may force someone to do a certain physical action against his will but he cannot be forced to believe against his will. Belief follows reason and understanding; and nothing but reason and understanding can create it.
>
> *(al-Tabataba'i, 1983)*

Abdullahi A. An-Na'im (b. 1946) is a Sudanese-born Muslim scholar of Islam who currently lives in the United States and teaches at Emory University. He studied the relation between Islam and human rights, on the one hand, and Islam and the secular State, on the other. According to him:

> it becomes imperative that the precise implications of religious liberty and the rights of religious minorities be authoritatively discussed and settled within the Islamic tradition. The Muslims are not to be allowed to treat religious minorities in this way because they believe that their own religious law authorizes them to do so. Otherwise, we would have to accept not only similar mistreatment of Muslim minorities in non-Islamic states, but also the complete negation of all the achievements of the domestic civil liberties and international human rights movement. If this type of argument is allowed, all forms and degrees of human rights violations, including torture and even genocide, may be rationalized or justified with reference to alleged religious or cultural norms. Cultural relativism can never be allowed to go this far.
>
> *(An-Na'im, 1987)*

Muhammad Sai'd al-'Ashmawy (1932–2013) was an Egyptian Supreme Court Justice and former head of the Court of State Security. He was a specialist in comparative and Islamic law at Cairo University and considered to be one of the most influential liberal Islamic thinkers today. He believed that not all the legal rules mentioned in the Qur'an are permanent but that some of them are temporary.

> A very specific example is slavery and slavery harems. Slavery and slave harems were mentioned in the Qur'an; as previously cited, they were not abrogated, yet they are not applied today and are forbidden by law. Even though the principle was not clear to him and to the Muslims of his time, the second caliph, 'Umar, stopped applying certain rules from the Qur'an. He also believes that all people have the right to choose their own faith without being threatened by the death penalty. Verses stating freedom of choosing one's faith have not been and never were abrogated from the Qur'an. According to the Qur'an, forcing someone to be or become a Muslim against his will is distorting the meaning of Islam and is a denial of human rights.
>
> *(al-'Ashmawy, 1998)*

Finally, two important international collective legal declarations – the Universal Islamic Declaration of Human Rights (1981) and the Cairo Declaration on Human Rights in Islam (1990) – were also considered to reflect Muslim reformism when initially written a generation ago. They both nominally affirm the idea of religious freedom but limit its protection to the freedom of conscience and worship. Yet, these documents limit the protection of all human rights, including freedom of religion, belief and worship, by retaining the requirements of normative traditional Islamic law (Anderson and Taliaferro, 2014: 6). These two declarations were the fruit of Muslim thinkers and scholars belonging to the current of Muslim reformism closer to holistic activist islamism.

That current within Muslim reformism is seen a generation later and very recently through the adoption of *The Charter of Makkah* (28 May 2019) – signed by more than 1,200 muftis and scholars of the Ummah from 139 countries – to have swayed, content-wise, toward the other side of Muslim reformism closer to Muslim liberal humanism.[6] Under the leadership of the Muslim World League, this momentous declaration may change the paradigm away from the up-till-recently dominant interpretation rooted in the theory of abrogation of *Sura al-Baqarah* 2:256 toward a new paradigm closer to Muslim liberal humanism, recognizing the right of religious freedom. Here are the five central principles of this recent declaration:

1. Men with their different ethnicities all have the same origin and are all equal in their humanity, Allah says (according to the meaning of the verses): 'O people, fear your Lord who created you from the same soul, created from her wife and then from them many men and women, and fear Allah, the One who will question you' (Women) Just as Allah has honored all human beings without exception, He says: 'We have honored Adam's sons, and carried them to the land and the sea, we gave them good things and preferred them to many of those whom We have created' (Isra).
2. The rejection of all forms of religious and ethnic racism, the denunciation of any form of arrogance based on an alleged preference granted. The best men are the most pious with their Creator, those who are most obedient to Him; as such the Prophet (peace be upon him) said, 'The best of you is the one that is most useful to people.' (Tabarâni)
3. The difference between human nations in their beliefs, cultures, natures and ways of thinking lies in the will and wisdom of Allah. It is a universal law that He has established. It is therefore much better to submit to it than to seek to oppose it, because that would establish harmony and peace. [...]
4. The religious and cultural divergence in societies does not necessarily imply conflict, but rather it should encourage civilization to cooperate, to establish positive relations for dialogue, to excel in order to be a service to humanity as well as to its happiness, to seek unifying common denominators, to invest in the construction of a global citizenship based on values, justice, legitimate freedoms, respectful exchanges and the search for good for all.
5. The basis of celestial religions is the same. It is in the One Allah without associating anything with it, in its laws and its different ways. Moreover, it is absolutely forbidden to mix religion with bad policies, no matter who it is.[7]

Examples from Muslim Liberal Humanism

Abdurrahman Wahid (1940–2009), an Indonesian Muslim religious and political leader who served as president of Indonesia from 1999 to 2001, argues:

> Sanctions against freedom of religious inquiry and expression act to stop the developmental process of religious understanding dead in its tracks. They conflate the sanctioning authority's current, limited grasp of the truth with ultimate Truth itself, and thereby transform religion from a path to the Divine into a 'divinized' goal, whose

6 See https://www.saudiembassy.net/sites/default/files/Charter%20of%20Makkah-%20Unofficial%20Translation.pdf.

7 See the *Charter of Mecca* translated into French, https://themwl.org/fr/node/36089.

features and confines are generally dictated by those with an all-too-human agenda of earthly power and control.

(Wahid, 2011: xxi)

Fazlur Rahman (1919–1988), a Pakistani modernist scholar and philosopher of Islam, advocates for the recognition of religious diversity in the Qur'an.

> In conformity with this strong rejection of exclusivism and election, the Qur'an repeatedly recognizes the existence of good people in other communities – Jews, Christians, Sabaeans – just as it recognizes the people of faith in Islam: 'Those who believe [Muslims], the Jews, the Christians, and the Sabaeans – whosoever believe in God and the Last Day and do good deeds, they shall have their reward from their Lord, shall have nothing to fear, nor shall they come to grief.' (Qur'an 2:62; cf. 5:69)
>
> In both verses, the vast majority of Muslim commentators exercise themselves fruitlessly to avoid having to admit the obvious meaning: that those – from any section of humankind – who believe in God and the Last Day and do good deeds are saved. They either say that by Jews, Christians, and Sabaeans here are meant those who have actually become 'Muslims' – which interpretation is clearly belied by the fact that 'Muslims' constitute only the first of the four groups of 'those who believe' – or that they were those good Jews, Christians, and Sabaeans who lived before the advent of the Prophet Muhammad – which is an even worse tour de force. [...] The logic of this recognition of universal goodness, with belief in one God and the Last Day as its necessary underpinning, demands, of course, that the Muslim community be recognized as a community among communities
>
> *(Rahman, 2009: 166).*

Saʿd al-Dīn al-Hilālī (b. 1954), a professor of Comparative Islamic Jurisprudence at the University of Al-Azhar, shows that:

> when it comes to the finalities and the supreme interests (*al-maqāṣid wa-l-maṣāliḥ al-'ulyā*) of the shari'ah, the preservation of the religion, as a goal of the šarī'a is translated by the protection of all the religions and consequently, by the defense of the freedom of belief (*ḥurriyyat al-i'tiqād*) of all citizens. The other purposes or objectives of the finalities and the supreme interests, such as the protection of human life and property, must also be applied to all human beings, regardless of their religious affiliation.
>
> *(Saleh, 2019)*

ʿAbd al-Ǧawwād Yāsīn (b. 1954), one of the most read Egyptian intellectuals after the Arab Spring, observes that:

> the dimensions of the text relating to the uniqueness of God and the invariable ethical framework have been transmitted independently of social references. In this sense, he sees the only texts that can be described as sacred, invariable and timeless. On the other hand, the other texts of both social and juridical nature, although they are in the Koran, are eminently temporal. In his daily practice, in his interference

> with the world that receives this text, religion is transformed into devotion, piety, religiosity. Therefore, religious practice (*tadayyun*) is a mutation of religion (*dīn*); part of the historical culture, which is intrinsically variable, is absolutized and becomes invariable; the conflict is inevitable and the tensions between the social world and the fixation of the devotional are chronic. Once religion interacts with the social, it is transformed and becomes a social factor that influences other social factors; it is in turn influenced by these factors, a socially and temporally marked influence.
>
> *(Saleh, 2019)*

Finally, for Fatḥī al-Maskīnī (b. 1961), a Tunisian university professor, philosopher and translator:

> free faith does not abandon our sources but changes the relationship with them. A free believer is rebellious but does not rely on any hatred in order to prove his freedom. Free faith does not require a ready consensus. It is not an accidental behavior. Today, the horizon of Western culture in its post-secular phase has confirmed that faith is a personal choice. But a free believer knows that there is no meaning to what is personal without living in a society that consecrates the individual. The history of the nation attests to the fact that it can be a 'person' (adult) without being an 'individual' (enjoying a free social or existential position). In a collective culture, what is individual may be perceived as dangerous. Therefore, while free faith rejects identity withdrawal, it still needs to belong. Hence, we understand how individuality can not be used as a pretext against belonging.
>
> *(Maskīnī, 2018)*

Fatḥī al-Maskīnī goes on to say that we must always take the concept of free faith

> as an interpretation workshop, not as a ready doctrine. This is why there is no culture that does not contain elements of free faith. But the readers of any tradition are not yet ready for free faith. Our relationship with the sources of ourselves is no longer doctrinal, but is about the model of life that it proposes to us. This is why there is no one confession to which we must belong automatically. However, this confession of our choice offers a unique moral/ethical framework that we must ourselves reconstitute freely. There is no supremacy of one culture above another; any culture allows a person to experiment free faith despite the content of this confession.
>
> *(Maskīnī, 2018)*

The current of holistic activist islamism invoking these same texts urges a return to an earlier, 'purer' Islam that forbids conversion away from Islam, as well as proselytism on the part of non-Muslims towards Muslims. This interpretation of Islam denies both non-Muslims and disfavored Muslims equal status in law and society. As for the current of Muslim reformism, it increasingly advocates an approach toward the Qur'an and Islamic jurisprudence that would place Islam on a path toward broader appreciation of religious freedom, including equality under the law for all religious individuals and groups. Finally, Muslim liberal humanism criticizes holistic activist islamism in its ability to manipulate religion in the realm of politics; it distinguishes between religion and religious devotion (*tadayyun*), deconstructs the authority of Islamic jurisprudence (*fiqh*) and develops a theory of human religious freedom in the name of Islam.[8] According to al-Hilâlî in particular, pluralism in *fiqh* can be a source of secularism and humanity in Islam. Similarly, according to Yâsîn, a post-text approach is able to free the Muslim from the control of the text and its interpretations (Saleh, 2019).

In concluding the first part of this chapter, we can say that each one of these three contemporary religiosities influences the ways its followers define Islam, and from there, their notion of human rights in general and the right of religious freedom in particular. The myriad perspectives from these three currents in contemporary Muslim religiosities demonstrate how contested this right of religious freedom remains to this day. While Qur'an 2:256 famously states that there is to be 'no coercion in religion,' other texts seem to endorse contradictory principles, appearing to enjoin coercion, sometimes even violent coercion, in matters of conscience and religious practice.

In the next part of this chapter, the focus will be on two very specific concepts related to religious freedom: apostasy (*ridda*) and heresy (*zandaqa*).

The question of apostasy and heresy in contemporary Islamic thought

As mentioned at the beginning of the previous section, early Islamic texts mention both that every human being must enjoy the freedom of belief, including the freedom not to enter Islam, and that Muslims ought not to have the freedom to exit Islam [i.e., apostasy (*ridda*)].[9] This difference emerged after the death of the Prophet, based on the canonical *hadith*, 'Whoever changes his religion, kill him.' On the basis of this *hadith* and similar traditions, the early Islamic schools of jurisprudence constructed a law of apostasy that prescribed the death penalty for offenders. The holistic activist islamism and the majority trend within Muslim reformism[10] thus hold that the death penalty for leaving Islam is 'divine law,' based on the teachings of the Qur'an and the practice (Sunna) of the Prophet Muhammad.

Al-Qaradawi (b. 1926), a holistic activist Islamist, demonstrates that there are degrees of prohibition within what is forbidden and what is allowed: the most important is undoubtedly the disbelief or denial of God, while the least important is a deplorable action. Furthermore, disbelief includes five degrees very different from each other: disbelief as atheism and denial; disbelief as associationism; disbelief of the People of the book; disbelief of apostates (the worst form of unbelief) and disbelief of hypocrites (Al-Qardâwî, 2007: 161–171).

---

8 We are aware that this trend is not yet dominant among Muslim intellectuals or in Muslim societies. Freedom of religion and worship has often been understood – and practiced – differently for Muslims than for non-Muslims. This has historical roots in the concept of dhimma , a protected but inferior status for non-Muslims granted in traditional Islamic law. Strains of thought in strong tension with a robust conception of religious freedom have been present in the Islamic tradition from the beginning, and they continue to exercise an important influence in many Muslim majority societies. See in particular Anderson and Taliaferro (2014: 6).

9 Apostasy, blasphemy and religious infidelity are interlinked: pronouncing certain words, expressing certain gestures, may imply an exit from Islam. The concept of harṭaqa [heresy] is of late introduction, by analogy with Christian discourse (Avon, 2019).

10 The most egregious example of the fact that the two streams often take the same position on the issue of apostasy is the case of Nasr Hamid Abu Zayd (1943–2010), who was an Egyptian Qur'anic thinker, author, academic, and one of the leading liberal theologians in Islam. Since Islamic law prohibits the marriage of a believer to an apostate, the courts declared his marriage to his wife Ebtehal null and void. A fatwa issued by Ayman al-Zawahiri from al-Jihad, the underground terrorist group responsible for assassinating Anwar Sadat, decreed that it was an Islamic duty that he be killed. A group of scholars, known as the Front of Al-Azhar Scholars, in an effort to force his repentance, called on the government to carry out the legal punishment for apostasy (i.e., death).

Concerning the disbelief of apostates, Al-Qaradawi confirms that according to Muslim scholars, the worst form of disbelief is apostasy. This is to abjure Islam after being guided by God. Apostasy is considered, in this case, a betrayal of Islam and its community, because of the ensuing changes of allegiance, and deviations that involve the passage from one community to another: it is like treason of the homeland since the individual presents his allegiance to another state and to another people, thus giving them his sympathy and support. It is for this reason that Islam has been very rigorous in the fight against apostasy. Apostates constitute a danger to the doctrinal foundations of a society, its core identity (Al-Qardâwî, 2007: 167–168).

> Some contemporary writers who are not versed in religious knowledge object to the penalty of proclaimed apostasy being death by saying that this penalty is not mentioned in the Qur'an. It is only mentioned in a hadith ahad (hadith that is narrated by people whose number does not reach that of the mutawatir, which is hadith that is narrated by such a large number of people that they cannot be expected to agree upon a lie, all of them together); and hadiths ahad, according to them, are not taken as evidences for the legal punishments prescribed by Shari'ah.
>
> But this objection is refutable in many aspects as follows. First, according to the scholarly consensus, the authentic Sunna is a source for applied rulings in shari'a. Almighty Allah says, [Say: Obey Allah and obey the Messenger] (AnNur 24:54). He also says, [Whoso obeyeth the Messenger obeyeth Allah] (AnNisaa' 4:80). As for the hadiths specifying the death penalty for apostates, they have been proven to be authentic. Besides, they were put into effect by the Companions in the era of the Rightly-Guided Caliphs.
>
> *(Al-Qaradawi, 2006)*

Ali Gomaa (b. 1952) is an Egyptian Islamic scholar, jurist and public figure who served as the eighteenth Grand Mufti of Egypt (2003–2013) through *Dar al-Ifta al-Misriyyah* and is considered a reformist. He says:

> They disregard the Muslim doctrine of freedom of belief expressed by God's words, 'There is no compulsion in religion. Truth stands out clear from error' (Qur'an 2:256). [...] These examples from the age of legislation caused Muslim jurists to understand the issue of 'executing apostates' as being unrelated to freedom of belief, freedom of thought, or persecution. The source texts that strictly called for the imposition of such a punishment do not refer to leaving Islam as much as coming out against Islam. Coming out against Islam is considered a crime against the public order of the state, just as it represents a coming out against the rulings of the religion that have been embraced by the community. In this case, apostasy is tantamount to high treason, which is forbidden by all legal systems, constitutions, and laws. [...] The execution of apostates was not just for apostasy. Rather, it was due to an additional factor that divides the Muslim community: using apostasy to cause Muslims to leave their religion.
>
> *(Gomaa, 2011, 83–85)*

As for one Shi'ite school of jurisprudence,[11] the judgments are very similar when it comes to men, based on the argument that apostasy constitutes a treason to Islam. The norm is that an apostate needs to be killed. Yet, according to Shaykh al-Mufid, al-Muqni'ah, there are four major differences between the above chart for Sunni Islam and the dominant position in Twelver Shi'ite Islam.

The first difference is that in Twelver Shi'ite Islam, the dominant position is to automatically distinguish between how to treat men versus women apostates: the latter is not subject to the death penalty. This position exists also in Sunni Islam, but only in the Hanafi school of jurisprudence.

The second difference is that Twelver Shi'ite Islam introduces a distinction in the category of *murtad* between:

1. 'Murtad Fitri' means a person who is born of a Muslim parent and then he rejects Islam. 'Fitrah' means creation. The term 'murtad fitri' implies that the person has apostated from the faith in which he was born.
2. 'Murtad Milli' means a person who converted to Islam and then later on rejected Islam. Milli is from millat which means religion. The term 'murtad milli' implies that the person has apostated from his religion and the Muslim community.

The murtad fitri is given the death penalty without any delay. The murtad milli is given a chance to repent only for three days.

The third difference is that in Twelver Shi'ite Islam, the dominant position is to give to any Shi'ite Muslim the right to apply the death penalty on the apostate. In Sunni Islam, the dominant position is to give this right only to those Muslims who carry political or juridical authority.

The fourth difference is that in the writings of some of the Shi'ah jurists, one gets the sense that the punishment of murtad is to be implemented only in dāru'l-Islām (i.e., the Muslim world), and that if the murtad flees to dāru 'l-kufr (i.e., the abode of kufr), then he is not to be pursued (al-Mufid, 1410: 781; at-Tusi, 1408: 424–425; al-Hilli, 1409: 961–962).

Another Twelver Shi'ite reference is that of Ayatollah Ruhollah Khomeini. He abounds in the same direction, with one additional distinction: he adds a section on the rights of minorities, understood as being constituted of two groups: (1) those apostates whose previous allegiance was with one of the people of the Book, and thus treated as the above *murtad milli*; and (2) those apostate whose previous allegiance was with communities other than Islam or with one of the people of the Book. In this latter case, they are to be considered 'not acceptable. Further, they will be counted among the hostile groups.' By deduction, it seems that those apostate who come from this second background are also to be treated with the death penalty (Khomeini, 1984).

The Muslim liberal humanist Mohammad Hashim Kamali (b. 1944) has summarized Ibn Taymiyyah's treatment of the Qur'anic evidence concerning the death penalty for blasphemy, and he ventures to say that it does not sustain the conclusions that he has drawn from it.

> The Qur'an has made no reference to the death penalty for blasphemy, and the text does not warrant the conclusion that it is a Qur'anic obligation, or a prescribed punishment or a mandate. [...] The scholastic doctrines of the madhahib treated blasphemy and apostasy on the same footing and viewed blasphemy as an extension of

11 See the transcript of the lectures of the late Ayatullāh al-Khu'ā by Shaykh al-Gharawi, *at-Tanqāh* , Vol. 3, 224–229 (Sayyid Muhammad Rizvi, Apostacy in Islam, in https://www.al-islam.org/articles/apostacy-islam-sayyid-muhammad-rizvi).

> apostasy, a position which is no longer justified. Furthermore, due to a change in the character of the nation-state, they can no longer be seen as political crimes in the first place, nor do they present a serious challenge to the security of the state. It would therefore be eminently justified for these changes to be reflected in the law that is applied to blasphemy and apostasy respectively.
>
> *(Kamali 1997: 243–250)*

Mohamed Talbi (1921–2017), a Tunisian historian and professor, and another Muslim humanist intellectual, thought that:

> From a Muslim perspective, and on the basis of the Qur'an's basic teachings, whose letter and spirit we have tried to adduce, religious liberty is fundamentally and ultimately an act of respect for God's sovereignty and for the mystery of God's plan for humanity, which has been given the terrible privilege of shaping entirely on its own responsibility its destiny on earth and hereafter. Ultimately, to respect humanity's freedom is to respect God's plan. To be a true Muslim is to submit to this plan. It is to put one's self, voluntarily and freely, with confidence and love, into the hands of God.
>
> *(Talbi, 2006, 105–117)*

Finally, Sa'd al-Dīn Al-Hilâlî (b. 1954) argues that apostasy is not to be understood as an aggression against Islam, but rather as a right existing in Islam, as was noted a long time ago by Omar ibn al-Khattâb (584–644), Al-Nakha'i (670–717) and Al-Thawrī (716–778). He notices also that *al-zandaqa* is a Persian word that is not cited in the Qur'an, nor in the Sunna. In the contemporary context of nation-states in which sovereignty belongs to the people, Al-Hilâlî argues that it is totally Islamic to understand that citizens have all the rights related to the practice of religious freedom (Al-Hilālī, 2012: 186–187).

Conclusion

A very broad range of arguments can be found in the rich Islamic tradition either in favor of or against various positions on the treatment to be given to apostates in Islam. These arguments go in almost all, and often contrary, directions. This chapter offered a small selection of past and present understandings about apostasy and heresy that are used among Muslims worldwide today. On that basis, it is possible to conclude that religious freedom in general is a contested human right within Islam. For example, while Qur'an 2:256 famously states that there is to be 'no coercion in religion,' other texts seem to endorse contradictory principles, appearing to enjoin coercion, sometimes even violent coercion, in matters of conscience and religious beliefs and practices. A reductionist logical tendency is to cite mostly only one or two Qur'anic verses and *ahâdîth* that seem to favor one's argument. The challenge is to look at the whole picture. In the Qur'an, there are 21 Meccan suras[12] and 28 Medinan suras[13] that touch upon questions of religious freedom alone (i.e., only one among many human rights). There are also at least 18

12 Qur'an 6:106-108; 6:164; 10:19; 10:40-43; 10:69-70; 10:99-100; 10:108; 11:118-119; 15:95-96; 16:82; 16:125-126; 26:3-4; 27:80-81; 27:92; 29:46; 35:23-24; 38:65-67; 39:41; 50:45; 88:21-24; 109:1-6. See Abdel Haleem (2005).

13 Qur'an 2:62; 2:109; 2:111-113; 2:135-136; 2:190-194; 2:216-218; 2:256; 3:75; 3:84-85; 3:110-115; 3:199-200; 4:59; 4:88-91; 4:136-138; 5:5; 5:32-34; 5:51; 5:57-58; 5:69; 8:39-40; 8:60-61; 9:5-6; 9:12-14; 9:29; 22:17; 22:39-40; 24:27-28; 60:7-9. See Abdel Haleem (2005).

ahâdîth on this same topic.[14] Roughly half of those Qur'anic verses can be literally interpreted to condone religious freedom, while the other half limit it to different degrees. When a contextual approach is used to interpret their meanings, it is possible to conclude that Qur'anic ethics supports religious freedom.

The best way to make sense of this diversity of opinions is to examine the underlying epistemological roots behind the hermeneutical arguments given by different sides. If the root is a positivist one, then the conclusion remains in line with the millennial-old tradition to administer the death penalty to the apostate. If the root is a historical-critical one, then many contemporary Muslims reach the conclusion that Islam does provide for all rights associated with Artcile 18 of the Universal Declaration of Human Rights that refers to freedom of religion, belief, and conscience. This latter approach allows us to understand how the still-dominant position of treating apostasy with the death penalty emerged during the early history of a fragile nascent community of Muslims in Arabia who felt threatened by any apostate men who could potentially take up arms against them. Whether then or now, identity and power dynamics have shaped the processes by which various competing religiosities have coexisted and developed within Muslim communities worldwide. These dynamics are at the center of how contemporary religiosities affect perceptions of what does or does not constitute human rights in general and the right to religious freedom in particular.

Further reading

Abu Zayd, N., 2004. On being accused of apostasy. In: N.A. Zayd, E. Nelson (Eds.), *Voice of an Exile: Reflections on Islam*. Praeger.

Khan, M.M., 1984. *The Translation of the Meanings of Sahih Al-Bukhari*, vols. 2–9. Kitab Bhavan.

Peters, R., 2005. *Crime and Punishment in Islamic Law. Theory and Practice from the Sixteen to the Twenty-first Century*. Cambridge University Press.

Picaudou, N., 2010. *L'Islam entre religion et idéologie. Essai sur la modernité musulmane*. Gallimard.

Saleh, W., 2016. *The State's Prism Design of the Link between Religious and Politics in Modern and Contemporary Egyptian Thought (2011–2015): Continuities, Evolutions and Breaks*. PhD dissertation. University of Montreal.

Sbat, H., 2016. *Les garanties de protection des non-musulmans dans le droit islamique*. Dar al-Kotob al-Ilmiya.

References

Abdel Haleem, M.A.S., 2005. *The Qur'an: A New Translation*. Oxford University Press.

Afifi, M.S., 1994. *al-Mujtama' al-islâmî wa huquq al-insân*. Dar al-Fikr.

Al-'Ashmawy, M.S., 1998. On conflicting Islamic views on human rights source. In: C. Fluehr-Lobban (Ed.), *Against Islamic Extremism: The Writings of Muhammad Sai'd al-'Ashmawy*. University Press of Florida, 123.

Al-Hilālī, S., 2012. *al-Islām wainsāniyat al-dawlah [Islam and Humanity in the State]*. al-Hay'ah al-Misriyah al-'Āmmah lil-Kitāb.

al-Hilli, M., 1409. *Sharā'I' al-Islām*, vol. 4. al-Istiqlāl.

al-Mufid, S., 1410. *al-Muqni'ah*. Jami'a Mudarrisin.

14 Sahih al-Bukhari: On Jewish Funerals; On the Treaty of Hudaibiya; On Jihad; On Non-Muslim Minorities; On Criminal Apostates; On the Punishment for Apostasy (I); On the Punishment for Apostasy (II); On Privacy; On the Fallible Judgment of Muhammad; On the Apostasy Wars; On a Bedouin Leaving Islam; On the People of the Book; Sahih Muslim: On Accusations of Unbelief; On Conduct in War; On the Execution and Expulsion of Medinan Jews; On Muslim Rulers; Ali ibn Abu Talib: on Rights and Government; On Treaties. See www.sunnah.com.

Al-Qaradawi, Y., 2006. *Apostasy Major and Minor*. Available at https://archive.islamonline.net/14930.

Al-Qardâwî, Y., 2007. *La science des priorités*. Maison d'Ennour.

Al-Tabataba'i, M.H., 1983. On Qur'an 2:256 ('There is no compulsion in the religion…'). In: S.A. Rizvi (Trans.), *Tafsir al-Mizan*. World Organization for Islamic Services.

Anderson, M., Taliaferro, K., 2014. *Islam and Religious Freedom: A Sourcebook of Scriptural, Theological, and Legal Texts*. Berkley Center for Religion, Peace & World Affairs Georgetown University.

An-Na'im, A.A., 1987. Religious minorities under Islamic law and the limits of cultural relativism. *Human Rights Quarterly*. 9(1), 1.

at-Tusi, I.H., 1408. *al-Wasilah ila Nayli 'l-Fadilah*. Maktaba as-Sayyid al-Mar'ashi.

Avon, D., 2019. *Du droit religieux dans le droit étatique, approche historique de la législation anti-blasphème dans les États à référence musulmane*. ICP.

Baber, J., 2004. The relationship between the constitution, the Sharīʻa and the Fiqh: the jurisprudence of Egypt's Supreme Constitutional Court. *Zeitschrift für ausländisches öffentliches Recht und Völkerrecht/Heidelberg Journal of International Law*. 64(4), 881.

Baderin, M., 2003. *International Human Rights and Islamic Law*. Oxford University Press.

Bin Laden, O., Al-Zawahiri, A., Rifʼai Ahmad Taha, A.Y., Mir Hamza, S., Rahman, F., 2005. The world Islamic Front's declaration of Jihad. In: B. Lawrence (Ed.), *Messages to the World: The Statements of Osama Bin Laden*. Verso, 59.

Diop, S., 1994. Islam et droits de l'Homme. Une problématique actuelle. Un impact certain. In: G. Conac, A. Amor (Eds.), *Islam et droits de l'Homme*. Economica.

Faraj, M.A., 1986. On apostasy and Jihad. In: *The Neglected Duty: The Creed of Sadat's Assassins and Islamic Resurgence in the Middle East* (J. J. G. Jansen, Trans.). Macmillan, 169.

Gauchet, M., 1998. *La religion dans la démocratie. Parcours de la laïcité*. Gallimard.

Gomaa, A., 2011. On apostasy. In: T. al-Ghawhary, N. Friedlander (Trans.), *Responding from the Tradition: One Hundred Contemporary Fatwas by the Grand Mufti of Egypt*. Fons Vitae, 83.

Kamali, M.H., 1992. The freedom of religion in Islamic law. *Capital Law Review*. 21(2), 63.

Kamali, M.H., 1997. *Freedom of Expression in Islam*. Islamic Texts Society.

Khomeini, A.R., 1984. On apostasy and non-Muslims. In: J. Borujerdi (Trans.), *A Clarification of Questions: An Unabridged Translation of Resaleh Towzih al-Masael*. Westview Press, 428.

Maskīnī, F., 2018. *al-Īmān al-ḥurr, aw, mā baʻda al-millah: mabāḥith fī falsafat al-dīn [Free Belief]*. Mu'minūn bi-lā Ḥudūd lil-Dirāsāt wa-al-Abḥāth.

Mawdudi, A., 1955. On the rights of non-Muslims in an Islamic state. In: A. Mawdudi (Ed.), *Islamic Law and Constitution*. Jamaat-e-Islami Publications.

Mawdudi, A., 1994. On the punishment of the apostate according to Islamic law. In: S. Husain, E. Hahn (Trans.), *The Punishment of the Apostate According to Islamic Law*. Available at http://www.answering-islam.org/Hahn/Mawdudi.

Mayer, A.E., 2007. *Islam and Human Rights. Tradition and Politics*. Westview Press.

Pansier, F.J., Guellaty, K., 2000. *Le droit musulman*. PUF.

Qutb, S., 1981. On the nature of Jihad. In: S. Badrul Hasan (Trans.), *Sayyid Qutb's Milestones*. International Islamic Publishers, 49.

Rahman, F., 2009. *Major Themes of the Qur'an*. University of Chicago Press.

Saddigh, A.M., 1979. *La conception islamique des droits de l'homme et leur mise en œuvre par le droit positif des Etats arabes*. Dissertation. Université de Nice.

Saeed, A., Hassan, S., 2016. *Freedom of Religion, Apostasy and Islam*. Routledge.

Saleh, W., 2019. Du droit musulman au droit humain au nom de l'islam. *Midéo* 34. Available at http://journals.openedition.org/mideo/2882.

Sālim, Ṣ., 2014. *al asatyr al mouassisa li al islam al siyassi [Les mythes fondateurs de l'islam politique]*, vol. 2. al-Hay'ah al-Miṣrīyah al-ʻĀmmah lil-Kitāb.

Şentürk, R., 2005. Sociology of rights: 'I am therefore I have rights': human rights in Islam between Universalistic and Communalistic perspectives. *Muslim World Journal of Human Rights*. 2(1), 1.

Talbi, M., 2006. On religious liberty. In: M. Kamrava (Ed.), *The New Voices of Islam: Rethinking Politics and Modernity*. University of California Press, 105.

Wafa, A., 1998. *Human Rights in Islam*. The World Islamic League.

Wahid, A., 2011. On anti-defamation legislation. In: N. Shea, P. Marshall (Eds.), *Silenced: How Apostasy and Blasphemy Codes are Choking Religious Freedom Worldwide*. Oxford University Press, xxi.

Waltz, S., 2004. Universal human rights: the contribution of Muslim states. *Human Rights Quarterly*. 26(4), 799.

10
Jewish perspectives

Matthew LaGrone

Introduction

Monarchy came late to Israel, relative to its Near Eastern peers. It arrived as an accommodation, a concession to human fallibility and weakness, the understandable desire for security and yet a troubling lack of faith. The Israelites demanded that the judge Samuel deliver a king, in order to be like the nations. 'To be like the nations' is biblical shorthand for idolatry, to engage in practices forbidden to the people Israel. Ideally, Israel was to be a theocracy, a commonwealth under the rule of God alone. God commands Samuel to appoint a king, but the people's discontent is not his fault: 'For it is not you that they have rejected; it is Me they have rejected as their king' (I Samuel 8: 7).[1]

Like the institution of kingship, freedom of religion or belief in Judaism – and any enduring faith tradition, I would say – is a kind of accommodation. Judaism, like its fellow Abrahamic faiths Christianity and Islam, is a religion of the final revelation. And if you claim to be the possessor of this singular revelation, and maintain that other revelations are flawed, imperfect at best, or fraudulent at worst, where does one find space for the freedom of religion for others? What do you do when you believe that the revelation you have received is uniquely true? Other faiths might teach prudential truths and truths that are conventional, practical, and available to reason. They might teach the natural law that precedes revelation, but they do not have the fullness of revelation. Looked at in this way, ought not members of that tradition try to compel others to accept it? Despite scattered exceptions such as forced conversions during Maccabean rule, the missionary impulse in Judaism has always been muted compared to Christianity and Islam (and Buddhism, for that matter). Pathways for conversion to Judaism exist, but rarely has this led to religious compulsion.

Yet, that same revelation contains directions for living with others outside the covenanted community and instructions regarding members of that community who have strayed from covenantal norms. Freedom of religion was not a cognitively or socially available category in the ancient world; the language simply wasn't there. However, the sources of Judaism – the Torah and Talmud, especially – are for this time and all times, responsive to need and changing conditions. We now have the language of freedom of religion and belief, and this essay is an

1 All biblical quotations are from *Tanakh*, 1985.

attempt to sort out how that language fits within Jewish scripture, legal traditions, and philosophical speculations.

Freedom of religion is not just about the relationship between Jews and gentiles, but also within Judaism itself. There is a (fruitful) tension between the belief in a commanding God and the belief in conscience. Several rabbinic parables traverse the knotty problem of God's omnipotence and the moral necessity of human free choice (whether for good or ill). We see this tension in a famous story from the Talmud (Shabbat 88a). God tells the wandering people, assembled at the foot of Mt. Sinai, that the mountain will be placed over them if they do not accept His commandments. The mountain would be their grave. There is a rabbinic protest: coercion cannot bring faithful adherence and acceptance. Only later, says one rabbi, during the time of Esther, did Jews, uncoerced by divine command, 'confirm that which they had already accepted.'[2]

A second rabbinic narrative indicates that the covenant was freely accepted by the Israelites, based on their historical experience of God's providential care:

> 'I the Lord am your God' (Exod. 20: 2). Why were the Ten Commandments not proclaimed at the beginning of the Torah? ... A parable: A human king entered a province. His servants said to him: Issue decrees upon the people. He answered: No! Once they have accepted my reign I shall issue decrees upon them. If they do not accept my reign, why should they accept my decrees?
>
> Similarly, God said to Israel: 'I the Lord am your God who brought you out of the land of Egypt. You shall have no other Gods.' He [thus] said to them: 'Am I He whose reign you have accepted in Egypt?' They replied: 'Yes;' [so he went on] – 'Now, just as you have accepted My reign, accept My decrees.'
>
> *(Lorberbaum et al., 2003: 27)*

The Torah commands worship of the one God, the God of Israel who is also the God of the whole world. The command to worship God alone gets its legitimacy from God's role in the liberation of the Israelites from Egyptian bondage. God is not Pharaoh. And while God chose Israel, the latter freely consented to God's sovereignty. This narrative demonstrates how space is created for the freedom of religion within a religion of revelation.

The biblical, rabbinic, medieval, and modern sources that we will address are not extended meditations on the nature of religious freedom or belief. What we will see throughout the texts surveyed here is a bewildering variety of divergent convictions and rationales about religious freedom. Of course, there are sociological and economic considerations in the development of a theory of freedom of religion, but it is the theological justifications that make that development interesting, the belief that the interpreter is following, through traditional hermeneutical techniques, God's command.

There are two regions for thinking through freedom of religion or belief. The first region is external; that is, how do Jews understand other religious practices and how they fit into the conceptual categories that Jews use. The other region is internal; that is, how Judaism defines its teachings and practices to its adherents and requires fidelity to those teachings and practices, and what are the consequences for nonadherence.

2 All Talmudic references are from https://www.sefaria.org, which is under license with Koren Publishers' translation of the Babylonian Talmud by Adin Steinsaltz. Steinsaltz's translation is by general acclamation the best English language translation.

To explain how the sources of Judaism discuss freedom of religion or belief, this essay highlights these key areas: covenant; idolatry; Noahide law; how to judge the status of gentiles, from pagans to Christians and Muslims; and, lastly, how to negotiate freedom of religion or belief in a liberal democratic order. The essay draws upon, among many other texts, essential sources such as the Torah, the foundation for any legitimate Jewish theology and philosophy; the Talmud, the authoritative rabbinic interpretation of the Torah; Maimonides' *Mishneh Torah*, the outstanding medieval work of Jewish thought and law; and Moses Mendelssohn's *Jerusalem*, which lays out a case for Jewish integration in the modern state, creating the terms for the Jewish debate over how to navigate choices in the contemporary liberal democratic order, hitched to discussions of how the creation of the state of Israel after World War II and the Holocaust would deal with Jewish sovereignty over non-Jews for the first time in almost 2,000 years.

Covenant

The relationship between God and Israel (the proper name for the Jewish people) is covenantal, a bond of shared trust, interest, and love. It is, writes Jonathan Sacks, 'the mutual commitment between God and the people Israel' (Sacks, 1992: 8). The covenant (*brit*) sets the moral and spiritual expectations for Jews in their connection to God, each other, and the world. Because the boundaries of ancient Israel's religious life were circumscribed by a series of covenants, religious freedom was not possible in the modern sense of the term, at least in the sense of total liberty in following one's own religious desires. In ancient Judaism (and for observant Jews today), the covenant between God and Israel determined what was allowed and what was forbidden for the community; religious choices and constraints were not creations of individual conscience or the state. In modern legal terms, the covenant was the bright-line test for the legitimate and the illegitimate, the measure by which Jews judge themselves and others, and will be judged by God.

The covenant exists perpetually, unlike a time-bound contract. Contracts have provisions for when one side or the other violates its terms: there may be redress by either eliminating the contract altogether or negotiating new terms. The covenant can be wounded, violated, or harmed, but its obligations remain in effect. Contracts are the result of negotiations; the covenant was not. The former is transactional, while the latter is indissolubly joined. As Richard Rubenstein notes, for traditional Jews 'obedience to the terms of the covenant is the path of life' (Rubenstein, 1988: 203).

Tradition identifies three major covenants in the Torah. First, there is a universal covenant made with Noah, who represents the human as such. The rabbis maintained that the covenant with Noah persists with his descendants; that is, all of us. While this covenant covers all peoples, it is especially significant for non-Jews. For gentiles, a wider range of religious options, including conversion to Judaism or the practice of ancestral faith, was available. So long as you didn't try to tempt Israelites into idolatry, you were (mostly) permitted to practice your own traditions. This is not the same thing as respect: the Prophets openly ridiculed pagan practice and the rabbis were skeptical about Roman morality. Nevertheless, the concept of the Noahide will allow for a fully dressed anthropology, a theory of how humanity, in its vexing imperfections, can still be morally good and on the path to the world-to-come (the common rabbinic term for heaven). The section on Noahide law will more fully enumerate its importance in developing a Jewish view on freedom of religion or belief.

The second covenant is made with Abraham and his family, sealed by the visible, physical sign of male circumcision. The Abrahamic covenant ('everlasting' per Gen. 17:14) comes with a three-fold blessing: land, descendants, and the promise that gentile nations will be blessed through him and his progeny. Abraham's grandson, Jacob, will take the name Israel, and this will be the name of the people going forward. By remaining faithful to the covenant and its terms, especially fidelity to God, Jews 'choose life' (Deut. 30: 19). Disobedience to the covenant brings curses (see Deut. 28 for the unnerving list of curses), imperiling the three-fold blessing to Abraham.

The third major covenant in the Torah forged Israel into a nation and a people. It was the memory of Egyptian slavery and God's providential release of the people from that bondage that confirmed the covenant, marked by Moses' reception of the Ten Commandments on Mt. Sinai. As slaves in Egypt, the Israelites could not have entered into the covenant, as they could not have consented freely. The Israelites are persistently reminded that their emancipation from Egypt created moral responsibilities beyond their own community: 'And a stranger you shall not oppress; for you know the feelings of a stranger, seeing you were strangers in the land of Egypt' (Ex. 23: 9). These covenants will set the initial conditions for understanding how Jews think through issues of religious freedom or belief.

Idolatry

For Jews, there is no permitted form of worship except that of the one God. Idolatry is the worship of something other than God or the worship of the one God in the wrong way. The Ten Commandments contain the initial prohibition: 'You should have no other gods before me. You shall not make a graven image or any likeness that is on the earth below, or that is in the water under the earth; you shall not bow down to them or serve them; for I the Lord your God am a jealous God' (Ex. 19: 3–5). A reminder appears later in Exodus: 'You shall not worship an alien god' (Ex. 34: 14). Monarchs seemed especially disposed to idolatry. Ahab is representative of this trend, with his veneration of Baal: 'Not content to follow the sins of Jeroboam son of Nebat, he took as wife Jezebel daughter of King Ethbaal of the Phoenicians, and he went and served Baal and worshiped him' (Kgs. 16: 31). The story of the Hebrew Bible is that of a people persistently tempted by idolatry, the central moral and ritual sin, and the often futile attempts of Prophets to guide them back to the good path.

The paradigmatic moment of idolatry is the fashioning and worshiping of the Golden Calf (Ex. 32); it was a very public denial of faith in the unseen God, aligned with worry that Moses would not return from Mt. Sinai. This scene contained all the essential elements of idolatry: the worship of something other than God; faithlessness in God's promises; imagining God in physical form; and using gentile modes of worship, here in imitation of Egyptian practices. For an illustration of the worship of the God of Israel but in the wrong mode, consider the account of Aaron's sons, Nadav and Avihu. In Lev. 10, they offered a 'strange fire' to God – an unsanctioned sacrifice – violating their roles as priests. The religious restrictions around sacrifice allowed no improvisation or personal choice. For those Israelites who participated in idolatrous cult or 'strange fire,' these transgressions merited death. Such examples could be multiplied many times over. The Torah reminds the people not to chase after the desires of their own hearts, and not to be driven by their desires, unanchored in Covenant. Beyond the fact that idolatry involved worship of something other than God, it was also regularly linked with (often sexual) immorality.

As mentioned in the foregoing, the consequences of idolatry are severe: if anyone "entice[s] you secretly, saying: 'Let us go and serve other gods,'... you shall surely kill him ... because he has sought to draw you away from the Lord your God, who brought you out of the land of Egypt, out of the house of bondage" (Deut. 13: 6–11). Again, the prohibition of idolatrous worship is tied back to God's freeing of the Israelites from slavery. That action created a legal-moral bond, and thus excludes desiring other gods. In Deut. 17, the accusation of idolatry, because of its gravity and its penalty, demands multiple witnesses; guilt cannot be determined on the testimony of one witness alone.

The rabbis of the Talmudic era deemed idolatry, along with murder and sexual immorality, as one of the sins that one must sacrifice her or his life for rather than commit (the *locus classicus* is Sanhedrin 74a). If idolatry is absolutely forbidden for Jews, and martyrdom is demanded, the situation is more complex for gentiles. At least in the Hebrew Bible, idolatry is mostly permitted to non-Jews outside of Israel (and thus outside of Israelite political sovereignty). The Bible is often contemptuous of gentile worship; such practice is described as useless and immoral. As the prophet Jeremiah wrote, 'Thus shall you say to them: the gods who did not make the heaven and the earth shall perish from the earth and from under the heavens. [...] Every man is stupid and without knowledge; every goldsmith is put to shame by his idols, for his images are false and there is no breath in them. They are worthless, a delusion' (Jer. 10: 11–15).

One famous rabbinic homily on the 'delusion' of idolatry embodies this notion. In *Genesis Rabbah*, a compilation of rabbinic sermons on the Torah's first book, Abraham's father, Terah, was an idolater. Terah owned a store that sold idols, and one day he left his son to oversee the store as Terah was away:

> A woman entered carrying a dish full of flour. She said to him: this is for you, offer it before them. Abraham took a club in his hands and broke all of the idols, and placed the club in the hands of the biggest idol. When his father returned, he asked: who did all of this? Abraham replied: I can't hide it from you - a woman came carrying a dish of flour and told me to offer it before them. I did, and one of them said 'I will eat it first,' and another said 'I will eat it first.' The biggest one rose, took a club, and smashed the rest of them. Terah said: what, do you think you can trick me? They don't have cognition! Abraham said: Do your ears hear what your mouth is saying?
> *(Katz and Schwartz, 2002: 50)*

We see in the rabbinic era growing reluctance to accept gentile ritual practice as merely ancestral worship, a continuance of the practice of their fathers. Instead, in a new situation where the Romans were always potential oppressors, Jews were without recourse to defense. While many Talmudic texts suggest there was a universal ban on idolatry, there was no mechanism, political or judicial, by which the rabbis could enforce this prohibition. Certainly, it helped to maintain social distance between Jews and gentiles. For instance, tractate Avodah Zarah, which contains the laws pertaining to idolatry, declares that 'three days before the festivals of the gentiles it is prohibited to engage in any business with them' (Avodah Zarah 2a). The reason: the gentile would earn money and, in his joy, would thank his god. Though he will deal differently with Christianity and Islam, Maimonides (1135–1204) walks a similar path to the rabbis. He reflects one end of rabbinic thought – the absolute prohibition of idolatrous practice because of its false concept of God and its tendency to immorality. In his great legal compendium, the *Mishneh Torah*, he wrote:

> No treaty is to be concluded with worshipers of an alien deity whereby we make peace with them while tolerating its worship; for it is said, 'Make no treaty with them' (Deut. 7:2); they must rather abandon its worship, or be killed. It is forbidden to pity them, as it is said: 'Show them no mercy' (Deut 7:2). So if one sees a gentile worshiper of an alien deity perishing or drowning in a river, one should not extricate him; if one sees him

> taken to [his] death, one should not rescue him. But to directly destroy [his life] or to push him into a pit, and the like, is prohibited, because he is not at war with us.
>
> You may thus deduce that it is forbidden to heal worshippers of an alien deity, even for a fee.
>
> *(Lorberbaum et al., 2003: 480–481)*

Because the corpus of Talmudic and related literature is so vast, there are rabbinic texts that extend a more charitable attitude to pagan religious practice, while always maintaining that it is proscribed for Jews. One text argues that 'gentiles outside of the land of Israel are not idolaters ... but only follow the traditions of their fathers' (Hullin 13b). Individuals were not to be held liable for cultural-religious elements that had been passed down to them; they knew nothing else. Other Talmudic sources suggest, much as the Torah does, that God does not worry over the idolatry of non-Jews, but rather the possibility of Israel falling into such practices.

Noahide law

The rabbis of the Talmud articulated a vision of how non-Jews fit into Judaism's covenantal narrative. This vision is not a fully dressed theory about gentiles, but rather a moral space, conceptual tool, and universal vision for understanding and judging individual non-Jews and gentile societies, a framework for gentile moral and political status. It is a robust, organic Jewish response to living with others who believe differently yet are as capable of truth and falsehood, good and evil as Jews themselves. Tractate Sanhedrin (56b) registers the seven commandments for what scholars later called the Noahide law. There is one positive commandment: to institute courts; the other six are negative commandments: the prohibition of idolatry, the cursing of God's name, murder, robbery, sexual immorality, and eating of a limb from a living animal. Crucially, and beyond the temporizing compromises of politics, the Noahide also provided a pathway to salvation, to the world-to-come, for gentiles. Fulfill the seven laws; your soul is redeemed, then, from the fires of Gehenna. 'A heathen who accepts the seven commandments,' Maimonides writes, 'and observes them scrupulously is a righteous heathen, and will have a portion in the world to come. ...' (Twersky, 1972: 221–222). Equally important, the concept of the Noahide means that gentiles have moral agency.

This rabbinic development of the Noahide laws was carved out of a creative explication of the story of Noah. In Gen. 9, after the flood, God promises never again to destroy the world by water. It is the initial covenant moment in the Torah, guaranteed by God placing a rainbow in the sky. God tells Noah and his sons: 'I now establish My covenant with you and your offspring to come, and with every living thing that is with you – birds, cattle, and every wild beast as well – all that have come out of the ark, every living thing on earth' (Gen. 9:8–10). We need not detail how the rabbis derived those seven laws for the construction (and construction is not invention) of the Noahide, but it is important to note that those laws are found in the Hebrew Bible prior to the revelation at Mt. Sinai. The latter formed Jews into a covenanted people, with a unique historical mission; prior to Sinai, in many ways, Jews were Noahides. The Noahide laws function at a very general level, whereas the revealed commandments (tradition sets the number of commandments at 613) operate at a high level of specificity. But this means that for individual gentiles and non-Jewish societies, the moral expectations of the personal and political order creates a lot of space for pluralism, religious and otherwise.

Some important historical context: in 70 CE, the Second Temple in Jerusalem was destroyed by the Romans; Jewish self-rule in the land of Israel ended. Roman rule had eroded

Jewish political and institutional sovereignty for over two centuries, but now even the reduced autonomy that Jews had in their own land was lost. From 70 to 1948, Jews lived under the yoke of someone else's authority, the exemplary diaspora people. In the absence of territorial and political sovereignty, novel approaches to issues of religious freedom or belief had to be articulated. The Noahide laws would be central. However, these laws had no functional or legal effect, whether as prescriptive rulings or descriptive of historical reality; they were – and are – theoretical and philosophical, part of a narrative of self- and other-understanding within Judaism. The Noahide is a way to grant political legitimacy to a regime, even if its religious practices are remote from Jewish monotheism. It is a kind of Jewish anthropology, an approach to recognizing what it is to human, and the social imperative that there be a basic structure for interhuman relations, even if this structure is 'thin.'

Noahide law is the Jewish version of natural law. Natural law, of course, is tied to no particular revelation, but represents the moral floor under which one must not fall. It is the moral standard that applies universally to everyone, at all times, everywhere. Natural law is derived from rational principles, as reason is a general faculty all humans share; revelation, on the other hand, is specific, available only to the community that receives and accepts it. Maimonides tells us that 'human reason approves of these precepts' (Twersky, 1972: 221–222). Made in the image of God, the Noahide is of equal moral worth, quality, and dignity as Jews. The central rabbinic insights about the Noahide are moral and not legal. As noted in the foregoing paragraph, prior to revelation, where God separated out Jews from the nations and yoked them to a special mission with unique moral and ritual demands, Jews themselves were Noahides.

Karaites

So far, we have considered how the textual sources of Jewish tradition have managed Jewish–gentile relations and relations between Jews. But it is worthwhile to briefly mention here a border case, that of the Karaites. The Karaites fell outside of normative Judaism, and medieval writers considered them a heretical group. Emerging out of the matrix of Jewish life in the early Islamic world, Karaism denied the Oral Law; that is, the divine (if indirectly so) origin of the Talmud, along with rabbinic authority. Karaites believed that the Talmud contradicted the Torah, and there was no way to reconcile the two. They were scripturalists, using the Hebrew Bible as the sole foundation of their traditions. By the middle of the ninth century, they were fully separated from rabbinic Judaism.

There was, and is, no consensus on how the Karaites fit within Judaism's self-understanding. Their rejection of the dominant rabbinic mode of Judaism certainly put them outside mainstream Judaism. But were they members of an altogether different religion? Or were later generations of Karaites misguided, coerced by factors outside of themselves and not halakhically responsible for their heresy? The following passage from Maimonides touches on those tensions:

> As soon as it is made public that he has repudiated the Oral Law, (he is cast into the pit and is not rescued from it), he is placed on par with heretics, epicureans, those who deny the divine origin of Scripture, informers, and apostates – all of whom are ruled out of the community of Israel. No witnesses or previous warning or judges are required. (Whoever puts any of them to death fulfills a great precept, for he removes a stumbling block.) This applies only to one who repudiates the Oral Law as a result of his reasoned opinion and conclusion ... But their children and grandchildren, who,

> misguided by their parents, were raised among the Karaites and trained in their views, are like a child taken captive and raised in their religion, whose status is that of an *anoos* ... Therefore efforts should be made to bring them back in repentance ... so that they may return to the strength-giving source, i.e. the Torah.
>
> *(Twersky, 1972: 210)*

Karaite beliefs held by a gentile would not rise to the level of heresy and, in fact, may even be seen as praiseworthy as those beliefs include monotheism and revelation. However, for a Jew, such beliefs carry with them the death penalty, according to Maimonides, without the usual judicial need for witnesses. But as long as one did not become or remain a Karaite based on philosophical consideration and commitment, then that person is categorized as one of the *anusim*, those that have been 'coerced' into belief because this is how their parents believed. By Jewish law, a person is not responsible if she or he has been coerced, and consequently the penalties for such heretical opinions are waived. For freedom of religion or belief, the category of *anusim* represents a key Jewish value: a child not legally or morally responsible for what her parents transmit to her.

Christians and Muslims

As Judaism entered the medieval era, we see significant shifts in views surrounding religious freedom, especially as Jewish contact with Christianity and Islam grew. However, these complex contacts were not simply relationships between oppressor and oppressed, gentiles bullying Jews, but also significant (and positive) economic, cultural, and social contacts.

The key turn in the medieval Jewish attitude toward gentiles was to see idolatry as something that, in general, pagans did rather than fellow monotheists. It was a thing of the past.

From its beginning, Islam was not considered idolatrous by Judaism. While Muslims rejected the authority of the Hebrew Bible (Christians did not), there was no question about their commitment to absolute monotheism. There was no theological or halakhic problem for living under Muslim rule; Muslims followed the Noahide law. Maimonides holds that Muslims 'are not at all idolators' (Blau, 1960: 725).

One somewhat unusual example illustrates the medieval Jewish attitude toward Islam. The Talmud regularly discusses the status of gentile wine. The rabbis knew that wine handled and sold by gentiles had often been used in their religious rituals and thus the wine itself was ritually tainted by pagan practice. The early medieval rabbis, however, allowed Jews to benefit from the wine of Muslims because there was no issue about their monotheism. Of course, Islamic commentators consider wine and other alcoholic beverages forbidden, yet clearly Jews in Muslim countries did purchase wine from Muslims. There is always some distance between elite, ideal religion and what the people actually do.

Menachem ha-Meiri (1250–1306) and other rabbis revised the legal status of Christianity, setting forth a radical reorientation of the Jewish views of its fellow monotheism. The older view was maintained by Maimonides. Maimonides, who approved of Islam's monotheism, appreciated Christian acknowledgment of the divine origin of the Torah, but their theology was problematic, especially their perceived compromised monotheism. They are to be treated as idolators:

> Know that this Christian nation, who advocates the messianic claim in all their various sects, all of them are [considered] idolaters. On all their various festivals it is forbidden for us to deal with them. All Torah restrictions pertaining to idolaters pertain to them. Sunday is included among their festivals. Therefore, it is forbidden to deal at all on

> Sunday with the believers in the messiah. We treat Sunday as an idolatrous festival.
>
> (Brill, 2010: 177)

His words could easily be mapped to the Roman pagans that the rabbinic sources discuss. All medieval Jewish authorities were troubled by essential Christian doctrines such as the Trinity and the Incarnation. These Christian mysteries violated the absolute uniqueness of God. However, the move away from seeing Christianity as idolatry occurs when rabbis like Meiri argue that when Christians swear by the Trinity or by the person of Jesus, they really intend the one true God that is behind reality. They err theologically in associating Jesus, Mary, or saints with God, but Christianity was in fact a monotheistic faith. The sixteenth-century Polish rabbi Moses Isserles sums up this change:

> Even though when they mention God they mean Jesus, they do not mention idolatry since they really mean the creator of heaven and earth. Even though they mention jointly God's name and another name, there is no prohibition to cause someone to jointly mention [or associate] God with another ... since this association is not forbidden to gentiles.
>
> (Brill, 2010: 179)

Christians saw the Torah or what they called the Old Testament as divinely revealed, so they worshiped the God of Israel, even if at great variance from the correct manner of worship.

Perhaps the best-known case of the medieval rethinking of the relationship between Jews and others is found in the story of the goring ox. In rabbinic literature, if the ox of a gentile gores that of a Jew, the gentile was liable for damages; if however, the ox of a Jew gores that of a gentile, the former had no legal obligations to recompense the latter. Meiri argued that this rabbinic prescription no longer held because Christians and Muslims – though they are gentiles like the Roman pagans that the rabbis knew – were not to be considered idolaters. Meiri said that those Talmudic laws applied only to idolatrous faiths. Among religions abiding by the Noahide law, there was to be no double standard. Meiri writes: 'This only applies to those nations not bound by the ways of the revealed religions and morality ... but anytime the law obligates them for the seven Noahide laws their case before us is like our case before us. We do not favor ourselves in the case' (Novak, 2011: 44). This move toward equality is a tentative extension for religious freedom.

Into modernity

The beginning of the modern era brings with it major transformations unimaginable in the rabbinic and medieval eras. Beginning in the eighteenth century in Europe, there were calls, both by Jews and gentiles, for Jews to receive equal rights in the slowly emerging nation-state. Certainly, by the end of the eighteenth century, we witness the slow, fitful transition from the restrictions of the ghetto (the authorized Jewish area in a town) to something resembling citizenship. This gain was offset by the loss of Jewish religious and cultural autonomy, with many Jews shedding their inherited identities and practices for a passport to gentile culture. The trade-off was this: Jews were no longer a corporate body, but rather individual citizens, and in theory had the same rights as gentiles. Religion was privatized, moved out of the public square – the arguments of a specific revelation were not to be used to formulate the political order or public policy. Jewish identity now became something that was voluntary, not necessarily inscribed from birth, and a burden or blessing to be carried; there were other possibilities and alternatives.

The run-up to this era, though, reveals that religious community had rights – and the ability to enforce them – that are prior to any notion of an individual's freedom of religion or belief. Unlike the constitutions of modern nation-states, which defer to the will of the people, the covenant is divinely revealed, although it can only be understood and implemented at the human scale. The distance between covenantal religion and the secular, liberal democratic order can be hard to bridge. Very far from Locke, Mendelssohn (about whom more is written below), and Mill – and not just the separation of centuries – is the medieval Rabbeinu Gershom ben Judah, an important early Ashkenazi rabbi. Referring to 'God's laws and His precepts' – the covenant – Rabbeinu Gershom maintained that:

> All Israelites are obligated to coerce and compel one another to live in accordance with truth, justice, God's laws and His precepts ... Therefore, if the kahal [the local, organized Jewish community] agrees together to enact decrees forming a fence around the Torah, an individual may not exclude himself from the collective and cancel the pronouncement of the many by saying that he did not agree to the enactment. The individual, being a minority, is himself cancelled: whereas the many are authorized to bind by oath, to decree, to place under a ban, expropriate his property, and enact any decree.
>
> If, God forbid, the inhabitants of another town transgressed the Torah or the law, or decided a point of law not in accordance with halakha, the inhabitants of another town might coerce them, and even pronounce the *herem* [ban of excommunication] against them, in order to force them to mend their ways.
>
> *(Lorberbaum et al., 2003: 394)*

Writing around the year 1000, Rabbenu Gershom's *tshuva* (rabbinic answer to a halakhic question) indicates the Jewish community had coercive power over its members, and perhaps the obligation to compel halakhic compliance elsewhere in cases of egregious transgression.

Six and a half centuries later, at the edge of modernity, these same corporate rights over the individual were on display in the case of the philosopher Baruch Spinoza, illustrating the perhaps inevitable tensions for religious freedom or belief. Spinoza's religious and philosophical beliefs were certainly heterodox, espousing views about God and the Bible that significantly drifted from how the tradition understood itself. The Amsterdam community in which Spinoza lived placed him under the ban (*herem*), similar to excommunication in Catholicism. He was to be denied ritual honors in the synagogue – and to be socially ostracized – until he had reconciled with the community, shelving his heretical views. The communal decree stated:

> ... [we] have long since been cognizant of the wrong opinions and behavior of Baruch d'Espinoza, and tried various means and promises to dissuade him from his evil ways. But as they effected no improvement, obtaining on the contrary more information every day of the horrible heresies which he practised and taught, and of the monstrous actions which he performed [...] they decided [...] that the same Espinoza should be excommunicated. [...]
>
> After the judgment of the Angels, and with that of the Saints, we excommunicate, expel and curse and damn Baruch de Espinoza with the consent of God, Blessed be He, and with the consent of all the Holy Congregation, in front of the holy Scrolls with the six-hundred-and-thirteen precepts which are written therein ... We order

> that nobody should communicate with him orally or in writing ... or read anything composed or written by him.
>
> *(Mendes-Flohr and Reinharz, 2010: 57)*

Is this a case of religious intolerance or is it the right of a religion to determine its boundaries and membership? In our time, we have tilted rights fundamentally toward the individual (and for good reason!), but historically – and in some places today – rights have favored the corporate/communal body. With Spinoza, very few doubted that the Jewish community had the right to expel or ostracize its members. Note one major difference from Rabbenu Gershom: the consequences for Spinoza were entirely social-religious, not economic, with no threat to undermine his employment or seize his property.

Use of excommunication was not limited to individuals such as Spinoza, who, as Orthodox Jews would say today, 'went off the *derech*,' leaving the right path of observance. In 1772, one group of traditional Jews placed another group of traditional Jews under the *herem*. In disagreement about religious practices, leading East European *mitnagdim* (literally, 'opponents' – opponents of Hasidism) ruled that the ritual deviations of Hasidic Jews had placed the latter beyond the pale of traditional Judaism. To overgeneralize matters for expediency, the *mitnagdim* were the 'rationalists' – committed to classical Talmud study – whereas the Hasidim were 'mystics,' with an emphasis on the charisma of the *rebbe* (Hasidic rabbi), interior states of religiosity, and a dedication to the study of mystical texts. Today, the differences between *mitnagdim* and Hasidim have diminished appreciably, to the loss of a kind of internal Orthodox pluralism. But, in the eighteenth century, the issues dividing the two groups led to a split in the traditionalist community, with one halakhically banning the other. As the *mitnagdic* Brody Proclamation declared:

> [...] Therefore the holy community has decreed by the great and awesome *herem* ... that, from this day onward, it is strictly forbidden for any one of the synagogues or fixed *minyanim* in our community to alter – God forbid – anything of our customary formula of Ashkenazi prayer. [...] Also it is forbidden for any individual to pray other than according to the Ashkenazi liturgy [...].
>
> *(Lorberbaum et al., 2003: 358–360)*

The foregoing situations would not go without challenge. The gap between the traditional and the embryonic modern conception of freedom of religion is best exemplified in the writings of Moses Mendelssohn (1729–1786). Though an observant Jew, Mendelssohn was committed to the modern liberal democratic state. His major work, *Jerusalem*, helped create the story of what religious freedom should look like, believing religious communities could give up their coercive privileges via the state while still remaining emotionally compelling and morally persuasive. He saw a need for a kind of civic faith, a place where atheism could have no foothold, but of course he was living at a time when there were very few open atheists. He imagined a secular public sphere that would not insist on bracketing one's prior religious commitments but rather drawing from them their universal insights such as wisdom and bringing that to bear on the issues of the day.

In terms of freedom of religion or belief, especially in its modern sense, the basic insight of Mendelssohn is this: states, institutions, and individuals cannot coerce conscience, and ought not to try. Mendelssohn considered *herem* to be a violation of both religious conscience and the social contract: 'Excommunication and the right to banish, which the state may occasionally permit itself to exercise, are diametrically opposed to the spirit of religion' (Mendelssohn, 1983: 73). Mendelssohn famously splits the responsibilities of church and state; they are separate domains, with different ontologies and teleologies: 'The state gives orders and coerces, religion teaches and persuades. The state prescribes laws, religion commandments. The state has physical power and uses it when necessary; the power of religion is love and beneficence' (Mendelssohn, 1983: 45). The state is concerned solely with the body: the *raison d'être* of the state is to create a proper political ordering of society. Its coercive power is a 'right through the social contract' (Mendelssohn, 1983: 45). The church – that is, any religious community – ought not to have coercive police power ['lays no claim to the right of coercion' [Mendelssohn, 1983: 45)] but rather focus on the soul. He writes:

> Insofar as men's actions and convictions can be made to serve the common weal through reasons arising from their relations to each other, they are a matter for the civil constitution; but insofar as the relations between man and God can be seen as their source, they belong to the church, the synagogue, or the mosque ... The only rights possessed by the church are to admonish, to instruct, to fortify, and to comfort; and the duties of the citizens toward the church are an attentive ear and a willing heart.
>
> *(Mendelssohn, 1983: 41, 59–60)*

Mendelssohn desired a kind of Lockean society where no person would be persecuted because of her religious beliefs. Toleration would be his beacon, similar to Locke who called toleration the 'chief characteristic mark' of the Church (Locke, 2003: 215).

One of the hallmarks of religion in the modern era is that it is voluntary; it is a choice no matter one's religious background. Even the obligation to practice and believe in a certain way is a choice; we are aware of other paths. By Jewish law, someone born of a Jewish mother or having converted to Judaism is Jewish. In that sense, the choice is not theirs, it is as indelible as baptism in Roman Catholicism. Yet, in reality, it was a functional choice, something one could embrace or reject, remix or forget. Such a reality brings with it a blossoming of pluralism, whether warmly received or not. We observe the loss of unity in the Jewish community at Emancipation, even if that unity had been at times gossamer-thin. Religious unity is exchanged for individual choice, a united community for fractious denominationalism. It would be a (unsatisfactory?) victory for religious liberty.

One of the hallmarks of religion in the modern era is that it is voluntary; it is a choice no matter one's religious background. The Assembly of Jewish Notables stressed to Napoleon that any conflict between the French civil code and Jewish law would be decided in favor of the former. They drew on the rabbinic principle of *dina d'malkhuta dina* (the law of the land is the law), originally formulated in the third century. The French state posed a series of questions to the Jewish community. The questions were designed to probe the loyalty of French Jews to France and its ideals. Echoing the revolutionary call for *égalité*, the Assembly stated that 'conduct prescribed towards Frenchmen not of our religion, is the same as that prescribed between Jews themselves; we admit of no differences but that of worshipping the Supreme Being, every one in his own way' (Mendes-Flohr and Reinharz, 2010: 130). The emphasis here on toleration and equality is notable and distinctly modern in its tone.

Conclusion

Most of Jewish history occurs in a vacuum of political sovereignty. Only for short stretches in ancient Israel and after 1948 did Jews have political power and authority in their own land. Different eras saw Jews have autonomy, especially over matters of personal status, within their communities, but it has always been a limited autonomy. They have lived under the rule, for good and ill, of gentiles for most of their history. Now, for the first time since the Roman destruction of the Second Temple, non-Jews live under the majority Jewish rule. This situation is both a challenge and an opportunity: a challenge because this is a novel situation and an opportunity because it has allowed for halakhic, theological, and philosophical innovations with Judaism, using sources creatively to unlock new ways of living with others and devise new interpretations of religious freedom.

The State of Israel has three significant populations: religious Jews, secular Jews, and Arab Muslims and Christians. Though perhaps an 'illiberal' democracy, Israel has freedom of religion or belief, even if imperfectly and unevenly implemented. But tensions exist. One can see this tension regarding religious freedom in the example of marriage. In Israel, marriage can only be legal if solemnized through official religious functionaries. And this is true not only for Jews but also for non-Jews. Matters of personal status, conversion, marriage, divorce, and adoption are controlled by religious authorities. The State of Israel at its beginning ceded to rabbinic control matters of personal status, which created conflicts between the religious and the secular. David Ben-Gurion and other early leaders proposed this grand bargain whereby religious Jews would receive political and economic privileges in return for support for the State and its policies. For instance, buses do not run on the Jewish Sabbath. We should ask: is this freedom of religion or belief? If the majority supports marriage only in a religious context, does that democratic decision deprive nonreligious people of rights? How do we properly balance the modern insistence on individual rights with the pre-modern claim by religious communities to precede – historically and ontologically – the state? There are no solutions to these permanent questions, only trade-offs, threading the needle between freedom of religion or belief for individuals and communities.

In the fateful year of 1967, Israel announced an important policy regarding holy (and contentious) sites. The Protection of Holy Places law declared, 'the Holy Places shall be protected from desecration and any other violation and from anything likely to violate the freedom of access of the members of the different religions to the places sacred to them or their feelings with regard to those places.'[3] This is probably the best any society can do, in the fullness of its imperfections.

I conclude with a final meta-ethical idea that is central to Judaism, as Jews reflect on their own sources about freedom of religion or belief. Theology assumes an anthropology. There must be some assumption about human nature and about dignity and moral worth. Others outside of one's community *matter*. In Judaism, this anthropology is radical and transformative: we are made in the image of God [*b'tselem elohim* (Gen. 1: 27)]. No matter the inequalities in this life (of wealth, beauty, strength, honor, et al.), no one can be owned by another – we are all God's children, Jew and gentile alike. In terms of religion or belief, sources tilt in many directions, and it matters what one choses to emphasize, but the preponderance of the textual evidence is consistent with the covenant, aligned to the core ethical idea that all humans are made in God's image.

Further reading

Maoz, A., 2006. Religious freedom as a basic human right: the jewish perspective. *Annuario DiReCom*. 5, 103.

3 See https://www.knesset.gov.il/laws/special/eng/HolyPlaces.htm.

References

Blau, Y. (Ed.), 1960. *Teshuvot Ha-Rambam*, vol. 2. Mekitse Nirdamim.
Brill, A., 2010. *Judaism and Other Religions: Models of Understanding*. Palgrave MacMillan.
Katz, M., Schwartz, G., 2002. *Searching for Meaning in Midrash: Lessons for Everyday Living*. Jewish Publication Society.
Locke, J., 2003. *Two Treatises of Government and A Letter Concerning Toleration* (I. Shapiro, Ed.). Yale University Press.
Lorberbaum, M., Walzer, M., Zohar, N. (Eds.), 2003. *The Jewish Political Tradition*, vol. 1. Yale University Press.
Mendelssohn, M., 1983. *Jerusalem: Or on Religious Power and Judaism* (A. Arkush, Trans.). Brandeis University Press.
Mendes-Flohr, P., Reinharz, J. (Eds.), 2010. *The Jew in the Modern World: A Documentary History*. Oxford University Press.
Novak, D., 2011. *The Image of the Non-Jew in Judaism*. Littman Library of Jewish Civilization.
Rubenstein, R., 1988. Evil. In: A. Cohen, P. Mendes-Flohr (Eds.), *Contemporary Jewish Religious Thought*. Free Press.
Sacks, J., 1992. *Crisis and Covenant: Jewish Thought After the Holocaust*. Manchester University Press.
1985 *Tanakh: The Holy Scriptures*, 1985. Jewish Publication Society.
Twersky, I. (Ed.), 1972. *A Maimonides Reader*. Behrman House.

11

Building an inter-religious notion of the right to freedom of religion: Dangers, opportunities, and goals

Arvind Sharma

Introduction

Do we really need to develop an interreligious notion of the right to freedom of religion? One must begin by asking whether one needs such a notion. The issue of developing an interreligious notion of freedom of religion would be redundant under the following three circumstances: (1) If a notion of freedom of religion already exists in human rights discourse, which suffices for all religions found in the world. (2) If a 'secular' concept of religion is so universally applicable that anyone, whether secular or religious by disposition, dealing with the issue of freedom of religion is likely to come up with similar formulations of it. For instance, if the idea that 'no one should be compelled to belong to any religion' is a broad enough formulation of the concept of religious freedom to be acceptable to all, then there is no point in developing an independent formulation of an interreligious concept of religious freedom because this, or a comparable formulation, suffices. (3) If a notion of religious freedom developed in any of the religions will basically be the same. That is to say, if Christians developed the notion of religious freedom and Muslims did the same, there would be such congruence between them that such a concept of religious freedom could be applied to any other religion. Such a 'religious' concept of freedom would also obviate any need to look further for an interreligious concept of freedom, inasmuch as the formulation of the concept of religious freedom in any one religion will do for all.

Let us now examine these three propositions. A concept of religious freedom as found in human rights discourse is articulated in Article 18 of the Universal Declaration of Human Rights (1948): 'Everyone has the right to freedom of thought, conscience, and religion; this right includes freedom to change his religion or belief, and freedom, either alone or in community with others and in public or private, to manifest his religion or belief in teaching, practice, worship and observance' (Brownlie, 1992: 25). This article, however, was challenged in the discussion at the United Nations by the Saudi Arabian delegate, who opposed it on the ground that this Article permits proselytization, which will ultimately lead to bloodshed (Glendon, 2001: 154). An objection more specific to Islam can also be cited against this clause, because, in classical Islam, the punishment for apostasy is death (Artz, 1996: 387). In other words, in the classical understanding, you cannot really change your religion once you are a Muslim. It is clear, therefore, that the existing formulation of religious freedom in human rights discourse, at least as found in the original UN document, does not suffice. It is true that an elaboration of this article in the International Covenant on Civil and Political Rights (1966) makes an attempt to respond to some criticisms of the formulation in the original Universal Declaration of Human Rights (UDHR) (1948). For instance, limitations to the freedom to manifest one's religion have been recognized by making that freedom subject to such limitations 'as prescribed by law [...] necessary to protect public safety, order, health, or morals or the fundamental rights and freedoms of others' (Brownlie, 1992: 132).

But these attempts to elaborate the original provision still leave it open to criticism and do not adequately take care of the objections raised earlier. Article 18 of the Covenant states: 'This right shall include freedom to have or to adopt a religion or belief of his choice.' This clause is obviously an attempt to rephrase the following section of Article 18 of the Universal Declaration: 'this right includes freedom to change his religion or belief.' Possibly, there was a problem with the word *change* in the UDHR, namely, that it does not similarly recognize the right to retain one's religion. The expression to have or to adopt a religion was introduced to soften the apparent bias in UDHR Article 18 in favor of missionary religions. The benefit of this new formulation is that you can become the follower of another religion without necessarily having to give up your own because you 'adopt it,' just as when you adopt another child you do not have to disown your existing children (Tahzib-Lie, 1996: 84–87). The problem, however, is that the freedom to retain one's religion is not clearly recognized, because to have a religion does not possess the force of the implication that someone is trying to take it away from you and therefore you need to retain it. There is a difference between 'having' and 'retaining or keeping.' The problem that many nonproselytizing religions have with the UDHR clause is that it does not protect their religious freedom in the face of the activities of the proselytizing religions. Moreover, indigenous religious freedom is not fully protected by this provision because of the nature of those religions. It has been argued, for instance, that religious freedom of indigenous people has not been fully protected by this clause as illustrated by the experience of indigenous people in the United States of America (Sharma, 2011: 233–250).

The second proposition, namely, that a secular concept of religious freedom (apart from the one proposed in human rights discourse and discussed above) would suffice also runs into difficulties. First of all, there is no one universally accepted definition of religion in the secular discourse which one could invoke (Hick, 1990). Moreover, some forms of secularism tend to be hostile to the very idea of religion, which makes relying on a secular definition of religion somewhat hazardous (Taylor, 2007). Therefore, this proposition is also problematic. It has now been widely recognized that the inadequacy of a secular concept of religion was largely responsible for the fact that the religious freedom of the indigenous peoples could not be protected. For example, the sentiment attached to land in indigenous religions is usually not reflected in secular definitions of religion. Most religions of the world do have *holy* places, but these do not compare to the importance the *sacred* land has in the regular worship of the indigenous peoples. For instance, in November 2017, plans for the development of a ski resort on land considered sacred by the Ktunaxa Nation of British Columbia, Canada, were accepted following the ruling of the Supreme Court, overruling the indigenous community's religious rights (Kassam, 2017).

The third proposition, that a definition of religious freedom found in any one religious tradition could be universally applicable, has its own problems. For instance, a concept of religious freedom based on Christian assumptions could emphasize the right of a person to change one's religion, but this could be challenged by the concept of religious freedom in Islam wherein as already noted, a change of religion is not permitted in its classical version. In fact, this position may also hold for Christianity. It has been suggested that according to the *doctrine* of Orthodox, Catholic and, in part, Protestant Christianity, the faithful of these denominations do not have the right to abandon their religion once they have been baptized. Moreover, as we shall soon discover, religions have been grouped into various categories, and the concept of religious freedom in these categories tends to have its own particular contour. Hence, the third proposition also becomes problematic.

It is, therefore, clear that we *do* need an interreligious notion of the right to freedom of religion.

Clarifying terms of reference

We do need to clarify the terms of reference as we try to build a notion of the right to freedom of religion across religions. The first concept we need to analyze is that of 'right' (Dershowitz, 2005). There are many definitions of a 'right' in the discourse of human rights, but most of them rely on the idea of an individual bearer of rights who can assert them over and against other individuals, or the state (Baxi, 2008). Rights can be both moral and/or legal. In the present discussion, both these dimensions will come into play.

We turn next to the idea of 'freedom.' Again, there can be many definitions of freedom, but I think we are well served by developing a minimal and maximal notion of freedom. A minimal notion involves absence of restrictions. That is to say, if I would like to enter a building, then I am not restricted from entering it. I am, therefore, free to enter it. A maximal notion of freedom would involve, on this metaphor, my freedom to go into as many buildings as I like.

On the question of 'religion,' we will take the term to mean anything that has come to be accepted as religion in the discourse of human rights. For instance, it has been argued in the study of religion that Marxism could also be considered a religion, but we will not be including it in our discussion because it is not considered so in human rights discourse. One may note here that UDHR Article 18, quoted above, is not restricted to the freedom of religion but includes freedom of conscience and freedom of thought and therefore also covers ideology because beliefs need not be only religious. The difference between religion and ideology consists of the fact that religions tend to have a transcendental referent, a feature which does not apply to ideologies. The problem of definitions is not restricted to religions; the problem of defining a religious tradition can be equally contentious (Satlow, 2006). In this matter also, we will be guided by current usage in the field.

Profiling ideas of religious freedom in various religions

It is clear then that we need an interreligious notion of the right to freedom of religion because all religions may not agree on what this right should be. Our next step should consist in examining the various notions of freedom of religion entertained by the major religions of the world and then to provide a formulation of 'freedom of religion' which would be acceptable to all or at least most of them. In order to do so, we will have to go into the nuances of this concept in the various religions of the world. Let us begin with indigenous religions and follow that up with an examination of the Abrahamic religious traditions, the Indic religious traditions, and the Far East religious traditions.[1]

1 For additional discussion of this point, see Chapter 7 of Arvind Sharma, *Problematizing Religious Freedom* (Dordrecht: Springer, 2012).

Indigenous religious traditions

There are two main aspects to the concept of religious freedom in Indigenous Religions. Such religions are typically small-scale with an oral rather than a written tradition and emphasize the solidarity of the community. Normally, a religious community forms around a set of doctrines and practices; in the case of primal religions, however, the religious practice itself tends to be an expression of the *communitas*. Thus, its close association is with the natural landscape not just on historical or esthetic grounds but ontological ones. That is to say, certain aspects of natural formations may have to be preserved for the religious rites to be performed. Most world religions, although they have holy centers, do not usually have such sacred sites and therefore it becomes important to recognize that an interreligious concept of religious freedom needs to be sensitive to this dimension. The second significant dimension of indigenous religions is that they tend to be inclusive in nature. In this case, if a person from one tribe finds himself/herself residing in another tribe, then that person does not feel any reluctance in participating in the rites and rituals of the host tribe. One interesting consequence of this is that when indigenous peoples convert to an exclusive religion, such as Christianity, they tend to look upon themselves as followers of both their indigenous religion and Christianity at the same time, which becomes problematic from a Christian point of view but poses little problem from the indigenous point of view. The phenomenon of belonging to two or more religious traditions at the same time may be compared to that of dual citizenship in civic life.

The Abrahamic religious traditions

The Abrahamic religious traditions consist of Judaism, Christianity, and Islam. The concept of religious freedom in Judaism is deeply influenced by the long history of the persecution of the Jews, of which the holocaust is the most glaring example. On the basis of this experience, the Jewish understanding of the concept of freedom of religion would tend to emphasize *absence* of religious persecution as a key element of religious freedom. The point to note is that absence of persecution is a negative right, whereas most phrasings of the right of freedom of religion emphasize the right to *exercise* freedom, which is a positive right. On the basis of the Jewish experience, one would be inclined to recognize (1) the freedom to follow one's own doctrines and practices without interference and (2) the desire not to be made an object of proselytization, as important components of religious freedom. It is also worth noting the generally held view, that Judaism is not a proselytizing religion which accepts converts but does not seek them (in fact even going to the extent of dissuading potential converts), has been questioned. Is has been argued that this attitude reflects an internalization of Judaism's own historical experience and that, at one point in its history, it was an actively proselytizing religion in the Mediterranean region. Be that as it may, Judaism is not a proselytizing religion at the moment. This comports with the fact that it does not wish to be made an object of proselytization. This sentiment is of course common to all religions but is particularly acute in the case of Judaism on account of the Jews being specially targeted for conversion by Christianity, and also by Islam to a certain extent. This would suggest that Judaism would be reluctant to admit freedom to proselytize as an integral element of religious freedom.

We turn next to Christianity. Christianity is an actively proselytizing religion, although Christians themselves prefer words like missionizing or evangelizing. That is to say, spreading the word is a very important element in its own understanding of itself, to the extent that it would consider any limitations on its right to proselytize a restriction on its religious freedom. This is confirmed by a glance at the 1974 Lausanne Covenant which actually invokes Article 18 of the UDHR as conferring on all Christians, especially Protestants, the right to proselytize as a component of religious freedom (Padilla, 1976).

The third member of the Abrahamic religious traditions, along with Judaism and Christianity, is Islam. Islam is a proselytizing religion although its legal system makes special provisions for the protection of non-Muslims living in an Islamic State, though not without certain restrictions. As some scholars have put it, although the non-Muslim is a second-class citizen in an Islamic state governed by Sharia Law, he or she has definite rights (Warner, 2010; Shepard, 2015). The Islamic concept of *ahl al-kitāb* is significant in this respect (Wahyudi, 1997). Nevertheless, the overall structure of Islam favors conversion to it. A striking aspect of Islamic law, which has a bearing on the present discussion, has already been mentioned, namely, that in its classical formulation the punishment for leaving it is death. In this sense, it is a religion with an entrance but no exit (we should note however that this provision has been much more refined in modern Islam and that other traditions, even if they do not have a legal provision for this, may nevertheless not spare the lives of those who have converted from them). This contrasts with Christianity in which leaving it does not usually invite such penalties, and in modern times imposes virtually none, exceptions notwithstanding.

It might be useful at this point to distinguish between legal and religious penalties for leaving a religion and that even in cases where no legal sanctions are involved for leaving a religion in the normal sense of the term, a religion may provide 'religious penalties' such as curses, the belief that such a person is condemned to hell, and so on. There is little doubt, however, that it is easier to exit from non-Abrahamic traditions than from the Abrahamic ones.

The overall picture then is that, from a Jewish perspective, religious freedom would mean the freedom to exist and to continue practicing one's religion without persecution as the main component of that freedom. From the Christian perspective, freedom of religion would include the freedom to convert people to Christianity. And for Islam, freedom of religion would consist of freedom to continue following a religion (which should involve in its classical formulation, freedom to enter Islam but not leave it). From the Jewish perspective, *one should neither be converted nor convert.* From a Christian perspective, *one should convert others and could get converted.* The issue of conversion from Christianity is a fraught one, and the actual provision may vary from one Christian denomination to another. But, given the rule of law prevailing in most Christian countries, and the relative preponderance of civil law over clerical law, such conversion would be hard to frustrate. And from an Islamic perspective, *one should convert but not be converted.* The thrust in Abrahamic traditions varies from no conversion either way in Judaism to conversion either way in Christianity and to conversion one way in classical Islam.

We turn next to the four religions of Indian origin, often collectively referred to as the Indic religious traditions, consisting of Hinduism, Buddhism, Jainism, and Sikhism.

The Indic religious traditions

Hinduism is usually considered a plural, diverse, and tolerant tradition. These characteristics have deeply influenced its concept of religious freedom. For it, religious freedom consists in the freedom to follow one's own religion, and leaving others free to follow their own. Religious freedom in Hinduism is very strongly associated with the idea that everyone should be allowed to tread their own religious and spiritual path without interference by others or interference in the affairs of others. There is no *theological* reason, according to modern Hinduism, for conversion either way because of its belief that all religions are valid and therefore there is no need to change one's religion (although there may be political, social, or cultural reasons hampering the free application of this principle). According to it, what one needs to change is not one's religion but one's life. Moreover, if it is not necessary to change, it is necessary not to change. What this means is the fact that a person belongs to a religion is not to be understood as a mere natal accident but the result of the working of karmic forces or God's will.

Buddhism is amongst the earliest missionary religions of the world. Religious freedom in Buddhism involves the freedom to spread one's word as in Christianity and Islam but with an important difference. To become an adherent of Buddhism, one does not have to disown one's earlier religion, with the result that Buddhism has become an integral component of the various cultures to which it has spread without replacing a religion or culture, although not without influencing them. In other words, the idea of dual or even multiple religious affiliations would be an important part of the Buddhist concept of religious freedom, along with the idea that one should be able to spread one's religion. It invites an interesting comparison with indigenous traditions inasmuch as both are not averse to the idea of dual or multiple religious identities.

Jainism is an ancient and persistent tradition in India which at one time enjoyed considerable influence in different parts of India but has now also spread to the West. One of its key doctrines is known as the 'manifoldness of reality,' and one of its key practices is that of nonviolence. Thus, religious tolerance will be a very significant element in the concept of religious freedom in Jainism. Moreover, Jainism, through its philosophical doctrines and reasoned practice of nonviolence, can help ground the idea of religious freedom intellectually.

Sikhism, in contrast to other members of Indic religious traditions, is a relatively young religion which appeared around the sixteenth century. It arose at a time when both Hinduism and Islam were present in the area of the Panjab in India, and Sikhism shares several ideas with both these religions. Even in its relatively short life, it has a history of persecution by the Moghul rulers of India. As in the case of Judaism, freedom from persecution would therefore be a very important component of religious freedom for it, as well as the idea of freedom to interact with other religious traditions without coercion. This seems typical of religions which have a history of being a minority religion such as Judaism, Sikhism, and to a limited extent Christianity. It is also remarkable that although the Moghuls were Muslims, the Sikh experience of persecution has not colored Sikhism's attitude of religious tolerance toward all religions, including Islam.

It can thus be said about the Indic religious traditions in general that all of its four members are strongly predisposed toward religious freedom. Out of these four, Hinduism, Jainism, and Sikhism are clearly nonproselytizing, and Buddhism, although it is missionary in nature, is also nonproselytizing in the sense that is does not require followers of other religions to disown their previous religious affiliation upon embracing Buddhism.

We turn now to the three religions of the Far East.

The religious traditions of the far East

Confucianism is strongly associated with Chinese history and culture. It is not a missionary religion per se; it did, however, spread to Korea and Japan with the spread of Chinese cultural influence in this region. However, the spread of Confucianism to these regions was more cultural than religious in nature. This may have an interesting bearing on modern developments in Hinduism as it is being increasingly identified as a culture rather than as a religion in India.

Daoism, like Confucianism, is also closely related with Chinese culture and spread to areas neighboring China as a part of the expansion of Chinese cultural influence in the region. Nature plays an important part in Daoism as a religion, suggesting some parallels with Indigenous religions. It is not a missionary religion per se, but, unlike Confucianism which is considered elitist in nature, it tends to flourish among the common folk whose needs it addresses through its belief in 'supernatural forces.' Religious freedom for it would then consist in the freedom to allow various strata of society to pursue their own religious beliefs and practices, which are sometimes threatened by the spread of elitist or proselytizing religions.

Shinto is the national religion of Japan and has remained culturally confined to it, although, in modern times, it has also gained some followers in the West. It is considered essentially ethnic in its orientation; therefore, religious freedom for it would consist in ensuring that ethnic religions are as free to follow their lifestyle as other forms of religiosity. This is confirmed by its historical response to the arrival of missionary Christianity. When Christianity reached Japan in the mid-sixteenth century, it was initially regarded by the Japanese as a form of Buddhism which may explain its initial success in Japan. But when the Japanese discovered its proselytizing nature and the threat it posed to their ethnic identity, of which Buddhism had already become a part, attempts were made to contain it (Amore and Ching, 1996: 315–316). Shinto has had a long history of interaction with Buddhism, Confucianism, and even Daoism, and most Japanese describe themselves as followers of both Shinto and Buddhism. In other words, dual or multiple religious identity is the norm in Japan and holds important lessons for us in the context of religious freedom (Reader, 1991: 202).

It may thus be said of the three religions of the Far East: Confucianism, Daoism, and Shinto, that all of them are predisposed to be religiously tolerant, which may be associated with their largely ethnic character, because an ethnic group tends to be organic in character and grows or declines in size by growth or decline in population rather than conversion and is therefore nonproselytizing by nature. Moreover, such religions are often designated as 'communitarian' because in them the community comes first and its beliefs and expressions are an expression of its togetherness. Such religions are distinguished from what are called 'associational' religions in which beliefs and practices come first and the community coalesces around it. Christian denominations would be a primal example of associational religion and primal religions of the communitarian kind. This statement may also apply to Hinduism, Jainism, and Sikhism. These three religions are, again, nonproselytizing, although this does not mean that their influence has not spread to other regions.

The significance of the families of religions in formulating a general notion of religious freedom

We have already noted that there are four major families of religion: (1) the indigenous religions, (2) the Abrahamic religious traditions, (3) the Indic religious traditions, and (4) the religions of the Far East. The list is not exhaustive, but it is fairly comprehensive, although illustrative, in nature.

It appears from the survey carried out on the concept of religious freedom in the previous section that there is a clear division among those religions in which proselytization is a key element in the formulation of the concept of religious freedom, and those for whom it is not. Our problem is complicated by the fact that the concept of religious freedom found in the Abrahamic religious traditions is the one which has gained salience in modern discussions of the topic, at the cost of overlooking the concept of religious freedom found in the three other families of religious traditions identified above.

The Abrahamic concept of religious freedom has two main features: (1) that one can adhere to only one religion at a time or can only possess a singular religious identity and (2) that religions should be free to proselytize (with the possible exception of Judaism). Both these features are embodied in the concept of religious freedom as propounded in Article 18 of the UDHR and in documents subsequent to it. These positions are not necessarily shared by the other families of religious traditions. Therefore, the problem of formulating an interreligious concept of religious freedom boils down to one of reconciling these differences. The two major points of friction are whether the right to proselytize is a defining element in the concept of religious freedom and whether religious identity must be exclusive.

The problem in a nutshell is that there are certain assumptions underlying what might be called the 'Western concept of religious freedom,' which seems to undergird the concept of religious freedom considered normative in human rights discourse but which does not sit well with the followers of the three other families of religious traditions. The fact that Christianity and Islam, between them, almost account for half of the population of the globe (with approximately over three billion adherents out of the seven billion total population of the world), the fact that they are proselytizing in nature, and the fact that Christian countries dominate the international arena has ensured that the very concept of religious freedom has come to be identified with the Western concept of religious freedom. This is the greatest obstacle in formulating a universal concept of religious freedom which will also be acceptable without reservation outside the Christian–Islamic sphere. What then precisely are the problems which religions other than Christianity and Islam have with the regnant concept of religious freedom?

There are two key distinctions which need to be analyzed before the genesis of the problem can be identified. The first is between proselytizing and nonproselytizing religions, and the second is between singular and multiple religious identity. Let us examine them by turn.

The issue of proselytization involves the attitude that a follower of a certain religion has toward the followers of a religion other than his/her own. The question we must ask is: How imperative is it for a religion to convert others as a part of its own concept of religious freedom? In other words, must the concept of religious freedom for a follower of such a religion mean the freedom to convert others? Does your religion direct you to convert others to it? This has to be understood with care. Not all the followers of a religion may feel like doing so but the question is: Does the religion ask them to do it? It also does not mean that a nonproselytizing religion does not *accept* followers, what it means is that it does not *seek* followers. The key idea underlying proselytization is whether your *religion* ideally requires you to *seek* converts.

Christianity and Islam, among the religions of the world, provide the classic example of a proselytizing religion. Both are required by their teachings to spread themselves over the world, to go global as it were. Because these religions regard proselytization as a key element in their religion, their concept of religious freedom necessarily means that religious freedom should include the right to *change* the religion of others. And because this understanding of religious freedom has become part and parcel of our understanding of religious freedom in public discourse, the very idea of religious freedom has come to be closely associated with the freedom of a religion to convert others to it. There are several religions of the world, however, which are essentially nonproselytizing. These include the indigenous religions, Judaism, Hinduism, Buddhism (which is missionary but not proselytizing), Jainism, Sikhism, Confucianism, Daoism, and Shintoism (Adcock, 2014: 3). In other words, the concept of religious freedom as it prevails in modern discourse does not take into account the views of half of the globe which lack the political clout of the proselytizing religions and whose views therefore tend to get overlooked, neglected, or marginalized.

The second major distinction, not unrelated to the first, is the distinction between singular and multiple religious identity. The key question here is: Can one belong to more than one religion at a time? The fact that such a question is a very unusual question to ask in a Western context sheds light on the issue. The Western notion of religion itself has become so captive to the idea of exclusive religious identity that it finds it difficult to even entertain such a question. The question borders on the absurd for the Abrahamic religious traditions. But it is a very reasonable question for many other religions of the world. We noted earlier how indigenous religions are quite comfortable with the idea of dual religious identity. It is well documented that multiple religious identity, or at least multiple religious participation if not affiliation, was a normal part of religious life in India in the pre-British period and still continues to be so despite the efforts of the British to impose a one-person one-religion concept in India almost on the lines of one-person one-vote.

The religious reality in pre-communist China also resembled the Indian, where Confucianism, Daoism, and Chinese Buddhism were not treated as watertight compartments. The cultured Chinese was familiar with all three, and his/her preference for one could change in the course of his/her life. The most striking evidence that this was probably the regnant reality of pre-modern Asia is provided by the case of Japan where even today, more than 90% of its citizens declare themselves followers of Shinto and more than 70% of the same population also declare themselves followers of Buddhism.

When the first distinction between proselytizing and nonproselytizing religions is placed alongside the distinction between singular and multiple religious identity, then the interesting insight emerges that proselytization religions tend to be associated with singular religious identity and nonproselytizing religions with multiple religious identity. The two interesting and instructive exceptions are Judaism and Buddhism. Judaism believes in exclusive religious identity but is not proselytizing, at least in its current form, and Buddhism welcomes converts but does not require that they give up their affiliation with their previous religious tradition. It is in this sense that it may be described as missionary without being proselytizing. The challenge before us is clear. We have to frame a universal concept of religious freedom which will do justice to both these halves of the globe.

A possible solution

It is obvious that something will have to give if we are to arrive at a universal concept of religious freedom because, to put it baldly, one half of the world thinks that religious freedom consists of freedom *for* conversion (i.e., the freedom to make others the object of proselytization), and the other half of the world feels that freedom of religion involves freedom *from* conversion (i.e., not to be made an object of proselytization). This obviously means that if we have to come up with a concept of religious freedom acceptable to both, each one of them will have to make compromises.

We propose a *principled compromise*. The principle on which it is based is that the positions of *both the parties*, although it may not be possible to retain them in the same form, must be taken into proper consideration. A key insight, which has so far eluded human rights discourse, may help us achieve this. It is a distinction between *my right* to change my religion and *someone else's right* to ask me to change my religion. If we examine the matter closely, my right to change my religion should really have no, or minimal, restrictions placed on it. *My* freedom to choose a religion, and if necessary to convert to it, should be unhindered and, as mentioned earlier, should have no, or very minimal restrictions, placed on it as it is everybody's right to choose their own religion. It is obvious to our intuition that a person should be free to follow any religion one chooses (so long as it is not by definition criminal in nature like claiming to kill somebody because that is one's religious view). This dimension of the issue is already adequately covered in human rights discourse. It should be noted clearly that the provisions against coercion in the context of religious freedom in human rights discourse are *not* understood explicitly as freedom from being made an object of proselytization. But the right of somebody else to ask me to change my religion cannot be left equally unqualified. I may not want to change my religion, I may not wish to be made an object of proselytization, I may not welcome an invasion of my privacy, and so on. Nobody has the right to ask me to change my religion if I don't want to.

The crucial point that emerges from this analysis is that any provision in human rights on this point should honor my right to change my religion, but *not* someone else's right to ask me to change my religion or to impose it onto me by either threat, inducement, or pressure of any kind. However, *proselytizing religions may object to such a formulation of religious freedom because they feel that their religion requires them to invite others to join them. They can certainly do so, but do they have the religious right to do so?*

One way of balancing the rival claims of the two parties would be to propose the formulation that *religious freedom consists of the freedom to retain or change one's religion and to belong to one, more than one, or to no religion.*

We still need to take into account the desire of the proselytizing religions to share their message with those who don't belong to their religion. We should honor this desire by treating it as a *manifestation of freedom of expression and not as a religious freedom.* The right to convert is not a religious right but a right of expression involving not freedom of religion but freedom of expression, which takes the form of an invitation which the other person is free to decline. This right is articulated in Article 19 of the UDHR as follows: 'Everyone has the right to freedom of opinion and expression; this right includes freedom to hold opinions without interference and to seek, receive and impart information and ideas through any media and regardless of frontiers' (Brownlie, 1992: 25).

The compromise which the proselytizing religions make in this formulation is to consider their right to approach others to join them as falling under the freedom of expression and not freedom of religion. The compromise nonproselytizing religions have to make is to accept the fact that the proselytizing religions can ask everyone, including them, to change their religion, an invitation they are free to turn down. Similarly, the formulation mentioned above also balances the right to have more than one religion with the right to have none. The provision that one may choose not to have a religion may also be seen as an attempt to balance religion with ideology and to accept the fact that people can choose to follow an ideology rather than a religion.

Nonproselytizing religions sometimes object to the aggression the proselytizing religions indulge in when members of a nonproselytizing religion are asked to change their religion. This issue also gets addressed when the right to ask somebody to change their religion is treated not as a matter of freedom of religion but as involving freedom of expression, inasmuch as aggression and politeness are more properly seen as matters of expression.

Limitations of freedom of religion

Let us now address the question whether religious freedom is completely unfettered because the UDHR (1948) mentions no restrictions on it in Article 18. It is significant that restrictions on religious freedom are mentioned in the International Covenant on Civil and Political Rights (1966). This covenant states that 'freedom to manifest one's religion or beliefs may be subject only to such limitations as are prescribed by law and necessary to protect safety, order, health, or morals, or the fundamental rights and freedoms of others' (Brownlie, 1992: 132). In fact, if we look at the matter closely, the problem regarding proselytization, which was discussed earlier, really involves the issue of the religious freedom of others. The Indian Constitution allows for the propagation of religion. When some states in India placed restrictions on the propagation of religion, by disallowing the use of coercion, inducement, or threat in the matter, some Christian organizations approached the Supreme Court of India with the complaint that such a provision interfered with their freedom of religion. The Supreme Court, in upholding the provisions, argued that the freedom of conscience of those who want to convert has to be balanced by the freedom of conscience of those whom they wish to convert. It is worth pointing out, however, that the formulation of religious freedom offered in this paper gives the proselytizing religions the right to try to convert others but does not treat it as a religious right but as a right falling under the freedom of expression.

Conclusion

At first blush, the concept of religious freedom appears to be a fairly self-evident one when understood as the freedom of everyone to follow a religion of their own choice. A closer look at the concept, however, leads us to identify a problem. The problem arises out of the fact that the followers of a religion might feel that they have an inherent right to bring others within their charmed circle. But this could involve interfering with the religious freedom of others who may not wish to be made an object of proselytization. The difficulty posed by this issue, we discovered, is further complicated by the fact that some religions of the world are proselytizing in nature but that others are not, so that an issue, which to begin with appears to be one of a personal right of freedom of religion and a right to privacy, turns into one that involves the very nature of the religious traditions themselves.

The historical survey of this issue led to the finding that some religions can be classified as proselytizing religions, of which Christianity and Islam are the main examples, while other religions are nonproselytizing religions including Judaism, Hinduism, Buddhism (a missionary rather than proselytizing religion), Jainism, Sikhism, Confucianism, Daoism, Shintoism, and the indigenous religions.

A third level of complication, in discussing the concept of religious freedom, is introduced by the demographic fact that almost half the population of the word adheres to the proselytizing religions of Christianity and Islam and the other half to the other religions enumerated above. That is to say, not only have the rights of the proselytizing and nonproselytizing religions been taken into account, but these categories of religions are also demographically balanced.

One possible way of negotiating this issue is to highlight the need for an 'ethics of conversion.' That is to say, the right of the proselytizing religions to proselytize could be accepted by the nonproselytizing religions if it was kept within universally accepted ethical guidelines such as a voluntary abstention from not using imbalances in resources or power to one's advantage while engaging in proselytizing activities. Some Christian denominations are known to have proposed such ethical guidelines. These efforts, however, have not reached a point where they could be seriously considered as a possible universally accepted solution in the matter. It, therefore, becomes necessary to incorporate the perspective of the nonproselytizing religions in the very framework of human rights discourse in order to balance the concept of religious freedom as found in both proselytizing and nonproselytizing religions.

The solution proposed by us for this resolution is that the right to proselytize not be included within the category of religious freedom, but within the category of the right of freedom of expression. This allows the proselytizing religions the right to ask others to change their religions without encroaching on the right to religious freedom of the nonproselytizing religions.

As we are invoking the right to freedom of expression in this context, it might be useful to consider the provision as found in Article 19 of the International Covenant on Civil and Political Rights (1966) in this respect:

1. Everyone shall have the right to hold opinions without interference.
2. Everyone shall have the right to freedom of expression; this right shall include freedom to

seek, receive and impart information and ideas of all kinds, regardless of frontiers, either orally, in writing or in print, in the form of art, or through any other media of his choice.

3. The exercise of the rights provided for in paragraph 2 of this article carries with it special duties and responsibilities. It may therefore be subject to certain restrictions, but these shall only be such as are provided by law and are necessary:

    a. For respect of the rights or reputations of others;
    b. For the protection of national security or of public order (ordre public), or of public health or morals (Brownlie, 1992: 132).

References

Adcock, C.S., 2014. *The Limits of Tolerance: Indian Secularism and the Politics of Religious Freedom*. Oxford University Press.

Amore, R.C., Ching, J., 1996. The Buddhist tradition. In: Oxtoby W.G. (Ed.), *World Religions: Eastern Traditions*. Oxford University Press.

Artz, D.E., 1996. The treatment of religious dissidents under classical and contemporary Islamic law. In: Witte J., Van der Vyver J.D. (Eds.), *Religious Human Rights in Global Perspective: Religious Perspectives*. M. Nijhoff Publishers. 727.

Baxi, U., 2008. *The Future of Human Rights*. Oxford University Press.

Brownlie, I., 1992. *Basic Documents on Human Rights*. Clarendon Press.

Dershowitz, A.M., 2005. *Rights from Wrongs: A Secular Theory of the Origins of Rights*. Basic Books.

Glendon, M.A., 2001. *A World Made New: Eleanor Roosevelt and the Universal Declaration of Human Rights*. Random House.

Hick, J., 1990. *Philosophy of Religion*. Prentice Hall.

Kassam, A., 2017. Top Canadian court rejects indigenous case against new ski resort. *The Guardian*. 3 November. Available at https://www.theguardian.com/world/2017/nov/03/canada-supreme-court-ski-resort-indigenous-sacred-land.

Padilla C.R., 1976. *The New Face of Evangelicalism: An International Symposium on the Lausanne Covenant*. Hodder and Stoughton.

Reader, I., 1991. *Religion in Contemporary Japan*. Macmillan.

Satlow, M.L., 2006. Defining Judaism: Accounting for 'religions' in the study of religion. *Journal of the American Academy of Religion* 74, 837.

Sharma, A., 2011. *Problematizing Religious Freedom*. Springer.

Shepard, W.E., 2015. *Introducing Islam*. Routledge.

Tahzib-Lie, B., 1996. *Freedom of Religion or Belief: Ensuring Effective International Legal Protection*. M. Nijhoff Publishers.

Taylor, C., 1999. *A Secular Age*. Belknap Press of Harvard University Press.

Warner, B., Center for the Study of Political Islam, 2010. *Sharia Law for the Non-Muslim*. Centre for the Study of Political Islam.

Wahyudi, J. 1997. *Ahl Al-Kitāb in the Qur'ān: An Analysis of Selected Classical and Modern Exegesis*. Dissertation: McGill University.

PART III

Geopolitics of the right to freedom of religion or belief

12

Geopolitics of the right to freedom of religion: Western perspectives

Gerhard Robbers

Ambiguities of concepts

The West

'The west' and 'western,' in their basic meaning, are mere geographical terms. In political discourse, the West and Western have become terms with a multitude of facets. They stand for Europe, the Americas, and Australasia. They signify cultural identity when pointing at differences between Orient and Occident.[1] In religion, there is the difference between Latin and Orthodox Christianity; for quite a while, there was political antagonism between the market economy identified with the West and communist systems identified with the East. Today, 'the West' has become a battle cry term also used to fuel confrontation between cultures coined by Christian traditions in one part and Muslim traditions in other parts of the world. Many other notions of 'the West' could well be added. They are ambiguous and all too easily misleading in their generalizing approach. In their political contexts, they can be dangerous tools when intensifying antagonisms and hampering mutual understanding by overstressing differences and covering similarities with other parts of the world.

In this chapter, 'Western' and 'the West' are used to describe a geographical area, a part of the world that includes Europe, the Americas, and Australasia. This definition is obviously open for flowing transitions; however, it can be useful as a first, yet vague approach to a manifold area.

This geographical concept of 'Western,' however, is immediately overlaid by cultural assumptions when it comes to historical developments that have led to or have hampered freedom of religion or belief. European settlement of the Americas and Australasia pushed aside previous populations and their cultures, and little is known about features of freedom of religion or belief in these cultures.

Analyzing freedom of religion or belief in this context does not intend to identify a distinct 'Western' approach as opposed to other approaches. The aim is rather to identify features of freedom of religion or belief as they exist in this area. These features may – or may not – be

1 For details and controversies, cf., e.g., Barzun, 2001; Daly, 2014; Stearns, 2003; Ankerl, 2000: 119–244; Huntington, 1996.

found in other parts of the world, perhaps with other names, intensity, or distinctness. This chapter tries to describe freedom of religion or belief from within the geographical area and not by segregation against other areas. The underlying assumption is that identity is constituted by one's own characteristics and qualities and not by delimitation against others.

Geopolitics

Examining freedom of religion or belief from the angle of geopolitics assumes that this freedom depends to a considerable extent on historical, philosophical, political, religious, economic, legal, and indeed geographical preconditions. The geographical area to be focused on is described by 'the West.' This approach rejects a narrow understanding of geopolitics as being the study of how geography affects politics and international relations (Devetak et al., 2012: 492), and it also rejects a perception as signifying merely the political relations of states or international organizations on a worldwide scale. Due to the lack of comprehensive studies based on such a broad approach, this chapter can merely present some examples and raise a number of questions which need deeper scrutiny.

In looking into geopolitical features which influence freedom of religion or belief, the assumption is that none of the features alone can explain the development, but together they form strong explanations for the factual appearance of freedom of religion or belief.

This includes the view that freedom of religion or belief has been used to implement economic, cultural, and political interests in other regions of the world; the allegation of this view is that freedom of religion or belief has been a tool for imperialism.[2] However, freedom of religion or belief has been developed and fought for in Europe, America, and Australasia internally. Equally, it was within this area that freedom of religion or belief was – and often still is – intensely under attack and facing strong and persistent opposition with the effect that emigrants were looking for places where they could practice their religion freely.

The idea of freedom of religion or belief as a human right, like the idea of human rights as such, holds freedom of religion or belief to be a value in itself, a value independent of all such geopolitical features. They may explain how freedom of religion as a human right came about, but they do not explain why this should in fact be so. They explain, but they do not legitimize.

It is to be assumed that freedom of religion or belief, on its part, does exert influence on geopolitical features. This influence may constitute a reason why freedom of religion or belief is not always welcomed or rather is under considerable threat by those who fear this influence.

Different geopolitical circumstances result in different shades of freedom of religion or belief. This is apparent in individual freedom of religion or belief as well as in its institutional or group-related relevance. In the United States of America, home schooling is regarded to be an important constituent of freedom of religion or belief, while in other states, the interest of public education to provide coherence of society and equal opportunities for rich and poor prevails (cf. Basham, Merrifiel, and Hepburn, 2007). In the United Kingdom, archbishops and bishops of the Anglican Established Church of England are by virtue of their church office members of the House of Lords and thus actors of state legislation. To the same effect, leaders of other religions are called into the House of Lords (McClean, 2019). In France, religion in general is regarded as a basically private matter and in this sphere it enjoys rather far-reaching freedom. Religion is less appreciated when it is visible in public or tries to interfere in the political process (Messner, 2019; Little, 2014). In contrast, in Germany the

2 For a contemporary issue, cf. Prodromou, 2006; Sullivan, Hurd, Mahmood, and Danchin, 2015; Su, 2016.

participation of religions in the public sphere is welcomed; religions are attributed by a number of state-religion treaties an explicit 'public task' which to a large extent is a result of the Nazi regime and its terror: After the breakdown of the Nazi regime, religions appeared as strong contributors to prevent Nazism to rise again.[3] The study of geopolitics of freedom of religion or belief may help to understand why such differences occur.

Approaches

This chapter explores geopolitical reasons for the development and existence of freedom of religion or belief. It thus looks primarily into supportive structures and activities. It must not be forgotten, however, that while freedom of religion or belief has become a foremost human right, there have been – and there still are – a multitude of efforts and views strongly opposing such freedom. A fair account of freedom of religion or belief has to take notice of these antagonistic elements as well. There is little doubt that many of the features which have positive effects on freedom of religion or belief can exert hampering influence as well.

General appearance of freedom of religion or belief

Come characteristics of freedom of religion or belief are common throughout the area described. The guarantee is perceived as being general and universal. It is viewed as a human right; thus, a fundamental importance is attributed to it. The legal guarantee answers to grave experiences of injustice and oppression which, on the other hand, may differ from region to region.

Moreover, freedom of religion or belief is part of major international treaties. It represents a value worth being protected by foremost political instruments. It also forms part of most state constitutions, a fact which also mirrors the high appreciation attributed to it.

There is obviously no common definition of *religion* in terms of the meaning of a fundamental right (see, e.g., Sandberg, 2018). Courts use a great variety of definitions and descriptions or avoid a definition altogether. Freedom of religion or belief remains an open freedom – open to developing concepts, ideas, and a multitude of situations.

A feature seemingly common to all approaches, however, is an understanding of a fundamental divide between the secular and the sacred, a notion of transcendence and beyond. A basic acceptance in law of at least some freedom of religion or belief represents appreciation while not necessarily acceptance of the worthiness of activities based on deep beliefs, be they religious or nonreligious. It is likewise generally accepted that the law protects both having as well as not having religious or nonreligious beliefs.

While there are great differences in describing the scope of freedom of religion or belief, it is generally accepted to protect opinions as well as actions based on religion or belief. The freedom covers both individual and institutional beliefs and activities.

Specific contents and consequences which are debated in the 2010s comprise issues such as labor law, home schooling, or wearing religious garments. These issues change quickly – only ten years before a broadly discussed issue was the rise of new religions and religious communities. An everlasting issue seems to be the separation of state and religious communities, what exactly that demands, and whether and to what extent religion or belief may be visible in the public sphere.

3 The 'Treaty of Loccum' of 21 March 1955. Available at https://www.religion-recht.de/2010/08/loccumer-vertrag-vertrag-des-landes-niedersachsen-mit-den-evangelischen-landeskirchen-in-niedersachsen.

In some regions, especially in Central Europe, an increase of secularization is noted (Pickel, 2013; Taylor, 2007). This observation reveals growing disregard and diminishing esteem for religious beliefs. Such disregard may also weaken the esteem for freedom of religion or belief as this freedom is perceived to affect only a smaller part of the population.

Geopolitical features of freedom of religion or belief

Geographical features

Freedom of religion or belief is necessary only where different convictions about religion exist. Such differences emerge and persist more easily when they are undergirded by geographical circumstances (Knott, 2005; Park, 1994; Büttner, 1985). In North America, developing in vast lands where – at the expense of the indigenous population – different religious groups could settle without interfering too much with each other, religious diversity could grow from the very beginning of modern immigration. The extended territories provided the possibility of emigration of religious groups and thus facilitated their survival and flourishing. Britain, being an island, developed and retained religious independence from Roman Catholic mainland Europe because of its remote geographical position.

The Alps provided a barrier between the Emperor of the Holy Roman Empire and the Pope and to some degree a geographical separation of State and Church which supported the power sruggle between the two and often prevented a final victory of one over the other. This geographical divide may well be regarded as a contribution to a general and early division of powers with checks and balances. It supported some degree of independence of one power from the others, an independence which served as a precondition to the development of freedom of religion or belief. This divide did not take place in the East Roman, or Byzantine Empire, where Emperor and Patriarch resided in the very same capital city.

Mountain ranges, broad rivers, and seas which served as natural barriers contributed to the rise of the nation-state which in turn contributed to growing religious diversity even within the same religious confessions. Religious diversity was thus solidified and persisted. In turn, freedom of religion or belief requires nondiscrimination in view of migrants' adherence to certain religions or beliefs. It was with this aim, to mention just one example, that an amendment bill to the Freedom of Religion Act in the United States had been introduced into the legislative process providing that an alien may not be denied entry, re-entry, or admission to the United States, or any other immigration benefit, because of the alien's religion or lack of religious beliefs.[4]

Geographical preconditions facilitate, encumber, or channel migration. Several phases of or rather continuous migration have shaped the religious demography in Europe, the Americas, and Australasia. Present immigration into the United States of America from predominantly Roman Catholic countries, migration into Europa from Islam-dominated regions, and former Calvinist immigration from France into Germany are examples that underscore the demand for freedom of religion or belief by intensifying religious diversity. Immigration influences the public atmosphere concerning freedom of religion or belief; immigration by adherents to religions which are regarded as alien to the local traditions have fed calls to limit freedom of religion or belief.

4 See https://www.congress.gov/bill/116th-congress/house-bill/590?q=%7B%22search%22%3A%5B%22CASE+Act%22%5D%7D&s=1&r=91.

Diversity of religions

Demographical religious facts seem to strongly influence the status of freedom of religion or belief.[5] Dominant religions mostly appear to be less appreciative of freedom of religion or belief as a general right than minority religions. Small religious groups with little overall influence usually seem to be more easily tolerated than minority religions which represent a stronger portion of the population and are regarded as a threat to the majority religion or belief or the majority culture. Muslim immigrants into Europe face intolerance, often with regard to the wearing of religious garments or the construction of mosques. Freedom of religion or belief appears to be stronger when there is no dominant religion or belief, but a number of more or less equally strong groups may form an equilibrium.

Some freedom of religion has been present throughout European history. While the dominant Christian religion prevailed, some other religions were more or less tolerated.

This applies to Muslim Tartars in Poland, Lithuania, and Belorussia, a current group of some thousand people that stem from immigrants in the fourteenth century.[6] It also applied to tolerated Jews[7] despite grave persecution throughout the centuries.

Diversity of religions thus has contributed to the rise of freedom of religion or belief. Such diversity was and is a strong public factor in the United States of America (see, however, Pew Research Center, 2014). It became an important factor in Europe during and after the Reformation which split the dominant church and resulted in a variety of different Christian confessions. However, because of the rise of nation-states with dominant confessions within them, this variety, while being a feature of Europe as a whole, was not significant in many individual nation-states. As a religious-demographic structure, diversity of religions was most visible in Switzerland, the Netherlands, and Germany; it has become a common feature throughout Europe.

However, diversity of religions does not necessarily foster freedom of religion or belief. A totalitarian regime can well regard religious diversity and religion as a threat to its rule, a fact which in Europe has been demonstrated by the anti-religious persecution of the German Nazi regime between 1933 and 1945.

Economic interests

Some authors argue that freedom of religion or belief serves as a strong factor in economic growth and prosperity. They believe that faith has a positive power on business and the economy.[8] While this could be misunderstood as subordinating freedom of religion or belief to mere economic interests, it points at an important factor that has supported free exercise of religion or belief in many a case, but also has counteracted this freedom throughout history. Freedom of religion or belief sets free energies and concentration to be employed for other ends than surviving in the religious sphere. If freedom of religion or belief is guaranteed, believers as well as non-believers have an important concern less to invest resources in. Moreover, religious hostilities and restrictions usually create climates of unrest or at least uncertainty that can drive

5 For diversity of religion in Europe, see, e.g., Botelho Moniz, 2019; see also Voltaire, 1733.

6 Cf. Harvard Encyclopedia of American Ethnic Groups, Polish or Lithuanian Tartars. Harvard University Press. 990.

7 As an introduction cf. Germany, Virtual Jewish History Tour, Jewish Virtual Library, https://www.jewishvirtuallibrary.org/germany-virtual-jewish-history-tour; United Kingdom Virtual Jewish History Tour, Jewish Virtual Library, https://www.jewishvirtuallibrary.org/united-kingdom-virtual-jewish-history-tour.

8 Cf. Brian Grim, The Religious Freedom & Business Foundation.

away local and foreign investment, which is likely to undermine sustainable development and to disrupt sectors of economies.

Religious institutions, distinct from secular ones, have contributed considerably and throughout the centuries to the common prosperity. Monastic orders have worked on drying vast swamp lands to win arable land (cf. Blackbourn, 2006), and church institutions have maintained schools and hospitals (cf. Ferzoco and Muessig, 2000; Bowers, 2007). While existing within the general prevailing Christian religion, religious orders provided at least some religious diversity.

Economic interests have been strong in allowing some freedom of religion for Jews in European history and at times safeguarding them against violent persecution. An example is the regal order of 1236 by Holy Roman Emperor Frederick II (Roth, 29917) which afforded imperial protection to Jews and at the same time imposed heavy payment obligations on them.

Trade interests also contributed to some freedom of religion or belief in Europe when it was divided into many territories. Economic exchange between the often only small territories with their different religious backgrounds made it necessary to tolerate different religions of traveling salesmen.

Largely due to economic reasons, in the aftermath of the Thirty Years War of 1618–1648, rulers called in Huguenots from France to repopulate many of the areas which had been almost completely depopulated by wartime events (Gilman, 1962; Candler, 1960; Scoville, 1952). They were granted freedom of religion and proved to be essential factors in rebuilding the economy. Such economic interest was supposedly also one, while not the only, component of Prussian religion policy which the Prussian king Frederick II expressed in 1740 in the words: All religions must be tolerated. Let every man seek heaven in his own fashion.[9]

In general, it can be said that freedom of religion attracts religious groups which are persecuted in other parts of the world; these are often people with strong economic potential who work hard in order to found a new and better existence. Furthermore, religions provide alternatives to existing society; they thus stand for innovation and progress in society. Minorities free to exercise their distinct religion or belief may well offer fruitful and innovative alternatives to the existing way of life.

This contribution to economic welfare, on the other hand, may lead to feelings of rejection in the existing local population that is afraid of new challenges and competition and can thus function as an obstacle to actual freedom of religion or belief. An example is the immigration of Muslim workers into Central Europe in the second half of the twentieth century, mostly from Turkey. This migration was first welcomed and actively endorsed when a workforce was needed, but these sentiments turned into some religious and cultural rejection when the workforce began to be viewed as competitors due to a decline in economic development.[10]

Peace function

A great variety of political interests affect freedom of religion or belief. Their positive or negative effects result from manifold components. Some have only short-term consequences, and some may cause long-term characteristics. Some may have direct consequences, and others only have indirect, but not inevitably less, impact.

9 Fredrick II, Rand-Verfügung des Königs zum Immediat-Bericht des Geistlichen Departements. Berlin 1740 Mai 22: Katholische Schulen und Proselytenmacherei, in Lehmann, 1881: 4.

10 A reportage in Gupte, 1984.

One of the predominant factors that lead to freedom of religion is the political interest of peace in society. While religious antagonisms have often led to violent confrontation, peace in society is best preserved when people can live their religion freely and without oppression. An atmosphere of mutual respect or tolerance between the different religions is a necessary element of such religious peace. Oppression of religion as such as well as oppression to specific religions has, in the longer run, always resulted in disorder and even violence.

There are ubiquitous past and present examples of this peace function of freedom of religion or belief.

Historically, this can be seen in Central Europe, in the Holy Roman Empire of the German Nation, which, after the exhaustion of the religious wars in the sixteenth and seventeenth centuries, needed religious peace to preserve its endangered unity. Similar experiences have been made in the English civil wars of the seventeenth century. In France, the 1598 Edict of Nantes brought temporary peace to the country by granting religious freedom to the Huguenots.[11] It was later revoked.

Contemporary examples of the important peace-keeping function freedom of religion or belief has are the United States of America and the multireligious situation of Western Europe. There is little religious strife in these countries; however, there is some religious intolerance, primarily against Muslim immigration, and resurgent anti-Semitism.

In a world that is growing smaller due technical progress which makes long distance travel take a matter of hours, diversity of religions is a determining factor of coexistence. Peace therefore depends on freedom of religion or belief worldwide.

Freedom of religion or belief has proven to be necessary for preserving peace in a religiously diverse society. It is an indispensable guarantee to avoid alienating parts of the population. Religious and belief convictions can be and usually are very strong. If a state does not succeed in accommodating religions and beliefs on its territory in a way that is acceptable to all its people, the very existence of this state, or at least public safety and order, are in danger. Freedom of religion is thus a prerequisite to the long-lasting and continuous harmony and well-being of a society.

Identity formation

The rise of the nation-state contributes to variations in the approach to freedom of religion or belief. Nations have defined their identity, their set of values, and their common bond often by recourse to a common religion. This is apparent in the history of the Polish people in retaining their national existence in the Catholic confession against Orthodox Russia and Protestant Prussia, and it is visible in Greece or Serbia retaining their national identity against Muslim Turkey. It is also a factor in the national self-understanding of Scandinavian countries keeping to Lutheranism or in England with its Anglican Church of England.

In the past and present, religion and freedom of religion or belief have thus been widespread elements of defining nations' identities. It often is an obstacle to freedom of religion or belief when a particular religious creed defines the identity of a people, a state, or a nation. On the other hand, it usually favors freedom of religion or belief when identity is found in this fundamental right. Freedom of religion or belief has often been declared one of the United States of America's most fundamental liberties and a central principle upon which the nation was founded.[12] It is not surprising that this nation endorses freedom of religion or belief in its overall

11 Edict of Nantes, https://www.culture.gouv.fr/Depot-legal-du-ministere-de-la-Culture/?lang=en&module=uc&fichier=00#/en/uc/02_00_00.

12 See https://www.aclu.org/issues/religious-liberty/free-exercise-religion/defending-rights-religious-minorities.

policies, while it must not be forgotten that specific details of freedom of religion or belief and their implementation may remain strongly controversial.

Other nations or political entities have found identity in identifying with one specific religion or confession. Some reminiscence of this is visible - while not distorting freedom of religion or belief any more - in some countries' constitutions when their preamble refers to the Almighty as in Switzerland or to the Holy Trinity as in Ireland.

More dangerous for freedom of religion or belief are state attempts to enforce unity of religion in supposing that such unity would serve as a guarantee for the nations coherence, while religious diversity would endanger social cohesion. Going to the very heart of what freedom of religion or belief stands for in a society, the European Court of Human Rights has held that freedom of thought, conscience, and religion is one of the foundations of a democratic society.[13] It is, in its religious dimension, as the Court states, one of the most vital elements that go to make up the identity of believers and their conception of life, but it is also a precious asset for atheists, agnostics, skeptics, and the unconcerned. The pluralism indissociable from a democratic society, which has been dearly won over the centuries, depends on it. While religious freedom is primarily a matter of individual conscience, it also implies, inter alia, freedom to manifest one's religion alone and in private or in community with others, in public, and within the circle of those whose faith one shares. Bearing witness in words and deeds is bound up with the existence of religious convictions. That freedom entails, inter alia, freedom to hold or not to hold religious beliefs and to practice or not to practice a religion.[14] The Court has also said that, in a democratic society, in which several religions coexist within one and the same population, it may be necessary to place restrictions on this freedom in order to reconcile the interests of the various groups and ensure that everyone's beliefs are respected.[15] However, in exercising its regulatory power in this sphere and in its relations with the various religions, denominations, and beliefs, the State has a duty to remain neutral and impartial. What is at stake here is the preservation of pluralism and the proper functioning of democracy, one of the principle characteristics of which is the possibility it offers of resolving a country's problems through dialog, without recourse to violence, even when they are irksome. Accordingly, the role of the authorities in such circumstances is not to remove the cause of tension by eliminating pluralism, but to ensure that the competing groups tolerate each other.[16]

Political structures

Freedom of religion or belief gradually grew in Central Europe not the least because this area was split in very numerous quasi independent territories. Local and regional princes as well as free cities enjoyed some and always an intensely contested degree of sovereignty under the umbrella of the Holy Roman Empire. It included the right of rulers to correct faulty conditions within the church in their territory when the church institutions were not able to act. This heterogeneous political landscape was favorable to the spreading of the Protestant

---

13 European Court of Human Rights, Case of Metropolitan Church of Bessarabia and others v. Moldova, judgment of 13 December 2001, 45701/99.

14 European Court of Human Rights, Kokkinakis v. Greece, judgment of 25 May 1993, Series A no. 260-A, p. 17, § 31; Buscarini and Others v. San Marino [GC], no. 24645/94, § 34, ECHR 1999-I.

15 European Court of Human Rights Kokkinakis v. Greece, judgment of 25 May 1993, Series A no. 260-A, p. 18, § 33.

16 European Court of Human Rights, Case of Metropolitan Church of Bessarabia and others v. Moldova, judgment of 13 December 2001, 45701/99.

Reformation from 1517 onward. Various princes were able to provide resources and refuge for the antagonistic confessions, Lutheran, Roman Catholic, and also Calvinist. This political situation contributed to the consolidation of the newly rising confessions and the increasing religious diversity.

The fragmented structure of Central Europe also gave some effectiveness to the right to emigrate as an early root and limited form of future freedom of religion or belief. While the 1555 Religious Peace of Augsburg had laid down the basic right of rulers to determine which confession, Roman Catholic or Lutheran, their subjects had to adhere to,[17] it also provided for the subjects' right to emigrate if they did not want to follow this determination.[18] It was often only a matter of a few miles, though hard enough, to change from one territory to another where one's own confession was the official one. This facilitated the right of Roman Catholic, Lutheran, and Calvinist individual believers in the 1648 Peace of Westphalia to retain their respective religious practice they had held in the year 1624 in territories of different confessional determination.[19] These early roots of some, though limited, freedom of religion were dictated by the very need to achieve and preserve peace in the deeply torn and heavily destroyed central European regions.

Diversity of approaches

Within the various nation-states, a variety of approaches to freedom of religion or belief could further develop. While in the United States of America a wall of separation between the state and religious communities prohibited state funding of religious activities, ample subsidies to religious activities are well accepted elsewhere. Depending on the point of view of the respective spectator, funding of specific religious activities appears to be discrimination for those who do not receive similar aid. Others view it as equal treatment with other, nonreligious activities such as sports or arts. Non-funding is regarded by some as discrimination of the religious sphere, while others cherish it as nonintervention into religion.

There are marked differences in the approach to separation between state and religious communities. While the wall of separation between the state and religious institutions is characteristic for the United States of America despite all specific exceptions to this basic concept, other states uphold state churches such as the United Kingdom or Denmark. Others prefer a system of cooperation between state and religious communities such as Italy, Spain, Austria, Hungary, Poland, or Germany in which there is cooperation on a basis of separation between the two institutions. Some states follow a policy of benevolent neutrality which allows support of religions; others declare a more distant relationship.

Differences in approach to freedom of religion or belief appear, for example, in labor law within religious communities when there is far-reaching autonomy of religious communities to frame labor law according to their specific religious convictions as in Germany (Robbers, 2019: 118). In other countries, like in Slovenia, the ordinary state labor law provisions were applied widely unchanged until recently also within religious communities.[20]

17 Sections 15, 16 Peace of Augsburg, https://web.archive.org/web/20080513031030/http://www.uoregon.edu/~sshoemak/323/texts/augsburg.htm.

18 Section 24 Peace of Augsburg, https://web.archive.org/web/20080513031030/http://www.uoregon.edu/~sshoemak/323/texts/augsburg.htm.

19 Article V. Section 31, Article VII IPO (Instrumentum Pacis Osnabrugensis, Treaty of Osnabrück).

20 Cf. for the development Sturm, 2005: 485; Sturm and Ivanc, 2019: 555.

Political organization in the form of a plurality of independent states has furthered diversity of approaches to freedom of religion or belief, and unification of states has exerted the contrary effect. Political organization of statehood affects freedom of religion or belief when, e.g. the European Union subjects all labor law within religious communities to state courts with the result of alignment of the laws of the European Union Member States. Important harmonizing effects in the law on religion within the European states are furthered also by the European Court of Human Rights.

The aforementioned are but examples for differing approaches in balancing competing rights within the general catalog of fundamental rights. Freedom of religion or belief, being one of the foremost fundamental rights, nevertheless stands in coexistence and often competition with other rights and freedoms which have to be brought into a valid balance. The results of these balancing processes differ from country to country due to a multitude of competing factors and differences in the levels of appreciation for the various interests; the European Court of Human Rights has attributed legitimacy to such differences by accepting a margin of appreciation of states on how to best accommodate opposing interests.[21]

Colonialism

Colonialism, by disrupting religious structures in the colonized regions, has been contrary to freedom of religion or belief (cf. Hackett, 2011). Arguably, on the other hand, in some European countries, colonialism, always bearing in mind its injustice and atrocities, has at least for some time contributed to freedom of religion or belief within the colonizing countries. This may hold true for the United Kingdom and France; immigration from colonized regions into these countries contributed to increased religious diversity; and immigrants mostly co-operated with the authorities of the colonizing state and were welcomed. On the other hand, such results were hardly visible in other European countries. However, these differences in immigration backgrounds seem to give some explanation of differences in approach to religious diversity and freedom of religion or belief in the various societies. Examples are the greater tolerance to Islam in the United Kingdom and French government efforts to accommodate Islam.

Opposition to freedom of religion or belief

Being important factors in the political process, religion and belief can be and are used in supporting political aspirations; often they are used to delegitimize political opponents as well as to motivate political followers. Religion and belief are strong components of political power. In this context, freedom of religion or belief as a universal right is easily regarded as a threat to one's own political power.[22]

Political opposition to freedom of religion or belief has been strong until now. Even when this freedom is basically accepted, there is ongoing debate about its limitations, and limitations are often easily implemented. While this limitation process is mostly due to competing legitimate interests in the relevant legal and political systems, it often is used to silence political opposition and exclude alternative positions from the political process.

---

21 European Court of Human Rights, Greece v. United Kingdom, 'Cyprus,' No. 176/56, 2 Yearbook of the European Convention 1958–1959, 176.

22 For further reading cf. Callaway, n.d.

Religious traditions

Freedom of religion or belief has often been opposed by religions and beliefs themselves with the exception of their own set of convictions. Freedom of religion or belief was and is frequently understood as merely allowing the true religion or belief to be freely exercised – it is freedom limited to following the (own) truth. No freedom was attributed to the (supposed) error and to other, mostly competing sets of beliefs. Such attitudes are not confined to religions or belief systems, but emerge also in the political field.

Religious convictions, on the other hand, have laid the groundwork for freedom of religion or belief not only for themselves, but also for believers of other theological concepts. The idea that only free belief is true belief leads to freedom of religion or belief for everyone. Today, the prevalent religions in the area described mostly teach freedom of religion or belief as an intrinsic value of their religion or belief (cf. Little, n.d.).

As an example, in 1965, the Second Vatican Council approved Dignitatis humanae, the Declaration on Religious Liberty. This document roots religious freedom in the teaching of the Roman Catholic Church on human dignity. It teaches that religious freedom is the cornerstone of a society that promotes human dignity; it is a fundamental human right, which follows the duty of all people to seek the truth about God.[23]

A step in this direction was taken when the Lutheran Reformation taught that the right religion should be spread 'sine vi sed verbo' (not by force, but through the word).[24] An earlier step was taken when in the second half of the thirteenth century Thomas of Aquino taught to respect the freedom even of a conscience that is mistaken about the truth of salvation.[25]

The area to be described in this chapter is deeply coined by Christianity in its various forms, predominantly Roman Catholic, Christian Orthodox, and Protestant with a multitude of further variations. Jewish as well as Muslim influences are also of high importance as is the basis of ancient Roman and Greek culture. They all have contributed in manifold ways to the present appearance of freedom of religion or belief. As example is the idea of symphonía between church and state in Christian Orthodox teaching, by which the state protects the church and the church supports the government (Harakas, 1993: 259 ff.). Another example is the passing on of ancient Roman law by the Catholic Church which contributes to the legal character of freedom of religion or belief. A further example is the Protestant tradition by which Martin Luther insisted in the 1521 Imperial Diet of Worms that his conscience was captive to the Word of God, and it was neither safe nor right to go against conscience.[26]

Freedom of religion or belief as an individual right was prepared by individualistic tendencies in theology, predominantly in Protestant teaching. It was the direct relationship between the individual person and God in which a clergy was no longer needed as a mediator for salvation that made an important contribution for individual freedom of religion or belief in particular and individual human rights in general.

While religiously based individualism has contributed to the development of modern individual human rights, religious traditions have also strengthened the idea of freedom of religion

23 Declaration on religious freedom Dignitatis Humanae on the right of the person and of communities to social and civil freedom in matters religious, December 7, 1965, http://www.vatican.va/archive/hist_councils/ii_vatican_council/documents/vat-ii_decl_19651207_dignitatis-humanae_en.html.

24 Confessio Augustana 28, English translation at https://redbrickparsonage.wordpress.com/2018/03/05/augsburg-confession-article-1-god/.

25 Thomas of Aquino, Summa theologiae, Ia-IIae, Quaestio 19, Art. 5–6.

26 Deutsche Reichstagsakten, Jüngere Reihe, Band II, n. 80: 581–582, https://archive.org/details/deutschereichst07kommgoog/page/n9.

or belief as a right of religious institutions. The idea of ecclesia, of community and representation of a religious group, has been an important factor in this approach. In several jurisdictions, the religious group does not only enjoy freedom of religion or belief as a representative of its individual members or adherents, but also as a group as such.

Philosophical traditions

Freedom of religion or belief has been an important subject of philosophy throughout at least modern times, and philosophy has in manifold ways contributed to its present manifestation.

The individualism which emerged strongly in theology and philosophy during the fifteenth century also formed the modern social contract theories.[27] Based on individual natural rights, these contracts legitimized and limited political power and conveyed civil and political rights to the individual including religious freedom. John Locke, outstanding and influential protagonist of this widely accepted theory, argued in the seventeenth century that the government was to protect life, liberty, and estate; interfering with the religious life of the citizens would mean to exceed its authority, and true belief could not be forced anyway (Locke, 2003). The exception from tolerance which John Locke made toward the Roman Catholic church may well be based in the geopolitical fear that foreign powers would intervene in British politics.

Historical experiences

Historical experiences shape attitudes toward freedom of religion or belief. They differ from country to country, from region to region (Davis, 2002). They influence approaches to rights and freedoms even when they exist only subconsciously. One of these common experiences in Central Europe was the religious wars of the sixteenth and seventeenth centuries which devastated vast areas. They contributed to the rise of nation-states as well as to a gradual secularization. It was the state that stepped into a vacuum of common legitimacy, a legitimacy which had been previously provided by the one Christian church, but which had vanished since competing confessions coexisted in basically the same territory. Where coexistence of competing religious systems had to be organized, freedom of religion was an option to pursue. The experience of success on this path reinforced the idea of freedom of religion or belief.

Another example of historical experience may be found in the memory of a religious institution overwhelmingly powerful in the public political sphere which in the course of history has been deprived of much of this power. Such experience may well have led to the exclusion of religions from the political public sphere or at least to diminishing their visible influence especially in France. Freedom of religion has then been reduced to appear in the private sphere, whereas in countries without such experience, religions are an accepted actor in the political democratic arena enlarging the scope of freedom of religion into another important sphere.

In more recent history, several countries in Europe have experienced communist rule which was openly hostile to religion. Communist governments aimed to eliminate religion altogether, viewing it as the opium of the people by alluding to Karl Marx (Marx, 1844: 3). In most of these countries, freedom of religion or belief has been (re)introduced and religions have enjoyed state support after the end of the communist rule in the 1990s. In several of these cases, the religious community, which had been dominant before the rise of communism, was again

27 For an introduction cf. Ainsworth, 2008.

put into a favored position, sometimes taking over the role of legitimizing state powers that had been left vacant after the breakdown of the communist party.

An exceptional historic experience is the persecution of the Jews by Nazi Germany between 1933 and 1945. While constituted by ethnic and racist prejudice, it was founded in long-lasting and widespread historic anti-Judaism. After the murder of millions of Jews, it was this experience of guilt, the acceptance of responsibility, and better insight that caused freedom of religion or belief to have a foremost place in the new constitution of (then West) Germany. Other religions and beliefs had also been severely persecuted under the Nazi rule. In view of all this moral breakdown, freedom of religion or belief was and is regarded as a stronghold against injustice, failure, and guilt.

Legal traditions

Deeply based in broader legal traditions, freedom of religion or belief usually figures among other rights and freedoms in catalogs of human rights. This is the case in Europe, North America, and in the states of Latin America. There seems to be no fundamental difference in the level of protection which would result from whether legal traditions are based in the European continental or in the common law tradition.

Human rights catalogs result from both early comprehensive contracts between rulers and (usually noble) subjects and the idea of constitutions as forming the fundamental law of a state. In this way, freedom of religion or belief can be and is limited, but also accompanied and thus strengthened by other human rights. It forms part of a network of rights and duties contributing to a well-balanced, harmonious, and peaceful society. However, freedom of religion or belief can well be upheld also in jurisdictions, such as Australia, which protects freedom of religion or belief in Article 116 of its federal constitution, where there is no formal bill of rights.

The actual appearance of freedom of religion or belief is also influenced by the tradition of independent state courts which decide on legal issues. The mostly secular courts define standards of religion in society. This is, when properly administered, a means of equality and nondiscrimination of religions. Freedom of religion or belief can be implemented and enforced in the individual case by state powers.

In societies with a strong state legal system that is able to implement general rules, freedom of religion or belief may well be more easily recognized. Weak legal systems would need other normative systems which prove able to enforce general rules. One such possible alternative is the normative system of religious communities. As a result, people have to be kept within common religious communities in order to implement such alternative general rules, a situation which may endanger freedom of religion or belief.

Institutions protecting freedom of religion or belief

The importance attributed to freedom of religion or belief has prompted states and international organizations to create a great variety of special institutions to oversee freedom of religion or belief in their own territories or abroad. Freedom of religion or belief belongs to the general set of human rights, the respect of which is often demanded by governments from foreign countries. Examples of such demands include the United States International Freedom of Religion Act that was passed to implement and uphold freedom of religion or belief abroad by means of sanctions.[28]

28 International Religious Freedom Act of 1998 text.

It has been widely questioned whether this use of sanctions is expedient or rather may trigger stronger opposition against freedom of religion or belief. In the field of freedom of religion or belief, sanctions remind many of enforcing religion – an approach which would be alien to freedom of religion or belief.

Furthermore, there is the institution of rapporteurs for freedom of religion or belief. Prominent are the United Nations Special Rapporteur on Freedom of Religion or Belief,[29] the Special Envoy for the promotion of freedom of religion or belief outside the European Union,[30] and, with a somewhat different institutional approach, the Panel of Experts on Freedom of Religion or Belief of the Organization for Security and Cooperation in Europe.[31] Individual States have also installed special rapporteurs such as the United States Ambassador at Large for International Religious Freedom,[32] or in Germany the Government Representative for Worldwide Freedom of Religion or Belief.[33]

Conclusion

The examples of roots, experiences, obstacles, and favorable conditions which have contributed to freedom of religion or belief, as it appears today, certainly have to be supplemented by a multitude of additional aspects. All of them form part of what can be regarded today as a key component of human rights. As freedom of religion or belief has been contested and more often than not violated, it is still a contested right today within the area described in this chapter. Despite the many differences among its appearance within the various regions and states, some common features which have emerged over time and space may well be identified.

One of those common features of freedom of religion or belief is its gradual development over time as a human right. It is not a technical construct invented at a certain point of time, but is a value that mirrors human needs which exist at all times and places. As such, it appears in different degrees and manifestations which are not always easily recognized as being part of this freedom. Today, freedom of religion is regarded as being indispensable for a democratic society. There is a widespread readiness to acknowledge failures, historical shortcomings, and accountabilities in the field of freedom of religion or belief.

One of the most significant features of freedom of religion or belief, as it evolved in the western world, may be that it appears today as a freedom of the individual without excluding the notion of group rights.

Perhaps the most visible and important contribution of freedom of religion or belief and its commonly accepted function is to be a strong component to ensure peace in a society. Some sort of separation between state and religious communities seems to be a common safeguard for freedom of religion or belief, while various forms of unity of the two seem to be compatible with freedom of religion or belief.

A common feature remains the plural vision of freedom of religion or belief. What exactly it requires depends on multiple conditions of a concrete region, state, and society. There is no solid overall opinion on it beyond some basic assumptions. Debate about the exact consequences in

29 See https://www.ohchr.org/en/issues/freedomreligion/pages/freedomreligionindex.aspx.

30 See https://ec.europa.eu/europeaid/sectors/human-rights-and-governance/democracy-and-human-rights/freedom-religion-or-belief_en.

31 See https://www.osce.org/odihr/271901.

32 See https://www.state.gov/bureaus-offices/under-secretary-for-civilian-security-democracy-and-human-rights/office-of-international-religious-freedom/.

33 See https://www.bundesregierung.de/breg-de/aktuelles/interview-gruebel-1652922.

individual cases and circumstances is a dominant feature of this freedom. It is always contested. The scope and legitimacy of limitations to freedom of religion or belief are a matter of constant dispute. It also is a common phenomenon that there is no fixed definition of what religion or belief is; freedom of religion or belief is a continually developing freedom.

Freedom of religion or belief requires nondiscrimination in religious and belief affairs, it is a freedom for individuals as well as for groups, it protects religious and nonreligious convictions, and it likewise protects having as well as not having any such convictions. Freedom of religion or belief is finally secured by a multitude of institutions and legal instruments, and yet it remains a highly vulnerable freedom.

References

Ainsworth, B.N. III., 2008. *Aspects of Individualism in Fourteenth and Fifteenth Century Medieval Texts*. Available from: https://scholarworks.montana.edu/xmlui/handle/1/806.

Ankerl, G., 2000. *Coexisting Civilizations: Arabo-Muslim, Bharati, Chinese, and Western*. Inu Press.

Barzun, J., 2001. *From Dawn to Decadence: 500 Years of Western Cultural Life: 1500 to the Present*. Harper Collins.

Basham, P., Merrifield, J., Hepburn, C.R., 2007. *Home Schooling: from the Extreme to the Mainstream*. Available from: https://www.fraserinstitute.org/sites/default/files/Homeschooling2007.pdf.

Blackbourn, D., 2006. *The Conquest of Nature*. Jonathan Cape Press.

Botelho Moniz, J., 2019. Diversity and secularization in Europe. Analyzing the correlation between indexes of religiosity and cultural diversity in Europe. *Revista Española de Sociología* 28(3, supl. 2), 45.

Bowers, B.S. (Ed.), 2007. *Medieval Hospital And Medical Practice*. Ashgate Publishing.

Büttner, M., 1985. *Grundfragen der Religionsgeographie*. Reimer.

Callaway, C., n.d. Religion and politics. In: *Internet Encyclopedia of Philosophy*. Available from https://www.iep.utm.edu/rel-poli.

Candler, W., 1960. *The Persecution of Huguenots and French Economic Development, 1680-1720*. University of California Press.

Daly, J., 2014. *The Rise of Western Power: A Comparative History of Western Civilization*. Bloomsbury.

Davis, D.H., 2002. The evolution of religious freedom as a universal human right: Examining the role of the 1981 United Nations Declaration on the elimination of all forms of intolerance and of discrimination based on religion or belief. *BYU Law Rev*. 2, 217.

Devetak, R., George, J., Percy, S. (Eds.), 2012. *An Introduction to International Relations*. Cambridge University Press.

Ferzoco, G., Muessig, C. (Eds.), 2000. *Medieval Monastic Education*. Leicester University Press.

Gilman, C.M., 1962. *The Huguenot Migration in Europe and America, Its Cause and Effect*. Arlington Laboratory for Clinical and Historical Research.

Grim, B.J., Clark, J., Snyder, R.E., 2014. Is religious freedom good for business?: A conceptual and empirical analysis. *Interdisciplinary Journal of Research on Religion*. 10(4), 2.

Gupte, P., 1984. *The Crowded Earth*. Norton.

Hackett, R.I.J., 2011. Regulating religious freedom in Africa. *Emory International Law Review*. 25, 853.

Harakas, S.S., 1993. *Living the Faith: The Praxis of Eastern Orthodox Ethics*. Light and Life Publishing Company.

Huntington, S.P., 1996. *The Clash of Civilizations and the Remaking of the World Order*. Simon & Schuster.

Knott, K., 2005. *The Location of Religion: A Spatial Analysis*. Equinox Publishing.

Lehmann, M., 1881. *Preussen und die katholische Kirche seit 1640. Nach den Acten des Geheimen Staatsarchives. 2. Theil*. Hirzel, pp. 1740–1747.

Little, D., 2014. *Christianity and Religious Freedom in the Modern Period*. Berkley Centre for Religion, Peace & World Affairs, pp. 1751–2011. Available from: https://berkleycenter.georgetown.edu/essays/christianity-and-religious-freedom-in-the-modern-period-1751–2011.

Little, D., n.d. *Religious Freedom and Christianity: An Overview*. Berkley Centre for Religion, Peace & World Affairs. Available from: https://berkleycenter.georgetown.edu/essays/religious-freedom-and-christianity-an-overview.

Locke, J., 2003. In: Shapiro I. (Ed.),*Two Treatises of Government and A Letter Concerning Toleration*. Yale University Press.
Marx, K., 1844. *A Contribution to the Critique of Hegel's Philosophy of Right*. Available from: https://www.marxists.org/archive/marx/works/download/Marx_Critique_of_Hegels_Philosophy_of_Right.pdf.
McClean, D., 2109. State and church in the United Kingdom. In: Robbers G. (Ed.), *State and Church in the European Union*. Nomos, 657.
Messner, F., 2019. State and church in France. In: Robbers G. (Ed.), *State and Church in the European Union*. Nomos, 213.
Park, C.C., 1994. *Sacred Worlds: An Introduction to Geography and Religion*. Routledge.
Pew Research Centre, 2014. *Global Religious Diversity*. Available from: https://www.pewforum.org/2014/04/04/global-religious-diversity.
Pickel, G., 2013. *Religion Monitor: Understanding Common Ground. An International Comparison of Religious Belief*. Bertelsmann Stiftung.
Prodromou, E.H., 2006. *Legislating International Religious Freedom*. Pew Research Center, Religion & Public Life. Available from: https://www.pewforum.org/2006/11/20/legislating-international-religious-freedom.
Robbers, G., 2019. State and church in Germany. In: Robbers G. (Ed.), *State and Church in the European Union*. Nomos, 118.
Roth, C., 1997. Antisemitism. *Encyclopedia Judaica*. Keter Publishing House.
Sandberg, R., 2018. Clarifying the definition of religion under English law: The need for a universal definition. *Ecclesiastical Law J*. 20(2), 132.
Scoville, W.C., 1952. The Huguenots and the diffusion of technology. *Journal of Political Economy*. 60(4), 294 and 60(5), 392.
Stearns, P.N., 2003. *Western Civilization in World History*. Routledge.
Sturm, L., 2005. State and Church in Slovenia. In: G. Robbers (Ed.), *State and Church in the European Union*. Nomos. 485.
Sturm, L., Ivanc, B., 2019. State and church in Slovenia. In: Robbers, G. (Ed.), *State and Church in the European Union*. Nomos. 555.
Su, A., 2016. *Exporting Freedom. Religious Liberty and American Power*. Harvard University Press.
Sullivan, W.F., Hurd, E.S., Mahmood, S., Danchin P. G. (Eds.), 2015. *Politics of Religious Freedom*. University of Chicago Press.
Taylor, C., 2007. *A Secular Age*. Harvard University Press.
Voltaire, 1773. *Letters on the English, Letter VI: On The Presbyterians*. Available from: https://www.gutenberg.org/files/2445/2445-h/2445-h.htm.

13
Freedom of religion: Asian perspectives

Jaclyn L. Neo and Arif A. Jamal

Introduction

Freedom of religion and belief (FoRB) is a ubiquitous, legally ascribed freedom entrenched in several international and regional human rights treaties, as well as in most constitutions in the world.[1] While the intellectual and political origins of FoRB, as currently framed, is distinctly European, the freedom has penetrated the legal landscape of Asia through the ratification of international instruments as well as through constitution drafting. Many of the international human rights instruments that have been ratified by countries in Asia contain binding commitments to the protection of the right to freedom of thought, conscience, and religion. These include the International Covenant for Civil and Political Rights (ICCPR), the International Covenant on Economic, Social and Cultural Rights (ICESCR), the International Convention on the Elimination of All Forms of Racial Discrimination (ICERD), the Convention on the Rights of the Child (CRC), and the Convention on the Elimination of All Forms of Discrimination against Women (CEDAW).[2] These instruments give rise to specific treaty obligations pertaining to freedom of thought, conscience, and religion. The diffusion of FoRB is further reflected in the inclusion of the right to freedom of thought, conscience, and religion in the region's only human rights document – the ASEAN Declaration of Human Rights, promulgated by the ten member-states of the Association of Southeast Asian Nations (ASEAN) in 2012.[3]

1 The proliferation of religious freedom clauses in domestic and international documents has been well documented. See Lerner (2000: 129) and Witte (2001: 709). Witte in particular notes that there is a corresponding increase in religious intolerance, discrimination, and conflict.

2 Office of the High Commission for Human Rights, United Nations Special Rapporteur on Freedom of Religion or Belief, 'Rapporteur's Digest on Freedom of Religion or Belief: Excerpts of the Reports from 1986 to 2011 by the Special Rapporteur on Freedom of Religion or Belief Arranged by Topics of the Framework for Communications,' 10 March 2011, at § 32. Available at https://www.ohchr.org/Documents/Issues/ Religion/RapporteursDigestFreedomReligionBelief.pdf.

3 For a critical examination of the AHRD's religious freedom protection, see Neo (2017a).

FoRB has also been given constitutional recognition; almost all Asian countries make some reference to the right to FoRB.[4] These constitutional provisions range from the most extensive such as in the Philippines constitution, which states that '[t]he free exercise and enjoyment of religious profession and worship, without discrimination or preference, shall *forever be allowed*,' to narrower formulations such as in Afghanistan where the constitution merely guarantees that '[f]ollowers of other faiths shall be free *within the bounds of law* in the exercise and performance of their religious rituals.'[5] Brunei, which is the only absolute monarchy in Asia, merely states in its constitution that 'all other religions may be practiced in peace and harmony by the persons professing them.' Another exception is the constitution of Maldives, which does not include any reference at all to FoRB. Instead, the Maldives constitution limits the right to freedom of thought, of communication, and of opinions and expression, which could be said to be closely related to FoRB, such that the exercise of this right must be 'in a manner that is not contrary to any tenet of Islam.'

Despite the diffusion of FoRB in Asia, critics often point to gaps between how FoRB is understood in international law and in Anglo-European states and how it is implemented (or not) in many Asian states. In fact, it is not uncommon for Asian states to be criticised for not living up to the expected standards of FoRB.[6] There is often a dissonance between what is promised under the international, regional, and/or constitutional instruments and the reality of how states control religion and belief. This is not helped by the fact that FoRB itself is a complex freedom that encompasses a whole range of obligations including non-interference, noncoercion, nondiscrimination, and more.[7] This chapter proposes that while FoRB, as a legal right, remains relevant to the contexts of Asia, its understanding and articulation will inevitably be calibrated to the differing conditions in – and within – Asia. In this chapter, we identify certain characteristics that could be said to give rise to distinctive Asian perspectives on FoRB and examine how the historical and political contexts of various Asian jurisdictions have given rise to certain types of FoRB issues and shaped the state's responses to these issues.

Thus far, we have spoken of Asia as if it is an unproblematic idea, and we should here preface the rest of our discussion by acknowledging otherwise. Depending on where one draws demarcations, Asia is a vast geographical region which could include the 'Middle East' (West Asia), the Sub-Continent (South Asia), Central Asia, Southeast Asia, North East Asia (perhaps including eastern Russia), and, on some accounts, even Oceania. Within this geography are massive populations of diverse ethnicities adhering to a tremendous range of cultures, religions, languages, and traditions. Encompassed within this space are the world's two most populous countries, China and India, which together comprise approximately four billion of the world's people, and whose populations speak hundreds of languages and dialects, and practice a whole range of different religions. Added to this demographic complexity are pluralistic legal systems influenced by different legal traditions and a wide spectrum of political arrangements ranging from democracies to absolute monarchies.

---

4 Readers may access the constitutional documents of each country on Constitute, at https://www.constituteproject.org.

5 Emphasis added.

6 See, e.g., 'Interim Report of the Special Rapporteur on Freedom of Religion or Belief: Elimination of All Forms of Religious Intolerance,' United Nations, A72/365 (28 August 2017); McDermid (2019).

7 Lindholm identified, for instance, eight components to what he considers to be the normative core of religious freedom: Lindholm (2014: 9–10). See also Lindholm et al. (2004: xxxvii–xxxix).

With such sheer scale and size, a real question arises as to whether 'Asia' is, and indeed can ever be seen to be, a coherent unit of analysis and discussion. In other words, does it make sense to think of 'Asia' and, *a fortiori*, an 'Asian perspective?' Indeed, in a curious way, confronting this question is an important initial step toward developing a view from Asia because in thinking about this issue seriously one is immediately made to reflect on the range and scope of Asia and to consider whether it is even possible to speak coherently about a region of this size, variation, and complexity. Furthermore, while one could conceive of important differences in which FoRB is implemented and even comprehended in different countries, it is not clear that a regional approach to understanding FoRB is necessarily a coherent or helpful endeavour.[8]

We nevertheless take the view that it is possible to identify Asian perspectives on FoRB on two grounds. The first is to accept the possibility that, notwithstanding its diversity, there might be a sort of Wittengensteinian 'family resemblance' that exists within Asia, at least when compared to areas outside of Asia. That is to say that there might be an 'Asia' when one considers the region in comparison to 'non-Asia,' like there may be a 'Europe' not because 'Europe' is the same but because one can discern a certain 'Europeanness' in the region when considering it against other parts of the world. The second is to accept that there has been a process of self-conscious coming together among various countries in Asia (Funabashi, 1993: 75), such that one could legitimately speak of the Asian perspective(s). This Asianization of Asia, as Funabashi calls it, has shaped an 'Asian consciousness,' which is animated by a gamut of factors including commitment to economic progress, political pragmatism, anti-colonialism/anti-West, and an apparent indifference to civil liberties (Funabashi, 1993: 75). This is perhaps most starkly reflected in the Asian Values discourse, where political leaders of otherwise feuding countries in Asia came together to present a supposedly cohesive, though not necessarily coherent, front against alleged Western imperialist human rights agenda.[9]

Accordingly, our approach in this chapter is to say that there is not *an* Asian perspective but rather a multiplicity of Asian perspective*s*, emphasising the plural. Seeing this is a specialist Handbook on FoRB, we will highlight specific issues concerning FoRB that could be said to arise from distinctive (though not necessarily unique) characteristics of Asian states.

Asian perspectives

One could identify several distinctive factors that may account for compliance gaps in FoRB in Asia. The extent to which FoRB is protected in a country depends on a wide variety of legal, social, and political factors, including the text of the constitution, the constitutional arrangement on state and religion, the type and stability of the political regime (Durham, 1996: 2), commitment to international human rights treaties, religious demography, the nature of the dominant religion, as well as the historical relationships among religious groups (Durham, 1996: 2). Economic factors may also be influential.[10] Here, we identify six distinctive features.

First, historically speaking, FoRB, as is more commonly conceptualized, developed as a distinctively Eurocentric phenomenon that was subsequently imported to Asia through the requirements of international law and imposed through the experience of imperialism and

8 See Dixon (2019) on intraregional comparisons.

9 See, e.g., Zakaria (1994), Kausikan (1993), and Neier (1993). For critique, see Thio (1999), Engle (2000), Donnelly (1999), and Tatsuo (1999).

10 See Barro and McCleary (2003) and Grim and Finke (2006). More generally, see Sen (1999) and Peerenboom (2004).

colonialism. One criticism is that FoRB transplanted poorly in non-European soil.[11] Asia's encounter with religion and consequently religious freedom was not primarily shaped by the political authorities' relationship with a powerful church establishment (Neo et al., 2019). Religious freedom thus did not emerge as part of a constitutional "settlement" between state and church in order to reconcile religious sectarian conflict, nor out of a need to defend against competing sovereignty claims from an all-powerful religious institution (the church) (Neo, forthcoming). In many countries in Asia, religion has always been in the foreground of politics and law, which affects the implementation of FoRB.

Second, one may argue that there is a fundamental difference between how the West and Asia conceive of religion and, concommitantly, FoRB. In reality therefore, FoRB in Asia may different forms due to local conditions and, in particular, due to variant understandings of the relation between the individual vis-à-vis the community and, in some places, because of the alignment of the state with a particular religion. Some critics like Prakash Shah have argued forcefully that '[w]hen certain kinds of legal ideas, embedded as norms within the Western culture, which is constituted by a religion, Christianity, enter non-Western cultures that do not have religion, those ideas break down, become distorted, absurd or nonsensical, and induce conflict' (Shah 2015: 81). To the extent that FoRB was developed with Christianity as the primary frame, this criticism could be similarly applied. Thomas DuBois warns against the 'often repeated, and suspiciously self-congratulatory narrative about how East Asia came to accept an essentially Western concept of religion' as both 'historically inaccurate and dangerously misleading' (DuBois, 2018: 47). He argues that long before Asian encounters and domination by Western intellectual ideas, East Asia had accumulated millennia of traditions about religion, its place in society, and its political regulation, even if the term 'religion' was not applied as such to the phenomenon (DuBois, 2018: 47). Accordingly, he has argued that the language of FoRB in these countries needs to be understood and interpreted according to historically and socially embedded notions of religion. Elizabeth Shakman Hurd's critique of international FoRB movements points to the tendency to overlook the subjectivity and historical contingency of the concept of religion to privilege a more individualistic notion of FoRB, coming from Western experience (Hurd, 2017).

Third, the religious demography itself may complicate the implementation of FoRB in Asia. Data show that the Asia-Pacific region is the most religiously diverse in the world, having adherents of major religions and a wide range of localised or folk religions. According to the Pew Research Centre's 2010 data 'half of the most religiously diverse countries are in Asia-Pacific region' (2014). The region has 24% Muslims, 25% Hindus, 12% Buddhists, 9% adherents of folk religions, 7% Christians, and 21% unaffiliated among its population (Pew Research Centre, 2014). In comparison, Europe and North America have moderate levels of religious diversity, while the Latin America–Caribbean and Middle East–North Africa regions have low degrees of religious diversity (Pew Research Centre, 2014; see also Keck, 2014). Accordingly, to the extent that FoRB was conceptualised to deal with intrareligious/sectarian conflict, rather than coexistence among a wide variety of different religions, some rethinking may be needed.

Fourth, most Asian jurisdictions, with the exception of the Philippines, do not have a dominant Christian majority. Instead, religions traditions such as Islam, Buddhism, and Hinduism are prominent and are professed by the majority in many Asian states. This, therefore, provides some demographic context that we need to think about when considering

11 For a critical view on this, see Shah (2015).

freedom of religion in Asia, noting in particular the different influences and the diversity and plurality. In this regard, Jonathan Fox's analysis of Southeast Asia is apposite, though not without problems. Fox argues that 'patterns of religious freedom differ significantly based on the country's largest religion' (2016: 28). He divides Southeast Asia into three groups: Christian majority countries (Papua New Guinea, the Philippines, and Timor); Muslim majority countries (Brunei, Indonesia, and Malaysia); and finally, Buddhist majority (or plurality) countries (Cambodia, Laos, Myanmar, Singapore, Thailand, and Vietnam). Using his religion and state dataset on various aspects of government policy affecting religion, he concludes that there are relatively low levels of religious regulation, religious discrimination, and religious support in the three Christian majority countries in Southeast Asia (Fox, 2016: 32–35). In comparison, he observes that in Muslim majority countries, there are high average levels of religious discrimination, regulation of Islam, and exclusive or near-exclusive support for Islam (Fox, 2016: 33–36). He further states that there is no consistent pattern of religious discrimination, regulation, or support among Buddhist majority/plurality states (Fox, 2016: 33). Fox's framework is helpful in identifying the role that religion plays in influencing religious freedom protection. However, it remains an important research question whether the type of majority religion itself is a sufficient factor in determining levels of religious freedom protection or whether it is the interplay of religion and constitutional arrangements. The actual religion that is in the majority could be a determining factor in constitutional design. For instance, it has been argued that secularism (or even more specifically, the claim of separationism) is rooted in Christian theology (Shah, 2010). The biblical invocation to render unto Caesar what is Caesar's and to render unto God what is God's is often used to justify jurisdictional demarcation or dualism crucial to secularism as separationism.[12] Thus, it is not inconceivable that the type of religion (i.e., non-Christian religion) may also account for the success or otherwise of certain types of constitutional state-religion regimes.

Fifth, most Asian states do not fully commit to the liberal prioritization of individual rights as would be the case in many European states. Instead, many are self-avowedly communitarian. Amitai Etzioni defines communitarianism as 'a social philosophy that builds on the assumption that the good should be defined socially.'[13] However, what is known as 'East Asian communitarianism' is also sometimes considered 'authoritarian communitarianism,' referring to a set of beliefs that prioritises social order and harmony over individual rights and political liberties (Etzioni, 2011). This means that FoRB is understood not, or at least not *only*, in terms of individual autonomy but in communitarian terms, whereby individual claims may be more likely to be subjected to the public good than would be the case in a liberal state (see Neo, 2017b). Instead of a concern for a Cartesian idea of the individual endowed with rights with an 'a priori affirmation of the normative worth of the individual' (Thio, 1997: 152), the attention is on concrete everyday relationships between individuals, groups, and the state premised upon an 'anti-liberal, communitarian or group centric ethos' (Thio, 1997: 152). In some cases, individual rights were not just met with ambivalence but with opposition. For example, Indonesian constitution makers were resistant to the incorporation of human rights protections which they saw as Western, liberal democratic ideas that were inherently imperialistic. They, in fact, deliberately omitted a comprehensive set of rights guarantees and instead adopted a 'Japanese-inspired ideology focusing on kinship and mutual cooperation.'[14] The protection of

12 See generally the section on Christian perspectives in Ahdar and Leigh (2013).

13 Etzioni (2011). See further generally Chua (2004).

14 Shah (2014). Despite this resistance to individual rights, the FoRB was included in the constitution attesting the importance placed on this value.

FoRB is therefore premised, not so much on the freedom of the individual believer, but rather the concerns of groups. Thus, in early independence Indonesia, Soepomo's resistance toward individual rights was trumped by his acceptance of the 'importance of religious freedom, particularly the freedom of every person to embrace his own religion and to worship according to his religion and beliefs' but this was on the basis that it was necessary to ensure that adherents of other religious beliefs would feel welcome in Indonesia (Shah, 2014). The focus was on ensuring social stability and cohesion rather than squarely on individual autonomy.

Finally, the implementation of FoRB cannot ignore the factors arising from the politics of identity in various Asian countries. These politics of identity may arise as a response to colonisation and decolonisation whereby 'restoring' the dominance of a particular religion is seen as necessary to rediscover a country's precolonial 'glory.' This in turn could have adverse impact on FoRB for those who are not adherents of that religion (Neo, forthcoming).

Defining religion

Asia's complex religious demography means that defining religion for the purposes of FoRB protection could be a difficult process that takes into account local particularities (Jamal, 2015). It also raises questions of whether 'religion' is a distinctive phenomenon, as opposed to being categorised as a cultural, social, or traditional institution, etc. (Jamal, 2017; Neo, 2018). Providing a workable legal definition for religion is widely admitted to be fraught with difficulties.[15] While jurisdictions like the United States have tended to give preference to the subjectivity of the applicant (e.g., judging the 'sincerity' of the applicant's views), several jurisdictions in Asia have not shied away from imposing an objective and often essentialist definition to *religion*. For instance, in Singapore, the courts have rejected the Jehovah's Witnesses' claim that the national pledge and anthem ceremony is religious despite their obviously sincere and strongly held belief. There, the Singapore Court of Appeal explicitly distinguished broader definitions accorded to religious belief in other jurisdictions, stating that it did not accept 'that any belief or thought potentially holds religious value.'[16] It declared that 'not every conviction or belief, including those held with what ironically may best be described as religious fervour, qualifies as a religious belief.'[17] Thus, the court stated that 'the pledge ceremony does not demand worship of the flag as a symbol' and that 'if a person held that understanding, that perception was a *philosophical choice*.'[18] Interestingly, the Singapore court still adopted an Abrahamic-centric idea of religion when it defined religion as 'a citizen's faith in a personal God, sometimes described as a belief in a supernatural being.'[19]

One interesting doctrinal development in Asia is the essential or integral practice test to allocate constitutional protection. This test, developed by the Indian Supreme Court, determines what are essential practices (and thereby deserving of constitutional protection) and what are not (and not deserving of constitutional protection). It has the potential to significantly

---

15 In the UK, see, e.g., *R (on the application of Hodkin) v. Registrar General of Births, Deaths and Marriages* [2013] UKSC 77 [2014] 1 AC 610 and *R v. Registrar General, Ex p Segerdal* [1970] 2 QB 697; in Australia, see, e.g., *Church of the New Faith v. Commissioner of Pay-Roll* [1983] HCA 40; in Canada, see, e.g., *Syndicat Northcrest v. Amselem* [2004] 2 S.C.R. 551, 2004 SCC 47.

16 *Nappalli Peter Williams v. Institute of Technical Education* [1999] 2 SLR(R) 529 (Court of Appeal, Singapore). In doing so, the court distanced itself from the approach taken by the Philippines court in *Ebralinag v. Division Superintendent of Schools of Cebu* 219 SCRA 256 [1993].

17 Ibid. at [27].

18 Ibid. at [28], emphasis added.

19 Ibid. at [26].

limit the scope of FoRB guarantee as it is not sufficient for practices to be accepted as 'religious,' but they also have to be essential in order to be constitutionally protected (Neo, 2018). It is interesting to note that the 1954 case of *The Commissioner, Hindu Religious Endowments, Madras v. Sri Lakshmindra Thirtha Swamiar*[20] first developed the essential or integral practice test in order to extend constitutional protection beyond beliefs to rituals, observances, ceremonies, and other modes of worship, which would include 'matters of food and dress.' There, the Supreme Court of India held that '[t]he guarantee under our Constitution not only protects the freedom of religious opinion but it protects also acts done in pursuance of a religion and this is made clear by the use of the expression "practice of religion" in Art 25.' Indeed, initial case law on the essential practice test suggested a more accommodative approach, which placed importance on community self-definition. In the 1962 case of *Sardar Syedna Taher Saifuddin Saheb v. State of Bombay*,[21] for instance, the Indian Supreme Court held that 'what constitutes an essential part of a religion or religious practice has to be decided by the courts with reference to the doctrine of a particular religion and include practices which are regarded by the community as a part of its religion.' In other words, the courts have to rely on the internal perspective of the religious group to determine what is essential.

However, in later cases, the courts have taken a more intrusive approach, employing the essential practice test to deny protection to a range of religious practices. Dhavan and Nariman have forcefully argued that the judges have assumed 'a power greater than that of a high priest, maulvi or dharmashastri' in taking on 'the theological authority to determine which tenets of a faith are "essential" to any faith' (Dhavan and Nariman, 2009: 259). Ronojoy Sen further criticises the employment of such 'religious fiat' as problematic as the test is used to shape a rational form of Hinduism by denying constitutional protection to religious practices that fall outside that imaginary (Sen, 2010: 40). This disciplining function of the essential practice test extends also to religious minorities; for instance, a majority in the Supreme Court of India recently held that triple talaq (final divorce by three pronouncements), which is accepted under certain interpretations of Muslim personal law, was not an essential practice and therefore not constitutionally protected.[22]

The overall effect of the essential practice test has been to allow judges to impose an objective review in allocating constitutional protection. The essential practice test has also been directly adopted in Malaysia to deny constitutional protection to serban-wearing schoolboys[23] and to the Catholic Church seeking to refer to God as 'Allah' in their Malay language publications. In both cases, the Malaysian courts held that these practices may be religious, but are not essential to the practice of Islam and Christianity, respectively. Jaclyn Neo has therefore proposed a qualified deferential approach which relies primarily on the self-definition of the religious claimant in order to reduce, if not remove, reliance on judicial assessment that could essentially deny the individual's religious truth. This is a qualified deferential approach because it involves a second stage of legal inquiry on whether the restrictions on religious belief or practice are constitutionally legitimate, outweigh the right to freedom of religion, or are proportionate. The approach seeks to give due regard to the status of FoRB as a fundamental

20 *The Commissioner, Hindu Religious Endowments, Madras v. Sri Lakshmindra Thirtha Swamiar* AIR 1954 S C 282.

21 *Sardar Syedna Taher Saifuddin Saheb v. State of Bombay* AIR 1962 SC 853.

22 *Shayara Bano v. Union of India* (2017) 9 SCC 1.

23 *Fatimah Bte Sihi & Ors v. Meor Atiqulrahman Bin Ishak & Ors (Minors, Suing Through Syed Ahmad Johari Bin Syed Mohd)* [2005] 2 MLJ 25 (Court of Appeal). The serban is a form of turban worn by some Muslim males. Since the 1970s in Malaysia, wearing a serban has been associated with a more conservative interpretation of Islam.

right, while mitigating (without eliminating) some of the difficulties that arise when secular courts become embroiled in religious questions (Neo, 2018).

The constitution and FoRB

The framing of constitutional texts can be an important, though not necessarily determinative, factor in how FoRB is protected in a country. As mentioned earlier, in Asia, most constitutions recognise and guarantee protection for FoRB but in varying forms. While most Asian constitutions include reference to the freedom to profess, of belief or of conscience (i.e., the *forum internum*), this does not always extend, for instance, to the freedom to not believe. Atheism, for instance, is a contentious issue in many Asian jurisdictions such as Indonesia, Malaysia, and Brunei. In contrast, the constitution of Vietnam explicitly extends freedom of religion to the freedom not to follow any religion (Art. 24). Besides beliefs and conscience, most constitutions in Asia also extend the constitutional protection to some aspect of the *forum externum* by including the freedom to 'practice,' 'worship,' and/or to 'free exercise.' Several constitutions also include the right to 'propagate' one's religion (for instance, article 15 of the Singapore Constitution).

However, as John Madeley observes, in most cases, 'constitutional promises of religious freedom provide only a distally uncertain indication of actual conditions pertaining to religious freedom and unfreeedom' (Madeley, 2015: 215). FoRB is also affected by the constitutional state religion arrangements in these countries. In the context of Sri Lanka, for instance, Benjamin Schonthal (2016) argues that constitutionalisation of religion aggravated interreligious and intrareligious disputes. Jaclyn Neo has broadly categorised Asian constitutional systems into three umbrella groups based on their constitutional relationship with religion, namely (1) states that explicitly prioritise religion, (2) statist or communitarian states that explicitly subordinate religion to state interests, and (3) states that explicitly commit to separation of state and religion (Neo, forthcoming). This conceptual grouping serves to highlight how specific state religion arrangements tend to give rise to certain types of religious freedom conflicts and claims (Neo, forthcoming). A survey of Asia shows that, even on formal terms, the separation of state and religion is the exception rather than the norm.[24] Within Asia, only the East Asian countries like Japan, Taiwan, and South Korea, in addition to the Philippines, claim to have formal separation of state and religion. For the East Asian states, while the state appears detached from religion, this does not mean that the state is nonreligious or commits to the separation of state and religion. Instead, as Thomas DuBois highlights, East Asian political traditions conceived of the state and society in terms that were 'essentially religious, but not confessional' (DuBois, 2018).

Furthermore, the majority of Asian constitutions prioritise religion. Islam is the religion of the state in Brunei ['official religion': Art. 3(1) of the 1959 const.], Bangladesh ['state religion': Art. 2A of the 1972 const.], Malaysia ['religion of the Federation': Art. 3(1) of the 1957 const.], Maldives ['religion of the State': Art. 10(a) of the 2008 const.], and Pakistan ['State religion': Art. 2 of the 1973 const.]. Constitutions that prioritise Buddhism are Cambodia ['state religion': Art. 43 of the 1993 const.], Bhutan ['good and compassionate society rooted in Buddhist ethos and universal human values': Art. 9(20) of the 2008 const.], Myanmar ('special position of Buddhism' as the faith professed by the majority: S. 361 of the 2008 const.), Sri Lanka ('Buddhism the foremost place' and it is 'the duty of the State to protect and foster the Buddha Sasana': Art. 9 of the 1978 const.), and Thailand (state obligation to 'support and protect

24 Note that Jonathan Fox (2016) has presented data showing that the separation of state and religion is the exception rather than the norm around the world, but this is based on actual practice. In contrast, many constitutions in Asia do not even formally commit to any separation of state and religion.

Buddhism and other religions': S. 67 of the 2017 const.). Indonesia's 1945 constitution is religious and pluralistic, declaring that '[t]he State shall be based upon the belief in the One and Only God.'[25] The close association between state and a particular religion or religions means that FoRB claims are likely to be viewed as closely related to the need to protect the priority or even dominance of the majority religion(s). Accordingly, in most of the countries that prioritise a majority religion, the freedom to choose one's religion tends to be severely limited. Malaysia, Pakistan, and Brunei have laws that seek to restrict religious choice, which are often tied up with the perceived need to control conversion out of the majority religion.[26] Myanmar's Religious Conversion Law 2015 regulates conversion through a registration scheme,[27] which has been criticised for potentially restricting the freedom to convert out of Buddhism.[28] There were also attempts to introduce an anti-conversion bill in Sri Lanka, but it was not passed.[29]

The constitutionalisation of religious dominance also tends to result in the perceived need to invoke state power to protect religious orthodoxy. Laws restricting the insulting of religion exist as part of the penal codes of Malaysia, Myanmar, Singapore, Pakistan, Bangladesh, India, and Sri Lanka. With the exception of Singapore, such laws have increasingly been deployed to protect the religious sensibilities of the majority. For instance, in Myanmar, owner and managers of a Yangon-based gastro bar were charged and convicted in 2015 for distributing a promotional flyer depicting an image of Buddha wearing headphones against a psychedelic backdrop. Their crime was outraging the religious feelings of Buddhists.[30] Indonesia also has a Blasphemy Law, which prohibits any public interpretation of a religion or conducting religious activities that deviate from the tenets of any one of its six officially recognised religions (Islam, Protestantism, Catholicism, Buddhism, Hinduism, and Confucianism).[31] This is supplemented by the Criminal Code which has a provision that makes it an offence to 'deliberately and publicly' express feelings or behave in a manner that 'involves hatred, misuse, or insulting of a religion followed in Indonesia' with the intention 'that a person should not practice any religion at all that is based on Belief in Almighty God.' The Blasphemy Law has been used in recent times to prosecute religious minorities, including minorities considered deviant to the majority Sunni Muslims, as well as adherents of folk religions (aliran kepercayaan or mystical belief).[32] In 2010, the Indonesian Constitutional Court upheld the Blasphemy Law against a constitutional challenge that the law violates the constitution's guarantees of FoRB.[33] The

25 See constitution of Indonesia, Article 29. There has been pressure to formally prioritize Islam, or more specifically include a provision in the constitution to privilege sharia (Lindsey and Kingsley, 2008; Black, 2008: 180).

26 Notably, several Indian states have adopted anti-conversion laws with the support and sponsorship of Hindu nationalists. See Osuri (2012).

27 Religious Conversion Law, unofficial translation by the Chin Human Rights Organization available at http://www.burmalibrary.org/docs18/2014-Draft_Religious_Conversion_Law-en.pdf.

28 Rahman and Zeldin (2015) and Zaw (2015). Restrictions on conversion have been linked to Islamophobia and Buddhist nationalism: see, e.g., Kyaw, 2016.

29 For further, see Hertzberg (2016).

30 *The Case of V Gastro Bar (Philip Blackwood, Htut Ko Ko Lwin, and Tun Thurein)* (17 March 2015). Case summary available at https://globalfreedomofexpression.columbia.edu/cases/the-case-of-v-gastro-bar-philip-blackwood-htut-ko-ko-lwin-and-tun-thurein.

31 The offence was first established by presidential decree in 1965 and subsequently promulgated as a law in 1969. Decree No. 1/PNPS/1965 on the Prevention of the Misusing/Insulting of a Religion and Law 5/1969 Declaring Several Decisions and Regulations of the President as Law.

32 For further analysis, see Crouch (2012).

33 Decision of the Constitutional Court No 140/PUU-VII/2009 concerning the Request for Judicial Review of the Blasphemy Law, dated 19 April 2010.

Constitutional Court upheld the law on public order grounds and on the basis that protecting religious values is a legitimate limitation on religious freedom under the constitution as allowing religious deviancy would lead to social chaos and disorder.[34]

Second, statist or communitarian states that do not adopt a particular religious commitment tend to see religion as a subject of state control, which tends to result in strong restrictions on FoRB. FoRB is often subordinated to state interests in public order, interethnic harmony, or national unity. This priority of state interests over religious freedom may be made explicit in the constitution such as in the constitution of China, which confirms that citizens shall enjoy 'freedom of religious belief' and that the state 'protects normal religious activities,' but that these are subject to the limitation that '[n]o one may make use of religion to engage in activities that disrupt public order, impair the health of citizens or interfere with the educational system of the state' (Art. 36 of the 1982 const.). Furthermore, the government sees itself as the final arbiter of what constitutes 'normal religious activities,' which would be protected, and which are not (Zhang and Zhu, 2011: 785). As Potter observes, China's regulation of religion reflects the Party's policies in 'granting limited autonomy for accepted practices while attempting to repress activities that challenge political orthodoxy' (Potter, 2003: 337). Recent developments have seen the securitisation of religious activities as well as increase in state oversight over religious activities, including online discussion of religious matters, all of which are justified as necessary to prevent the spread of 'extremist' ideology and to protect China's national security against threats from religious groups.[35] Indeed, statist/communitarian states tend to conceptualise religion as a suspect subject that needs to be controlled. Accordingly, the state does not eschew entanglement with religion but sees such entanglement as necessary to exercise control over religion (Neo, forthcoming).

Finally, where the constitution explicitly separates state and religion, FoRB issues tend to arise conjunctively with the constitutional claim to realise this separationist arrangement. In Asia, as alluded to earlier, only three Asian constitutions expressly separate state and religion: the Philippines ('[n]o law shall be made respecting an establishment of religion, or prohibiting the free exercise thereof' and that '[t]he separation of Church and State shall be inviolable:' Art. III s. 5 of the 1987 const.); South Korea ('[n]o state religion shall be recognized, and church and state shall be separated:' Art. 20 of the 1987 const.); and Japan ('[n]o religious organization shall receive any privileges from the State, nor exercise any political authority' and that '[t]he State and its organs shall refrain from religious education or any other religious activity:' Art. 20 of the 1947 const.). FoRB issues are thus commonly linked to the requirement to ensure against the establishment of religion. For instance, in South Korea, when a local court decided that it is against the freedom of religion for a private Christian high school to dismiss a student from the school for protesting Christian education, it also found that there was violation of the constitution's separation requirements.[36] Similarly, in the Philippines, the courts have held that the state should not intervene in ecclesiastical affairs, which would involve 'matters of faith, religious doctrines, worship and governance of the congregation.'[37] Indeed, in holding for

34 A high-profile blasphemy case against a popular Christian governor of Jakarta in 2017 attracted widespread international criticism. The Indonesian government has stated an intention to review the laws. Chan (2017).

35 'China tightens regulation of religion to 'block extremism.' Reuters. 7 September 2017. Available at https://www.reuters.com/article/us-china-religion/china-tightens-regulation-of-religion-to-block-extremism-idUSKCN1BI1IH.

36 Judgment of the Seoul Central Local Court, 2005, Ka-Dan 305176, 5 October 2007, discussed in Kim (2015: 471).

37 *Pastor Dionisio Austra v. National Labor Relations Commission* , GR No 124382 (16 August 1999).

Jehovah's Witnesses who were unconstitutionally expelled from a Cebu public school for refusing to salute the flag, sing the national anthem, and recite the patriotic pledge, Justice Cruz of the Supreme Court of the Philippines stated in his concurring judgment that religion is 'forbidden territory that the State ... cannot invade.'[38] The Court held that religious freedom is a 'fundamental right which is entitled to the highest priority and the amplest protection among human rights, for it involves the relationship of man to his Creator.'[39]

Religious nationalism and polarisation

Another important context impacting Asia is the emergence of heightened polarisation resulting from more assertive (or some might say 'fundamentalist') expressions of religious traditions. These expressions are manifesting themselves in different countries in Asia and across a range of religious traditions. Examples of this phenomenon are well known and include the alignment between the BJP government and Hindu nationalism in India, which some see as advancing a pro-Hindu (and anti-non-Hindu and perhaps particularly anti-Islam) agenda, the touting of 'political Islam' by political parties in Malaysia, or 'political Buddhism' in Myanmar and Sri Lanka.[40]

The effects of these manifestations can result in polarisation in at least three ways. First, they may add to the polarisation between those who express adherence to a religion versus those who do not. This is especially when religious views are presented in assertive terms that may seem either aggressive or intolerant or to be making excessive demands on public life to those who do not hold religious views. Second, even for those who do hold religious views, and indeed, even for those of the same religious tradition, forms of religious expression that are especially assertive can be off-putting; in other words, they can cause others within the same tradition to be alienated from their co-religionists. Third, assertive religious expression is often linked to a sense of a 'purified' form of any one religious tradition and thus more strongly demarcating the boundaries between one tradition and another. This can limit the syncretic space of religious plurality and hybridity and so more starkly polarise the distinctions between religions.

In sum, these forces may result in a multidimensional polarisation emerging in the socio-political environment, with external and internal dimensions; externally, between those of religion and those not; and internally within different understanding of a religious tradition. As 'assertive' religion becomes emergent in different part of Asia today (e.g., India, Myanmar, Sri Lanka, Malaysia, and others), these different facets of polarisation must be reckoned with.

Conclusion

Globally, as well as in Asia, the data suggest that what we are seeing are conditions of heightening plurality – among religious traditions and among those with and without religious affiliation – which is captured in enhanced global religious diversity. This diversity is especially prominent in the Asia-Pacific region. In the result, it is likely that FoRB issues will only

38 *Ebralinag v. Division Superintendent of Schools of Cebu*, GR No 95770 (1 March 1993), 219 SCRA 256 (1993) Supreme Court, Philippines.

39 Ibid.

40 For a discussion of Sri Lanka, see Schonthal (2016); for a discussion of Indonesia, Malaysia, and Sri Lanka, see Shah (2017); and for Myanmar, see Kyaw, 2019. For an analysis from the perspective of judicialisation of religion, see Moustafa (2018).

become more important and more contested in the future in Asia as well as worldwide. Indeed, besides interfaith diversity, intrafaith diversity, based on different interpretation or approaches *within* a faith tradition, will also become a point of contention in FoRB protection in the future. In the context of many Asian jurisdictions where several states unabashedly regulate religion to advance public interests or the common good, this means that internal plurality will continue to pose a challenge for understanding FoRB in Asia. This challenge has both regulatory as well as definitional aspects to it. For instance, in Asian states, regulation often entails the simplification of diversity into corporate bodies [e.g., Christians, Hindus, Buddhists, etc., which could then be dealt with as single entities (Jamal, 2019)].

Asian responses will also continue to be shaped by a range of constitutional, political, and regulatory factors. Taking all the above into account, it is evident that in looking at Asia we must be alert to its identifiably different contexts. Concomitantly, we must also recognise that while there cannot be said to be one Asian approach, we should understand the distinctive conditions that feed into the experiences and choices (plural required) of present-day Asia and its future.

References

Ahdar, R., Leigh, I., 2013. *Religious Freedom in the Liberal State*. Oxford University Press.

Barro, R.J., McCleary, R.M., 2003. Religion and economic growth across countries. *American Sociological Review*. 68(5), 760.

Bell, D., Bauer, J.R., 1990. (Eds.), *The East Asian Challenge for Human Rights*. Cambridge University Press.

Black, E.A., 2008. Finding the role for Sharia law in post-reformasi Indonesia. *Lawasia J*. 165.

Chan, F., 2017. Indonesia to review anti-blasphemy laws. *Straits Times*. 17 May. Available from: <http://www.straitstimes.com/asia/se-asia/indonesia-to-review-anti-blasphemy-laws>.

Chua, B.H. (Ed.), 2004. *Communitarian Politics in Asia*. Routledge.

Crouch, M.A., 2012. Law and religion in Indonesia: The constitutional court and the blasphemy law. *Asian Journal of Comparative Law*. 7(1), 1.

Dhavan, R., Nariman, F., 2009. The Supreme Court and group life: Religious freedom, minority groups, and disadvantaged communities. In: Kirpal B.N., Desai A.H., Subramanian G., R. Dhavan , R. Ramchandran (Eds.), *Supreme but not Infallible: Essays in Honour of the Supreme Court of India*. Oxford University Press, 256.

Dixon, R., 2019. (Why) comparative constitutional amendment in South-East Asia. *Journal of Comparative Law*. 14 (1), 205.

Donnelly, J., 1999. Human rights and Asian values: A defense of 'Western' universalism. In: Bauer, J.R., Bell, D.A. (Eds.), *The East Asian Challenge for Human Rights*. Cambridge University Press, 60.

DuBois, T.D., 2018. Religious freedom in East Asia: historical norms and the limits of advocacy. *Journal of Religious and Political Practice*. 4(1), 46.

Durham Jr, W.C., 1996. Perspectives on religious liberty: A comparative framework. In: van der Vyver J.D., Witte Jr. J. (Eds.), *Religious Human Rights in Global Perspective: Legal Perspectives*. Martinus Nijhoff.

Engle, K., 2000. Culture and human rights: The Asian values debate in context. *Int. Law Polit*. 32, 291.

Etzioni, A., 2011. Communitarianism. In: Badie, B., Berg-Schlosser, D., Morlino, L. (Eds.), *Int. International Encyclopedia of Political Science*. Sage, 327.

Fox, J., 2016. Freedom of religion in Southeast Asia: An empirical analysis. *Review of Faith & International Affairs*. 14(4), 28.

Funabashi, Y., 1993. The Asianization of Asia. *Foreign Affairs*. 72(5), 75.

Grim, B.J., Finke, R., 2006. International religion indexes: Government regulation, government favoritism, and social regulation of religion. *Interdisciplinary Journal of Research on Religion*. 2, 1.

Hertzberg, M., 2016. The rhetorical shadows of the anti-conversion bill: Religious freedom and political alliances in Sri Lanka. *Nordic Journal of Human Rights*. 34(3), 189.

Hurd, E.S., 2017. *Beyond religious freedom: The new global politics of religion*. Princeton University Press.

Jamal, A.A., 2015. The impact of definitional issue on the right to freedom of religion and belief. In: Ferrari, S. (Ed.), *Routledge Handbook of Law and Religion*. Routledge, 91.

Jamal, A.A., 2017. Considering freedom of religion in a post-secular context: Hapless or hopeful? *Oxford Journal of Law and Religion*. 6(3), 433.

Jamal, A.A., 2019. Regulatory markers. In: Neo, J.L., Jamal, A.A., Goh, D.P.S. (Eds.), *Regulating Religion in Asia: Norms, Modes and Challenges*. Cambridge University Press, 19.

Kausikan, B., 1993. Asia's different standard. *Foreign Policy* 92, 24.

Keck, Z., 2014. Asia leads world in religious diversity. *The Diplomat*. 9 April. Available from: <https://thediplomat.com/2014/04/asia-leads-world-in-religious-diversity>.

Kim, S.Y., 2015. Religion and the secular state in Korea. In: Martínez-Torrón, J., Durham, W.C. (Eds.), *Religion Oxford and the Secular State: National Reports Issued for the Occasion of the Xviiith Congress of the International Academy of Comparative Law*. Servicio de Publicaciones de la Facultad de Derecho de la Universidad Complutense de Madrid, 467.

Kyaw, N.N., 2016. Islamophobia in Buddhist Myanmar: The 969 movement and anti-Muslim violence. In: Crouch, M. (Ed.), *Islam and the State in Myanmar: Muslim-Buddhist Relations and the Politics of Belonging*. Oxford University Press, 183.

Kyaw, N.N., 2019. Regulating Buddhism in Myanmar: The case of deviant Buddhist sects. In: Neo, J.L., Jamal, A.A., Goh, D.P.S. (Ed.), *Regulating Religion in Asia: Norms, Modes and Challenges*. Cambridge University Press, 169.

Lerner, N., 2000. *Religion, Belief, and International Human Rights*. Orbis Books.

Lindholm, T., Durham, W.C., Tahzib-Lie, B.G., Sewell, E.A., Larsen, L. (Eds.), 2004. *Facilitating Freedom of Religion or Belief: A Deskbook*. Springer.

Lindholm, T., 2014. Freedom of religion or belief from a human rights perspective. In: Gravaas, A. et al. (Eds.), *Freedom of Belief and Christian Mission*. Regnum, p. 3.

Lindsey, T., Kingsley, J., 2008. Talking in code: Legal Islamisation in Indonesia and the MMI Shari`a criminal code. In: Bearman, P., Heinrichs, W., Weiss, B.G. (Eds.), *The Law Applied: Contextualizing the Islamic Shari'a*. IB Taurus, 295.

Madeley, J.T.S., 2015. Constitutional models and the protection of religious freedom. In: Ferrari, S. (Ed.), *Routledge Handbook of Law and Religion*. Routledge, 209.

McDermid, C., 2019. Asia is 'new hotbed of Christian persecution' with situation in China worst since cultural revolution. *South China Morning Post*. 16 January. Available from: <https://www.scmp.com/news/asia/southeast-asia/article/2182260/asia-new-hotbed-christian-persecution-situation-china-worst>.

Moustafa, T., 2018. *Constituting Religion: Islam, Liberal Rights, and the Malaysian State*. Cambridge University Press.

Neier, A., 1993. Asia's unacceptable standard. *Foreign Policy*. 92, 42.

Neo, J.L., 2017a. Realizing the right to freedom of thought, conscience, and religion: The limited normative force of the ASEAN human rights declaration. *Human Rights Law Review*. 17(4), 729.

Neo, J.L. 2017b. Secularism without liberalism: Religious freedom and secularism in a non-liberal state. *Michigan State Law Review*. 333.

Neo, J.L., 2018. Definitional imbroglios: A critique of the definition of religion and essential practice tests in religious freedom adjudication. *International Journal of Constitutional Law*. 16(2), 574.

Neo, J.L. (forthcoming). Religious Freedom. In: Law D. et al. (Eds.), *Oxford Handbook of Comparative Constitutional Law in Asia*.

Neo, J.L., Jamal, A.A., Goh, D.P.S., 2019. Introduction. In: Neo, J.L., Jamal, A.A., Goh, D.P.S. (Eds.), *Regulating Religion in Asia: Norms, Modes and Challenges*. Cambridge University Press, p. 1.

Osuri, G., 2012. *Religious Freedom in India: Sovereignty and (Anti) Conversion*. Routledge.

Peerenboom, R., 2004. Show me the money: The dominance of wealth in determining rights performance in Asia. *Duke Journal of Comparative and International Law* 15, 75.

Pew Research Center, 2014. Global religious diversity. Available from: <http://www.pewforum.org/2014/04/04/global-religious-diversity>.

Potter, P.B., 2003. Belief in control: Regulation of religion in China. *China Quarterly*. 174, 317.

Rahman, S., Zeldin, W., 2015. Burma: Four 'race and religion protection laws' adopted. *The Global Legal Monitor*. 14 September. Available from: <http://www.loc.gov/law/foreign-news/article/burma-four-race-and-religion-protection-laws-adopted>.

Schonthal, B., 2016. *Buddhism, Politics and the Limits of Law: The Pyrrhic Constitutionalism of Sri Lanka*. Cambridge University Press.

Sen, A., 1999. Human rights and economic achievements. In: Bauer, J.R., Bell, D.A. (Eds.), *The East Asian Challenge for Human Rights*. Cambridge University Press, 88.

Sen, R., 2010. *Articles of Faith: Religion, Secularism, and the Indian Supreme Court*. Oxford University Press.

Shah, P., 2010. The Indian dimension of An-Na'im's Islam and the secular state. In: Foblets, M.-C., Carlier, J.-Y. (Eds.), *Islam and Europe: Crises Are Challenges*. Leuven University Press.

Shah, D.A.H., 2014. Constitutional arrangements on religion and religious freedom in Malaysia and Indonesia: Furthering or inhibiting rights. *Indonesian Journal of International and Comparative Law*. 1, 260.

Shah, P., 2015. The difference that religion makes: Transplanting legal ideas from the West to Japan and India. *Asian Journal of Comparative Law*. 10(1), 81.

Shah, D.A.H., 2017. *Constitutions, Religion and Politics in Asia*. Cambridge University Press.

Tatsuo, I., 1999. Liberal democracy and Asian orientalism. In: Bauer, J.R., Bell, D.A. (Eds.), *The East Asian Challenge for Human Rights*. Cambridge University Press, 27.

Thio, L., 1997. An 'i' for an 'I'? Singapore's communitarian model of constitutional adjudication. *Hong Kong Law Journal*. 27, 152.

Thio, L., 1999. Implementing human rights in ASEAN countries: Promises to keep and miles to go before I sleep. *Yale Human Rights and Development Law Journal*. 2, 1.

Witte Jr, J.R., 2001. A Dickensian era of religious rights: An update on religious human rights in global perspective. *William and Mary Law Review*. 42, 707.

Zakaria, F., 1994. Culture is destiny: A conversation with Lee Kuan Yew. *Foreign Affairs*. 73(2), 109.

Zaw, H.Y., 2015. Myanmar's president signs off on law seen as targeting Muslims. *Reuters*. 31 August. Available from: <www.reuters.com/article/us-myanmar-politics-idUSKCN0R011W20150831>.

Zhang, Q., Zhu, Y., 2011. Religious freedom and its legal restrictions in China. *Brigham Young University Law Review*. 783.

14

The right to freedom of religion or belief: African perspectives

Idowu A. Akinloye

Introduction

Research has widely established the religiosity of most Africans (see, for instance, Agbiji and Swart, 2015; Awolalu, 1976; Mbiti, 1990). Further, in keeping with the global trends, almost every African State includes a bill of rights, which includes the right to freedom of religion in their respective national constitutions.[1] Numerous states are also signatories to some international instruments that guarantee the protection of the right.[2] Accordingly, the idea of freedom of religion as an aspect of human rights in most African States is assumed to primarily follow international instruments, which are conceived to be a Western idea. In this context, the right to freedom of religion and belief implies a state's duty to refrain from interfering with an individual's or community's pursuit of a chosen religious belief; a right to choose and change one's religion without force and coercion, including the freedom to manifest and practise the religion or belief individually or in fellowship with other believers.

While Africa's growing enthusiasm for human rights awareness and culture seems to be increasing, the number of scholarships that explore freedom of religion on a country-specific basis is limited (see generally Nsereko, 1992; Nwauche, 2008; van der Vyver, 1999a; Mutangu, 2008), and an evaluation of the phenomenon from the broad African point of view has remained largely unexplored. Furthermore, although freedom of religion provisions form part of the constitution of most African States, there is a growing concern that most of the provisions do not translate into actual practice (Hackett, 2011). For instance, one such group whose right to freedom of religion is perceived to be regularly violated is the adherents of the African Traditional Religions (ATR). The above issues raise some questions that need attention. Can it be argued that the failure to translate the provisions on freedom of religion into practice in African States is due to the noncompatibility of the freedom of religion provisions with Africans' understanding of how religion should be practised? Are there common standards and approaches to freedom of religion that are unique to

1 In this chapter, the expression 'freedom of religion' is intended also to include freedom of belief, save where the context suggests otherwise.

2 See the Universal Declaration of Human Rights (General Assembly Resolution 217 A) 1948; African Charter on Human and Peoples' Rights 1981; Declaration on the Elimination of All Forms of Intolerance and of Discrimination Based on Religion or Belief (General Assembly Resolution 36/55 of November 1981); International Covenant on Civil and Political Rights (General Assembly Resolution 2200A XXI) 1966.

Africans? Can these approaches be identified, promoted or adapted to enhance the effectiveness of freedom of religion on the African continent and/or contribute to the global debate on freedom of religion? This chapter focuses in particular on providing answers to these questions. Accordingly, the chapter adopts a historical, comparative and analytical research approach to achieve its objectives. The chapter is structured as follows. After the introduction, the next section briefly examines Africa's religious demography. The third section discusses if and how freedom of religion was deployed in precolonial and colonial Africa. It investigates whether there are approaches to freedom of religion that are distinctive to precolonial Africa. The fourth section highlights some factors that informed the adoption of freedom of religion in the legal instruments of postcolonial African States. It evaluates how the various African States currently regulate freedom of religion and identifies similar and different legal and deployment patterns of the right by these states. It further interrogates the role that religion and freedom of religion play in the political discourse, strategies, structure and governance among African States. The section concludes with a brief examination of the implication of the current approaches of regulating freedom of religion among the African States for ATR. The last section gives a summary of the findings and then the conclusion.

An overview of Africa's religious demography

In precolonial Africa, the religions that were predominantly practised are those developed in Africa by Africans for Africans. These religions are commonly referred to as African Traditional Religions (ATR). As observed later in this chapter, Islam and Christianity have now influenced the religious demography of the continent. Currently, there is no accurate estimate of the composition of religious groups on the continent. We are left with mere projections (Pew Research Centre, 2015) and conjectures.[3] However, it is generally acknowledged that Christianity and Islam are the dominant religions (Hackett, 2011: 857). Of the estimated population of over 1.2 billion on the continent, the adherents of Christianity are said to be approximately 50.9%,[4] Islam 43.3%[5] and others 5.8%.[6] Other religions that are practised on the continent include Judaism, Buddhism, Hindu, Bahai faith, Sikhism and Rastafarianism, among others. A substantial number of people still practice ATR. It is further asserted that the religious beliefs of the aforementioned dominant religions are sometimes characterised with syncretism with the ATR.[7] It is widely acknowledged that Muslims dominate North African countries and Christians dominate most of sub-Sahara countries.[8] Nigeria can, however, be singled out as the only country with an estimated equal proportion of Christians and Muslims (see Stonwaski et al., 2016). As will be observed shortly, the religious

3 Hackett, 2011. Professor Hackett observes that the 'Statistics on religion in Africa are limited, unreliable (due to changing or multiple associations), and often contested for their political manipulation.' See also Barrett et al., 2001.

4 The prominent Christian denominations on the continent include the Roman Catholic Church, Anglican Communion, Baptist Church, Seventh Day Adventists, the Methodist Church, Jehovah's Witnesses and a large number of Evangelical and Pentecostal churches, many of whom are indigenous with no links to the West.

5 The prominent Muslim sect on the continent is Sunnis. Other Muslim sects include Shiites and Ahmadiyah, among others.

6 See the simplified map of Africa's religions at https://brilliantmaps.com/simple-africa-relgions.

7 Awolalu, 1976; Rutanga, 2011: 1–39. Rutanga revealed from his empirical research conducted in Uganda that the people lived dual or multiple religious lives. They worshipped African gods in secrecy and were Christians or Muslims openly. They found having different religions neither contradictory nor conflictual but rather empowering, and at times enabling of their maneuverability, concealment and benefits.

8 The sub-Sahara countries with a Muslim majority population include Chad, the Comoros, Djibouti, Somalia, Sudan, Burkina Faso, Ivory Coast, Gambia, Guinea, Mali, Guinea Bissau, Mauritania, Niger, Sierra Leone and Senegal. It is interesting to note that most of these countries are francophone countries.

demography of most countries typically influences their constitutional and legal approaches to the reception and deployment of freedom of religion of African States.

Freedom of religion in precolonial Africa

Although the current geography of the over 50 African States is mostly the creation of the colonialists, there are accounts that precolonial Africa comprised 'highly developed kingdoms and empires' that had 'established and settled systems of government' (Emiola, 2011: 2) that equate to modern sovereign states (Meredith, 2006; Mokhtar, 1990). Examples of such kingdoms include the Ashantis, Konkonbas and Akans in Ghana; the Zulus, Kurumans and Bantus in Southern Africa; the Gikuyu, Kigezi, Bunyoro and Oruganda in present-day East Africa; the Oyo and Benin empires in Nigeria; the Dogon in Mali; and so on. While some of these communities were 'cephalous,'[9] others were 'acephalous.'[10] But each community was characterised by people knitted together by culture and language.

There are further reliable accounts and a consensus among scholars of the history of religions that a variety of traditional beliefs and religions as well as established religious communities existed in the precolonial Africa era.[11] These religious communities may not necessarily have been structured in any formal way, but their adherents were knitted together by common religious beliefs or commitment. For example, the Mende people of Sierra Leone were known to believe in and worship *Ndogbouoi* (the mountain god), the Akan of Ghana worshipped *Asase Yaa* (the earth goddess of fertility), the Igbos in Nigeria worshipped the *Ota Miri* (the deity who owns all the waters), the indigenous people in Namibia worship *Kalunga ya Nangombe* (the cattle god), and so on. While some of these religious beliefs were exclusive to certain families,[12] ethnic groups, communities or territories; others were shared across societies (Oguntola-Laguda, 2005: 26). But a salient element of these precolonial religions, which to some extent still exists, is that they are closely merged with the culture and traditions of the people. To this end, Oguntola-Laguda, a Nigerian professor of African Religions, explains that African religions are 'often expressed daily in practices and activities';[13] Jacob Olupona, a professor of indigenous African Religions, made a similar comment that 'African spirituality simply acknowledges that beliefs and practices touch on and inform every facet of human life, and therefore African religion cannot be separated from the everyday or mundane.'[14] In fact, it is averred that the distinction between religious and cultural practices was unknown in precolonial Africa (see Amoah and Bennett, 2008). Thus, it may be

9 'Cephalous' means 'with head or leader.' This form of government is said to be prevalent in most of the southern African kingdoms. See generally Sansom, 1974 and Mayhm, 1987.

10 'Acephalous' means 'without leader or central authority.' This form of government is practiced among the Igbos in Nigeria.

11 Agbiji and Swart, 2015: 3; Bennett, 1993: 31; Mbiti, 1990. Mbiti states, 'We speak of African Traditional Religions in the plural because there are one thousand African Peoples (tribes) and each has its religious system.'

12 Within the African context, a family consists of all those who are related by blood known as the 'extended family'; it includes a group of closely related people, known by a common name and consisting usually of a man and his half-brothers and their wives and children, and possible other relations. See generally Green, 1941: 43; Bennett, 1993: 32–33.

13 Oguntola-Laguda, 2005: 18; Mbiti, 1990: 15. Mbiti similarly says this religious worldview informs the philosophical understanding of African myths, customs, traditions, beliefs, morals, actions and social.

14 Olupona states further, 'For starters, the word "religion" is problematic for many Africans, because it suggests that religion is separate from the other aspects of one's culture, society, or environment. But for many Africans, religion can never be separated from all these. It is a way of life, and it can never be separated from the public sphere. Religion informs everything in traditional African society, including political art, marriage, health, diet, dress, economics, and death.' See the interview with Professor Jacob Olupona in Chiorazzi, 2015.

logical for us to describe the precolonial religious practices as 'religio-cultural practices.' A substantiation of such religio-cultural practices that is still in vogue in contemporary time is a practice of adding prefixes or suffixes to the names given to children born in certain families or communities to reflect their religious identity. For example, the worshippers of *Ogun* (the god of iron) among the Yorubas in Nigeria give names like *Ogun*bodede, *Ogun*tunde, and so on, to reflect the religion to which their children are born. Implicit in this practice is that the religious identity of a child is immediately tied to his or her family's religion at birth. This probably prompted Agbiji and Swart to submit that 'in African traditional life, an individual is immersed in religious participation that starts before birth and continues after death' (Agbiji and Swart, 2015: 3).

Although there is a dearth of accounts and scholarships on how freedom of religion was conceived in precolonial Africa, the above features that characterised precolonial African religions offer some assistance in discerning how freedom of religion was conceived and deployed in that era. The elements that are discerned are highlighted and briefly discussed below.

a. The fact that culture and religions overlap and are inseparable and because an individual is immediately tied up with his or her family's or community's religion at birth illustrates that no African can be without a religious belief since an individual must necessarily be born into a certain religion. This submission has two implications. On the one hand, it aligns with the European notion that conceives every human as 'homo-religious,' meaning, religion is inborn and innate; it forms part and parcel of human nature (Vasile, 2013; Stoker, 2000; see also Raz, 1978: 272–273). A state only needs to recognise it as a human right (McDougal et al., 1976; Evans, 2001: 29–32). On the other hand, it derogates from the European conception that seeks to protect the status of the nontheistic and atheistic under the right to freedom of conscience, opinion and belief. It was unthinkable for an African to be nonreligious or an unbeliever during precolonial Africa.

   Since religion can be exclusive to a family or community, and several families form a kingdom, it thus indicates that religious pluralism existed in precolonial African societies. And indeed, there are accounts of coexistence and accommodation of religions during this era. Writing about the multiplicity and nature of religious beliefs from the West African context, Oguntola-Laguda says, 'It is rather difficult to determine the number of divinities and spirits recognized by the people most of who have their own priests and priestess as well as devotees. Each of these divinities have their own rules, doctrines, taboos, totems, symbols liturgy and days of worship.'[15] For example, in the Oyo Empire among the Yoruba people in Nigeria, there was coexistence of various traditional religions, such as worshippers of *Ogun* the god of iron, *Sango* the god of thunder, and *Yemoja* the sea goddess, among others. The coexistence of religions, even if not formally called, is indicative of protection of group religious freedom as well as religious tolerance among the various religious groups. Nsereko's account on this issue is apt. He states: 'Most traditional African societies were pluralistic in the matter of religion and boasted a number of deities that were worshipped by Africans. The devotees of a given deity recognized the right of others to worship their own deities in their own way without hindrance.'[16] As will be discussed, the religious pluralism that is being evoked in this context denotes the coexistence of different religions within the same community or political entity, not pluralism within the same family.

15 Oguntola-Laguda, 2005: 31. Olupona also emphasises: 'Indigenous African religions are by nature plural, varied, and usually informed by one's ethnic identity, where one's family came from in Africa.' See Chiorazzi, 2015.
16 Nsereko, 1986: 269 (emphasis added). See also Walser, 1982: 236.

b. In addition, there is little or no evidence of religious discrimination, bigotry, proselytisation or conversion from one religion,[17] or the predominance of one religion over another in precolonial Africa.[18] There was neither categorisation of religions into minority and majority, nor inferior and superior religions.[19] Thus, Bennett submits, 'in Africa people suffered no systematic discrimination or oppression.' It can therefore be concluded that members of each family or community had the opportunity to manifest and practice their religio-cultural practices without undue constraints imposed by the political powers. This is what Amoah and Bennett described as 'cultural liberty' (Amoah and Bennett, 2008). On his part, Nsereko (1986) says it is 'religious liberty.' What can be identified as a close instance of discrimination in precolonial Africa is a 'group caste system' practiced by some ethnic groups such as the Osu people in eastern Nigeria.[20] But even then, a 'group caste' is at best a discrimination founded on social class, not religious.
c. Since a child is born, surnamed, nurtured and groomed into a family or community's religious space, the exercise of his or her religious right is encapsulated in the family or community's religious freedom. The family's religious affiliation automatically infects a child born into the family as the child becomes tied up with the shared family's religio-cultural practices. This implies that the prospect of a family member to change to another religion is limited since he or she cannot change his or her family except perhaps through marriage. Put differently, the individual religious right was less recognised and protected. In precolonial Africa, religion was not a mere private and internal concern but a group affair. Thus, Agbiji and Swart submit that religion is 'organised and practised in a community, instead of being an individual or personal affair' (Agbiji and Swart, 2015: 2). In the same vein, Bennett says, 'In Africa individualism would not be valued as it is in the west. Rather, a person would be expected to compromise his or her interests for the good of the larger unit; to stand on one's rights would be thought anti-social. It follows that whenever rights were an issue they would be the concern of the family as a group' (Bennett, 1993: 33; see also Holleman, 1969: 2–6 and Gluckman, 1972: 4–5).

Freedom of religion in colonial Africa

A new chapter on religion and freedom of religion was opened in Africa with the introduction of Islam and Christianity to the continent by Arab Muslims and European colonialists and missionaries, respectively. The settlement of Arabs Muslims and spread of Islam started around

17 Onyeidu similarly argued that Africans are generally not converted to traditional religion or received into membership of a religious community; rather, they are born into it, they live it, and they practice it. See Onyeidu, 1999: 54.

18 Mosoma, 1993: 49. Mosoma submits that Africans perceive religions as the 'wholeness of life'; thus, rendering coercion and discrimination on the basis of religion is unimaginable.

19 See also Bennett, 1993: 31; Asante, 1969: 73–74. Asante submits that 'The notion of due process of law permeated indigenous law; deprivation of personal liberty or property was rare; security of the person was assured, and customary legal process was characterized not by unpredictable and harsh encroachments upon the individual by the sovereign, but by meticulous, if cumbersome, procedures for decision-making. The African conception of human rights was an essential aspect of African humanism sustained by religious doctrine and the principle of accountability to the ancestral shades.'

20 What appears to be the only form of individual religious freedom is a self-imposed caste. Emiola describes this as 'those who bind themselves on oath to the service of their gods for as long as they live. This caste belongs to religious rather than social sects ... members dedicate themselves to a life of piety and live in seclusion in monasteries and abbeys ... such case members' legal status is fully recognized by the community because the apparent limitation they seem to suffer is self-imposed.' See Emiola, 2011: 59.

the seventh century AD among the Berbers of Maghrib, the indigenous people of North Africa. The Arab Muslims originally came to North Africa to trade. They later settled and married Africans and converted some of them to Islam. The Africans' inclination to religious diversity and accommodation probably aided the ease with which the Arab Muslims settled and proselyted Islam among Africans. The significance of this account is that it began religious proselytisation and religious conversion on the continent. At this initial period, ATR and Islam coexisted (Trimingham, 1962: 16; Fuglestad, 1978). But later, the Arab Muslims invaded and conquered the Berbers of Maghrib and imposed Islam on them. With this, the Arab Muslims again introduced religious violence, discrimination and bigotry on the continent. The conquest and success of the business of the Arab merchants in North Africa gave them a strong impetus to extend their trade through the trans-Saharan and consequently increase their degree of penetration to the remaining regions of the continent. In the eleventh century, the Arab Muslims with some of their African converts launched a militant reforming movement aimed at conquering and converting West Africa, starting from Sudan (Onwubiko, 1982: 115–117). By the nineteenth century, most of the indigenous people of Ghana, Mali, Kanem-Bornu, Fulani and Hausa land in West Africa had been converted from ATR to Islam through proselytisation and *jihad* (Onwubiko, 1982: 118–120; Trimingham, 1962: 16).

In a similar vein, the Europeans originally came to the continent to trade. They later proceeded to colonise and Christianise Africans. But while Christianisation succeeded in sub-Sahara Africa, it did not in North Africa. The difference between the approaches of Arab Muslims and European colonialists was that the former used physical violence and the latter used nonphysical coercion in converting Africans.[21] Christianity was integrated as part of the colonisation policies, such as through education and control of religious groups through registration and legislative and judicial policies,[22] among others. For example, many religio-cultural practices of Africans were struck down by the courts and colonial statutes on the grounds that they were repugnant to public policy and were incompatible with the contemporary idea of human rights (Taiwo, 2009; Kiye, 2015; Quashigah, 2016). Some of these colonial policies are still reflected in the contemporary constitutional and regulatory arrangements of most African States. Van der Vyver, writing from the South African context, confirms that 'the rights and freedoms protected by the constitution have been dictated by internationally recognized norms of right and wrong, which are in many instances not in conformity with the moral perceptions and customary practices of large sections of the South African population' (van der Vyver, 2011: 12). He argued further that 'Some of the laws that have been drafted to implement the principles of human rights from time to time provoke strong voices of protest from groups within the country whose age-old customs may fall prey to the concerned legal reform measures.'[23]

21 It was only the apartheid policy in South Africa that seemed to introduce Christianity by force.

22 For instance, Professor Hackett noted that the regulations of the British colonialists in Ghana effectively limited the religious freedom of the indigenous people of Ghana to practice ATR. See Hackett, 2011: 872.

23 van der Vyver, 2011: 12. See also Hackett, 2011: 862–863. Hackett submits that the 'Patterns of strict regulation of religious groups can sometimes be traced back to colonial practices or the manipulation of the status of religious groups according to the political needs of the postcolonial ruler.' Professor Emiola, however, argues that most of the precolonial religious and cultural practices that were struck down on the account of repugnancy test were not against public policy. He contended: 'It (customary law) is a law based on principles of natural justice and equity in its general and widest sense. There is nothing basically inequitable in the contents of most African customary law. Some of the rules of customary law struck down by the application of the doctrine of repugnancy can be explained away by reference to history when the rules were the most equitable by the popular feelings of the time' (Emiola, 2011: 16).

The primary conclusion that can be drawn from the above account is that during colonial Africa, the dominance of one religion over another emerged on the continent; and of course, Islam and Christianity enjoyed the benefit of being the dominating religions over ATR.

Freedom of religion in postcolonial Africa

At their independence or immediately after their independence, virtually all the African States included freedom of religion provisions in their national constitutions, albeit with different features in terms of wording, scope and limitations. Different factors necessitated such constitutional insertion. Regarding Nigeria, for instance, the religious demography of the country resulting in the fear of domination of majority religious groups over minority religious groups necessitated the introduction of freedom of religion provisions in the country's constitution. At about the time of Nigeria's independence in 1960, some minority ethnic and religious groups expressed the fear of domination by majority groups. This prompted the British colonial government of Nigeria to set up the Willink Commission to look into the agitation. The Willink Commission found that this fear was genuine and suggested that a bill of rights be entrenched in the Independence Constitution of Nigeria, 1960. This suggestion was accepted and a bill of rights following the European Convention for the Protection of Human Rights and Fundamental Freedoms was included in the Constitution of the Federation of Nigeria, 1960.[24] These provisions were later entrenched in the country's 1979 Constitution and now in the 1999 Constitution, the extant constitution.[25] With regard to South Africa, the sensitivity to the discriminatory and racist regimes that the country experienced during apartheid influenced the introduction of freedom of religion provisions in the country's constitution to protect, manage and integrate religious pluralism with the goals of the new democratic state, underpinned by equality and nondiscrimination (preamble to the 1996 const.). Other reasons for including freedom of religion provisions in the constitution of some other African countries include pressure from political and nonstate actors, and so on.

An attempt to analyse the constitutional arrangements in the over 50 African States is no small task. It will also be a prolix exercise given the limited length of this chapter. Thus, three major observations that can be made from the analysis of the constitutional arrangements on freedom of religion in some states are briefly discussed below.

First, it is observed that nearly all the over 50 African States have freedom of religion provisions and limitations in their constitutions. The major differences lie in the wording and limitation approaches. Furthermore, virtually all the constitutions have a faith confession that makes reference to God or Allah. This constitutional feature in itself is a *prima facie* evidence that supports African religiosity. However, this constitutional feature is discriminatory against the members of the irreligious group.

Second, the North African countries and some other countries with a Muslim majority population appear to have similar approaches. Although their constitutions recognise the right to religious freedom of other religions, Islam is made the state religion with a commitment to

24 Report of the Commission Appointed to Enquire into the Fears of Minorities and the Means of Allying Them, Command paper 505, 18 August 1958. London: H.M.S.O.

25 See Matthew Hassan Kukah, Homily delivered on 11 February 2020, at the funeral mass of seminarian Michael Nnadiwho who was kidnapped and murdered by the Boko Haram terrorist group at the Good Shepherd Seminary Kaduna. Kukah says 'The persecution of Christians in northern Nigeria is as old as the modern Nigerian state. Their experiences and fears of northern, Islamic domination are documented in the Willinks Commission Report way back in 1956. It was also the reason why they formed a political platform called, the Non-Muslim League.'

Islamic law. For instance, Islam is declared the state religion in Egypt,[26] Libya (Art. 1 of the 2011 Constitutional Declaration), Algeria (Art. 2 of the 1989 const.), the Comoros (preamble to the 2001 const.), Somalia (Art. 2.1 of the 2012 const.), Tunisia (preamble and Art. 1 of the 2014 const.), Mauritania (preamble and Arts. 1 and 5 of the 1991 const.) and Morocco (preamble and Art. 3 of the 2011 const.). Furthermore, the legal conditions under which other religions can manifest their religious practices in these countries are onerous, thereby making the exercise of freedom of religion meaningless. For example, the Constitution of the People's Democratic Republic of Algeria (1989) declares that 'freedom of creed and opinion is inviolable' (Art. 36). But its Article 9 disallows 'practices that are contrary to the Islamic ethics.' Similarly, Article 17 of the Constitution of the Federal Republic of Somalia, 2012, provides that 'every person is free to practice his or her religion.' However, Article 2.2 stipulates that 'no religion other than Islam can be propagated in the country,' and Article 2.3 provides that 'No law can be enacted that is not compliant with the general principles and objectives of Shari'ah.'[27] The constitutional preference for a particular religion and the above limiting provisions will technically impede the flourishing of other religions since Islamic doctrine and jurisprudence typically inhibit the manifestation of other religions. Meyer has rightly observed that Islam characteristically disapproves missionary activities in the interest of non-Muslim religions, but proselytising efforts to convert non-Muslims to Islam are welcomed (1987: 149). In the same vein, Abdullahi An-Na'im (1987) pointed out that the standing of non-Muslims under *Shari'ah* is inferior, and constitutions which proclaim *Shari'ah* to be a foundation of law consequently approve discrimination against religious minorities.

Third, as was previously noted, many of the countries in sub-Sahara Africa have a Christian majority population. But unlike the approach adopted by the countries with Muslim majority populations considered above, their constitutions do not make their countries Christian states. Rather, they commonly adopt a religious neutral approach. Only the Constitution of Zambia (2016) declared the country 'a Christian nation while upholding a person's right to freedom of conscience, belief or religion' (preamble). Some other countries with a Muslim majority population in the sub-Sahara such as Djibouti (Arts. 1 and 3 of the 1992 const.), Ivory Coast (Arts. 1, 4, and 19 of the 2016 const.), Niger (Arts. 8 and 30 of the 2010 const.), Liberia (Art. 14 of the 1984 const.), Congo (Art. 1 of the 2005 const.), Senegal (Arts. 1 and 8 of the 2001 const.) and Togo (Art. 2 of the 1992 const.) also have a constitutional commitment to operating a neutral state. Since the adoption of religious neutrality cuts across both the Muslim majority and Christian majority States in sub-Sahara Africa, it may be problematic to conclude that the basis for adopting neutrality by these States is connected exclusively either to Islamic or Christian doctrine. The basis for the States' adoption of religious neutrality may, however, be predicated on two possible factors. The first is that it is a legacy of European colonialism. Abbink shares this view when he asserts that 'despite its ambiguous origin under colonial regimes, the "secular model" was held onto by (African) postcolonial political leaders as they believed it would facilitate religious freedom and dampen religious conflict' (Abbink, 2004: 92). The second view is to see the adoption of the neutrality by the States as a means of building on the religious pluralism and nondiscrimination previously said to characterise precolonial African societies. However, while these sub-Sahara countries provide for religious neutrality, they strangely have

26 Article 2 of the Constitution of the Arab Republic of Egypt, 2014. The provision states, 'Islam is the religion of the State and Arabic is its official language. The principles of Islamic Sharia are the main source of legislation.'

27 See similar contradictory provisions in Articles 2 and 64 of the Constitution of the Arab Republic of Egypt, 2014; Article 3 of the Constitution of the Kingdom of Morocco, 2011 and Articles 1 and 6 of the Constitution of the Tunisian Republic, 2014.

vague and far-reaching limiting provisions that make it easy for political authorities to undermine freedom of religion.[28] The obvious assumption that underlies these limiting provisions is what Ellis and ter Haar described as the political actors' use of religions as a dubious and opportunistic tool to suppress freedom in order to keep power and influence others.[29] Accordingly, van der Vyver observes that 'the constitutional protection of religious freedom in many African countries provided cold comfort to religious groups disapproved of by the political authorities' (Van der Vyver, 1999b: 140; Hackett, 2011: 859).

Furthermore, religion and freedom of religion play a role in the political discourse, strategies, structure and governance among African states. The next section briefly describes how this is played out in some African countries.

Religion, freedom of religion and state relations in Africa

Religion and state relations within Africa have been explored by a number of scholars (Devenish, 2005: 88; Nsereko, 1986). Most of these writings focused on the degree of religious neutrality in African States. Devenish, for instance, identifies three approaches to religion and state relation.[30] The first approach is where a state adopts an official religion as in the case of Egypt, Libya, Algeria, the Comoros, Somalia, Tunisia, Mauritania and Morocco where Islam is adopted as the state religion. In this category, religious freedom can be easily inhibited. The second is where there is a strict separation between all religious activities and the state, which is a secular state. This appears to be the approach in the constitutions adopted by most of the sub-Sahara countries. For instance, countries like Benin (Art. 2 of the 1990 const.), Burkina Faso (Art. 31 of the 1991 const.), Burundi (Art. 1 of the 2005 const.), Cape Verde (Art. 48.3 of the 1980 const.), Cameroon (Art. 2 of the 1972 const.), Chad (Art. 1 of the 1996 const.), the Congo (Art. 1 of the 2005 const.), Ivory Coast (Art. 49 of the 2016 const.), Guinea (Art. 1 of the 2010 Fundamental Law), Guinea-Bissau (Art. 1 of the 1991 const.), Madagascar (Art. 1 of the 2010 const.), Mali (preamble to the 1992 const.), Namibia (Art. 1.1 of the 1990 const.), Senegal (Art. 1 of the 2001 const.), Togo (Art. 1 of the 1992 const.), Angola (Art. 10.1 of the 2010 const.), Mozambique (Arts. 12.1 and 12.2 of the 2004 const.), Ethiopia (Art. 11 of the 1995 const.), Niger (Art. 3.2 of the 2010 const.), the Democratic Republic of Sao Tome and Principe (Art. 8 of the 1975 const.) and Madagascar (Art. 2 of the 2010 const.), among others give a constitutional commitment to religious neutrality. In this instance, the state has no official religion. However, contrary to what is literally provided in these countries' constitutions, the states and political powers have a history of interfering and influencing the religious space (van der Vyver and Green, 2008: 346–347). In reciprocity, religions also constitute a strong force in determining the political terrain of most African States (Abbink, 2004; Ellis and ter Haar, 2007). This reality probably forms the basis of Devenish's third approach. This third approach is premised on a state's accommodation of religions, where there is neither established religion

28 See, for instance, Article 5 of the Constitution of Senegal, 2001; Articles 18 and 30 of the Constitution of Niger, 2010; Article 45 of the Constitution of the Federal Republic of Nigeria, 1999; Article 25 of the Constitution of Togo, 1992; Articles 19 and 21.2 of the Constitution of Namibia, 1990; Article 48.1 of the Constitution of Cape Verde, 1980; Article 22 of the Constitution of the Democratic Republic of Congo, 2005; Article 41 of the Constitution of Rwanda, 2003 and Articles 19, 30 and 31 of the Constitution of Tanzania, 1977.

29 Ellis and ter Haar, 2008; Abbink, 2004: 93. Further, Hackett said 'inefficient and poorly funded court systems may also be to blame' (2011: 860).

30 Devenish, 2005: 88. However, Nsereko identifies three broad categories of church–state relations that exist among African countries as follows: (1) separation of church and state; (2) supremacy of religion over the state and (3) subordination of religion to the state. See Nsereko, 1986.

nor coercion, but a close cooperation prevails between the state and religions (Devenish, 2005: 88). Hackett, while quoting Durham (1996: 16–17), observes that Africa may be closer to Europe and Scandinavia than to the United States in its approach to religion–state relationships. There is a 'far greater acceptance of state involvement with religious affairs as long as this is done in a fair and transparent way' (Hackett, 2011: 860).

It is worth noting that regardless of the approach that is expressly recognised in each country's constitution, studies confirm that religion plays a role in the political discourse and structure in African States. However, evidence shows that the dominant religions or the dominant religious sects exercise more influence in the legal and political spheres to the detriment of the minority religions (Ward, 1995: 82). For instance, some political offices are constitutionally reserved for Muslims in some states with a Muslim majority population. In the Comoros (Art. 41 of the 2001 const.) and Morocco (Art. 41 of the 2011 const.), a Council of *Ulemas*[31] are assigned executive powers in certain matters that affect the States. In Mauritania (Art. 23 of the 1991 const.) and Tunisia (Art. 74 of the 2014 const.), the president must, as a matter of constitutional design, be a Muslim. Similar instances are obtained in States with a Christian majority population. Van der Vyver and Green explain:

> Although the 1996 Constitution of Botswana designated that country to be a secular state, statutory provisions proclaiming Ascension Day, Easter and Christmas public holidays — according to one analyst — 'makes the country unofficially a Christian country' ... Zimbabwe is constitutionally a secular state but, we were told, is in reality a Christian state. And the list goes on (van der Vyver and Green, 2008: 343–344).

On this issue of religion and state relations, the Nigeria case deserves special mention since it is a country where Islam and Christianity, which are the majority religions, are estimated to be of equal population. It is an 'unwritten agreement' of the Nigerian constitution that any person vying for the post of president or vice president must identify with either Christianity or Islam. Where a Muslim is vying for the seat of president, the vice president must be a Christian, and vice versa. Meanwhile, the provision of Article 10 of the Nigerian 1999 Constitution *prima facie* adopts a religious neutral approach. The provision states: 'The Government of the Federation or of a State shall not adopt any religion as state religion.' This provision has led to two opposing views of Nigeria's status as a secular state. Some scholars and public commentators argue that Section 10 of the Constitution makes Nigeria a secular state in which there is no interference from the state in any religious affairs (Tyus, 2004: 205; see also Nwabueze, 1992: 282; Iwobi, 2004: 133–135). In contradistinction, other scholars argue that the prohibition of a national or state religion is not a clear indication that Nigeria is a secular state. The comment of Nwauche, one such proponent of the latter position, is very relevant here:

> Section 10 of the 1999 Constitution prohibits the adoption, by the federal or a state government, of any religion as a state religion. It is often said that because of this provision, Nigeria is a secular state. This would be a wrong conclusion if it were to mean that religion does not play a role in public policy. Nigeria is a *de facto*

31 Council of Ulama consists of senior religious clerics and scholars with special knowledge of Islamic jurisprudence and theology.

> religious state where Islam and Christianity are integrated into public policy—in the recognition of marriages, the observance of public holidays, and the resolution of conflicts.[32]

The activities of the successive governments in Nigeria further make it easy to conclude that the government overtly, but unjustifiably, supports Christianity and Islam. And this has disproportionately affected other religions that are practised in the country, particularly ATR. Several facts substantiate this assertion. First, only Christian and Islamic holidays are mentioned and approved in the Public Holidays Act (Act 31 of 1979). In addition, following the provisions of the legislation, the government annually declares Good Friday, Easter and Christmas as public holidays for Christians and *Eid-el-Maulud*, *Eid-el-fitri Sallah* and *Eid Al-Adha* as public holidays for Muslims. The federal government further allocated plots of land free of charge at the Federal Capital Territory, Abuja for the building of the national mosque and the Christian ecumenical centre. Furthermore, the Constitution recognised the creation of the Sharia Court of Appeal as a superior court of record (Arts. 6.5 (f) and (g), 260, 275). The government further established the National Christian Pilgrim Commission[33] and National Hajj Commission[34] as government agencies to organise, facilitate and subsidise from government funds Christian and Muslim pilgrimages, respectively, to religious sites globally.

The continued political support for the dominant religions among most African states is discriminatory to other religions and limits their flourishing. It is unfortunate that the ATR is mostly affected. Beginning from the colonial era until now, the ATR that enjoyed prominence in precolonial Africa has been devalued to the status of a minority religion and endured political assaults and social stigmatisation. On the state of ATR in Africa today, Olupona emphasises: 'That's a mixed bag. Indigenous African spirituality today is increasingly falling out of favour. The amount of devotees to indigenous practices has dwindled as Islam and Christianity have both spread and gained influence throughout the continent ... The success of Christianity and Islam on the African continent in the last 100 years has been extraordinary, *but it has been, unfortunately, at the expense of African indigenous religions*.'[35] But it is worth noting that Islamisation and Christianisation of the continent are not the only reasons for the relegation of ATR; it coincided with other modern phenomena, such as capitalism, industrialisation, urbanisation and labour migration. All these have impacted the ties of kinship and fragmented families and communities, the premise on which the sustenance of ATR rests.

Conclusion

This chapter aimed to uncover some elements of freedom of religion that are distinctive to Africa and perhaps more importantly to discover how these features may contribute to the dialogue on freedom of religion. The chapter explored freedom of religion from a three-phase development of Africa — precolonial, colonial and postcolonial. The common trend

32 Nwauche, n.d. See also Kawu, 2016: 4; Tabiu, 2001. Tabiu argues: 'We can see that the section does not establish ... [the] claim that the Constitution describes Nigeria as a secular state. In fact, the Constitution does not use the word secularism or any of its derivatives at all. How then can they build an argument, alleging a violation of the Constitution, merely on their personal interpretation of such a word of varied and controversial meaning, which is not even in the Constitution?'

33 Article 1 of the Nigerian Christian Pilgrim Commission Act 74 of 2007.

34 Article 1 of the National Hajj Commission of Nigeria (Establishment) Act 2006.

35 Chiorazzi, 2005. Emphasis added.

that runs through the three phases supports the widely held view of African religiosity. However, each phase has its unique features. Among the three phases, precolonial Africa best reflects the African perspective on freedom of religion. In this era, an individual right to religious freedom received little or no protection; rather, the focus was on group religious freedom. No one can choose to be without a religious belief, change his or her religious belief or have beliefs system contrary to the group belief system. This feature possibly forms the basis for why the right to freedom of sexual orientation, a right deeply rooted in individual freedom, still grapples to flourish in many African States and religious institutions. This is simply because such an individualistic right has no place in African religio-cultural practices. However, an effective and religious pluralism and religious accommodation featured prominently in precolonial Africa. Although the ATR dominated the religious space in this era, there were little or no accounts of religious violence, religious discrimination, proselytisation or conversation from one religion to another. Given the above, freedom of religion cannot be said to be completely imported into Africa; it was only the individual religious freedom that the colonialists introduced to the continent.

The second phase witnessed the introduction of foreign religions — Islam and Christianity. The foreign religions whittled down the elements of freedom of religion that characterised the precolonial African religions. The continent further experienced a radical change in the co-existence of religions and religious accommodation. The seed of religious violence, religious tension, discrimination and bigotry were sown during this era. This phase also began the de-valuation of the ATR on the continent.

The postcolonial phase was built on the legacy of the colonial era. While in theory, freedom of religion is entrenched in the grundnorm of most states, such introduction is a mere façade. In this era, it is observed that religious institutions are 'religionising' the political spheres, while the political actors are politicising the religious spheres. Because religion overlaps with the socio-political and economic spheres of states, the political class hides behind the limitation clauses to undermine both group and individual religious rights, particularly that of the minority religions to gain political scores. Dominant religions and religious sects also use their political influence to violate minority religions. In the same vein, religious violence, religious tension and discrimination and bigotry have been on the increase during this phase. Given that freedom of religion best flourished in precolonial Africa, in the construction and reconstruction of freedom of religion, the need to focus on each societal context may become indispensable for freedom of religion to flourish effectively.

References

Abbink, J., 2004. Religion and politics in Africa: The future of the 'the secular. *Africa Spectrum* 49(3), 83.

Agbiji, O.M., Swart, I., 2015. Religion and social transformation in Africa: A critical and appreciative perspective. *Scriptura* 114(1), 1.

Amoah, J., Bennett, T., 2008. The freedom of religion and culture under the South Africa constitution: Do traditional African religions enjoy equal treatment. *Journal of Law and Religion*. 24(1), 1.

An-Na'im, A.A., 1987. Religious minorities under Islamic law and the limits of cultural relativism. *Human Rights Quarterly*. 9, 1.

Asante, S.K.B., 1969. Nation building and human rights in emergent African nations. *Cornell Law Journal*. 2, 72.

Awolalu, J.O., 1976. What is African traditional religion? *Studies in Comparative Religion*. 10(2), 1.

Bennett, T.W., 1993. Human rights and the African cultural tradition. *Transformation*. 22, 30.

Barrett, D.B., Kurian, G.T., Johnson, T.M. (Eds.), 2001. *World Christian Encyclopedia: A Comparative Survey of Churches and Religions in the Modern World*. Oxford University Press.

Chiorazzi, A., 2015. The spirituality of Africa. *The Harvard Gazette*. Available from: https://news.harvard.edu/gazette/story/2015/10/the-spirituality-of-africa.
Devenish, G.E., 2005. *The South African Constitution*. Lexisnexis Butterworths.
Durham, W.C., 1996. Perspectives on religious liberty: A comparative framework. In: van der Vyver, J.D., Witte, J., Jr. (Eds.), *Religious Human Rights in Global Perspective: Legal Perspectives*. Martinus Nijhoff Publishers, p. 1.
Dworkin, R., 1978. *Taking Rights Seriously*. Harvard University Press.
Ellis, S., ter Haar, G., 2007. Religion and politics: Taking African epistemologies seriously. *Journal of Modern African Studies*. 45(3), 385.
Ellis, S., ter Haar, G., 2008. Religion and politics in sub-Saharan Africa. *Journal of Modern African Studies*. 36(2), 175.
Emiola, A., 2011. *Principles of African Customary Law*. Emiola Publishers.
Evans, C., 2001. *Freedom of Religion under the European Convention on Human Rights*. Oxford University Press.
Fuglestad, F., 1978. A reconsideration of Hausa history before the Jihad. *Journal of African History*. 19(3), 319.
Gluckman, M., 1972. *The Ideas in Barotse Jurisprudence*. Manchester University Press.
Green, M.M., 1941. *Land Tenure in an Ibo Village*. Berg Publishers.
Hackett, R.I.J., 2011. Regulating religious freedom in Africa. *Emory International Law Review*. 25, 853.
Holleman, J.F., 1969. *Chief, Council and Commissioner: Some Problems of Government in Rhodesia*. Royal Van Gorcum Ltd.
Iwobi, A.U., 2004. Tiptoeing through a constitutional minefield: The great Shari'a controversy in Nigeria. *Journal of African Law*. 48, 111.
Kawu, S.D., 2016. Religious rights in a pluralistic world: The Nigerian experience. *A paper presented at the 23rd Symposium on Law and Religion organised by the International Centre for Law and Religion*. Brigham Young University, Provo (UT), 1–4 October 2016.
Kiye, M.E., 2015. The repugnancy and incompatibility tests and customary law in Anglophone Cameroon. *African Studies Quarterly*. 2, 85.
Mayer, A.E., 1987. Law and religion in the Muslim Middle East. *American Journal of Comparative Law*. 35, 127.
Mayhm, P., 1987. *A History of the African People of South Africa*. David Philip.
Mbiti, J.S., 1990. *African Religions and Philosophy*. Heinemann.
McDougal, M.S., Lasswell, H.D., Chen, L., 1976. The right to religious freedom and World public order: The emerging norm of non-discrimination. *Michigan Law Review*. 74, 865.
Meredith, M., 2006. *The fate of Africa – A Survey of Fifty Years of Independence*. Public Affairs.
Mokhtar, G. (Ed.), 1990. *UNESCO General History of Africa, vol. 2*. University of California Press.
Mosoma, D.L., 1993. Religious liberty: An African perspective. In: Kilian, J. (Ed.), *Religious Freedom in South Africa*. Unisa Press, p. 48.
Mutangu, T., 2008. Religion, law and human rights in Zimbabwe. *African Human Rights Law Journal*. 8, 526.
Nsereko, D.D., 1986. Religion, the state and the law in Africa. *Journal of Church and State*. 28, 269.
Nsereko, D.D., 1992. Religious liberty and the law in Botswana. *Journal of Church and State*. 1992, 843.
Nwabueze, B.O., 1992. *Military Rule and Constitutionalism*. Spectrum Law Publisher.
Nwauche, E., 2008. Law, religion and human rights in Nigeria. *African Human Rights Law Journal*. 8, 568.
Nwauche, E., n.d. *Nigeria: Introductory Notes*. Institute for International and Comparative Law in Africa. Available from: http://www.icla.up.ac.za/images/country_reports/nigeria_country_report.pdf.
Ocheni, S., Nwankwo, B., 2012. Analysis of colonialism and its impact in Africa. *Cross-Cultural Communication*. 8(3), 46.
Oguntola-Laguda, D., 2005. *Divinities in West African religion*. Free Enterprise Publishers.
Onwubiko, K.B.C., 1982. *History of West Africa AD 1000–1800*. Africana Educational Publishers.
Onyeidu, S.O., 1999. *African Traditional Religion: The Problem of Definition*. Ben Quality Printers.
Pew Research Center. 2015. *The Future of World Religions: Population Growth Projections, 2010–2050*. Available from: https://www.pewforum.org/2015/04/02/religious-projections-2010–2050.
Quashigah, K., 2016. Justice in the traditional African society within the modern constitutional set-up. *International Journal of Legal and Political Thought* 7(1), 93.
Raz, J., 1978. *The Morality of Freedom*. Clarendon Press.
Rutanga, M., 2011. *Politics, Religion, and Power in the Great Lakes Region*. Fountain Publishers.

Sansom, B., 1974. Traditional rulers and their realms. In: Hammond-Tooke, W.D. (Ed.), *The Bantu-Speaking Peoples of Southern Africa*. Routledge & Kegan Paul, p. 246.

Stoker, W., 2000. Are Human Beings Religious by Nature: Schleiemacher's Generic View of Religion and the Contemporary Pluralistic, Secular Culture. *Journal in Philosophy and Theology*. 61(1), 51.

Stonawski, M., Potančoková, M., Cantele, M., Skirbekk, V., 2016. The changing religious composition of Nigeria: Causes and implications of demographic divergence. *Journal of Modern African Studies*. 53(3), 1.

Tabiu, M., 2001. *Shari'a federalism and Nigerian constitution*. A paper presented at the International Conference on Shari'a, London.

Taiwo, E.A., 2009. Repugnancy clause and its impact on customary law: Comparing the South African and Nigerian positions – some lessons for Nigeria. *Journal for Juridical Science*. 34(1), 89.

Trimingham, J.S., 1962. *A History of Islam in West Africa*. Oxford University Press.

Tyus, J., 2004. Going too far: Extending Shari'a law in Nigeria from personal to public law. *Washington University Global Studies Law Review*. 3, 199.

van der Vyver, J.D., 1999a. Constitutional perspective of church-state relations in South Africa. *Brigham Young University Law Review*. 2, 635.

van der Vyver, J.D., 1999b. Religious freedom in African constitutions. In: An-Na'im A.A. (Ed.), *Proselytization and Communal Self-Determination in Africa*. Orbis Books, p. 109.

van der Vyver, J.D., 2011. The right to self-determination of cultural, religious and linguistic communities in South Africa. *Potchefstroom Electronic Law Journal*. 14(4), 2.

van der Vyver, J.D., Green, M.C., 2008. Law, religion and human rights in Africa: Introduction. *African Human Rights Law Journal*. 8, 337.

Vasile, C., 2013. Homo religiosus – culture, cognition, emotion. *Procedia – Social and Behavioral Sciences*. 78, 658.

Walser, F., 1982. *Luganda Proverbs*. Dietrich Reimer Verlag.

Ward, K., 1995. The church of Uganda amidst conflict: The interplay between church and politics in Uganda since 1962. In: Hansen, H.B., Twaddle, M. (Eds.), *Religion and Politics in East Africa: the Period Since Independence*. James Curry, p. 72.

PART IV

Mapping the right to freedom of religion or belief

15

Freedom of religion: Constitutional patterns of protection

Johan D. van der Vyver

The legal and constitutional dimensions of religion have many, quite distinct, ramifications, including the following:

a. Freedom of religion or belief, which is an individual right and includes (i) the right to believe, and (ii) the right to manifest one's religion or belief in teaching, practice, worship, and observance;
b. Freedom from discrimination based on religion or belief, which is an individual right and includes an obligation of the state (i) to display in its laws and practices objectivity toward all religions, and (ii) to outlaw unfair discrimination and to take action against persons who discriminate in the public sphere against persons on grounds of religion;
c. The relationship between the state and religious organizations, including church institutions, which is an institutional group right (that is, it vests in a religious institution as such) and that requires of the state not to interfere in the internal affairs of religious institutions; and
d. the right to self-determination of religious communities, which is a collective group right (that is, it vests in individuals as members of a religious community) and includes (i) the right to practice one's religion in association with other members of the religious community, and (ii) the right to form, join and maintain religious associations.

In the Canadian case of *R. v. Big M. Drug Mart (Ltd.)*, Dickson C.J.C. encapsulated as follows the gist of religious freedom:

> The essence of the concept of freedom of religion is the right to entertain such religious beliefs as a person chooses, the right to declare religious beliefs openly and without fear of hindrance or reprisal, and the right to manifest religious belief by worship and practice or by teaching and dissemination.[1]

1 *R. v. Big M. Drug Mart (Ltd.)*, [1985] 13 C.R.R. 64, at 95; and see also the South African cases of State v. Lawrence; State v. Negal; State v. Solberg, para. 92, 1997 (4) SA 1176, 1997 (10) BCLR 1348 (CC); Christian Education South Africa v. Minister of Education, para. 18, 2000 (4) SA 757, 2000 (10) BCLR 1051 (CC).

This chapter contains a rather synthetic overview of constitutional arrangements in countries from different regions of the world relating to the above dimensions of freedom of religion. Classifying those constitutional arrangements in scholarly compartments is no easy task, because of the great variety of such constitutional arrangements. We have laid special stress in the first section of this chapter on constitutional preferences afforded to certain denominations in particularly Muslim countries, but also in a number of Western states that afford special constitutional recognition to certain Christian denominations based on long-standing traditions rather than the spiritual dictates of those denominations. The second section is devoted to constitutional secularism and secularity with special emphasis on the American perceptions of the separation of church and state and on religion and law. The final section is centered upon constitutional objectivity in relation to religious diversity, which requires the state to protect all religions on the basis of the principle of equal treatment. This principle applies irrespective of the historical religious commitments of the state or the religious affiliations of a majority of the people in the countries concerned.

Religious selectivity

It is not uncommon for counties with a Muslim majority to embed references to Islam and perhaps also to Islamic law into their constitutional provisions. For example, the Constitution of the Islamic Republic of Iran of 1979, as amended in 1989, thus proclaims: 'The government of Iran is an Islamic Republic,' [Art. 1] and the Saudi Arabian Basic Law of Governance of 1992 similarly proclaims this kingdom to be 'a sovereign Arab Islamic state with Islam as its religion' [Art. 1].

Similar provisions exist in African countries with Muslim majorities. Islam is thus proclaimed to be the religion of the state in Algeria [Art. 2 of the 1989 const.], the Comoros [preamble to the 2001 const.], Egypt,[2] Libya [Art. 2 of the 1969 Constitutional Proclamation], Mauritania,[3] Morocco,[4] Somalia [Art. 2.1 of the 2012 const.], and Tunisia.[5] In its Transitional Constitution of 1985, Sudan proclaimed its constitution in the name of 'Allah, the Compassionate and merciful,' [preamble] but in its Interim National Constitution of 2005, it adopted a more religiously neutral stance by describing the Republic as 'a democratic, decentralized, multi-cultural, multi-racial, multi-ethnic, multi-religious, and multi-lingual country, where such diversities co-exist' [Art. 1(1)] and furthermore proclaimed that 'religion, beliefs, transitions and customs are the source of moral strength and inspiration for the Sudanese people' [Art. 4(b)].

Several countries in the East also proclaims a constitutional commitment to Islam. Afghanistan thus proclaimed its constitution (2004) 'In the name of Allah, the Most Beneficent, the Most Merciful' [preamble] and defined the country as 'an Islamic Republic' [Art. 1]. It further provides: 'The sacred religion of Islam is the religion of the Islamic Republic of

2 Article 2 of the constitution of the Arab Republic of Egypt (2014). Egypt proclaimed its constitution of 2014 'In the name of Allah, Most Gracious, Most Merciful.'

3 Article 5 of the constitution of the Islamic Republic of Mauritania (1991) proclaims: 'Islam is the religion of the people and of the State.' In the preamble, Mauritania confesses the 'omnipotence of Allah' and depicts the Mauritanian nation as 'a Muslim, African and Arab people.' In Article 1, Mauritania is described as 'an Islamic, indivisible, democratic and social Republic.'

4 Article 3 of the constitution of the Kingdom of Morocco (2011). See also the preamble proclaiming the country to be 'a sovereign Muslim State.'

5 Article 1 of the constitution of the Tunisian Republic (2014). See also the preamble proclaiming the constitution '[i]n the name of God, the Compassionate and the Merciful,' and further testifying to 'the people's commitment to the teachings of Islam and its aims characterised by openness and moderation.'

Afghanistan' [Art. 2]. Malaysia similarly provides in its constitution (1957) that 'Islam is the religion of the Federation' [Art. 3(1)], and Bangladesh in a similar vein ordains that Islam is the state religion of the country.[6]

In some instances, Muslim countries added substance to their commitment to Islam by sanctioning, as part of the administrative state structure, certain religious institutions and/or expressly requiring high-ranking state officials to be Muslims. In the Comoros [Title VI of the 2005 const.] and Morocco [Art. 41 of the 2011 const.], a Council of Ulemas (religious scholars with special knowledge of Islamic sacred law and theology) have been entrusted with jurisdiction in certain executive matters. In Mauritania [Art. 23 of the 1991 const.] and Tunisia [Art. 74 of the 2014 const.], the president must, as a matter of constitutional compulsion, be a Muslim, and Morocco, again, requires the king, 'Commander of the faithful,' to ensure 'the respect for Islam' [Art. 41 of the 2011 const.]. The constitution of Bangladesh proclaims 'equal rights in the practice of the Hindu, Buddhist, Christian and other religions' [Art. 2A].

Almost all Muslim countries guarantee religious freedom in one form or another, but in most instances that freedom is subjected to often sweeping conditions. The constitution of Algeria (1989) thus proclaims 'freedom of creed and opinion' to be inviolable [Art. 3], but at the same time forbids 'practices contrary to Islamic morals and the values of November Revolution' [Art. 9]. In the Comoros, the people 'solemnly proclaim their aspiration to draw from Islam, the permanent inspiration of the principles and laws that shall govern the State and its institutions' [preamble to the 2005 const.]. The constitution of Egypt (2014) seemingly contains an unqualified guarantee of the freedom of belief and the freedom of practicing religious rituals [Art. 64] (thereby, incidentally, also emphasizing the free exercise of religious freedom, which is not common in Muslim countries[7]), but at the same time states that Islamic jurisprudence shall be 'the main source of legislation' [Art. 2]; and Islamic jurisprudence places radical restrictions on the free exercise of religion, or at least the spread of religion, by non-Muslims in Islamic countries. By instructing the legislature to found its enactments on Islamic jurisprudence, the constitution mandates state intervention to curb proselytizing efforts by proponents of non-Muslim religions. Freedom of 'religious creed and worship' must in the Sudan be exercised within the 'requirements of law and public order' [Art. 38 of the 2005 transitional const.]. The constitution of Afghanistan (2004) affords to followers of faiths other than Islam the freedom to exercise and perform their religious rituals but only 'within the bounds of law' [Art. 2].

Freedom of religion is not expressly mentioned in the constitution of Mauritania. The constitution of Mauritania (1991) does make provision for the freedom of opinion and of thought (that may be limited by law) [Art. 10]. Such freedoms can be taken to include particular religious opinions and thought, but the sanctioning of legislative intervention to curtail those freedoms clearly leaves the door open for the legislature to subject the constitutional freedom and the free exercise guarantee to restrictions that can be quite radical. In Morocco, the constitution (2011) guarantees 'the free exercise of beliefs [*cultes*]' in the same context as the assertion that 'Islam is the religion of the State' [Art. 3].

6 Article 2A of the constitution of Bangladesh (1972, reinstated in 1986). However, it should be mentioned that the preamble makes a reference to the ideal, inter alia, of secularism, and Article 12 also references the principle of secularism.

7 But see also Article 6 of the constitution of the Sudan (2006), Article 6 of the constitution of Morocco (2011) protecting 'freedom of worship,' and Article 17.1 of the constitution of the Federal Republic of Somalia (2012) referring to freedom of every person 'to practice his or her religion.' Article 3.1 of the federal constitution of Malaysia states that 'Islam is the religion of the Federation; but other religions may be practised in peace and harmony in any part of the Federation.'

There is a similar guarantee in the constitution of Somalia (2012) of an entitlement of '[e]very person ... to practise his or her religion' [Art. 17.1], but the constitution then goes on to provide that '[n]o religion other than Islam can be propagated in the Federal Republic of Somalia' [Art. 17.2]. The constitution is also quite explicit in providing that '[n]o law can be enacted that is not in compliance with the general principles and objectives of Shari'ah' [Art. 2.3]. The constitution of Tunisia (2014) makes special provision for 'the free exercise of religious practices and the neutrality of mosques and places of worship from all partisan instrumentalisation,' but also in the same context proclaims the state as 'the guardian of religion' [Art. 6].

Though still rare in Muslim countries, such concessions are indeed indicative of increasing tolerance in the Muslim world toward non-Islamic religions. It is worth noting that several Muslim states, notably the Comoros, Egypt, and Somalia, included in their respective constitutions, equal protection clauses 'without regard to religion or belief' (or similarly defined) and without further qualification.[8]

Although the Libyan constitution (2011) proclaimed Islam to be the religion of the state and 'Islamic *Shari'ah* shall be the main source of legislation,' it added: 'The State shall guarantee for non-Muslims the freedom to practise their religious rituals' [Art. 1]. Initially, only the law of inheritance was governed by *Shari'ah* [Art. 8 const.], but in 1976 the Holy Koran was elevated to the level of constitution of the Socialist People's Libyan Arab Jamahiriya.[9] More recently, in 1991, the General People's Congress of Libya ordained: 'Religion is a direct relationship with the Creator, without an intermediary. It is prohibited to claim monopoly over religion or to exploit it for any purpose.'[10] And, as noted above, the Libyan constitution of 2011 affords to non-Muslims freedom to practice their religious rituals.

Missionary activity in the interest of non-Muslim religions is generally frowned upon by Islam, whereas missionary efforts to convert non-Muslims to Islam are encouraged (Mayer, 1987: 149; Sahlieh, 1985: 642). This becomes particularly precarious in countries where *Shari'ah* has been afforded the status of the main or principal source of legislation – as is the case in Egypt [Art. 2 of the 2014 const.] and Somalia [Art. 2.3 of the 2012 const.]. Here, the protection of human rights is inevitably undermined by *de facto* discrimination and repression. This is evidenced, in general, by the status afforded to non-Muslim religions in the concerned countries. As pointed out by Abdullahi An-Na'im, the status of non-Muslims under *Shari'ah* is inferior (1987: 10; see also 1992: 147), and constitutions which proclaim *Shari'ah* to be a source of law therefore in effect sanction discrimination against religious minorities (1987: 10–14).

Constitutional preference for a particular religion is not confined to Muslim states, but also prevails in other political communities, as evidenced by the institution of established churches: the Evangelical Lutheran Church in Denmark [Art. 4 of the 1953 const.], Finland,[11] Iceland [Art. 62 of the 1944 const.] – and not so long ago also in Norway and Sweden; the Anglican Church in England,[12] and the Presbyterian Church in Scotland.[13] The Roman Catholic Church is still an established church, or is afforded special constitutional recognition, in Liechtenstein [Art. 37 of the 1921 const.], Malta [Art. 2 of the 1964 const.], and Monaco

8 Article 3 of the constitution of the Federal Islamic Republic of Comoros (1996); Article 53 of the constitution of the Arab Republic of Egypt (2014); Article 6 of the constitution of the Federal Republic of Somalia (1979); see also Article 29 of the constitution of the People's Democratic Republic of Algeria (1996) and Article 6 of the Constitutional Proclamation of the Socialist People's Libyan Arab Jamahiriya (2011).

9 Article 2 of the Declaration on the Establishment of the Authority of the People (1976).

10 Article 5 of Libya's General People's Congress Law 20 of 1991 on the Consolidation of Freedom.

11 Article 76 of the constitution of Finland (1999) making special mention of the Evangelical Lutheran Church.

12 See Submission of the Clergy Act, 25 Hen. 8, c. 19 (1533); Act of Supremacy, 1 Eliz. I, c. 1 (1558).

13 See the Union with Scotland Act, 5 Ann, c. 8 (1706).

[Art. 9 of the 1962 const.]. The Eastern Orthodox Church of Christ is singled out as '[t]he prevailing religion' in Greece [Art. 3 of the 1975 const.]. The Russian Federation based its constitution on the principle of secularism, but this constitutional commitment was contradicted in the Preamble to the Law of 1997 On the Freedom of Conscience and on Religious Associations, which recognized 'the special contribution of Orthodoxy to the history of Russia and to the development of Russia's spirituality and culture' and promised respect for 'Christianity, Islam, Buddhism, Judaism and other religions and creeds which constitute an inseparable part of the historical heritage of Russia's people' (see Barberini, 2003: 14). Proclaiming Israel to be a Jewish state[14] also has religious freedom implications.

Since early times, Roman Catholicism has been the dominant religion in Latin American countries, and allegiance to the Roman Catholic Church has come to be a special feature of many constitutions of countries in that region. The constitution of Argentina (1853) thus proclaims: 'The Federal Government supports the Roman Catholic Apostolic religion' [Art. 2]. In Title VI of the constitution of Costa Rica (1949) dealing with 'Religion,' it is stated: 'The Roman, Catholic, Apostolic Religion is that of the state, which contributes to maintenance, without preventing the free exercise in the Republic of other beliefs that do not oppose themselves to the universal morality of good customs' [Art. 75]. El Salvador officially affords constitutional recognition of the juridical (legal) personality of the Catholic Church, while requiring of other religions a duty to obtain recognition of their legal personality 'in conformity with the law' [Art. 26 of the 1983 const.]. Guatemala similarly recognizes in its constitution the juridical or legal personality of the Catholic Church, and goes one step further by extending to the Catholic Church titles of ownership of its real assets without any cost [Art. 37 of the 1993 const.]. Panama affords constitutional recognition to the fact 'that the Catholic religion is practiced by the majority of Panamanians' [Art. 35 of the 1972 const.].

Several Latin American constitutions do not specifically refer to Roman Catholicism, but do proclaim their creation and/or substance on religious assumptions. The constitution of Peru (1993) maintain in its Preamble that the Democratic Constitutional Congress could enact the constitution by invoking 'All-mighty God' [preamble]. The constitution of Brazil (1988) was promulgated 'under the protection of God' [preamble]. The constitution of Costa Rica (1949) was similarly sanctioned by 'invoking the name of God' [preamble]. Panama composed its constitution (1972) while 'invoking the protection of God' [preamble].

Constitutional confessions of faith is also quite common in African countries. Ghana thus proclaimed its constitution (1992) 'in the name of Almighty God' [preamble]. Liberia testified of its 'gratitude to God' and recognized 'His Divine Guidance for our survival as a nation' [preamble to the 1984 const.]. The people of Seychelles confessed their gratitude to Almighty God 'that we inhabit one of the most beautiful countries in the world' and expressed their conscious pride for having learned as descendants of different races to live together as one Nation under God [preamble to the 1993 const.]. Zaire, while professing to be a secular state [Art. 1 of the 1990 const.], acknowledged its 'responsibility before God' [preamble].

Secularism and the separation of religion and law

Javier Martínez-Torrón and Cole Durham made a commendable distinction between secularism and secularity (2012: 3). Secularism entails a certain hostility to religion, while secularity

14 Article 7 A(a)1 of Israel's Basic Law: The Knesset (1958), referring to 'the State of Israel as a Jewish and democratic state.'

applies to a state that does not entirely distance itself from religion but makes provision for some degree of religious freedom. The American concept of the separation of church and state is a matter of secularity.

Several countries testify in their constitutions to being secular states, including in the European context, France,[15] Russia [Art. 14 of the 1993 const.], and Turkey [Art. 2 of the 1982 const.]; and yet another group, including Albania [Art. 10 of the 1998 const.], Ireland [Art. 44.2 of the 1937 const.], Slovakia [Art. 1 of the 1992 const.], and Spain,[16] proclaim their neutrality in respect of religion. Several Eastern European countries, notably Estonia [Art. 40(2) of the 1992 const.] and Lithuania [Art. 47(3) of the 1992 const.], asserted in their respective constitutions the absence of a state church or state religion. An increasing number of African states similarly proclaim the secularity of the state, including Benin,[17] Burkina Faso [Art. 31 of the 1991 const.], Burundi [Art. 1 of the 2005 const.], Cameroon [Art. 14 of the 1972 const.], Chad [Art. 1 of the 1996 const.], the Congo [Art. 1 of the 2015 const.], Ivory Coast [Art. 49 of the 2016 const.], Guinea [Art. 1 of the 2010 const.], Guinea-Bissau [Art. 1 of the 1991 const.], Madagascar [Art. 1 of the 2010 const.], Mali [preamble to the 1992 const.], Namibia [Sec. 1(1) of the 1990 const.], Senegal [Art. 1 of the 2009 const.], Togo [Art. 1 of the 1992 const.], and Zaire [Art. 1 of the 1990 const.]. Within the confines of Latin America, the constitution of Nicaragua (1987) in a similar vein simply proclaims: 'The State has no official religion' [Art. 14].

As far as the Far East is concerned, special mention can be made of India, which in its constitution (1949) proclaims the country to be 'a Sovereign Socialist Secular Democratic Republic' [preamble] and makes ample provision for freedom of conscience and freedom to profess, practice and propagate religion, subject only to the dictates of 'public order, morality and health' [Art. 25(1)]. The constitution of Japan (1948) also upholds freedom of religion, which entails a prohibition of privileges afforded by the state to religious organizations and also renders unlawful the exercise of political authority by religious organizations; compelling persons to take part in religious acts, celebrations, rites, or practices; and religious education or other religious activities conducted by the state [Art. 20].

China similarly proclaimed freedom of religious belief of all its citizens [Art. 36(1) of the 1982 const.]. It expressly prohibits state organs, public organizations, and individuals to compel citizens of the state to believe, or not to believe, in any religion [Art. 36(2)]. Discrimination based on religion is strictly prohibited,[18] and religion may not be used as the basis of engaging in activities that disrupt the public order, impair the health of citizens, or interfere in the public education system [Art. 36(3)]. Foreign domination of religious bodies or religious affairs in China is also not permitted [Art. 36(4)].

More common usage is allegiance to the separation of religion and law. This allegiance derives from the constitution of the United States of America, which postulates in its First Amendment that 'Congress shall make no law respecting an establishment of religion, or prohibiting the free exercise thereof,' and which allegedly created a wall of separation between church and state which, in the celebrated words of Mr. Justice Black, 'must be kept high and impregnable.'[19]

---

15 Article 1 of the constitution of France (1958) upholding the principle of *laïcité*.

16 Article 16(3) of the constitution of Spain (1978), but with special mention of the state maintaining 'the appropriate cooperation relations with the Catholic Church and other confessions.'

17 Article 2 of the constitution of the People's Republic of Benin [Law No. 90–32, 1990].

18 Article 36(2) of the constitution of the People's Republic of China (1982). The conditions of adherents to Falun Gong, Tibetan Buddhists,and Muslim Uyghurs in northeastern China suggest that this provision, at present, may be being adhered to only in its breach.

19 *Everson v. Board of Education*, 330 US 1, p. 18 (1947).

The separation of religion and law, based on the First Amendment was imitated, as far as European countries are concerned, in the constitutions of Ireland,[20] Poland [Art. 25(3) of the 1997 const.], Portugal [Art. 41(4) of the 1996 const.], and Russia [Art. 14(2) of the 1993 const.].

Several Eastern European countries – Bulgaria [Art. 13(2) of the 1991 const.], Croatia [Art. 41(1) of the const.], Slovakia [Art. 24(3) of the 1991 const.], Slovenia [Art. 7(1) of the const.], and Hungary [Art. VII(2) of the 2011 const.] – also proclaimed the typical American notion of the separation of church and state. The Romanian constitution (1991) refers to the autonomous status vis-à-vis the state of religious cults [Art. 29(5)], while the Polish constitution (1997) emphasizes impartiality of the state in matters of personal convictions [Art. 25(2)], and of the autonomous and mutual independence of church and state [Art. 25(3)]. The Russian Federation enunciated in its constitution (1993) the secular disposition of the state [Art. 14(1)], the non-existence of a state-sponsored or mandatory religion in the Federation [Art. 14(1)], the principle of separation of church and state, and the equality before the law of religious associations [Art. 14(2)]. Albania, likewise, proclaims the absence of an 'official religion' [Art. 10(1) of the 1998 const.], neutrality of the state in matters of religion [Art. 10(2)], and mutual respect for the independence of church and state [Art. 10(4)].

In Africa, the separation of the state and religious denominations is proclaimed in the constitution of Angola [Art. 10(1) of the 2010 const.], Mozambique,[21] Ethiopia [Art. 11(1) of the 1995 const.], Niger [Art. 3.2 of the 2010 const.], and the Democratic Republic of Sao Tome and Principe [Art. 8 of the 1975 const.]. The constitution of Madagascar (2010) in a similar vein refers to the neutrality of the state toward different religions [Art. 2].

These principles, taken from mainly American sources, are not applied with the same emphases and (relative) consistency as evidenced by their original source. For example, while Bulgaria in church–state relations sided with the separationist position, it nevertheless afforded constitutional recognition to Eastern Orthodoxy as the 'traditional religion' of the country [Art. 13(3) of the 1991 const.]. Lithuania testified in its constitution (1992) to the absence of a state religion, but nevertheless promised to recognize 'traditional Lithuanian churches and religious organizations,' as well as others provided they have 'a basis in society' and their teachings and rituals do not contradict 'morality and the law' [Art. 43(1)]. Drafters of the Polish constitution (1997) saw fit to make special mention of its concordat with the Holy See regulating a special place in the country for the Roman Catholic Church [Art. 25(4)].

In its equality provisions, the constitution of Angola (2010) outlawed discrimination based, among other things, on religion, and also prohibited the granting of privileges or the deprivation of rights on the basis of, among other things, religion [Art. 23(2)]. It promised respect for different religious faiths 'which shall be free to organise and exercise their activities,' but subject to the constitution and the laws of the country, the substance of which remained undefined in the constitution itself [Art. 10(2)]. The state promised to protect churches, faiths, and their places and objects of worship, but again subject to the constraint that they 'do not threaten the Constitution and public order and abide by the Constitution and the law' [Art. 10(3)]. It likewise proclaimed freedom of conscience, religion, and worship to be inviolable [Art. 41(1)]. Questioning of persons with regard to their convictions or religious practices must be confined to the accumulation of statistical data [Art. 41(4)]. The constitution further guarantees that 'no-one shall be deprived of their rights, persecuted or exempted from obligations due to their

20 Article 44.2 of the constitution of Ireland (1937) proclaiming that the state 'guarantees not to endow any religion.'

21 Article 12.2 of the constitution of the People's Republic of Mozambique (2004) referring to Mozambique in Article 12(1) as 'a lay State.'

religious beliefs' [Art. 41(2)]. An exception is seemingly made to the rule against exemption from obligations where, in the very next subsection 'the right to be a conscientious objector' is guaranteed [Art. 41(3)]. It might be noted that recognition of the right to conscientious objection is seemingly in conflict with a provision in the equal rights provision which states that no one may be exempted from any duty based on, among other things, his or her religion [Art. 23(2)]. This anomaly perhaps bears evidence of the fact that Angola has not quite come to grips with the persecution of pacifist religious groups, such as the Jehovah's Witnesses, who refused to participate in military activity during the Angolan civil war that erupted after independence in 1975.

The constitution of Mozambique (2004) also guarantees the right to conscientious objection [Art. 54(5)]. It furthermore prohibits discrimination based on 'faith or religious persuasion or practice' [Art. 54(2)]. The Mozambican constitution also addressed a problem of special significance for religious freedom, namely the autonomy of religious institutions to mind their own internal affairs. It provides that religious denominations shall have the right to pursue their respective religious aims and to own and acquire assets for the purpose of achieving their objectives [Art. 54(3)], and it guarantees the protection of places of worship [Art. 54(4)]. In a unique free exercise clause, the constitution speaks of freedom of all citizens to practice or not to practice a religion [Art. 54(1)].

Mozambique also sided with a number of francophone African states, such as Gabon [Art. 13 of the 1997 const.], Niger [Art. 8 of the 2010 const.], and Senegal [Art. 5 of the 2001 const.], that in their constitutions rendered religious discrimination punishable – with the added rider in the case of Mozambique that such discrimination shall be punished 'in terms of the law' [Art. 39 of the 2004 const.]. The constitution of Tanzania (1977) touches upon many of the same themes. It defines the government's task of securing equal opportunities to all citizens regardless of, inter alia, religion.[22] It proclaims the right of everyone to freedom of conscience or faith, including the freedom to change one's religion or faith [Art. 19(1)], but subjects the protection of this right to provisions prescribed by law 'that are of importance to a democratic society for security of peace in the society, integrity of the society and the national coercion' [Art. 19(2)]. It is perhaps worth noting that in the original text of the Tanzanian constitution (1977) one found the first provision thus far addressing the question of proselytizing in express terms: promotion of religion, worship, and evangelization will be free and matters of personal voluntary choice – Tanzania proclaimed – but '[w]ithout jeopardising the laws applicable in the Union Republic. ...'[23] The laws that could not be jeopardized were not bound to any substantive human rights criteria, and the right to promote one's religion through worship and evangelization was furthermore subordinated to additional general directives outlined elsewhere in the constitution. The provision relating to evangelization was deleted from the constitution by subsequent amendments of the bill of rights.[24] Protection of the constitutional rights and freedoms remained subject to general constraints. They may not be exercised in any way that will result in interference with, or curtailment of, the rights and freedoms of others, or with the public interests [Art. 30(1)]. The constitutional rights and freedoms must not trump any statutory provision or executive act ('lawful acts') enacted or performed with a view to a long list of objectives, to ensure

22 Constitution of the United Republic of Tanzania (1977), Article 9(1)(g) and Article 13(1), read with Article 13(5) (the equal protection and nondiscrimination clause).

23 Article 19(2) of the constitution of the United Republic of Tanzania (1977); and as to limitations, see also the sweeping provisions of Articles 30 and 31.

24 See in particular Act 15 of 1984, Sec. 6 (Tanzania).

'that the rights and freedom of other people or of the interests of the public are not prejudiced by the wrongful exercise of the freedoms and rights of individuals' [Art. 30(2)(a)] and that 'the defence, public safety, public order, public morality, and public health, rural and urban development planning, the exploitation and utilization of minerals or the increase and development of property or any other interests for the purpose of enhancing the public benefit' will not be prejudiced [Art. 30(2)(b)].

As far as Latin America is concerned, Mexico must be singled out as the country that took a lead in the separation of church and state in that region of the world. The Mexican constitution of 1917 marked the end of the revolution that had ravaged that country since 1910 and was specially noted for restricting – and indeed denying – the privileged status of the dominant (Catholic) religion. The constitutional arrangement is based on '[t]he historical principle of the separation between State and religion,' but affords an exclusive competence to the legislature to enact laws 'on matters of public worship, churches and religious groups;' it renders the legal status of religious associations subject to registration procedures; it prohibits governmental interference in the internal affairs of religious associations; it subjects the competence to become ministers of any religious denominations to requirements established by law; it deprives ministers of religion to be elected and to hold public office; it denies ministers of religion the right to participate in the election processes in favor of particular candidates, to oppose the laws of the country, and to insult patriotic symbols in public, in worship, or in religious literature; and much more.[25] It furthermore proclaimed marriage to be a civil contract [Art. 130 const.], thereby presumably denouncing the traditional Catholic assumption that marriage is a holy sacrament.

The Mexican trend probably influenced constitutions such as the one of Honduras which provides: 'Ministers of the various religions may not hold public office or engage in any form of political propaganda invoking religious motives or, as a means to such end, thus taking advantage of the religious beliefs of the people' [Art. 77 of the 1982 const.]. The constitution of Costa Rica similarly proclaims that no clergymen or laymen may invoke religious motives or exploit religious beliefs as a mechanism of political propaganda in any form [Art. 28 of the 1949 const.].

The Republic of Chile proclaimed more elaborately in its constitution of 1980 the freedom of conscience and authorized the manifestation of all creeds and the free exercise of all religions that are not opposed to 'morals, good customs or public order' [Art. 19(6)]. Religious communities are endowed with a constitutional competence 'to erect and maintain churches and their facilities in accordance with the conditions of safety and hygiene as established by laws and ordinances' [Art. 19(6)]. Churches and religious communities and institutions are granted the rights acknowledged by the laws in force [Art. 19(6)]. Churches and their facilities assigned exclusively for religious activities are exempted from all taxes [Art. 19(6)]. It must be emphasized that these entitlements apply equally to all religious denominations.

Having proclaimed freedom of conscience of every person which includes 'freedom of religion, freedom to change his religion or belief and freedom, either alone or in community with others, and both in public and in private, to manifest and propagate his religion or belief in worship, teaching, practice and observance' [Art. 11(1)], the constitution of Belize (1981) specifically protects all persons from receiving religious instruction and from taking part in, or attending, a religious ceremony or observance related to a religion other than his own [Art. 11(2)]. This applies in particular in the context of education and to persons detained in a

25 Article 130 of the constitution of Mexico (1917); and see van der Vyver, 2004.

prison or correctional institution or serving in the sea, land, or air forces of the country [Art. 11(2)].

As far as the Far East is concerned, the constitution of Singapore (1959) perhaps deserves special mention. It prohibits discrimination against citizens of the country based on religion, which extends to 'any law or in the appointment to any office or employment under a public authority or in the administration of any law regulating the acquisition, holding or disposition of property or the establishing or carrying on of any trade, business, profession, vocation or employment' – subject only to exceptions expressly authorized by the constitution [Art. 12(2)]. The constitution rather strangely affords to the Legislature a competence to regulate by law 'Muslim religious affairs' and makes special provision for a Council 'to advise the President in matters relating to the Muslim religion' [Art. 153].

Constitutional objectivity in respect of religious diversity

There is a clear tendency in the world today for non-Muslim states to move away from religiously based constitutional testimonies. Some time ago, Zambia reversed this trend of eliminating constitutional commitments to Christianity. An amendment of its constitution that entered into force on 1 May 1996, included a clause in the preamble declaring that 'the Republic is a Christian nation while upholding the right of every person to enjoy that person's freedom of conscience and religion.'[26] Proclaiming a state to be 'Christian' still enjoys some appeal in many countries where Roman Catholicism predominates, but even there, one finds the tendency to do away with the established status of the Church.[27] Except in the context of an established church, ideological statements in a constitution of non-Muslim states have very little juridical relevance, if any relevance at all.

The tendency to discard confessions of faith in constitutional instruments may be illustrated with reference to developments in the Republic of South Africa. The South African governments of yesteryear had always claimed that the country represented a Christian state and sought to testify to its religious commitment with all kinds of quite nonsensical provisions, such as the one which proclaimed that '[t]he people of the Republic of South Africa acknowledge the sovereignty and guidance of All-mighty God.'[28] South Africa proclaimed its 1983 constitution '[i]n humble submission to God' [preamble]. This phrase has altogether been omitted from the 1996 constitution, which in its preamble only appeals to God – citing the words of the national anthem – to 'protect our people.'

The current South African constitution deals elaborately with religious freedom, the relationship between law and religion, and religious diversity within the South African community and can in general be described as one of profound toleration and accommodation. It in general allocates to church institutions the rights in the bill of rights to the extent required by the nature of the right and the nature of the church as a legal person [Sec. 8(4)]; it guarantees the free exercise of religion [Sec. 15(1)]; it protects the right to self-determination

26 Constitution of Zambia, as amended by Act 18 of 1996, Preamble. It might be noted that the president at that time, Frederick Chiluba, and his vice president, General Miyanda, who were the driving forces behind this constitutional amendment, were both 'Born Again Christians.'

27 See van der Vyver, 1996: xl. However, there are recent signs in countries like Poland, Hungary, and Italy that seem to indicate an inversion of this trend. The same is true, among nonChristian countries, for India.

28 Section 2 of the constitution of the Republic of South Africa [Act 110 of 1983].

of religious communities [Secs. 33 and 235] and makes provision for a Commission for the Promotion and Protection of the Rights of Cultural, Religious and Linguistic Communities;[29] and it envisaged the establishment, by means of national legislation, of a Pan South African Language Board charged, inter alia, with promoting and ensuring respect for 'Arabic, Hebrew, Sanskrit and other languages used for religious purposes in South Africa' [Sec. 6(5)(b)(ii)].

The South African constitution is indeed not based on the principle of secularism, or on the separation of church and state or the proscription of state action in matters of religion. Constitutionalism in South Africa places an obligation on the state to accommodate, and indeed to promote, religion, but must do so on the basis of objectivity, which, according to Francois Venter, rejects the predominance within the structures of the law and good governance of a particular religion but requires instead that the state affords to all religions a place in the sun on the basis of equality and nondiscrimination, thereby maintaining 'a constant balance between the state's responsibility of maintaining social order, religious preferences and legal certainty' (Venter, 2015: 212–213).

Several other African countries (including some with a Muslim majority population) – Djibouti [Art. 1 of the 1992 const.], Ivory Coast,[30] Niger [Art. 9 of the 1992 const.], Liberia [Art. 14 of the 1984 const.], Senegal,[31] and Togo [Art. 2 of the 1992 const.] – similarly promised to respect all religious beliefs.

Special mention should also be made of the Indian constitution which upholds, similar to its South African counterpart, the principle of sphere sovereignty of religious institutions; that is noninterference by the state in the internal affairs of religious organizations. Under the heading of 'Freedom to manage religious affairs,' the Indian constitution (1949) affords to every religious denomination or any section thereof the competence 'to establish and maintain institutions for religious and charitable purposes; to manage its own affairs in matters of religion; to own and acquire movable and immovable property; and to administer such property in accordance with the law,' subject only to the dictates of 'public order, morality and health' [Art. 26].

Concluding observation

The Constitutional Court of South Africa has on several occasions emphasized the vital importance of religion as a component of South Africa's constitutional democracy. In *Christian Education South Africa v. Minister of Education,*[32] Justice Albie Sachs identified religion as 'the key ingredient of any person's dignity' and as 'a framework for individual stability and growth,' which as such 'affects the believer's view of society and founds the distinction between right and wrong.' But there is more to it than just that. Religion is also of great importance to the state. In *Minister of Home Affairs v. Fourie*; *Lesbian and Gay Equality Project v. Minister of Home Affairs*, Justice Albie Sachs, delivering the unanimous decision of the court, noted the many difficulties attending 'the relationship foreshadowed by the Constitution between the sacred and the secular,' but went on to say:

29 Sections 181(1)(c), 185, and 186 of the constitution of the Republic of South Africa (1996); and see the Commission for the Promotion and Protection of the Rights of Cultural, Religious and Linguistic Communities Act 19 of 2002.

30 Article 6 of the constitution of the Republic of Cote d'Ivoire [Law No. 60–356, 1960].

31 Article 1 of the constitution of the Republic of Senegal [Law No. 63–22, 1963].

32 *Christian Education South Africa v. Minister of Education*, 2000 (4) SA 757; 2000 (10) BCLR 1051 (CC) para. 36.

> Religious bodies play a large and important part in public life, through schools, hospitals and poverty relief programmes. They command ethical behaviour from their members and bear witness to the exercise of power by State and private agencies; they promote music, art and theatre; they provide halls for community activities, and conduct a great variety of social activities for their members and the general public. They are part of the fabric of public life, and constitute active elements of the diverse and pluralistic nation contemplated by the Constitution. Religion is not just a question of belief or doctrine. It is part of the people's temper and culture, and for many believers a significant part of their way of life. Religious organizations constitute important sectors of national life and accordingly have a right to express themselves to government and the courts on the great issues of the day. They are active participants in public affairs fully entitled to have their say with regard to the way law is made and applied.[33]

Constitutional protection of freedom of religion cannot be achieved by affording preference to a particular religion, or by distancing the state from religion through secularity or the separation of religion and law, but requires of the political structures of the state to promote religions of all kinds on the basis of objectivity and therefore without affording constitutional preference to any particular religion.

Further reading

Durham Jr, C.W., Ferrari, S., Cianitto, C., Thayer, D. (Eds.), 2013. *Law, Religion, Constitution. Freedom of Religion, Equal Treatment, and the Law.* Routledge.

References

An-Na'im, A.A., 1987. Religious minorities under Islamic law and the limits of cultural relativism. *Human Rights Quarterly*. 9, 1.

An-Na'im, A.A., 1992. Cross-cultural support for equitable participation in Subsaharan Africa. In: Mahoney, K.E., Mahoney, P. (Eds.), *Human Rights in the Twenty-First Century A Global Challenge.* Martinus Nijhoff, p. 133.

Barberini, G., 2003. Religious freedom in the process of democratization of central and Eastern European states. In: Ferrari, S., Durham, C.W., Jr, Sewell, E. (Eds.), *Law and Religion in Post-Communist Europe.* Peeters, p. 7.

Martínez-Torrón, J., Durham, W.C., 2012. Religion and the secular state. In: Brown, K.B., Snyder, D.V. (Eds.), *General Report of the XVIIIth Congress of the International Academy of Comparative Law Rapports Généraux du XVIIIème Congrès de l'Académie Internationale de Droit Comparé.* Springer, 1.

Mayer, A.E., 1987. Law and religion in the Muslim Middle East. *American Journal of Comparative Law*. 35, 127.

Sahlieh, A.A., 1985. Les Droits de l'Homme et l'Islam. *Revue Générale de Droit International Public* 89, 626.

Van der Vyver, J.D., 1996. Introduction: Legal dimensions of religious human rights: Constitutional texts. In: van der Vyver, J.D., Witte, J. Jr (Eds.), *Legal Perspectives: Religious Human Rights in Global Perspective.* Martinus Nijhoff. p. xi.

Van der Vyver, J.D., 2004. *Leuven Lectures on Religious Institutions, Religious Communities and Rights.* Peeters.

Venter, F., 2015. *Constitutionalism and Religion.* Edward Elgar.

33 *Minister of Home Affairs v. Fourie; Lesbian and Gay Equality Project v. Minister of Home Affairs*, 2006 (1) SA 524; 2006 (3) BCLR 355, para. 93.

16

The right to religious freedom in international human rights law: A brief overview and exploration of its positive dimension

Laurens Lavrysen and Eva Brems

This chapter will map the right to religious freedom in international human rights law. Indeed, religious freedom is among the classic 'civil and political rights,' and as such has been included in numerous human rights conventions and soft law documents. The exercise of 'mapping' can be either of a synthetic nature, summing up and categorising well-known facts, or of a more explorative or even adventurous nature – mapping as cartography – visualising hitherto unknown territory. In this chapter, we try our hand at both. The first section will provide a quick roadmap to the international legal framework on freedom of religion. After that, the second section, will explore an underdeveloped area in the law and scholarship on freedom of religion, which is the field of positive obligations.

A roadmap to the international legal framework on freedom of religion

This section will explain the essentials of the international legal framework on freedom of religion. That is to say, it will focus on the most important human rights texts in this regard and highlight the characteristic features of the relevant provisions.[1] Successively, we will examine the protection of freedom of religion at the United Nations level and in regional human rights protection systems, before zooming in on the scope of freedom of religion under international human rights law.

The UN human rights regime

In 1948, in the aftermath of the Second World War, the Universal Declaration of Human Rights (UDHR) was adopted by the General Assembly of the United Nations. Article 18 of the UDHR proclaims:

1 For a general overview, also see Tahzib, 1996; Evans, 1997; Boyle, 2007; and Lerner, 2012.

> Everyone has the right to freedom of thought, conscience and religion; this right includes freedom to change his religion or belief, and freedom, either alone or in community with others and in public or private, to manifest his religion or belief in teaching, practice, worship and observance.

Also relevant from the viewpoint of religious freedom is Article 2 of the UDHR, which prohibits discrimination on grounds of *inter alia* religion.

Albeit formally not a legal binding document, the UDHR is generally considered a powerful source of moral obligation in the field of human rights. Its importance is reflected by the fact that the manner in which human rights have been framed in the UDHR has subsequently exercised a strong influence on the drafting of legally binding human rights provisions at the international, regional and national levels.

In 1966, with a view to translating the rights enshrined in the UDHR into sources of legal obligation, two International Covenants were adopted within the UN framework: the International Covenant on Civil and Political Rights (ICCPR) and the International Covenant on Economic, Social and Cultural Rights (ICESCR). Both Covenants entered into force in 1976 and enjoy wide ratification by 172 and 169 States, respectively (as of September 2018). Of particular importance is Article 18 § 1 of the ICCPR, which strongly resembles the corresponding provision from the UDHR:

> Everyone shall have the right to freedom of thought, conscience and religion. This right shall include freedom to have or to adopt a religion or belief of his choice, and freedom, either individually or in community with others and in public or private, to manifest his religion or belief in worship, observance, practice and teaching.

The second paragraph holds that '[n]o one shall be subject to coercion which would impair his freedom to have or to adopt a religion or belief of his choice.' The third paragraph spells out the conditions for permissible limitations of the freedom to manifest one's religion or beliefs. Finally, the fourth paragraph obliges States 'to have respect for the liberty of parents and when applicable, legal guardians to ensure the religious and moral education of their children in conformity with their own convictions.' The latter paragraph corresponds with Article 13 § 3 of the ICESCR, which is the provision guaranteeing the right to education. Article 18 of the ICCPR by and large contains the most important legal standard protecting freedom of religion at the international level. For this reason, it is relevant to draw attention to the fact that, in 1993, the Human Rights Committee, which is the treaty body responsible for monitoring implementation of the ICCPR through consideration of State reports and individual complaints, issued an authoritative interpretation of Article 18 of the ICCPR by means of General Comment No. 22.[2]

A number of other provisions also contain references to religion as a prohibited ground of discrimination: Article 26 of the ICCPR[3] bans discrimination in all spheres, whereas Article 2 §1

---

2 Human Rights Committee (HRC), 27 September 1993, General Comment (GC) No. 22 (Art. 18), CCPR/C/21/Rev.1/Add.4.

3 'All persons are equal before the law and are entitled without any discrimination to the equal protection of the law. In this respect, the law shall prohibit any discrimination and guarantee to all persons equal and effective protection against discrimination on any ground such as race, colour, sex, language, religion, political or other opinion, national or social origin, property, birth or other status.'

of the ICCPR[4] and Article 2 § 2 of the ICESCR[5] concern discrimination in the exercise of human rights, and the reference in Article 24 § 1 of the ICCPR[6] specifically deals with discrimination regarding protection measures for children.

Finally, Article 27 of the ICCPR must also be mentioned, which recognises minority rights, including those of persons belonging to religious minorities:

> In those States in which ethnic, *religious* or linguistic *minorities* exist, persons belonging to such minorities shall not be denied the right, in community with the other members of their group, to enjoy their own culture, to profess and practise their own religion, or to use their own language (emphasis added).

The Human Rights Committee has clarified that Article 27 is a right 'conferred on individuals,' rather than a collective right.[7] In this regard, it is debated whether, in its religious dimension, it even adds anything to Article 18 (Tahzib, 1996: 91). At the UN level, Article 27 is complemented by the (legally nonbinding) 1992 Declaration on the Rights of Persons Belonging to National or Ethnic, Religious and Linguistic Minorities, which is considered as enshrining minority rights that go beyond the scope of individual rights (Lerner, 2012: 45–46).

A number of specialised UN human rights treaties, dealing with the rights of specific groups, also contain provisions explicitly recognising the freedom of religion or prohibiting discrimination on the ground of religion. For instance, Article 5 of the 1965 International Convention on the Elimination of All Forms of Racial Discrimination guarantees

> the right of everyone, without distinction as to race, colour, or national or ethnic origin, to equality before the law, notably in the enjoyment of the following rights: [...] (d), (vii) The right to freedom of thought, conscience and religion ...

It must be noted that the Committee on the Elimination of Racial Discrimination – the treaty body monitoring the implementation of this Convention through consideration of State reports and individual complaints – has regularly dealt with questions of freedom of religion as it considers there to be a close nexus between racial and religious discrimination (Tahzib 1996: 401–402).

The 1989 Convention on the Rights of the Child in turn recognises the right of the child to freedom of thought, conscience and religion (Art. 14) and the right of children belonging to religious minorities to profess and practice their religion (Art. 30), and it requires States to respect and ensure the rights set forth in this Convention without discrimination of any kind, including on the ground of the child's or his or her parent's or legal guardian's religion (Art. 2 § 1).

---

4 'Each State Party to the present Covenant undertakes to respect and to ensure to all individuals within its territory and subject to its jurisdiction the rights recognized in the present Covenant, without distinction of any kind, such as race, colour, sex, language, religion, political or other opinion, national or social origin, property, birth or other status.'

5 'The States Parties to the present Covenant undertake to guarantee that the rights enunciated in the present Covenant will be exercised without discrimination of any kind as to race, colour, sex, language, religion, political or other opinion, national or social origin, property, birth or other status.'

6 'Every child shall have, without any discrimination as to race, colour, sex, language, religion, national or social origin, property or birth, the right to such measures of protection as are required by his status as a minor, on the part of his family, society and the State.'

7 HRC, 26 April 1994, GC No. 23 (Art. 27), CCPR/C/21/Rev.1/Add.5, para. 3.1.

Finally, the 1990 International Convention on the Rights of All Migrant Workers and Members of Their Families recognises the principle of nondiscrimination on the grounds of *inter alia* religion in the enjoyment of the rights set out in that Convention (Art. 7) and recognises the right to freedom of thought, conscience and religion of migrant workers and members of their families (Art. 12).

In the realm of soft law, attention must also be drawn to the Declaration on the Elimination of All Forms of Intolerance and of Discrimination Based on Religion or Belief adopted by the UN General Assembly in 1981. Even though the title suggests this Declaration to be primarily concerned with spelling out obligations in the field of nondiscrimination on the ground of religion (see Arts. 2–4), it also contains a number of provisions guaranteeing the right to freedom of thought, conscience and religion and specifying the scope thereof (see Arts. 1 and 5–6). While not legally binding, it has nonetheless been considered as 'particularly valuable as a normative source in conjunction with the Human Rights Committee's General Comment on Article 18 of the Covenant' in the area of freedom of religion (Boyle, 2007: 47). Originally, the Declaration was conceived by many as a stepping-stone toward the adoption of a legally binding Convention, which would provide for a treaty-based body comparable to, for instance, the Committee on the Elimination of Racial Discrimination (Tahzib, 1996: 192). However, given the difficulties in reconciling the different ideological and religious positions of the various States – the Declaration itself had already taken over two decades to adopt – efforts to strive toward such a Convention never gained traction and by now it is unlikely that such a Convention will ever be adopted (Boyle, 2007: 46–47). In 1986, the former UN Commission on Human Rights appointed a Special Rapporteur on religious intolerance (since 2000 known as the Special Rapporteur on freedom of religion or belief) with the mandate to examine incidents and governmental actions that are inconsistent with the 1981 Declaration and to recommend remedial measures.[8]

Regional human rights protection systems

The main regional human rights protection systems are those in the Council of Europe, the Organisation of American States and the African Union. These systems are characterised by the adoption of human rights conventions and supervision mechanisms that include supranational courts.[9]

The 1950 European Convention on Human Rights (ECHR), the 1969 American Convention on Human Rights (ACHR) and the 1987 African Charter on Human and Peoples' Rights (ACHPR) all contain provisions guaranteeing the freedom of religion and the principle of nondiscrimination on the grounds of *inter alia* religion.

Article 9 § 1 of the ECHR stipulates the right to freedom of thought, conscience and religion in a manner that almost verbatim corresponds with Article 18 of the UDHR. The second paragraph spells out the conditions under which restrictions of the freedom to manifest one's religion or beliefs are permissible. Article 14 of the ECHR prohibits discrimination in the enjoyment of ECHR rights on any ground, including religion. In addition, Article 1 of Protocol No. 12 to the ECHR – which has only been ratified by 20 out of 47 Council of

8 The current mandate of the Special Rapporteur is defined by Human Rights Council, 14 December 2007, Resolution 6/37. On the work of the Special Rapporteur, see Evans, 2003.

9 Regional human rights documents that do not possess these characteristics will therefore not be discussed in this section (e.g., the 1990 Cairo Declaration on Human Rights in Islam and the 2012 ASEAN Human Rights Declaration).

Europe Member States (as of September 2018) – is broader in that it prohibits discrimination on any ground, including religion, in the enjoyment of 'any right set forth by law.' Finally, Article 2 of Protocol No. 1 to the ECHR, which guarantees the right to education, stipulates that 'the State shall respect the right of parents to ensure such education and teaching in conformity with their own religious and philosophical convictions.'

Article 12 of the ACHR, in turn, closely resembles Article 18 of the ICCPR, both in terms of structure and content of the provision. The main differences lie in the fact that the right is labelled the 'freedom of conscience and religion' rather than the 'freedom of thought, conscience and religion' and the fact that the right to change as well as the freedom to profess or disseminate one's religion or beliefs are mentioned explicitly in Article 12. Article 1 § 1 ACHR requires States to guarantee the free and full exercise of the rights guaranteed in the ACHR without any discrimination, including on the grounds of religion. Religion is also explicitly mentioned in the provisions concerning the freedom of association and the freedom of movement and residence. Article 16 § 1 ACHR guarantees 'the *right to associate freely for* ideological, *religious*, political, economic, labour, social, cultural, sports, or other *purposes*.' Article 22 § 8 ACHR prohibits the deportation or return of a person to a country in which '*his right to life or personal freedom is in danger of being violated because of his* race, nationality, *religion*, social status, or political opinions.'

While the wording of the relevant provisions in the ECHR and the ACHR strongly resemble those from the International Bill of Human Rights, Article 8 of the ACHPR is drafted somewhat differently:

> Freedom of conscience, the profession and free practice of religion shall be guaranteed. No one may, subject to law and order, be submitted to measures restricting the exercise of these freedoms.

Article 2 of the ACHPR spells out the principle of nondistinction, including on the grounds of religion, in the enjoyment of the rights and freedoms recognised in the ACHPR. Finally, religion is referred to in Article 12 § 5 of the ACHPR, which deals with mass expulsion of non-nationals:

> The mass expulsion of non-nationals shall be prohibited. Mass expulsion shall be that which is aimed at national, racial, ethnic or religious groups.

In addition, specialised conventions and soft law instruments proliferate at the regional levels as well. Of particular note in this context is the 1994 Framework Convention for the Protection of National Minorities of the Council of Europe, which includes several provisions regarding the protection of minorities' religious identity.

Scope of freedom of religion

Given the multilayered and fragmented nature of human rights law, there is inevitably some divergence in the interpretation thereof by the various relevant enforcement actors and monitoring bodies (see below and Brems, 2014). Nonetheless, there seems to be sufficient consensus about the content of the right to freedom of religion to enable discussing the broad lines of these provisions together.

First, the right to freedom of thought, conscience and religion protects the freedom of believers and nonbelievers alike. In the words of the Human Rights Committee, it 'protects theistic, non-theistic and atheistic beliefs, as well as the right not to profess any religion or belief.'[10]

Second, despite some small textual differences, the ICCPR, ECHR and ACHR all explicitly refer to the fact that freedom of religion can be exercised 'either individually or in community with others.' This is sometimes considered in terms of the individual and collective aspects of freedom of religion. The individual aspect comprises questions such as worship (e.g., ritual and ceremonial acts), observance (e.g., dietary regulations or the wearing of distinctive clothing and headwear), practice and teaching.[11] Both the Human Rights Committee and the European Court of Human Rights have moreover interpreted the freedom of religion as encompassing a right to conscientious objection to military service.[12] The collective aspect of freedom of religion, on the other hand, protects the peaceful functioning of religious communities against arbitrary interference.[13] It protects 'acts integral to the conduct by religious groups of their basic affairs, such as, *inter alia*, the freedom to choose their religious leaders, priests and teachers, the freedom to establish seminaries or religious schools and the freedom to prepare and distribute religious texts or publications.'[14]

Third, a distinction is made between the so-called *forum internum* and *forum externum*. The *forum internum* relates to the freedom to have or to adopt a religion or belief of one's choice, including, explicitly or implicitly, the freedom to change one's religion.[15] The *forum internum* is absolute in that it does not allow for any limitations. Consequently, it is prohibited to use brainwashing or other acts of coercion to make a person change his or her beliefs (Vermeulen and Van Roosmalen, 2018: 378) or to compel a person to reveal his or her thoughts or adherence to a religion or belief.[16] On the other hand, with respect to the *forum externum* – i.e., the freedom to manifest religion or belief – the relevant human rights provisions typically provide for the possibility to limit this manifestation freedom under certain conditions. Article 18 § 3 ICCPR, Article 9 § 2 ECHR and Article 12 § 3 ACHR all provide that the freedom to manifest one's religion or beliefs can be subjected to limitations on the condition that such limitation is 'prescribed by law' and is 'necessary (in a democratic society)' to protect the legitimate aims of public safety, order, health or morals or the rights and freedoms of others. While limitations of the manifestation freedom are typically optional, some limitations may even be mandated by international human rights law (Evans, 1997: 226). In this respect, under the ICCPR and ACHR, States are obliged to prohibit by law 'any advocacy of national, racial or *religious hatred*' that constitutes incitement to 'discrimination, hostility or violence' (Art. 20 § 2 ICCPR) or 'violence or to any other similar action against any person or group of persons' (Art. 13 § 5 ACHR).

In the assessment of whether or not any particular restriction of religious freedom constitutes a violation of that right, there is room for each supranational monitoring body to adopt its own approach. Such assessment reflects not only that body's interpretation of religious freedom, but also the body's mandate, its view on its role in relation to national authorities, and its tendency

10 HRC, GC 22, o.c., para. 2. Similarly, ECtHR, 25 May 1993, Kokkinakis v. Greece, no. 14307/88, para. 31.

11 HRC, GC. 22, o.c., para. 4.

12 HRC, GC, o.c., para. 11; and ECtHR (Grand Chamber), 7 July 2011, Bayatyan v. Armenia , no. 23459/03, paras. 92–111.

13 E.g., ECtHR (Grand Chamber), 26 October 2000, Hasan and Chaush v. Bulgaria, no. 30985/96, para. 62.

14 HRC, GC 22, o.c., para. 4.

15 The freedom to change one's religion is either explicitly mentioned in the relevant Convention provision (see Art. 9 § 1 ECHR and Art. 12 § 1 ACHR), or it can be implicitly be derived from it, see HRC, GC 22, o.c., para. 5, with respect to Article 18 ICCPR.

16 HRC, GC 22, o.c., para. 3.

toward restraint or activism. This occasionally results in divergent solutions for similar problems. The most striking example is the different approach of the UN HRC, as compared to the ECtHR, with regard to bans on religious dress. The ban on religious dress worn by pupils in French public schools was considered a violation of religious freedom by the HRC, whereas the ECtHR found no violation, based on its principled decision to accord a wide margin of appreciation to the national authorities.[17] A similar discordance arose with regard to other French bans – regarding religious headgear on photographs for identity documents[18] – and the ban on face veiling in public space.[19]

Exploring uncharted waters: Positive obligations for religious freedom

However, the issue of state interference with a right covers only one side of state obligations under human rights, obligations of state restraint, known as negative obligations or obligations to *respect* rights. In addition, all human rights also entail positive obligations (i.e., obligations of the State to take action in order to ensure human rights).[20] While in general, there is quite some conceptual clarity about the relevant principles that govern negative obligations under the freedom of religion and other civil and political rights – discussions tend to focus mainly on the application in concrete cases – the same does not hold true for positive obligations. The reason for this lies in the fact that the orthodox view on civil and political rights places emphasis on negative obligations with a focus on the protection of the individual against the intrusive State. However, gradually it has been recognised that the State may cause as much harm to the rights of the individual by failing to intervene as by acting (Kreimer, 1983: 1395). By now, it is accepted that

> human rights hold out more than just the promise of freedom from State interference with their exercise. Human Rights are based on a much richer view of freedom, which pays attention to the extent to which individuals are in a position actually to exercise those rights (Fredman, 2008: 1).

In human rights law, this has resulted in the gradual development of positive obligations under virtually every human right,[21] albeit not necessarily to the same extent in relation to each respective right.

We proceed to present an overview of the relatively limited positive obligations that have been developed under the freedom of religion and to explain why the development of positive obligations in this context has been less elaborate than in some other areas of human rights law. Before doing so, it is necessary first to draw attention to the tripartite typology that is often invoked when discussing State obligations under UN human rights instruments.

---

17 HRC, 1 November 2012, Bikramjit Singh v. France (CCPR/C/106/D/1852/2008), and ECtHR (inadm.), 30 June 2009 Aktas v. France, No. 43563/08. In the context of university education, the Court had already accepted in the case of ECtHR (Grand Chamber), 10 November 2005, Leyla Şahin v. Turkey, no. 44774/98, that such ban could fall within the State's (wide) margin of appreciation.

18 ECtHR (inadm.), 13 November 2008, Mann Singh v. France, no. 24479/07 and HRC, 26 September 2013, Mann Singh v. France, CCPR/C/108/D/1928/2010.

19 ECtHR (Grand Chamber), 1 July 2014, SAS v. France, 43835/11 and HRC, 17 July 2018, Yaker v. France and Hebbadj v. France, CCPR/C/123/D/2747/2016 and CCPR/C/123/D/2807/2016.

20 For a critical discussion of the distinction between both in the context of the ECHR, see Lavrysen, 2016.

21 See, generally, Fredman, 2008. Specifically under the ECHR, where this development has been most evident, see Mowbray, 2004 and Lavrysen, 2016.

In this respect, it is assumed that all human rights give rise to three types of obligations: obligations to respect, to protect and to fulfil human rights.[22] In terms of the positive/negative obligations dichotomy, the obligation to respect (i.e., requiring States to refrain from interfering with human rights) corresponds with the negative obligation, whereas the obligations to protect and fulfil correspond with the category of positive obligations. In what follows, the categories of obligations to protect and obligations to fulfil will be used as analytical tools for mapping the development of positive obligations in this area.[23] Generally, the obligation to protect requires the State to prevent human rights violations by third parties, and the obligation to fulfil requires States to take appropriate legislative, administrative, budgetary, judicial and other measures towards the full realisation of human rights.[24] The latter obligation is sometimes further divided into the obligation to facilitate individuals' enjoyment of their human rights, the obligation to provide a certain good when this is necessary for the enjoyment of a human right[25] and the obligation to promote for example through the provision of appropriate education on the exercise of the right.[26]

The obligation to protect

Before turning to the wholly uncharted waters of the positive obligations to fulfil the right to freedom of religion, an overview will be given of the somewhat better developed positive obligations to protect this right. It must first be noted that the Human Rights Committee's General Comment No. 22 on Article 18 of the ICCPR, although being almost silent on positive obligations, does mention that:

> The Committee wishes to be informed of *measures* taken by States parties concerned *to protect the practices of all religions or beliefs from infringement and to protect their followers from discrimination* (emphasis added).[27]

General Comments of the Human Rights Committee have the dual objective of, on the one hand, providing an authoritative interpretation of the ICCPR and, on the other hand, providing guidance to the States on what their reports to the Committee should focus on. This quote clearly pertains to the latter objective, thereby doing little to elucidate the scope of any positive obligation to protect that might be derived from the right to freedom of religion.

---

22 In particular, the work of Asbjørn Eide on the right to adequate food has been influential in this respect (1987).

23 It is submitted that not all positive obligations neatly fall in these categories. For instance, in the context of Article 9 ECHR, the European Court of Human Rights has recognized a positive obligation to provide the applicant with an effective and accessible procedure to have established whether he can benefit from the status of conscientious objector under domestic law (ECtHR, 12 June 2012, *Savda v. Turkey*, no. 42730/05, para. 99). It is difficult to consider this obligation in terms of either the obligation to protect or the obligation to fulfil. In fact, one may wonder whether it would not have been more appropriate to examine this as a procedural safeguard to protect an individual against unjustified State interference (i.e., from the viewpoint of negative obligations). In the landmark case on conscientious objection of ECtHR (Grand Chamber), 7 July 2011, *Bayatyan v. Armenia*, no. 23459/03, the Court in fact examined the case through a negative obligations lens.

24 Maastricht Guidelines on Violations of Economic, Social and Cultural Rights, adopted by a group of academic experts meeting in Maastricht on 22–26 January 2007.

25 E.g., Committee on Economic, Social and Cultural Rights (CESCR), 12 May 1999, General Comment No. 12 on the right to adequate food, E/C.12/1999/5, para. 15.

26 E.g., CESCR, 20 January 2003, General Comment No. 15 on the right to water, E/C.12/2002/11, para. 25.

27 HRC, GC, o.c., para. 9.

Article 18 of the ICCPR must, however, also be read in light of General Comment No. 31 which clarifies in general terms that the positive obligations under the Covenant require the State to protect individuals 'against acts committed by private persons or entities that would impair the enjoyment of Covenant rights.'[28] The Committee further specifies the scope of the obligation to protect by holding States to be under an obligation to 'take appropriate measures or to exercise due diligence to prevent, punish, investigate or redress the harm caused by such acts by private persons or entities.'[29] It must be noted that General Comment No. 31 teaches us little about what kinds of acts can be considered as 'impairing the enjoyment' of Article 18 of the ICCPR to such an extent as to trigger such positive obligations, but it can safely be assumed that at the very least States are required to take measures to protect individuals against violence targeting the exercise of their freedom of thought, conscience and religion.

Compared to General Comment No. 22, in General Comment No. 23 on Article 27 ICCPR, the Human Rights Committee has been more explicit in recognising the existence of positive obligations to protect ethnic, religious and linguistic minorities:

> Positive measures of protection are [...] required not only against the acts of the State party itself, whether through its legislative, judicial or administrative authorities, but also against the acts of other persons within the State party.[30]

So far, the Human Rights Committee has not yet dealt with obligations to protect either Article 18 or Article 27 in its individual communications procedure.

Finally, at the UN level, the 1981 UN Declaration also provides for positive obligations to protect against discrimination on the grounds of religion. Article 2 § 2 prohibits not only State but also private discrimination:

> No one shall be subject to discrimination *by any* State, institution, *group of persons, or person* on grounds of religion or other beliefs (emphasis added).

The State obligations in this regard are further specified in Article 4 of the Declaration:

1. All States shall *take effective measures to prevent and eliminate discrimination* on the grounds of religion or belief in the recognition, exercise and enjoyment of human rights and fundamental freedoms in all fields of civil, economic, political, social and cultural life.
2. All States shall make all efforts to *enact or rescind legislation where necessary to prohibit any such discrimination*, and to *take all appropriate measures to combat intolerance* on the grounds of religion or other beliefs in this matter (emphasis added).

At the regional level, only the European Court of Human Rights has dealt with obligations to protect freedom of religion. Under the ECHR,[31] the obligation to protect is the most established with respect to situations in which believers have been targeted by violent acts on account of their beliefs. According to the Court, 'where religious beliefs are opposed or denied in a manner which inhibits those who hold such beliefs from exercising their freedom to hold

28 HRC, 26 May 2004, GC No. 31 on The Nature of the General Legal Obligation Imposed on States Parties to the Covenant, CCPR/C/21/Rev.1/Add.13, para.8.

29 Ibid.

30 HRC, GC 23, o.c., para. 6.1.

31 On positive obligations under Article 9 ECHR, see Ferri, 2017.

or express them ... the State may be called upon to ensure the peaceful enjoyment of the rights guaranteed under Article 9 to the holders of those beliefs.'[32] The case of *Begheluri and Others v. Georgia,* for instance, concerned a group of Jehovah's Witnesses who had been humiliated and physically attacked by private individuals because of their religious beliefs. According to the Court,

> it was incumbent on the national authorities to fulfil their positive obligation not only to ensure that a legal *framework was put in place to safeguard freedom of religion*, but first and foremost, to guarantee that *effective measures* would be taken *to implement* that right (emphasis added).[33]

The Court found a violation of Article 9, because the State had failed to discharge its positive obligation 'to take the necessary measures to ensure that Jehovah's Witnesses were able to exercise their right to freedom of religion.'[34] The State is under an obligation to not only take operational steps to ensure the effective and peaceful exercise of Article 9 ECHR but also to give a 'meaningful response' when violent infringement of this right has taken place, including by identifying and prosecuting those responsible.[35]

A highly controversial issue is the question of a potential positive obligation on the state to protect the religious sentiments of believers, or even religion itself, against hate speech or 'defamation of religion.' In the United Nations, Islamic states campaigned for the recognition of the latter concept.[36] This campaign largely subsided in 2011 with the Human Rights Council's adoption of a consensus resolution on 'combating intolerance, negative stereotyping and stigmatization of, and discrimination, incitement to violence and violence against, persons based on religion or belief.'[37] This resolution refocused the discussion on the protection of members of a religious group. Protective measures against hate speech targeting individuals or groups on account of their religion are mandated under some human rights provisions[38] but not under provisions of freedom of religion as such.

It is however not excluded that a positive obligation to take measures to protect religious feelings against the defamation of religion might be recognised under freedom of religion. In a 1997 decision, the now defunct European Commission for Human Rights, stated that

> the manner in which religious beliefs and doctrines are opposed or denied is a matter which may engage the responsibility of the State to ensure the peaceful enjoyment of the right guaranteed under Article 9 of the Convention to the holders of those beliefs

32 ECtHR, 7 October 2014, Begheluri and Others v. Georgia, no. 28490/02, para. 160.

33 Ibid., para. 164.

34 Ibid., para. 165.

35 ECtHR, 24 February 2015, Karaahmed v. Bulgaria, no. 30587/13.

36 On this issue, see Blitt, 2011.

37 Human Rights Council, 12 April 2011, Resolution 16/18.

38 E.g., Article 20 (2) ICCPR, stating that 'Any advocacy of national, racial or religious hatred that constitutes incitement to discrimination, hostility or violence shall be prohibited by law.' Also, under the Convention on the Elimination of Racial Discrimination (CERD), the need for protection against racist hate speech has been understood to encompass 'hate speech targeting persons belonging to certain ethnic groups who profess or practice a religion different from the majority, including expressions of Islamophobia, anti-Semitism and other similar manifestations of hatred against ethno-religious groups,' Committee on the Elimination of Racial Discrimination, 26 September 2013, General Recommendation No. 35, 'Combating racist hate speech,' CERCD/C/GC/35, para. 6.

> and doctrines. Thus, the respect for the religious feelings of believers as guaranteed in Article 9 may in some cases be violated by provocative portrayals of objects of religious veneration [...]. As a consequence, there may be certain positive obligations on the part of a State inherent in an effective respect for rights guaranteed under Article 9 of the Convention, which may involve the adoption of measures designed to secure respect for freedom of religion even in the sphere of the relations of individuals between themselves [...]. Such measures may, in certain circumstances, constitute a legal means of ensuring that an individual will not be disturbed in his worship by the activities of others.[39]

While neither the Commission nor the Court has ever found a violation of Article 9 on this ground, this line of reasoning is not dead, as testified by the recent case of *E.S. v. Austria*. In this case, the ECtHR validated an application of national legislation on defamation of religion. In this context, when examining whether this interference with Article 10 ECHR (the freedom of expression) was justified, the Court referred to positive obligations, stating that 'the Convention States are even required, under their positive obligations under Article 9 of the Convention, to ensure the peaceful co-existence of religious and non-religious groups and individuals under their jurisdiction by ensuring an atmosphere of mutual tolerance.'[40]

The Court has moreover required the State to intervene in private law relations in order to protect the individual's freedom of religion. This is particularly relevant in the case of the private employment relationship. A prominent example concerns the case of *Eweida and Others v. the United Kingdom*, in which one of the applicants had been suspended from her job as a flight attendant for British Airways for wearing a cross at work in violation of the company's uniform policy. The Court found a violation of Article 9 because it considered that the domestic courts had attributed too much weight to the company's wish to project a certain corporate image and too little to the applicant's freedom to manifest her religion.[41] *Mutatis mutandis*, it can be assumed that whenever a domestic court is required to rule on a private law dispute in which the freedom of religion of one of the parties is at stake, the Convention requires it to properly balance the individual's Article 9 right against the other competing interests that may be at stake.

The obligation to fulfil

While there is thus no doubt as to the existence of positive obligations to protect freedom of religion, positive obligations to fulfil this right are far less established. For instance, the Human Rights Committee's General Comment on Article 18 does not even mention positive obligations to fulfil at all. The General Comment on The Nature of the General Legal Obligation Imposed on States Parties to the Covenant, on the other hand, does refer to the requirement under Article 2 ICCPR that States Parties must 'adopt legislative, judicial, administrative, educative and other appropriate measures in order to fulfil their legal obligations.'[42] However, it fails to specify how this may translate into concrete obligations in relation to specific human rights, let alone how the scope of any such obligations can be determined. With respect to Article 27, the Committee has been more generous in its recognition of positive obligations

39 ECmHR, 18 April 1997, Teresa Dubowska and Tomasz Skup v. Poland, No. 33490/96-34055/96, para. 2.
40 ECtHR, 25 October 2018, E.S. v Austria, No. 38450/12, para. 53.
41 ECtHR, 15 January 2013, Eweida and Others v. the United Kingdom, nos. 48420/10 etc., para. 94.
42 HRC, GC 31, o.c., para. 7.

to fulfil the rights of members of (religious) minorities. It has explained that in order to ensure 'the ability of the minority group to maintain its culture, language or religion,'

> positive measures by States may also be necessary to protect the identity of a minority and the rights of its members to enjoy and develop their culture and language and to practice their religion, in community with the other members of the group.

Article 4 of the Declaration on the Rights of Persons Belonging to National or Ethnic, Religious and Linguistic Minorities goes even further, stating that:

> States shall take measures to create favourable conditions to enable persons belonging to minorities to express their characteristics and to develop their culture, language, religion, traditions and customs, except where specific practices are in violation of national law and contrary to international standards.

While it is not specified what kind of measures States are required to create for such 'favourable conditions,' arguably measures of facilitation or even provision are hereby envisaged.

In its jurisprudence under the individual communications procedure, the Committee has not further developed positive obligations to fulfil either Article 18 or Article 27. In the *Waldman v. Canada* case, concerning religious education, one Commissioner did suggest that 'Article 27 imposes positive obligations for States to promote religious instructions in minority religions.'[43] The majority however simply observed that 'the Covenant does not oblige States parties to fund schools which are established on a religious basis,' but only requires that any public funding that is provided to religious schools is made available without discrimination.[44] While in the case of *Prince v. South Africa*, the applicant, an adherent to Rastafarianism, did invoke a positive obligation to provide an exception to the general prohibition on the possession and use of cannabis, the Committee examined the case from the viewpoint of negative obligations, by considering whether this limitation of the applicant's freedom to manifest his religion complied with the criteria set out in Article 18 § 3.[45]

At the regional level, the obligation to fulfil freedom of religion has not yet appeared in the African or Inter-American jurisprudence. In the case law of the European Court of Human Rights, the obligation to fulfil the freedom of religion is most evident in cases concerning prisoners. For instance, in the case of *Jakóbski v. Poland*, prison authorities had refused to provide a Buddhist prisoner with a vegetarian diet in accordance with his beliefs. As the Court did not consider that this 'would have entailed any disruption to the management of the prison or to any decline in the standards of meals served to other prisoners,' it considered that a fair balance had not been struck between the applicant's right to manifest his religion and the interests of the prison authorities, in violation of Article 9 ECHR.[46] More generally, the case law suggests that there may be a positive obligation to provide a prisoner with particular facilities to manifest his or her religion whenever a failure to do so would affect the 'very essence' of the manifestation

43 HRC, 3 November 1999, Waldman v. Canada, no. 694/1996, individual opinion by Martin Scheinin.

44 Ibid., para. 10.6.

45 HRC, 31 October 2007, Prince v. South Africa, no. 1474/2006, paras. 3.1 and 7.2-7.3. Similarly, African Commission on Human and Peoples' Rights, 7 December 2004, Prince v. South Africa, no. 255/02.

46 ECtHR, 7 December 2010, Jakóbski v. Poland, no. 18429/06, paras. 52-55. Similarly ECtHR, 17 December 2013, Vartic v. Romania (No. 2), no. 14150/08.

freedom.[47] The rationale for holding the State to be under enhanced positive obligations vis-à-vis detainees is probably the fact that they do not have the possibility to cater for their religious needs themselves (Lavrysen, 2014: 80–81).

Outside the prison walls, the Court has rejected all claims based on alleged positive obligations to fulfil the freedom of religion. The Court has for instance held that Article 9 ECHR cannot be interpreted as encompassing a right for a religious community to obtain a place of worship from the public authorities.[48] If a religious community however exercises a lawful right to occupy a place of worship, a decision or measure affecting the enjoyment thereof would be examined under the State's negative obligations.[49] The Court has also held that Article 9 does not confer on religious communities or their members an entitlement to secure funding from the State budget.[50] However, under Article 14 (the prohibition of discrimination) in combination with Articles 9 and 11 (the freedom of association), the Court has added that:

> Where, in pursuit of its perceived positive obligations with regard to Articles 9 and 11, the State has voluntarily decided to afford entitlement to subsidies and other benefits to religious organisations [...] it cannot take discriminatory measures in the granting of those benefits.[51]

Under the ECHR, differential treatment is not as such prohibited, but it is considered to be discriminatory if it has no objective and reasonable justification.[52] As a result, the ECHR does not necessarily exclude that States, based on their historical–constitutional tradition, maintain a close relationship with particular religions (e.g., a State–Church system)[53] and even vest them with certain secular functions (Evans and Thomas, 2006: 713). However, any material or financial benefits granted to them may not be excessive (i.e., 'clearly disproportionate to those received for comparable activities by other organisations in a given society').[54]

The Court did consider that 'there is a positive obligation incumbent on the State to put in place a system of recognition which facilitates the acquisition of legal personality by religious communities.'[55] However, this merely regards the possibility of acquiring legal capacity as civil law entities; the State is not required to accord them a specific public law status[56] or a special fiscal status.[57] Again, if the State has created a legal framework in order to grant religious communities a special status entailing specific privileges, it must comply with the principle of

47 Mutatis mutandis ECtHR (inadm.), 31 January 2012, Kovalkovs v. Latvia, no. 35021/05, para. 67.

48 ECtHR (inadm.), 8 January 2013, Juma Mosque Congregation and Others v. Azerbaijan , no. 15405/04, para. 61.

49 Ibid., para. 62 with reference to ECtHR, 26 September 1996, Manoussakis and Others v. Greece, no. 18748/91.

50 ECtHR, 8 April 2014, Magyar Kereszteny Mennotina Egyhaz and Others v. Hungary, nos. 70945/11 etc., para. 106.

51 Ibid., para. 107.

52 ECtHR (Grand Chamber), 24 April 2016, Izzettin Doğan and Others v. Turkey, no. 62649/10, para. 164.

53 ECtHR, Magyar Keresztény Mennotina Egyhaz and Others v. Hungary, o.c., para. 100.

54 Ibid., para. 100.

55 Ibid., para. 90.

56 Ibid., para. 91.

57 ECtHR, 24 May 2016, Association for Solidarity with Jehovah's Witnesses and Others v. Turkey, nos. 36915/10 and 8606/13, para. 97.

nondiscrimination by ensuring 'that religious groups have a fair opportunity to apply for this status and that the criteria established are applied in a non-discriminatory manner.'[58]

With the ambiguous position of religious minority rights as an outlier, it is fair to endorse Nieuwenhuis' findings that 'freedom of religion, in general, gives no grounds for facilitating religious communities' (2012: 164). In theory, however, there is no reason why it would not be possible to develop such obligations under the right to freedom of religion. In the context of the ECHR, it is for instance illustrative to compare Article 9 jurisprudence with case law under Article 8 (the right to respect for private and family life). While the Court has been quite hesitant to impose far-reaching obligations to fulfil under this provision, it has nonetheless accepted that the State may be under an obligation to provide for particular goods or services when there is 'a direct and immediate link between the measures sought by an applicant and the latter's private and/or family life.'[59] There is nothing inherent about Article 9 of the ECHR that would exclude claims for similar limited obligations to fulfil from the scope of this provision altogether. The categorical denial to recognise such obligations under this provision is in the first place a question of judicial policy. Ferri explains that this is rooted 'in the fact that, in the Court's view, the adoption of some State positive measures in favour of one religion could compromise the principle of State neutrality and impartiality' in religious matters (Ferri, 2017: 319). However, this principle fails to explain the denial of obligations to fulfil as State neutrality and impartiality is not compromised when positive measures in this sphere are implemented in a nondiscriminatory manner, as required under Article 14 in combination with Article 9. What however does explain such denial is the risk that recognising obligations to fulfil in this area may ultimately reduce the scope of permissible diversity regarding how the relationship between State and religion can be regulated. The human rights instruments discussed above 'do not require a particular degree of separation or attachment between religions and the State' (Evans and Thomas, 2006: 699). The Grand Chamber of the Court has reaffirmed its position on these matters in 2016, holding that

> no single model exists in Europe governing relations between the State and religious communities. States have a certain margin of appreciation in choosing the forms of cooperation with the various religious communities.[60]

Leaving such a margin of appreciation to the State is particularly important '[i]n matters of general policy, on which opinions within a democratic society may reasonably differ widely.' This holds true in particular in this area, as 'practice in European States is characterised by a wide variety of constitutional models governing relations between the State and religious groups.'[61] The Court has therefore recognised that a variety of models, going from a strict separation between State and church to a system based on State religion, may be compatible with the Convention, on the condition that 'each system must include specific safeguards for the individual's freedom of religion.'[62] As long as such safeguards are in place and as long as the State complies with the principle of nondiscrimination, the ECHR leaves States the choice of whether or not to intervene at all in order to facilitate the exercise of religious freedom. To hold otherwise would have prevented States from adhering to a strict separation model,

58 ECtHR (Grand Chamber), Izzettin Doğan and Others v. Turkey, o.c., para. 164.
59 ECtHR, 24 February 1998, Botta v. Italy, no. 21439/93, para. 34.
60 ECtHR (Grand Chamber), Izzettin Doğan and Others v. Turkey, o.c., para. 162.
61 Ibid., para. 112.
62 Ibid., para. 163.

which is widely accepted as a permissible model governing relations between State and religion. In the absence of an authoritative interpretation by UN and regional human rights bodies pointing in the other direction, arguably the same holds true for other UN and regional human rights provisions guaranteeing the freedom of religion.

References

Blitt, R.C., 2011. Defamation of religion: Rumors of its death are greatly exaggerated. *Case Western Reserve Law Review*. 62, 347.

Boyle, K., 2007. Freedom of religion in international law. In: Rehman, J., Breau, S. (Eds.), *Religion, Human Rights and International Law*. Martinus Nijhoff Publishers, p. 23.

Brems, E., 2014. Should pluriform human rights become one? Exploring the benefits of human rights integration. *European Journal of Human Rights*. 4, 447.

Eide, A., 1987. *Report on the Right to Adequate Food as a Human Right*. UN Doc E/CN.4/Sub.2/1987/23. Available from https://digitallibrary.un.org/record/139080.

Evans, C., 2003. The special rapporteur on freedom of religion or belief. In: Ghanea, N. (Ed.), *The Challenge of Religious Discrimination at the Dawn of the New Millenium*. Martinus Nijhoff Publishers, p. 33.

Evans, C., Thomas, C. 2006. Church-state relations in the European Court of Human Rights. *Brigham Young University Law Review* 3, 699.

Evans, M., 1997. *Religious Liberty and International Law in Europe*. Cambridge University Press.

Ferri, M., 2017. The Dogan et al. v. Turkey case: A missed opportunity to recognise positive obligations as regards the freedom of religion. *European Papers*. 2, 311.

Fredman, S., 2008. *Human Rights Transformed*. Oxford University Press.

Kreimer, S., 1983. Allocational ssanctions: The problem of negative rights in a positive state. *University of Pennsylvania Law Review* 132, 1293.

Lavrysen, L., 2014. Protection by the law: The positive obligation to develop a legal framework to adequately protect ECHR rights. In: Haeck, Y., Brems, E. (Eds.), *Human Rights and Civil Liberties in the 21st Century*. Springer, p. 69.

Lavrysen, L., 2016. *Human Rights in a Positive State – Rethinking the Relationship between Positive and Negative Obligations under the European Convention on Human Rights*. Intersentia.

Lerner, N., 2012. *Religion, Secular Beliefs and Human Rights*. Martinus Nijhoff Publishers.

Mowbray, A., 2004. *The Development of Positive Obligations under the European Convention on Human Rights by the European Court of Human Rights*. Hart Publishing.

Nieuwenhuis, A., 2012. State and religion, a multidimensional relationship: Some comparative law remarks. *International Journal of Consitutional Law (I*CON)*. 10, 153.

Tahzib, B., 1996. *Freedom of Religion or Belief: Ensuring Effective International Legal Protection*. Martinus Nijhoff Publishers, The Hague.

Vermeulen, B., Van Roosmalen, M., 2018. Freedom of thought, conscience and religion. In: Van Dijk, F., Van Hoof, F., Van Rijn, A., Zwaak, L. (Eds.), *Theory and Practice of the European Convention on Human Rights*. Intersentia, p. 375.

17

The right to freedom of and from religion in non-State legal orders: The case of indigenous peoples

Martin Ramstedt

Preliminaries

The present handbook seemingly departs from the bold assumption that the right to freedom of religion can truly be seen as a universal right, with historical roots that are traceable in all major cultures of the world. As an anthropologist, however, I am quite aware that all supposedly universal concepts are in fact culturally, politically and historically situated, and thus need to be 'culturally translated' in order to be able to globalize. Hence, I would like to shift our perspective – and thus methodology – a bit, by highlighting the entanglement of different historical trajectories that has enabled, not the universalization, but the globalization of the right to freedom of religion.

Universality of the right to freedom of religion: A shift in perspective

The right to freedom of religion is undoubtedly a '[concept] in motion' that has had world-making power (see also Gluck, 2009: 3). In other words, it has helped set global standards, 'without prematurely homogenizing the globe' (Lowenhaupt Tsing, 2009: 11). That is to say, as a concept in motion, the right to freedom of religion has arguably become a global reference point, even though certain states deny their citizens this freedom, or have narrowed – sometimes to a considerable degree – the original meaning of either 'freedom' or 'religion', or both. Inasmuch as this right has been adapted to changing sociocultural, political and historical contexts, the concept has been 'taking and making meanings' across the boundaries of its original context (Gluck, 2009: 5).

Projects of tracing concepts in motion do not only allow us to better understand how global connections have been formed in concrete travel routes. They also enable us to appreciate where certain standards might have broken down, where they have not yet been (fully) established, and why (Lowenhaupt Tsing, 2009: 11). By moving, a certain 'traveling concept' (Bal, 2002) might have changed its meaning to such a degree that it has become but a caricature of its original design; or that its original meaning has remained culturally untranslatable with respect to actual situations on the ground. In a recent article, I proposed a methodological specification, whereby we can actually trace what happens, and why, when concepts 'travel', that is, when they are 'translated' to alien cultural contexts:

> We should, first of all, inquire into the concrete socio-political events that prompted the traveling of a certain concept beyond its culture of origin. This also includes events that account for the local rejection of a certain traveling concept just as much as instances of partial translation. We then have to study the history and range of meanings of the traveling idea, as well as the history and meaning of the associated institutions and practices. This has to be supplemented with a study of the history and range of meanings of the concepts, institutions and practices the traveling concept has been translated to. In a third step, we need to ask who controls the cultural translation, and whether there are rival, or alternative translation processes with regard to the same traveling concept. Last but not least, our analysis should highlight what is lost, and what might have been gained in the course of the translation processes. This also entails an inquiry into the effects of a particular cultural translation on the different stakeholders (Ramstedt, 2017: 53).

Many historiographies that trace the development of the concept of the right to freedom of religion foreground 'the West' as the place, where governments 'slowly stepped away from religious impositions and persecution' from the seventeenth century onwards (Blackford, 2012: 2). Contrary to the design of the present handbook, however, such historiographies commonly neglect comparable developments in other parts of the world, and in other historical cultures, such as, for instance, the millet system in the Ottoman Empire. They also usually lack analyses on why a certain culture did not develop the right to freedom of religion, or did indeed reject it as an alien concept that traveled from elsewhere. With regard to the Middle Eastern 'postcolony' (Mbembe, 2001), for instance, we need to bear in mind that religious liberalism is often equated with moral libertinism supposedly rampant in a culturally degenerate, yet overpowering West. It is no accident, hence, that, in the Middle East, the concept of 'religion' has stayed congruent with orthodox Islamic notions of the term, and their in-built view that apostasy is heinous. If we want to fathom how the right to freedom of religion has fared among indigenous cultures, we need to inquire into the culturally situated tacit assumptions that have determined the concrete routes this right has traveled, in order to become applicable to indigenous contexts (see also Cohen, 2010; Loenhoff, 2011).

If we want to ascertain a distinct historical locus, from which the right to freedom of religion has traveled in the shape of a modern fundamental human right, it does make sense to take 1948, the year of the proclamation of the Universal Declaration of Human Rights, which also contains Article 18 on the Right to Freedom of Religion (UDHR Universal Declaration of Human Rights, 2015: 38), as our point of departure. The United Nations website gives a succinct summary of the historical context in which the Declaration arose. It clearly states that the latter was informed by the appalling experiences of the crimes against humanity during World War II. It also attests to the fact that the process of drafting the Declaration was heavily influenced by US leadership, irrespective of the fact that the drafting committee had an international membership. While Eleonor Roosevelt, the widow of former US President Franklin D. Roosevelt, chaired the committee, the other members comprised delegates only from France, Lebanon, China and Canada. Apparently, the Chinese delegate, Dr. Peng Chung Chang, was alone in stressing the point that the Declaration should reflect more than just Western ideas. When the Declaration was finally adopted by the General Assembly of the United Nations, which in 1948 had 58 member states (GUNM, n.d.), eight states had abstained from the vote (UDHR-HoD, n.d.).

From 1948 until today, UN membership has grown to some 190 members (GUNM, n.d.). Whereas human rights activists tend to aver that the translation of the Universal Declaration of

Human Rights into international law constituted an absolute break with colonialism, critical scholars of international law, such as Antony T. Anghie (Professor of Law at the National University of Singapore and Secretary-General of the Asian Society of International Law) and Balakrishnan Rajagopal (founding Director of the Program on Human Rights and Justice at the Massachusetts Institute of Technology and Associate Professor of Law and Development at the MIT Department of Urban Studies and Planning), emphasize that international law has developed around a certain set of strongly interlinked universalist concepts (including human rights, along with 'development', 'nationalism' and 'good governance') that has governed postcolonial international politics in a way very similar to the manner colonial universalist ontologies had informed the governance of native populations. While it is true that many postcolonial non-Western social movements, including indigenous rights movements, have frequently used human rights rhetoric to their advantage, human rights in the non-West is still largely associated, if not with Western neocolonial aspirations, then at least with Western claims to cultural hegemony. Such claims are intrinsic to the notion of 'modernization' that is so strongly suggested by the interlinkage between human rights and the concepts of development, good governance and nationalism within postcolonial international law (Anghie, 2004: 199–211, 254–263; Rajagopal, 2006: 767–770).

Western concepts that still tacitly inform contemporary human rights become very much apparent when we turn to the right to freedom of religion. Let us start with the notion of religion itself. The right of freedom of religion has traveled in both a geographical and a temporal sense from its original sociocultural context of production (i.e., war-worn mid-twentieth century Western liberal democracies), in which the notion of 'religion' was still very much informed, if not anymore by traditional Christendom, then at least by the late nineteenth century Western notion of 'world religions.' In these very same Western liberal democracies, 'religion' has become, over the period of a few decades, a rather fuzzy concept indeed. In twenty-first-century Western societies, 'religion' is being used as some sort of 'a blanket term, which covers myriad beliefs and practices' (Trigg, 2012: 16). This is due to mass immigration by adherents of alien religions, along with the advent of New Religious Movements and New Age spirituality, as well as cultural tourism, which have all played their part in palpably altering the traditional religious landscape of Western societies.

While 'religion' has acquired a much broader range of meanings in early twenty-first-century Western liberal democracies, the concept continues to refer to a separate and private realm of culture. Separating out 'the religious' from 'the social' is indeed one of the hallmarks of secular Western societies. In contrast, indigenous cultures, at least before the advent of alien settlers, were marked by a complete absence of the concept of a separate religious sphere. Religious practices and beliefs were in point of fact very much 'interwoven into everyday thought and action,' to the extent that they were 'not even noticeable as a separate sphere' (Blackford, 2012: 5). Indigenous religions must therefore be conceived of as a whole way of life. They transcend the narrow field of 'the religious' in Western liberal democracies, by expanding right into spheres that lie at the heart of modern state sovereignty, like jurisdiction, governance or natural resource management.

Moreover, current Western mainstream societies not only mean 'religion' to demarcate a separate cultural sphere, but they also use 'religion' as an umbrella term for everything that cannot be conceived of, described or classified in secular scientific terms, such as afterlife, soul, divinity and the like. This has rendered 'the religious' as something very abstract and cut off from the ordinary experiences that constitute the frame of reference for people's daily life. Due to their interwovenness with even the most minute detail of each group's way of life, indigenous spiritual taxonomies, on the other hand, are not at all abstract but rather exhaustive and concrete. This is why traditionalist members of the Dene Tha, a First Nation Group in Northern Alberta, Canada, like members of many other indigenous peoples, describe 'what Euro-North Americans would consider a religious or mystical experience [...] not as a believer but as someone who "knows"' (Goulet, 1998: xxix). Contrary to the aloof and often rather inconsequential privatized beliefs of contemporary Westerners, indigenous religions thus have a high degree of world-making power – this side of life. Here, every change in the religious or spiritual topography matters in the sense that it immediately impacts on the very institutions and routines that guarantee a life worth living for, as well as the cultural, and sometimes also physical survival of the respective group.

The rationale for the modern right to freedom of religion, last but not least, lies in 'safeguarding those [individuals] who may suffer from the "tyranny of the majority"' (Trigg, 2012: 43, 69). The right to freedom of religion is indeed, as we know, an individual, and not a collective right, and has traveled, or globalized as such. Because in Western liberal democracies, each individual right is limited by other rights as well as the rights of others, 'religious freedom' is granted to a much higher degree to – ultimately inconsequential – private religious convictions, than to world-making and invasive indigenous or tribal spiritual practices (see also Trigg, 2012: 2–3, 13, 97). Indigenous religions are, after all, about real-life collective interventions that are believed to guarantee 'good living,' or *buen vivir*. From a legal reasoning point of view, it is therefore highly problematic to apply a 'right to freedom of religion' framework to the protection of indigenous worldviews and their associated ways of life.

The right to the freedom of practicing the whole range of their own traditional rituals has indeed hardly ever been granted to indigenous peoples after their subjugation to the colonization and/or nationalization processes in the respective settler countries, as well as colonial and post-colonial states they were finding themselves in. It is only since the 1950s that pro-indigenous rights activism has succeeded in casting considerable doubt among an increasing number of global citizens on the righteousness of the destruction of indigenous spiritual cultures, brought about by political and social disenfranchisement, the growing devastation of their natural environments in the name of progress, as well as by forced conversion to an alien worldview, often to Christianity, less so to Islam, Hinduism, Buddhism, or any of the varieties of secular scientism, like Communism, etc. Special mention must be made here, too, of the trauma caused by the long-standing practice of abducting indigenous children by either Christian missionaries, or secular states (e.g., Jacobs, 2009; Toulouze Kotljarchuk 2017: 216–217).

Since the 1980s, international indigenous rights activism increasingly garnered the support of cosmopolitan urban dwellers in both the global north and the global south, who have experienced the growing fragility of sociocultural bonds under neoliberal conditions. These seemingly improbable supporters of indigenous causes have lent legitimacy to indigenous rights activism, by connecting or rather translating it to a whole range of modern spiritual and secular discourses, such as environmentalism, alternative healing, neopaganism and communitarianism (Niezen, 2009: xiv–xv). The indigenous rights movement of today therefore consists of highly diverse marginalized groups in countries of both the global north and the global south, as well as their nonindigenous urban supporters. Over the past few decades, indigenous rights activism has clearly developed the legal, organizational and technical wherewithal to harness culture in a global discourse for local political ends (Goodale, 2006: 635–642; Niezen, 2009: 11–19, 32–42).

The moral legitimacy of indigenous calls for justice notwithstanding, if the right to freedom of religion was granted to indigenous peoples, the ramifications would challenge both the logic of the international human rights framework and that of the indigenous cosmologies themselves. Much more would be at stake than 'just' the right to publicly display individual religious identity markers, like indigenous equivalents to veils, crucifixes, and so on. This is illustrated by a whole array of recent cases, in which indigenous traditions have been successfully juridified.

However, before I zoom in on one case of juridification in terms of freedom of and from religion, I will recapitulate in broad-brush terms the conflicts, and here particularly their 'religious' dimensions, that boosted the development of the global indigenous rights movement. We will see, that in the course of the globalization of the indigenous rights movement, the concept of 'indigenous' also traveled, 'taking and making meaning' (see above) in the process.

Development of global indigenous rights activism

The roots of the contemporary global indigenous rights movement reach back to the inchoate and rather localized forms of indigenous resistance against the physical, religious and political encroachment by European newcomers in the classical settler countries, comprising the Americas, Australia, New Zealand and the Russian Empire, as well as its successor state, the Soviet Union. A first step toward an international form of indigenous rights activism was made, though, when the International Labour Organization (ILO) was founded in 1919. In the pre-World War II period, the ILO focused on improvement of the excruciating working conditions of indentured laborers on South American plantations, many of whom were members of indigenous peoples. It also sought to address the lack of equal citizen rights for members of indigenous communities choosing to adhere to their traditional way of life, as suffrage was typically only granted to those who had 'detribalized,' that is, who had severed all ties with their native community, in order to lead a fully assimilated life among 'whites' instead (Hall, 1995: 2; Chesterman and Galligan, 1997: 2–10; Rollings, 2004: 126–127; Rathgeber, 2013: 6–7).

However, fair treatment of indigenous laborers and the granting of suffrage to the adult members of indigenous peoples was signed into law only after World War II. ILO Convention No. 107 from 1957 concerning the Protection and Integration of Indigenous and Other Tribal and Semi-Tribal Populations in Independent Countries enabled 'the said populations to benefit on an equal footing from the rights and opportunities which national laws or regulations grant to the other elements of the population' (ILO C107, 1957: Art. 2.2a). The Convention furthermore ensured them 'Enjoyment of the general rights of citizenship, without discrimination' (ILO C107 C107 – Indigenous and Tribal Populations Convention No. 107, 1957: Art. 3.3). Finally, it is noteworthy that the Convention extended 'indigenous rights' also to 'tribal' and 'semi-tribal' peoples, that is, to populations 'whose social and economic conditions are at a less advanced stage than the stage reached by the other sections of the national community, and whose status is regulated wholly or partially by their own customs or traditions or by special laws and regulations' (Art. 1.1). The range of potential receivers of indigenous rights was thus considerably broadened. Incidentally, no mention was made about indigenous or tribal religions, which were rather subsumed under secular container terms, such as 'custom' and 'tradition.'

ILO Convention No. 107 was never ratified by either of the classical settler states. In fact, it only ever received 27 ratifications (Ratifications of C107, 1996–2017), which means that, apart from the settler states, most decolonized countries were also not prepared to grant separate rights to the tribal and semitribal groups in their territories, as this would have seriously impeded their nation-building process. For the classical settler countries, ratification would have entailed a grave modification of their legal and administrative structure, involving the adoption of a significant degree of legal pluralism as well as granting regional autonomy to the respective groups. ILO C107 Art. 7, for instance, stipulated that 'In defining the rights and duties of the population concerned regard shall be had to their customary laws' (Art. 7.1). What is more, it also allowed indigenous peoples to retain 'The right to ownership, collective or individual, [...] over the lands which these populations traditionally occupy' (Art. 11).

Even though the classical settler states did not support ILO Convention No. 107, they were nevertheless prepared to grant standard citizenship rights to their indigenous population. This coincided with a growing awareness of the fact that a significant number of indigenous men had rendered military service to their countries during the war (Hall, 1995: v–vi, 4–11; Rollings, 2004: 137–138). However, government policies generally continued to be geared toward a mode of 'integration' that required the cultural assimilation of indigenous, tribal and semitribal groups. In other words, these groups were still commonly expected to modernize, which more often than not included conversion to one or the other forms of Christianity (Brock, 2005).

Christianization had already been widely deployed during the colonial period as a means to bring the blessings of modernity to colonized local populations, particularly those adhering to so-called 'animist' cosmologies and 'primitive' lifestyles (Veer, 1996: 7–9; Rooden, 1996: 69–70, 83; Keane, 1996: 138, 145). 'Animist' groups revering nature, ancestor and guardian spirits, etc., had often been marginalized even by non-Christian majority populations in the colonies, embracing Islam, a variety of Hinduism or Buddhism. Through conversion to a dominant religion, particularly Christianity, former animists profited considerably in terms of education, health care, as well as economic and political advancement from the fringe to a more comfortable place in colonial societies. Some former animists later became themselves Christian missionaries, successfully converting other groups at the margin to a 'better life.'

Indigenous or tribal groups converting to some sort of Christian modernity in the colony and postcolony included the Karen and Hmong in mainland Southeast Asia (Thawnghmung, 2011: 14; Ngô, 2016), so-called Adivasi populations in India (Bauman, 2013: 634; Lefebure, 2013: 33–35), ethnic groups inhabiting remote mountain and forest areas, or faraway islands in Indonesia, such as the Dayak, Batak, Toraja, Papua, non-Muslim Moluccans (Aritonang and Steenbrink, 2008: 99–177) and similar groups in other parts of the world.

From the 1960s onward, indigenous rights activism was increasingly geared to cultural rights advocacy, which included claims to religious freedom and parental rights. For, even after the war, indigenous children had been taken away from their families and put into orphanages, mission schools or industrial schools, in order to save them from their 'primitive' relatives, who were often being criminalized for adhering to their traditional ways (Chesterman and Galligan, 1997: 8, 24–52; Irwin, 1997: 41–42). It is worth mentioning that it was only in the beginning of the 1990s that a majority of anthropologists were prepared to publicly highlight the 'culturally destructive effects of missionary activities' at a professional gathering in the US (Benthall, 1995: 1). And it was not until 2007 that an agency of the United Nations, that is, the United Nations Permanent Forum on Indigenous Issues, founded in 2000, recommended that research be made by an expert on the subject of boarding schools for indigenous children all over the globe and the related question of child abduction (Smith, 2009: 3). In 2009, a comprehensive report was submitted to the Eighth Session of the United Nations Permanent Forum on Indigenous Issues by the expert, Andrea Smith. The report states that boarding schools for indigenous children were frequently established in cooperation with Christian missions. These schools had the expressed goal of Christianizing indigenous peoples, particularly in the Americas, the Arctic and the Pacific, in order to assimilate them into the dominant societies of the countries in which they lived. There were regional differences regarding such assimilation policies. Whereas it was 'full-blood' native American and First Nations children who were forcibly abducted from their families in Canada and the US, it was children of mixed ancestry who were repeatedly targeted in New Zealand and Australia. Their boarding school education was to prepare them for their designed role as an elite within their indigenous communities that was to take over the leadership of the respective groups. According to a report on a Boarding School Healing Project in South Dakota (US) of 2007, children were given inadequate food and medical care in the past, so that hundreds of children died because of malnutrition and ill health. Moreover, many children, boys and girls alike, were sexually abused and regularly assigned arduous chores. We have similar reports from Canada and Australia (Smith, 2009: 3–11, 29). For lack of space, I do not want to go deeper into the issue. Suffice it to say that the secular boarding schools in Africa were hardly ever attended by children of tribal groups, while those in the Middle East were principally opened for Bedouin children, in order to enable them to negotiate with the colonial administrations, under whose jurisdiction they fell (Smith, 2009: 3–4). While in the 1960s the system of boarding schools began to peter out in many areas of the world, it has continued in some countries, albeit generally – although, alas, not everywhere – under a more caring and emancipatory regime (Smith, 2009: 20, 33–48).

In the US, the counterculture and civil rights movements of the 1960s were linked to a growing awareness of the right to freedom of religion for indigenous peoples. One of the first US laws recognizing such a right was the American Indian Religious Freedom Act (AIRFA) from 1978, signed by US President Jimmy Carter. It protects the rights of Native Americans, Inuit, Aleut and Native Hawaiians 'to believe, express, and exercise' their traditional religions (Irwin, 1997: 35). AIRFA was enacted in order to balance the many federal laws that had proven detrimental to indigenous spiritual practices. Because the latter 'are so culturally removed' from Christianity and Judaism, the religions of mainstream Americans (NARF, 1979: 1), they had just not been taken into account by the lawmakers. Such indigenous practices involved the taking of hallucinogenic drugs, like Peyote, the use of feathers or hides, etc., from protected species, and sojourns in nature reserves forbidden to the public. AIRFA hence revoked – for members of certain indigenous groups only – the anti-drug legislation criminalizing the use of Peyote and the laws for the preservation of wildlife and the protection of wilderness areas, which had previously made it impossible for Native Americans, Inuit, Aleut or Native Hawaiians to collect eagle feathers, hunt certain animals, gather herbs and other ingredients for their ceremonies or access certain sacred sites situated in national parks, etc., for the performance of rituals (NARF Native American Rights Fund, 1979: 3–6).

However, not all native Americans have benefited from AIRFA, because not every group who self-identifies as Native American is recognized as such by the US federal government. The latter to date recognizes altogether 567 groups, mostly through historic treaties and the positive evaluation of factors, such as 'the extent of Indian [i.e., indigenous] governmental control over individual lives and activities, the extent to which the group exercises political control over a specific territory, and the continuity of the group's history' (AIL, n.d.). There are, for instance, about 20 different Native American groups in the state of Virginia. However, only one group among them (i.e., the Pamunkey) gained official recognition in 2016. Suffering from systematic destruction of their records in the past, the other groups cannot come up with the required 'individual genealogies that show direct descent from individuals listed in nineteenth century federal Indian registers' (Hilleary, 2017; Lawrence, 2004: 3–4).

Sometimes, even recognized groups have factually not been granted protection of their religion under AIRFA. In *Sequoyah v. Tennessee Valley Authority 480 F. Supp. 608 (E.D. Tenn 1979)*, for instance, Cherokee leaders sought in vain to obtain an injunction against government plans to flood their sacred homeland, which then led to the complete inundation of medicine gathering sites, important burial sites from the nineteenth century and other sacred sites. Due to their Judeo-Christian concept of 'religion' as well as their entrenched respect for existing property rights, the judges failed to acknowledge the relevance of these sites for the religious life of the Cherokee, opining that 'The free exercise clause is not a license in itself to enter property, government-owned or otherwise, to which religious practitioners have no other legal right of access' (*Sequoyah v.* Tennessee Valley Authority, 1979; see also Kuppe, 2009: 53).

In 1989, the International Labour Organization, which 'in 1946 [had] become the first specialized agency associated with the newly formed United Nations,' and on its 50th anniversary in 1969 had been awarded the Peace Nobel Prize (ILO, 2007: 2), issued the first and to date only internationally enforceable law seeking to protect the rights, customs and institutions of indigenous peoples: ILO Convention No. 169 on Indigenous and Tribal Peoples in Independent Countries. It stipulates 'self-identification as indigenous or tribal [...] as a fundamental criterion for determining the groups to which the provisions of this Convention apply' (ILO C169 C169, 1989: Art. 1.2). The Convention furthermore promulgates that 'the social, cultural, religious and spiritual values of these peoples shall be recognized and protected, and due account shall be taken of the nature of the problems which face them both as groups and as individuals' (ILO C169 C169 – Indigenous and Tribal Populations Convention No. 169, 1989: Art. 5.a). C169 thus exceeds by far the extent of the right of freedom to religion granted to recognized Native American groups in the US. However, it was again not ratified by the classical settler states. A mere 23 countries ratified the Convention, most of them Latin American ones (Ratifications of C169, 1989).

In 1989, the year of the issuance of ILO C169, the Soviet Union was rapidly disintegrating. With its final dissolution at the end of 1991, many of the 30 some indigenous peoples, distributed over northern Russia, Siberia, and the Russian Far East, began to revitalize their traditional spiritual beliefs and practices. These were invariably defined by Shamanism (Ivashchenko, 2017: 264, 277; Kotljarchuk and Sundström, 2017: 21–25; Kusber, 2016: 243; Toulouze, 2017: 153–154). Since the seventeenth century, the indigenous shamanic communities had been exposed to some degree of Russification. However, Catherine II, who ruled the Russian Empire in the second half of the eighteenth century, was an enlightened ruler. She abolished forced conversion, granting all indigenous peoples under her sway religious tolerance if they remained loyal to her (Kusber, 2016: 252). Yet, in the last decades of the nineteenth century, more and more Russians moved into indigenous territories after the opening of the Trans-Siberian Railway. In Siberia, they eventually greatly outnumbered the indigenous population (Kusber, 2016: 254).

In the first years after the October Revolution, the Bolsheviks favored a kind of nativization policy, which promised indigenous communities that they could participate in a Soviet modernity, without having to compromise their cultures, including shamanism (Kusber, 2016: 255; Kotljarchuk and Sundström, 2017: 19, 24; Kotljarchuk, 2017: 89; Toulouze, 2017: 155–156; Bulgakova and Sundström, 2017: 230–231). This policy, however, drastically changed at the end of the 1920s, when Stalin began to enforce collectivization and a sedentary way of life upon indigenous peoples, in order to modernize and de-ethnicize them. Shamans were deprived of their civic rights, material sustenance and spiritual influence, so that those who were not killed or deported to the Gulag were forced to go underground or survived at the margins of their communities (Bulgakova and Sundström, 2017: 225–227, 232–251; Toulouze et al., 2017: 206, 211, 217–218). Several indigenous groups then killed their herds and fled into China, never to return. The majority of the groups, however, succeeded in retaining a nomadic lifestyle until the 1950s (Kusber, 2016: 259–260; Kotljarchuk and Sundström, 2017: 15, 19–20, 25–26; Toulouze, 2017: 157; Toulouze et al., 2017: 204).

At the end of the 1950s, the Central Committee returned to the initial treatment of indigenous groups shortly after the October Revolution. It more strongly included them into local development projects, while encouraging them to continue their cultural traditions. The ban on shamanism still existed, yet people could circumvent it and practice shamanic rites secretly in cellars or other secluded locations. In this way, shamanism could survive well into the 1970s (Kusber, 2016: 260; Ivashchenko, 2017: 265–266). Thereafter, shamanism declined due to the fact that modern innovations had crept into local traditions that were undermining the charisma shamans had wielded before (Ivashchenko, 2017: 276).

After the dissolution of the Soviet Union, shamanism was revitalized among many indigenous communities in the Russian Federation (Ivashchenko, 2017: 264, 277). Article 96 of the latter's Constitution furthermore increased the status of a certain range of indigenous peoples: 'The Russian Federation shall guarantee the rights of indigenous small peoples in accordance with the universally recognized principles and norms of international law and international treaties of the Russian Federation' (ConRussFed, 1993). The rights granted to small indigenous peoples in the Russian Federation concern tax exemption, privileged access to natural resources and possible material compensation for the extraction of natural resources on indigenous territory. The adjective 'small' added to 'indigenous peoples' defines the size of each of the communities benefiting from these rights as not exceeding 50,000 people. This limit is clearly at odds with the United Nations' concept of indigenous peoples, which followed the model of ILO C169 and is hence predicated upon self-identification. The Constitution of the Russian Federation, on the other hand, prevents larger ethnic groups, such as the Tuvans or Buryats, from ever being recognized as 'indigenous peoples.' This has not impeded the revitalization of shamanism among larger ethnic groups, such as the Tuvans and Buryats, though (Kusber, 2016: 244–245).

In Buryatia, for instance, the revitalization of shamanism has been consciously deployed, in order to bring about a renaissance of the Buryat language and culture. Since 1992, the Republic of Buryatia, which is part of the Russian Far East, has enjoyed a large degree of independence within the Russian Federation. And since then, shamanism can be practiced openly again. Today, Buryat shamanism is strongly interlinked with cultural tourism that brings the much-needed revenue in support of the revitalization of Buryat culture. However, this cultural revival has been accompanied by innovations that have significantly altered the ritual tradition, so much so that traditionalist Buryats openly doubt the authenticity of many contemporary shamans and their performances. Many Buryat shamans have organized themselves into nontraditional organizations. There is, for instance, the new Shamanic Center in Ulan-Ude, the capital of Buryatia, catering to a largely urban and multiethnic clientele seeking healing for personal illnesses and troubles that have sprung from modern life. Other Shamanic Centers have taken on students, who are often not even Buryat, but Russian, German and so forth. (Wierucka, 2013: 101, 104, 107, 109–111, 114–116; Quijada et al., 2015: 258–262). Foreign students of Buryat shamanism can climb the ladder of consecutive initiations and may eventually become shamans in their own right (Quijada and Stephens, 2015: 6, 7, 10, 14).

It is noteworthy in this respect that – in contrast to US federal laws on Native Americans or the UNESCO World Heritage program – the Universal Declaration of the Rights of Indigenous Peoples (UNDRIP) from 2007 does allow for self-determined innovation, as long as it does not contravene the law or any human rights standards (DRIPS, 2007: 14–15). Article 11.1, for example, stipulates that:

> Indigenous peoples have the right to practise and revitalize their cultural traditions and customs. This includes the right to maintain, protect and develop the past, present and future manifestations of their cultures, such as archaeological and historical sites, artefacts, designs, ceremonies, technologies and visual and performing arts and literature (DRIPS United Nations Declaration on the Rights of Indigenous Peoples, 2007: 6).

And Article 33.2 clearly states that:

> Indigenous peoples have the right to determine the structures and to select the membership of their institutions in accordance with their own procedures (DRIPS United Nations Declaration on the Rights of Indigenous Peoples, 2007: 12).

After decades, or even centuries, of subjugation under foreign cultural, political and religious regimes, which has resulted in the development of more or less creole or hybrid cultures and religions, how would indigenous peoples be able to emancipate themselves, without (re)inventing their traditions that then '[establish] themselves with great rapidity' (Hobsbawm, 1983: 1)? Due to the increasing success of the indigenous rights movement in the international public sphere, it today consists, as I said, of highly diverse, marginalized groups in countries of both the global south and the global north. These groups are united in sentiments of rage, hopelessness, and disappointed expectations that are rooted in a common long-term exposition to structural disempowerment, dispossession, discrimination and destruction (Niezen, 2009, 11–18, 32–43; see also Stavenhagen, 2013: 46–48). Even if indigenous emancipation involves romantic attachment to an imaginary 'tradition,' we should not underestimate the social-psychological healing potential of such religious freedom, as long as adherence to the invented traditions in question is self-determined.

The growing global awareness of indigenous rights and the increasingly accepted need for protecting vulnerable indigenous communities against overbearing outside influence might have informed the balanced media reaction to the recent killing of the young American missionary John Allen Chau, who relentlessly pursued his goal to proselytize the Sentinelese, until they violently retaliated. The Andaman and Nicobar Islands Protection of Aboriginal Tribes Regulation, promulgated by Rajendra Prasad, president of India, in 1956, lists the Sentinelese among the local 'aboriginal tribes.' They inhabit North Sentinel Island, which belongs to one of seven union territories of India, that is, the Union Territory of the Andaman and Nicobar Islands (CoI Census of India, 2011: 4, 7). North Sentinel Island has been classified as a 'reserved area,' in order to protect the Sentinelese against harm caused from the outside, particularly against foreign diseases, to which they do not have any resistance (ANI Protection Act, 1956: 1–2, 6; Corderoy, 2018).

In November 2018, Chau made an illicit voyage to the island, with the explicit goal to convert the Sentinelese to Christendom. He tried three times to reach the shore by stealth. The first time, he approached the shore with a canoe, leaving the motored boat and crew he had hired further away from the coastline. Upon sight, Sentinelese tribesmen greeted him with arrows, so that he had to paddle back to his boat. The second time, tribespeople destroyed his canoe, which forced him to swim back to the boat. He nevertheless returned again to the island, which was when he finally met his death (Chavez, 2018).

By entering the island, Chau had in fact violated Article 7 of the Andaman and Nicobar Islands Protection of Aboriginal Tribes Regulation, which prohibits

> [...] any person other than a member of an aboriginal tribe or any class of persons other than members of an aboriginal tribe from entering a reserved area except on the authority and subject to the observance of the conditions and restrictions of a pass granted by the Deputy Commissioner or by such officer as the Deputy Commissioner may authorize in writing in this behalf (ANI Protection Act Andaman and Nicobar Islands Protection of Aboriginal Tribes Regulation, and Rules Framed Thereunder, 1956: 3).

While his violation of Article 7 is obviously no excuse for his murder, Chau had clearly not considered the mortal danger his mere presence would pose to the tribespeople, quite apart from the fact that he might have arguably interfered with their right to freedom of religion.

Juridification of indigenous cosmologies

On the other hand, it is quite instructive to inquire more deeply into what the consequences – in terms of the right to freedom of religion – would be, if UNDRIP Article 25 was actually heeded. The article takes into account all the world-making implications inherent in the concept of 'indigenous religion:'

> Indigenous peoples have the right to maintain and strengthen their distinctive spiritual relationship with their traditionally owned or otherwise occupied and used lands, territories, waters and coastal seas and other resources and to uphold their responsibilities to future generations in this regard (DRIPS United Nations Declaration on the Rights of Indigenous Peoples, 2007: 10).

A case most congruent with UNDRIP Article 25 is the juridification of the hybrid Hindu-Balinese cosmology in the context of the Indonesian governance reform that followed the demise of ex-President Suharto's 'New Order' regime in the wake of the Asia Crisis of 1997–1998. While Indonesia paid more attention to 'indigenous rights' in its constitutional amendments from 1999–2002 and also signed UNDRIP (Suryani, 2016: 101), it continues to reject the term 'indigenous peoples' for the respective groups in its territory, arguing that the vast majority of the country's population would also be indigenous. The Indonesian government uses the term 'customary law community,' or *masyarakat hukum adat*, instead (Ramstedt, 2017: 56–60).

Balinese religious and political leaders joined the indigenous rights movement in the early 1990s, when the Indonesian central government started to convert more and more patches of Balinese land into tourism development zones, which involved forced displacement of local fishing communities. Moreover, like other 'indigenous people' in the archipelago, the Balinese have been considered 'animists' and practitioners of 'ancestor worship' by the predominantly Muslim Indonesian mainstream society (Ramstedt, 2014: 54). In order to discourage further in-migration by Muslim Indonesians from other islands and further influx of foreign investment that would continue to alienate sacred communal land as well as valuable rice paddies, the Balinese enacted an array of new provincial regulations that revitalized local customary law communities at the village level in accordance with local spiritual cosmologies. Newly endowed with a significant degree of administrative, fiscal and religious autonomy, these new village jurisdictions are grounded in modified customary law institutions. As new criteria for local citizenship were established, there arose a strong and discriminatory distinction between indigenous and non-native members of village communities. This distinction has not only undermined the constitutional provision that grants every Indonesian equal citizenship rights, but it has also infringed upon several human rights standards, particularly gender equality and the right to freedom of religion. Infringements on the latter for instance consist in the requirement for all residents of Balinese villages to participate financially and actively in the performance of numerous recurrent religious rituals that are geared to placate hostile nature and ancestor spirits, and thus to protect local communities against disaster, illness and loss. All residents are strongly encouraged, if not forced, to do so, regardless of their professed religion and conviction (Ramstedt, 2013: 111, 118–119).

Conclusion

The increasing global support for the indigenous rights movement has resulted in a growing awareness for the vulnerability of indigenous spiritual traditions. However, when indigenous cosmologies are translated into national law, they are pressed into a complex legal system of a modern state, which espouses unambiguous and fixed definitions and distinctions, as well as rigorously standardized procedures. The original range of interpretive possibilities inherent in indigenous cosmologies has thus been considerably narrowed. The Balinese case has clearly shown that the juridification of indigenous beliefs and practices may entail the loss of citizenship rights for non-indigenous residents in indigenous jurisdictions, which is aggravated by the fact that the new rigidity, which juridification commonly bestows on juridified indigenous beliefs and practices, is no longer counterbalanced by more lenient or flexible interpretations. The juridification of indigenous traditions therefore needs to be balanced by the translation of human rights – including the individual right to freedom of and from religion – into the respective local law. As a counterbalance to revitalized traditionalist worldviews, the modern quality inherent in contemporary human rights, including the right to freedom of religion, is for certain individuals undoubtedly quite liberating. Again, the individual right to freedom of religion does not lend itself to further the emancipation of indigenous spiritualities. It rather remains a safeguard against the 'tyranny of the majority,' in our Balinese case the majority of privileged local citizens.

Further reading

Bauman, C., 2013. Hindu-Christian conflict in India: Globalization, conversion, and the coterminal castes and tribes. *Journal Asian Studies*. 72(3), 633.

References

AIL (American Indian Law). n.d. Cornell Law School, Legal Information Institute. Available from: <https://www.law.cornell.edu/wex/american_indian_law>.

Anghie, A., 2004. *Imperialism, Sovereignty and the Making of International Law.* Cambridge University Press.

ANI Protection Act (Andaman and Nicobar Islands Protection of Aboriginal Tribes Regulation, and Rules Framed Thereunder), 1956. Office of the Chief Commissioner. Available from:<http://www.and.nic.in/archives/C_Charter/Dir_tw/2012/PAT1956.pdf>.

Aritonang, J.S., Steenbrink, K., 2008. *A History of Christianity in Indonesia*. Brill.

Bal, M., 2002. *Travelling Concepts in the Humanities*. University of Toronto Press.

Benthall, J., 1995. Missionaries and human rights. *Anthropology Today* 11(1), 1.

Blackford, R., 2012. *Freedom of Religion and the Secular State*. Wiley-Blackwell.

Brock, P., 2005. Introduction. In: Brock, P. (Ed.), *Indigenous Peoples and Religious Change*. Brill, p. 1.

Bulgakova, T., Sundström, O., 2017. Repression of Shamans and Shamanism in Khabarovsk Krai: 1920s to the early 1950s. In: Kotljarchuk, A., Sundström, O. (Eds.), *Ethnic and Religious Minorities in Stalin's Soviet Union: New Dimensions of Research*. Södertörn University (Södertörn Academic Studies 72), p. 225.

Chavez, N. 2018. Indian authorities struggle to retrieve US missionary feared killed on a remote island. *CNN*. 26 November. Available from: <https://edition.cnn.com/2018/11/25/asia/missionary-john-chau-north-sentinel-island-sentinelese/index.html>.

Chesterman, J., Galligan, B., 1997. *Citizens Without Rights: Aborigines and Australian Citizenship*. Cambridge University Press.

Cohen, E., 2010. Anthropology of knowledge. *Journal Royal Anthropological Institute*. 16(s1), S193.

CoI (Census of India), 2011. District Census Handbook, Part A: South Andaman District, North & Middle Andaman District and Nicobars District. Directorate of Census Operations.

ConRussFed (The Constitution of the Russian Federation). 1993. Available from: <http://www.mid.ru/en/foreign_policy/official_documents/-/asset_publisher/CptICkB6BZ29/content/id/571508>.

Corderoy, J., 2018. Traumatic history of isolated tribe who killed American missionary. *News Corp Australia Network*. 25 November. Available from:<https://www.news.com.au/world/asia/traumatic-history-of-isolated-tribe-who-killed-american-missionary/news-story/75120b92130bcea44642156bffd60059>.

DRIPS (United Nations Declaration on the Rights of Indigenous Peoples), 2007. United Nations. Available from: <https://www.un.org/esa/socdev/unpfii/documents/DRIPS_en.pdf>.

Gluck, C., 2009. Words in motion. In: Gluck, C., Lowenhaupt Tsing, A. (Eds.), *Words in Motion: Towards a Global Lexicon*. Duke University Press, p. 3.

Goodale, M., 2006. Reclaiming modernity: Indigenous cosmopolitanism and the coming of the second revolution in Bolivia. *American Ethnologist*. 33(4), 634.

Goulet, J.-G.A., 1998. *Ways of Knowing: Experience, Knowledge, and Power among the Dene Tha*. University of Nebraska Press.

GUNM (Growth in United Nations Membership, 1945-present), n.d. United Nations. Available from:<https://www.un.org/en/sections/member-states/growth-united-nations-membership-1945-present/index.html>.

Hall, R.A., 1995. *Fighters from the Fringe: Aborigines and Torres Strait Islanders Recall the Second World War*. Aboriginal Studies Press.

Hilleary, C., 2017. US government decides which are, are not, legitimate native American tribes. *Voice of America (VOA) Public Relations*. Available from: <https://www.voanews.com/a/us-government-decides-which-are-are-not-legitimate-native-american-tribes/3834462.html>.

Hobsbawm, E., 1983. Introduction: Inventing traditions. In: Hobsbawm, E., Ranger, T. (Eds.), *The Invention of Tradition*. Cambridge University Press, p. 1.

ILO (International Labour Organization), 2007. *The ILO at a Glance*. International Labour Office, Department of Communication and Public Information.

ILO C107 (C107 – Indigenous and Tribal Populations Convention (No. 107)), 1957. International Labour Organization. Available from: <https://www.ilo.org/dyn/normlex/en/f?p=NORMLEXPUB:12100:0::NO::P12100_ILO_CODE:C107>.

ILO C169 (C169 – Indigenous and Tribal Populations Convention (No. 169)), 1989. International Labour Organization. Available from: <https://www.ilo.org/dyn/normlex/en/f?p=NORMLEXPUB:12100:0::NO::P12100_ILO_CODE:C169>.

Irwin, L., 1997. Freedom, law, and prophecy: A brief history of native American religious resistance. *American Indian Quarterly*. 21(1), 35.

Ivashchenko, Y., 2017. Where have the Amur region's Shamans gone?. In: Kotljarchuk, A., Sundström, O. (Eds.), *Ethnic and Religious Minorities in Stalin's Soviet Union: New Dimensions of Research*. Södertörn University (Södertörn Academic Studies 72), p. 263.

Jacobs, M.D., 2009. *White Mother to a Dark Race: Settler Colonialism, Maternalism, and the Removal of Indigenous Children in the American West and Australia*. University of Nebraska Press, pp. 1880–1940.

Keane, W., 1996. Materialism, missionaries, and modern subjects in colonial Indonesia. In: van der Veer, P. (Ed.), *Conversion to Modernities: The Globalization of Christianity*. Routledge, p. 137.

Kotljarchuk, A., 2017. Propaganda of hatred and the great terror: A Nordic approach. In: Kotljarchuk, A., Sundström, O. (Eds.), *Ethnic and Religious Minorities in Stalin's Soviet Union: New Dimensions of Research*. Södertörn University (Södertörn Academic Studies 72), p. 89.

Kotljarchuk, A., Sundström, O., 2017. Introduction: The problem of ethnic and religious minorities in Stalin's Soviet Union. In: Kotljarchuk, A., Sundström, O. (Eds.), *Ethnic and Religious Minorities in Stalin's Soviet Union: New Dimensions of Research*. Södertörn University (Södertörn Academic Studies 72), p. 15.

Kuppe, R., 2009. Religious freedom law and the protection of sacred sites. In: Kirsch, T.G., Turner, B. (Eds.), *Permutation of Order: Religion and Law as Contested Sovereignties*. Ashgate, p. 49.

Kusber, J., 2016. Sibiryaks and indigenous peoples: Indigeneity in nineteenth- and twentieth century Siberian discourse. In: Banerjee, M. (Ed.), *Comparative Indigenous Studies*. Universitätsverlag Winter, p. 241.

Lawrence, B., 2004. *'Real' Indians and Others: Mixed-Blood Urban Native Peoples and Indigenous Nationhood*. University of Nebraska Press.

Lefebure, L.D., 2013. Catholics on the margin in India. *Journal Dialogue Culture*. 2(1), 33.

Loenhoff, J., 2011. Tacit knowledge in intercultural communication. *Communication Studies*. 20(1), 57.

Lowenhaupt Tsing, A., 2009. Worlds in motion. In: Gluck, C., Lowenhaupt Tsing, A. (Eds.), *Words in Motion: Towards a Global Lexicon*. Duke University Press, p. 11.

Mbembe, A., 2001. *On the Postcolony*. University of California Press.

NARF (Native American Rights Fund), 1979. 'We also have a religion' – The American Indian religious freedom act and the religious freedom project of the Native American rights funds. *Announcements.* Winter.
Ngô, T.T.T., 2016. *The New Way: Protestantism and the Hmong in Vietnam.* University of Washington Press.
Niezen, 2009. *The Rediscovered Self: Indigenous Identity and Cultural Justice.* McGill-Queens University Press, Montreal.
Quijada, J.B., Stephen, E., 2015. Performing 'culture': Diverse audiences at the International Shamans' Conference and Tailgan om Ol'khon Island. *Études mongoles et sibériennes, centrasiatiques et tibétaines* 46, 1.
Quijada, J.B., Graber., K.E., Stephen, E., 2015. Finding 'their own': Revitalizing Buryat culture through Shamanic practices in Ulan-Ude. *Problems Post-Communism.* 62, 258.
Rajagopal, B., 2006. Counter-hegemonic international law: Rethinking human rights and development as a third world strategy. *Third World Quarterly.* 27(5), 767.
Ramstedt, M., 2013. Religion and disputes in Bali's new village jurisdictions. In: von Benda-Beckmann, F., von Benda-Beckmann, K., Ramstedt, M., Turner, B. (Eds.), *Religion in Disputes: Pervasiveness of Religious Normativity in Disputing Processes.* Palgrave Macmillan, p. 111.
Ramstedt, M., 2014. Converging ontologies, flattening of time – discordant temporalities and feeling rules in Bali's new village jurisdictions. In: Stodulka, T., Röttger-Rössler, B. (Eds.), *Feelings at the Margins: Dealing with Violence, Stigma and Isolation in Indonesia.* Campus, p. 53.
Ramstedt, M., 2017. Cultural translation, traveling law, and the transposition of indigenous rights to Indonesian contexts. *Translation Translanguaging Multilingual Contexts* 3(1), 47.
Rathgeber, T., 2013. Einführung in die ILO 169 und internationaler Überblick. In: Häfner, D., Laschewski, L., (Eds.). *DieRechte indigener Völker an natürlichen Ressourcen und die Sorben/Wenden.* Cottbus: BTUCottbus-Senftenberg, p. 5.
Ratifications of C107 (Ratifications of C107 – Indigenous and Tribal Populations Convention, 1957 (No. 107)), 1996-2107. International Labour Organization. Available from: <https://www.ilo.org/dyn/normlex/en/f?p=1000:11300:0::NO:11300:P11300_INSTRUMENT_ID:312252>.
Ratifications of C169 (Ratifications of C169 – Indigenous and Tribal Populations Convention , 1989 (No. 169)), 1989. *International Labour Organization.* Available from: <https://www.ilo.org/dyn/normlex/en/f?p=1000:11300:0::NO:11300:P11300_INSTRUMENT_ID:312314>.
Rollings, W.H., 2004. Citizenship and suffrage: The Native American struggle for civil rights in the American West, 1830-1965. *Nevada Law Journal.* 5, 126.
Rooden, P. van, 1996. Nineteenth-century representations of missionary conversion and the transformation of Western Christianity. In: van der Veer, P. (Ed.), *Conversion to Modernities: The Globalization of Christianity.* Routledge, p. 65.
Sequoyah vs. Tennessee Valley Authority) Sequoyah v. Tennessee Valley Authority, 480 F.Supp. 608. (E. D. Tenn.1979). Available from https://law.justia.com/cases/federal/district-courts/FSupp/480/608/1531244.
Smith, A., 2009. *Indigenous peoples and boarding schools: A comparative study (E/C.19/2009/CRP. 1).* Prepared for the Eighth Session of the Permanent Forum on Indigenous Issues in New York. 18–29 May. Available from: https://www.un.org/esa/socdev/unpfii/documents/E_C_19_2009_crp1.pdf
Stavenhagen, R., 2013. *The Emergence of Indigenous Peoples.* Springer.
Suryani, D., 2016. Structural violation of indigenous human rights in Indonesia: A case study of Merauke integrated food and energy estate (MIFEE) in Papua. *Jurnal Masyarakat Budaya.* 18(1), 97.
Thawnghmung, A.M., 2011. *Beyond Armed Resistance: Ethnonationalist Policies in Burma (Myanmar).* East-West Center.
Toulouze, E., 2017. A long great ethnic terror in the Volga region: A war before the war. In: Kotljarchuk, A., Sundström, O. (Eds.), *Ethnic and Religious Minorities in Stalin's Soviet Union: New Dimensions of Research.* Södertörn University (Södertörn Academic Studies 72), p. 153.
Toulouze, E., Vallikivi, L., Leete, A., 2017. The cultural bases in the north: Sovietisation and indigenous resistance. In: Kotljarchuk, A., Sundström, O. (Eds.), *Ethnic and Religious Minorities in Stalin's Soviet Union: New Dimensions of Research.* Södertörn University (Södertörn Academic Studies 72), p. 199.
Trigg, R., 2012. *Equality, Freedom, and Religion.* Oxford University Press.
UDHR (Universal Declaration of Human Rights), 2015. United Nations. Available from https://www.un.org/en/udhrbook/pdf/udhr_booklet_en_web.pdf.

UDHR-HoD (Universal Declaration of Human Rights: History of the Document), n.d. United Nations. Available from: <https://www.un.org/en/sections/universal-declaration/history-document/index.html>.
van der Veer, P. (Ed.), 1996. Introduction. In: *Conversion to Modernities: The Globalization of Christianity*. Routledge, p. 1.
Wierucka, A., 2013. Modern forms of Buryat Shaman activity on the Olkhon Island. *Anthropological Notebooks*. 19(3), 101.

PART V

The dynamics of the right to freedom of religion or belief

18

The organic unity of human rights and the place of freedom of religion or belief: Challenge and response

David Little

Challenge

In discussing the findings of their book, *The Price of Freedom Denied: Religious Persecution and Conflict in the Twenty-First Century*, Brian Grim and Roger Finke emphasize the interconnection of religious freedom and other human rights:

> Although our focus has been on religious freedoms, these freedoms are embedded within a larger bundle of civil liberties … Our analysis of the most recent data … graphically displays the relationships that religious freedoms and the well-being of residents in various countries. The association between religious freedoms and other civil liberties, press freedoms, and political freedoms are especially striking. The highly significant and strong correlations (exceeding 0.6) suggest that the freedoms are closely intertwined.[1]

Grim and Finke are right to urge further consideration of how the right to religious freedom is related to other human rights. Many advocates have long believed that the wide array of civil and political rights (including the right to religious freedom), as well as economic, social, and cultural rights contained in the international human rights documents, form an indivisible whole.[2]

However, such beliefs have been, and continue to be, vigorously challenged. For one thing, a currently influential group of scholars severely doubt that the right to religious freedom, as expressed in the documents, has a proper place in the human rights corpus because it favors the

---

1 Grim and Finke, 2011: 205, 210. The authors make clear that the terms of reference for their reflections on religious freedom and other 'civil liberties, press freedoms, and political freedoms,' are international human rights standards (see 26–27, 206).

2 Vienna Declaration, adopted 25 June 1993, by the World Conference on Human Rights, declares that 'All human rights are universal, indivisible and interdependent and interrelated' (part I, para. 5).

beliefs and interests of some groups over others, and thus works against, rather than for, the cause of human rights. Particularly pertinent here is the work of Elizabeth Shakman Hurd in *Beyond Religious Freedom: The New Global Politics of Religion* (2015), together with a volume, *Politics of Religious Freedom*, edited by Hurd and three colleagues (Sullivan et al., 2015).

These scholars complain that existing formulations of Article 18 of the Universal Declaration of Human Rights (UDHR) and the International Covenant on Civil and Political Rights (ICCPR) – guaranteeing the right 'to have or to adopt a religion or belief of [one's] choice' – are the product of a highly parochial cultural and religious tradition, namely, Western European and American Protestant Christianity, and, accordingly, do not apply universally, as human rights terms are supposed to do. Not all religious expression takes the form of rationalized doctrine or principle, nor is it regarded as institutionally segregated or the product of personal choice tied to an idea of individual conscience, as in the case of Protestant Christianity. Much religion the world over is of the 'lived' variety, meaning it is naturally acquired in the same way a native language is, and is nondoctrinaire, flexible in nature, loosely organized, and expresses itself in ceremony and ritual that is often interwoven in the web of daily life. For Hurd and her colleagues, all this means that the official version of the right to religious freedom is 'impossible' to apply legally because it represents a partial and distorted version of how the complex reality of religion, in its manifold forms, is actually expressed.

Although not mentioned by these scholars, another related objection to the language of Article 18 pertains to the words, 'freedom to change [one's] religion or belief.' Controversy concerning that language was probably the most contentious issue confronted in the drafting of Article 18, and disagreement over it has, subsequently, not abated. The Saudi delegate to the drafting committee, Jamil al'Barudi, offered inconsistent complaints about the language (discussed in Gunn, 2020, 149–152). For one thing, he thought it unnecessary, since the right to reject a religion or belief is implicit in the very idea of the freedom of belief. But he also predicted, in a much more contrarian spirit, that Muslim majority countries would oppose such language undoubtedly because of the powerful influence of the religious objections of Islamic jurists to any suggestion of a legal right to leave Islam.[3] What is more, al'Barudi was joined by the Egyptian delegate, Wahid Fikry Raafat, in opposing the language because of a concern about the disruptive societal effects of Christian missionaries, mainly their efforts to try to convert to their own beliefs the masses of the population of the Orient. The implicit complaint that the language about freedom to change religion seriously threatens social stability and communal loyalty by permitting Christians and other missionaries to engage in proselytism has also

3 John Kelsay, in an email comment clarifying his claim that for al'Barudi 'the right to change one's religion, at least for Muslims, was not recognized by Islamic law' (1988: 36). Kelsay's view is that jurisprudential objections assuredly underlay al'Barudi's prediction regarding Muslim opposition to the right to change religion. Kelsay states that standard historical Sunni jurisprudence cites the wording of Qur'an 2:256, appearing to limit the celebrated statement about 'no compulsion in religion' to Muslim converts, as a basis for not applying the rule to apostates. According to that interpretation, apostates are not exempt from compulsion. Kelsay also emphasizes the probable influence of the Wahhabi predilections of the Saudi state on al'Barudi's thinking about the disruptive social effects of the freedom to change religion, a major theme in Wahhabi theology (38–41). Kelsay's interpretation is reinforced by a comment by al'Barudi reported in Schabas, 2013: Vol. 3, 2505: al'Barudi inquires whether the Muslim peoples of North Africa and other French territories had been consulted before the words favoring the freedom to change religion had been accepted. Were the colonial powers, he asks, 'not afraid of offending the religious beliefs of their Muslim subjects by imposing [those words] on them?' Morsink adds that the vote in the drafting committee to retain language concerning the freedom to change religion was accomplished 'over the strong objections of Muslim delegations led by Saudi Arabia to abstain in the final vote on the Declaration,' which only Saudi Arabia wound up doing, proving how profoundly committed it was to opposing the freedom to change religion (see Morsink, 1999: 261–262).

been embraced by representatives of 'ascribed religions' like Judaism, Hinduism, and many indigenous religions, for which membership depends largely on birth (Casanova, 2010: 15–16; see also Mutua, 1996). 'The human rights corpus should outlaw those forms of proselytization used in Africa, because their purpose and effect have been the dehumanization of an entire race of people,' meaning, most importantly, adherents of African indigenous religions (Mutua, 1996: 440).

The deleterious practical consequences of the language and interpretation of Article 18 of the UDHR cited by the opponents of the freedom to change religion overlap with the more general criticisms. 'To understand the contested historical genealogy of the concept of religious liberty, we believe it is important to grasp the ways in which this seemingly obvious and neutral right has yielded mutually contradictory and often discriminatory results' (Sullivan et al., 2015: 2). Hurd elaborates the point by charging that 'religious freedom elites' – namely, national and international government officials, along with academics, lawyers, and members of nongovernmental groups, who advocate and implement religious freedom standards around the world – 'risk exacerbating the [very] social tensions, forms of discrimination, and inter-communal discord' the effort is supposed to alleviate (Hurd, 2015: 64). They do this by rendering 'invisible less established religions, collective ways of life, and modes of being and belonging that do not qualify as "religious" [in the accepted sense]. Nontraditional religions, unprotected religions, and nonreligious [minorities] are pushed into the wings' (Hurd, 2015: 49–50). Acting in that way, she claims, exacts serious 'costs in human dignity' and amounts to a 'modern attempt at mind control' (Sullivan et al., 2015: 55).

But the challenge to the indivisibility of human rights is still greater. For a long time, considerable skepticism has existed about the possibility of ever establishing a unified theory of human rights. Not only does the right to religious freedom not fit together with other rights, but the whole corpus of human rights itself lacks any principled coherence. As early as 1949, Jacques Maritain, a member of a group of experts working on human rights under UNESCO auspices, summarized doubts over finding a common justification: 'We agree about the rights but on the condition that no one asks us why' (cited in Glendon, 2001: 77).

More recently, human rights scholars such as Michael Ignatieff have argued that no unifying theory is needed or possible since human rights are not intended to serve as 'an ultimate trump card in moral argument' or 'for the proclamation and enactment of eternal verities.' Rather, they are designed 'for the adjudication of conflict,' and therefore constitute a quite prosaic, down-to-earth language of political 'trade-offs and compromises' (Ignatieff, 2001: 20, 84). Other scholars, like Samuel Moyn in *The Last Utopia: Human Rights in History*, take a more radical view. Moyn claims that human rights language as formulated in the late 1940s was intrinsically incoherent and impractical. It consisted of words that were 'victims of their own vagueness' and 'empty vessel[s] that could be filled by a wide variety of different conceptions.' Contrary to popular opinion, the language was not composed in reference to Nazi atrocities in the Holocaust and elsewhere. It took on that connotation only years later and was thus thoroughly 'utopian' in its origins for being unrelated to real-world problems.[4]

Although Charles Beitz, in an acclaimed volume, *The Idea of Human Rights*, does not forswear the possibility of a normative theory of human rights, he rejects all unitary proposals, according to which the authority of human rights is based on 'a single, more basic value or interest. There is no clear reason to hold that human rights should be explicable in terms of a single master value. Perhaps the pressure to regard them in this way derives from a desire to see them all as standards of

4 Moyn, 2010: 7, 51, 64, 83, 89. For a further elaboration of that line of argument, see Moyn's more recent book (2015) and Posner, 2014.

the same generic kind. But … an account of their normativity need not be embarrassed to appeal to a variety of distinct justifying considerations' (Beitz, 2009: 128, 138).

While it is no doubt possible to connect the various human rights provisions enumerated, say, in the Universal Declaration of Human Rights (UDHR) without referring to a 'single master value,' it does seem reasonable to infer, as Beitz does, that affirming such a value would lead to conceiving of the different provisions as being of 'the same generic kind.' Conversely, positing, with Beitz, 'distinct justifying considerations,' or, with Ignatieff and Moyn, no common justifying considerations at all, would appear to foster intense skepticism as to whether human rights provisions are closely bound together by some set of generic characteristics.

It is worth recalling that debates about the coherence of the various human rights standards laid out in the UDHR go back to the drafting period of the later 1940s. Johannes Morsink, in his definitive account of the legislative history of the UDHR, discusses at length disagreements over the 'organic unity of the document,' particularly in regard to the relationship between the so-called 'old' and 'new' human rights, namely, civil and political rights and economic, social, and cultural rights, both of which were included in the final version of the UDHR (see Morsink, 1999: 222–238). It must be added, of course, that the two sets of rights were later separated into two different international human rights treaties that entered into force in 1976: the ICCPR and the International Covenant on Economic, Social, and Cultural Rights (ICESCR). The separation made it possible for countries such as China and the United States to ratify one and not the other and thereby posed again the question of the coherence of the two sets of rights.[5]

Response

The position to be developed in what follows is that the foregoing claims are mainly mistaken. The first step in the response is to try to show that contrary to the various assertions just sketched there is a plausible theory that explains and justifies the 'organic unity' of the UDHR, as well as of the two covenants – the ICCPR and the ICESCR – that elaborate its contents and reinforce its legal authority. The second step is to try to show how the right to religious freedom fits in as part of that unity, and in the process to indicate why the charges against it are largely unfounded.

The best place to start is to point out that the original language of human rights should in fact be seen as an ardent moral and legal reaction against fascist, and especially Nazi, behavior during the World War II period.[6] Two arresting passages set beside each other in the Preamble to the UDHR epitomize what the various rights enumerated in the UDHR, and later developed and elaborated in the ICCPR and ICESCR, all have in common:

> *Whereas* disregard and contempt for human rights have resulted in barbarous acts which have outraged the conscience of [humankind],[7] and the advent of a world in

5 See Steiner and Alston, 2000: 137–320 for a detailed discussion of the process of development from the UDHR (1948) to the two treaties, the ICCPR and ICESCR (1977). China has ratified the ICESCR, but not the ICCPR. For the United States, the reverse is true.

6 This is the convincing interpretation put forward by Morsink, 1992: esp. chapter 2 ('World War II as Catalyst'). Morsink's evidence conclusively refutes Moyn's denials, mentioned above, that human rights language was composed in response to the persecution of the Jews by the Nazis. See Little, 2015: chapter 2. Morsink has just published a new book further substantiating his claims (Morsink 2019).

7 In keeping with the prevailing, but inconsistently applied, opinions among the drafters concerning the difficulty with gender-specific language, the words 'mankind' in the first passage and 'if man is' in the second should be changed as proposed. See Lash, 1972: 70, for an important discussion of those attitudes.

which human beings shall enjoy freedom of speech and belief and freedom from fear and want has been proclaimed as the highest aspiration of the common people,

Whereas it is essential, if [all human beings][7] are not to be compelled to have recourse, as a last resort, to rebellion against tyranny and oppression, that human rights should be protected by the rule of law,

The passages make clear that human rights are to be understood in response to 'tyranny and oppression,' taken to mean two aspects of the same thing: the 'cruel and arbitrary exercise of power or control,'[8] as manifested in a shocking and extensive record of 'barbarous acts.' The real-world fascist personification of tyranny and oppression, with relentless 'disregard and contempt for human rights,' was not in doubt to the drafters of those passages, nor was the conviction that, *precisely in reaction to the consistent practice of gross violations*, 'a world made new'[9] by means of the acceptance and advancement of human rights – summarized in the first passage as freedom of speech and belief and freedom from fear and want – had become 'the highest aspiration of the common people.'

More specifically, the passages are about the legitimate and illegitimate use of force. By acknowledging that under tyranny and oppression, human beings might see fit to take up arms in rebellion, the second passage presupposes that such actions would be justified as a *legitimate* use of force – undertaken 'as a last resort' – in response to an *illegitimate* use of force – one that is 'cruel and arbitrary' – by tyrants and oppressors.[10] It further suggests that the measure most appropriate for preventing such an occurrence is the establishment of 'the rule of law,' namely, the suppression of arbitrary force by subordinating the use of force to well-defined and established laws, impartially administered and enforced, and including the protection of human rights.[11]

The right of self-defense as morally foundational

Assumed here is the idea of subjective rights, meaning that all individuals, simply as human beings, possess an entitlement to claim (or have claimed for them) a certain performance or forbearance under threat of sanction for noncompliance. Also assumed are inferred duties to respect rights. In the second passage, the key reference is to the *right of self-defense*, to be defined as the right to use reasonable or defensive force to protect oneself or others against arbitrary force, where *arbitrary force* means (at a minimum) the intentional infliction of death, impairment, severe pain/suffering, or involuntary confinement primarily for self-serving or unfounded reasons. As mentioned, the relevant sanction available to an individual or group exercising the right of self-defense against such a threat is the use of force under certain strict conditions – necessity, imminence,

8 Meaning of 'tyranny' (2002); one meaning of 'oppression' is very close: 'unjust or cruel exercise of authority or power.'

9 A favorite phrase of Eleanor Roosevelt's, celebrated by Glendon, 2001.

10 See Morsink, 1999: 307–312. I disagree with the interpretation of Morsink's account of the debate by Hessbruegge, 2017: 81 and 327–328.

11 My definition of 'rule of law' reconstructed from several available definitions to reflect what is an accurate understanding of the intended meaning of those terms as they appear in our second passage from the Preamble to the UDHR.

proportionality, and right intention[12] – conditions that spell out the meaning of 'reasonable or defensive force.' The imposition of conditions indicates that force may be used only if no less violent means are available to thwart an unwarranted attack. They are indispensable for preventing a use of force from itself becoming an arbitrary act.

The term *arbitrary force* needs to be broadened to include features also typically exhibited by tyrants and oppressors, and of special pertinence to the World War II setting against which human rights language was composed and adopted. The broader version may be called *arbitrary deprivation/neglect*, meaning enforcing laws and policies aimed at withholding or negligently disregarding the means necessary for basic human survival primarily for self-serving or unfounded reasons. The means in question would include the opportunity to make a living and have adequate sustenance, housing, clothing, health care, education, and assistance 'in the event of unemployment, sickness, disability, widowhood, old age or other lack of livelihood in circumstances beyond [one's] control.'[13] If means like these are available and are forcibly withheld or disregarded primarily for self-serving or unfounded reasons, such actions are the proper target of resistance, including the use of defensive force.

The clear implication of the two passages, so understood, is that the right of self-defense is *morally foundational* to the whole system of human rights. Words used in the passages, such as 'contempt for,' 'barbarous acts,' 'outraged the conscience of humankind,' 'tyranny,' and 'oppression,' are unquestionably moral utterances in the sense that they presuppose fundamental standards by which to condemn what is wrong and bad, and to justify what is right and good as regards protecting and supporting basic human welfare.[14] Accordingly, arbitrary force, expanded to include arbitrary deprivation/neglect, is believed to be morally condemnable, and efforts and means, including the use of defensive force, to protect against them to be morally justifiable.

The important point is that force may be justified only by a certain set of reasons. Given the universally unwanted effects of force – death, impairment, severe pain/suffering, and involuntary confinement, whether inflicted directly or as the result of withholding or ignoring the means to avert them – everyone everywhere has a presumed good reason to avoid or resist those effects. Therefore, if force is ever to be used, very much better overriding reasons must be offered. 'Because I want to' or 'because it gives me pleasure' or 'because it serves my interest' are *no reasons at all*. Neither, obviously, are unfounded reasons, and prevaricating or offering mistaken claims about the use of force is particularly egregious since so much is at stake.

Giving justifying reasons presupposes a set of shared rational standards sensitive to the common interests of all parties involved and has as its objective bringing about consensual agreement among the parties. To refer primarily to one's own interest, or to tell lies or mislead, in support of using force is blatantly offensive because the references in no way address the severely unwanted effects of the act upon the victim; such actions leave the victim's damaged or deprived condition altogether out of account, as well as rule out any opportunity for informed dissent or consent. Accordingly, such a statement could not possibly be a justification. In that respect, arbitrary force overlaps with the idea of cruelty, which means callous indifference to or pleasure in causing pain and suffering. It need

12 See Fletcher, 1988: 18–29. For a comparable discussion of the conditions on the right of self-defense, see Hessbruegge, 2017: 65–68.

13 Article 25 of UDHR.

14 Moral language is taken to mean statements addressing matters of human welfare that are held to be of great importance and to be based on standards of justification (a variation of the formulation in Little, 2015: 34).

hardly be mentioned that what has just been described is very close to Nazi and other fascist practice during the World War II period.[15]

Conversely, the right of self-defense is morally justifiable since good reasons can be given in its support, namely the great value of acting in a measured way to resist and subdue a '*summum malum*': the exercise of arbitrary force, whether as inflicting death, impairment, severe pain/ suffering, or involuntary confinement directly, or as withholding or ignoring provisions for basic human survival.[16]

However, the second passage also implies a profound complication. No matter how morally justified armed rebellion in self-defense against tyranny and oppression might be, it is something, if possible, to be avoided. That is because of the precariousness of the idea. On the one hand, self-defense against arbitrary force, undertaken under strict limits, is morally justified. On the other hand, if practiced widely and regularly, its exercise, ironically, would likely increase the incidence of arbitrary force, since defenders take the law into their own hands. They become their own judges, juries, and enforcement officers in a 'state of nature,' typically subject to passion and fear and therefore to conditions that are altogether unconducive to judicious and measured (nonarbitrary) action.

According to the second passage, the complication is resolved by subjecting the right of self-defense to governmental control based on the rule of law and the protection of human rights. Monopolizing force in accord with established laws, fairly administered by impartial legislative, judicial, and enforcement officials, and aimed at protecting individual citizens against acts of arbitrary force constitutes an enormous public good. It represents a surer guarantee of the personal security and welfare of all citizens than allowing individuals to be laws unto themselves. In acknowledgment of the moral primacy of the right of self-defense, rule-of-law governments do continue to permit a remarkable, if limited, exception to their authority. Citizens retain the right to defend themselves, forcibly if necessary, in the face of threats of arbitrary force where the police cannot protect them, though the government still reserves to itself final authority to determine whether such acts are carried out within the proper bounds of defensive force.

15 Hitler's role, as he saw it, was not to convince, but to mobilize his followers by achieving submission to his will through any utterance or action necessary. '[Hitler's] twelve years' dictatorship was barren of all ideas save one – the further extension of his own power and that of the nation with which he had identified himself … Hitler constantly exalted force over the power of ideas and delighted to prove that men were governed by cupidity, fear, and their baser passions. The sole theme of the Nazi revolution was domination, dressed up as the doctrine of race ... What Hitler constantly aimed at was arbitrary power' (Bullock, 1964: 206, 806). 'The dissolution of conventional forms of government was accelerated by Hitler's tendency to appoint special agents to take care of what he considered the most urgent tasks. As a rule, they were responsible neither to the party nor to the government administration, but rather only to Hitler personally. Their authority was based solely on the Fuhrer's faith in them' (Ullrich, 2016: 581). '[T]he rightness of fascism does not depend on the truth of any of the propositions advanced in its name. Fascism is 'true' insofar as it helps fulfill the destiny of the chosen race or people or blood, locked with other peoples in a Darwinian struggle, and not in the light of some abstract and universal reason' (Paxton, 2004: 16). Moreover, Hitler saw no problem in falsifying his reasons for invading other countries, as he did regularly. 'The invasion of Belgium, Holland, and Luxembourg [by Nazi forces] was entirely without justification. It was … made without any other consideration than the advancement of the aggressive policies of Germany' (Judgment of the International Military Tribunal for the Trial of German Major War Criminals. London: His Majesty's Stationery Office, 1951).

16 The words 'summum malum' are used by Shklar, 1989: 29. Shklar means by the term 'arbitrary, unexpected, unnecessary, and unlicensed acts of force and by habitual and pervasive acts of cruelty and torture performed by military, paramilitary, and police agents in any regime.' We would expand the reference to include forcible acts of arbitrary deprivation/neglect.

The crucial implication of the second passage is that governments must be held accountable according to the standards of the rule of law insofar as those standards protect human rights, which is to say, protect the security and welfare of all citizens against the threat of arbitrary force, broadly understood.

Is the right of self-defense a human right?

None of the major international human rights documents specifically lists the right of self-defense as a human right (Hessbruegge, 2017: 78). Furthermore, the drafters of the UDHR moved reference to the right to the Preamble after debating and rejecting a proposal to include it among the articles of the declaration (Morsink, 1999: 307–312). In the debate, there was strong support for recognizing an explicit right of *both* individuals and groups to defend against tyranny and oppression, but the opposition persistently invoked the abiding peril to law and order of endorsing such a right without qualification. Consequently, a compromise was reached. The right of self-defense was affirmed, but in a way that was slightly disguised or 'barely submerged' so as to avoid official encouragement of rebellion (Morsink, 1999: 308).

Still, despite these facts, the right is referred to explicitly in the European Convention of Human Rights (ECHR)[17] and the Statute of the International Criminal Court.[18] More importantly, the personal right of self-defense is 'recognized in all of the world's major legal systems,' and, accordingly, constitutes a binding general principle of international law derived from domestic law (Hessbruegge, 2017: 58–59). Though there are variations in application, the same basic conditions defining a legitimate act of self-defense – necessity, imminence, proportionality, and right intention – 'are found in virtually every legal system in the world.'[19] As such, the right is consistently recognized and applied in human rights jurisprudence affecting private citizens, as well as police and military personnel, around the world (Hessbruegge, 2017: 235–243 and Chapters 4 and 5). In addition, an 'inherent' collective right of self-defense is recognized in Article 51 of the UN Charter, and the conditions of defensive force are obligatory in international humanitarian law.[20]

Superficially, the right of self-defense is not explicitly identified as a human right in the international documents (or in most domestic constitutions) because of the social disorder that could result from officially authorizing it. But the real reason, though not unrelated, is deeper than that. The right of self-defense, whether individual or collective, occupies a unique, if precarious, status. It provides, as we have argued, the moral foundation of the entire human rights corpus; it is not simply one right among many. Just because of its precariousness – its potential for causing social disorder – it can only satisfactorily be secured by proper governmental regulation, namely, by means of a political-legal system dedicated to 'human rights protected by the rule of law.'

Human rights and the right of self-defense

The words in the first passage, 'freedom of speech and belief and freedom from fear and want,' recall the 'four freedoms' famously declared by President Franklin D. Roosevelt on January 6, 1941, and further elaborated on in his 'second Bill of Rights' proposed three years later.

17 See fn. 23 below.

18 Statute of the International Criminal Court, Article 31(1)(c).

19 Fletcher, 1988: 27. Cf. Hessbruegge, 2017: 32, for a similar conclusion.

20 Article 51 of Protocol I of the 1977 Protocols to the Geneva Conventions.

Emphasizing that traditional civil and political rights by themselves 'proved inadequate,' he outlined a set of economic and social rights, supplementary to civil and political rights, as the 'new basis of security and prosperity' 'established for all – regardless of station, race or creed.'[21]

Accordingly, President Roosevelt provided the drafters of the human rights documents with a rhetorical warrant for combining 'old' and 'new' human rights, affirming that, together, they constituted an indispensable bulwark against tyranny and oppression. He thereby set the stage for the moral primacy of the right of self-defense against the forms of arbitrary force represented by the fascist powers operating at the time. To be sure, he perceived the grave danger represented by 'the new order of tyranny' to the 'old' rights that guaranteed civil and political freedoms. Nobody, he said, 'can expect from the dictator's peace ... freedom of expression, or freedom of religion,' and for that reason it was necessary to commit to 'the preservation of civil liberties for all.' At the same time, he called attention to 'the economic and social problems which are the root cause of the social revolution' enveloping the world at the time, and concluded that because 'people who are hungry and out of a job are the stuff of which dictatorships are made,' the 'new' social and economic rights must also be defended with great urgency.[22]

Morsink's account of the provenance of human rights language leaves no doubt that the drafters of the UDHR shared Roosevelt's outlook. The selection and articulation of each of the provisions, both civil/political and social/economic/cultural, can only be understood in light of 'the experience of the war.' Morsink discusses other influences, such as the Cold War, the Western natural rights tradition, and Latin American socialism, but 'none of them match the Holocaust in importance' (Morsink, 1999: 37).

The original human rights corpus, at least the UDHR and the ICCPR, was conceived as an urgent effort to impose stringent restrictions on governments that would prevent the recurrence of the kind of arbitrary injury and arbitrary deprivation/neglect that was practiced by Hitler and other fascists. The ICESCR was a somewhat different story. While the rights it contained were drawn from the UDHR and thus bore the stamp of the World War II period, the interpretation and implementation of that document, for special reasons, would not achieve a comparable level of stringency and urgency until the late 1980s.

Article 4 of the ICCPR declares that even during times of public emergency, consistently invoked by Hitler, the following civil/political rights are 'non-derogable' – not subject to suspension under any conditions: those that prohibit discrimination based on race, color, sex, language, religion, or social origin; extrajudicial killing; torture or 'cruel, inhuman, or degrading treatment or punishment'; enslavement; denials of legal due process; and violations of the freedom of conscience, religion, or belief (though this right, to be discussed presently, is partially subject to limitations)[23]. These provisions represent fundamental protections of the right of self-defense since performing any of the prohibited practices readily allows or directly involves the infliction of death, impairment, severe pain/suffering, or involuntary confinement for primarily self-serving or unfounded reasons.

The rest of the rights in the ICCPR are classified as 'derogable' rights which means two things. One is that they stand as instrumental or conditional protections; rights, for example, like freedom of speech, assembly, and participation in democratic government (Arts. 19–21)

21 See http://www.worldfuturefund.org. See Sunstein, 2004.

22 'Without the consequences of the Great Depression, which hit Germany particularly hard, the [Nazi Party] would never have become a mass movement. And it was [Hitler] who best understood how to articulate and exploit people's desires for a savior who would inject order into chaos, create an ethnic-popular community in place of party squabbling and class warfare and lead the Reich to new greatness' (Ullrich, 2016: 378).

23 Referring, respectively, to Article 4(1) and Articles 6, 7, 8, 11, 15, 16, and 18.

guarantee opportunities to hear, debate, and pass judgment upon a government's reasons for its laws and policies, thereby helping to make sure that the government's use and regulation of force is duly justified.[24] Because of their importance in protecting against the violation of nonderogable rights, instrumental rights such as these 'are the first ones dictators will seek to deny and destroy' (Morsink, 1999: 69).

Secondly, derogable rights may temporarily be suspended, though only under the most extreme and stringent conditions. Only public emergencies or severe threats to national security, public safety, order, or health, or protecting the rights and freedoms of others, can justify suspension. According to Article 4, the reasons for the scope and duration of any suspension of rights during an emergency must be shown to be 'strictly required by the exigencies of the situation … ,' implying both that governments bear a heavy burden of proof, and that any deviations from human rights law must be subject to the conditions of defensive force – necessity, imminence, proportionality, and right intention. Similarly, special limitations that apply to derogable rights must be 'prescribed by law' and consistent with some of the conditions of self-defense; they must be 'necessary to protect public safety, order, health, or morals, or the fundamental freedoms of others,' and 'must be directly related and proportionate to the specific needs on which they are predicated.'[25] Finally, there was a relatively strong monitoring system for holding governments to account.

Despite the fact that the 'new' economic, social, and cultural rights contained in the UDHR were composed against the background of the Nazi record of arbitrary deprivation/neglect, the ICESCR, designed to implement the 'new' rights included in the UDHR, did not contain the same degree of precision and stringency as the ICCPR. There were several problems: a lack of conceptual clarity in the language, seeming permission for extensive governmental discretion in complying with the provisions, 'ambivalence of most governments [involved in the drafting] towards economic, social, and cultural rights *qua* rights,' the lack of a significant body of national legal experience and of academic and nongovernmental attention that was available in regard to the 'old' rights, and a very ineffectual monitoring committee. Unlike the ICCPR, there is no list of nonderogable rights, nor any set of strict requirements regarding the suspension of rights during emergencies or in the name of protecting public safety, health, order, and the rights of others.[26] The shortcomings were partly explained by 'strong ideological undertones [in the drafting] debate' on the part of the opposing leaders of the Cold War (Alston, 1992: 474). By the 1950s, the United States had turned its back on President Roosevelt's vision and 'oppos[ed] the very concept of economic, social, and cultural rights,' and the USSR was worried that intrusive monitoring would threaten its national sovereignty (Alston, 1992: 487).

All this would begin to change with the formation in 1987 of an active and effective expert monitoring committee. The newly constituted committee started doing two things. One was to introduce serious, systematic scrutiny of the reports required of State Parties regarding their compliance with the standards of the ICESCR. The other was to clarify and explicate the normative content of the rights recognized in the Covenant by issuing General Comments that sharpened and elaborated the requirements implied in the document and thereby helped recover something of the original inspiration that animated the inclusion of the 'new' rights in the

---

24 To suggest that derogable rights are justified instrumentally or conditionally in a human rights framework does not exclude that they may also be justified independently on other grounds.

25 United Nations Human Rights Committee General Comment No. 22 (48) (Art. 18), para. 8.

26 Article 4 of the ICESCR is much vaguer in referring to limitations on rights than the corresponding article in the ICCPR.

first place. If rights against arbitrary deprivation/neglect exist, governments duty-bound to uphold them must be held to account.

That can best happen by setting practicable standards that define 'minimum essential levels of each of the rights' 'incumbent upon every State Party,' and accordingly place the burden of proof squarely on the State Parties to demonstrate how their laws and policies meet those minimum standards. For example, General Comment 14, issued in 2003, enumerated a set of 'nonderogable obligations' requisite for complying with Article 12, which guarantees 'the right of everyone to the enjoyment of the highest standard of physical and mental health.' The idea would be that if within the jurisdiction of a State Party any group of citizens is 'deprived of essential foodstuffs, ... essential, primary health care, ...basic shelter and housing, or the most basic forms of education,' the government 'is, *prima facie*, failing to discharge its obligations under the Covenant' (Alston, 1992: 495). The implication is not that governments must themselves directly supply all the requisite goods and services. Private sector arrangements are typically indispensable, up to a point, in enabling citizens to provide for themselves. Governments are, however, ultimately responsible for how well nongovernmental arrangements meet the minimum standards, and for making up the difference where those arrangements fall short. They are also responsible for making remedies available to citizens deprived of their economic, social, and cultural rights.[27]

There is the possibility that not all governments are capable of meeting even the minimum standards and thus may be excused temporarily from the obligations. That is true, incidentally, in regard to both 'old' and 'new' rights. The implementation of civil and political rights entails political, judicial, and law enforcement officials and institutions typically as expensive to provide as the goods and services required for enforcing social, economic, and cultural rights. Even if they are excused, such governments are, of course, bound to show efforts toward compliance. Still, according to the approach taken in this essay, the first concern in the human rights corpus is with those governments that already possess the resources to implement both sets of rights, since the emphasis is on *preventing* the exercise of the arbitrary use of force, either in deliberately inflicting injury or in willfully depriving or neglecting basic survival goods and services. There is another implication of that emphasis, as well. In the interest of advancing the cause of human rights and the rule of law, affluent governments bear a second responsibility, namely, to offer coordinated assistance to those governments incapable of meeting their obligations.[28]

Freedom of religion or belief and the right of self-defense

It is of the utmost importance that the right of freedom of religion or belief was singled out by President Roosevelt in his list of 'four freedoms' and was included as one of the nonderogable rights in Article 4 of the ICCPR. That is because, like the other nonderogable rights – protecting the right to life, prohibiting torture, cruel treatment or punishment, enslavement, etc., freedom of religion or belief defends 'everyone' against a particularly egregious form of arbitrary force. A key practice of the Nazis was the relentless imposition by force of a specific set of beliefs and practices on everyone under their control. That was a severe violation because force is not a justification for believing the truth or rightness of anything. Uttering the words, 'believe what I tell you or I'll punish you,' is an obvious instance of failing to give good reasons for using force.

The legislative history of Article 18 in the UDHR – 'Everyone has the right to freedom of thought, conscience and religion; this right includes freedom to change [one's] religion or

27 UDHR, Article 8; ICCPR, Article 2(3)(a). See Kent, 2005: chapter 7 ('Accoutability Mechanisms') for a thoughtful discussion of this matter.
28 See Morsink, 2009: chapter 4 ('Human Rights Cosmopolitanism') for an elaboration of this point.

belief' – makes clear that the drafters were deeply concerned about the inviolability of fundamental commitments regarding what is right and true, which in this context is the common meaning of the terms 'thought,' 'conscience,' 'religion,' or 'belief.' Freedom of thought comes first in the series because, according to Morsink, it was intended to modify 'conscience' and 'religion' by guaranteeing the right to challenge with impunity expressions of either one, thereby making room, alongside many different religious adherents, for atheists, nontheists, and freethinkers (Morsink, 1999: 261), positions that would also be covered by the concept 'belief.'

But freedom of thought meant something else. It also meant 'the right not to be compelled to profess a belief or ideology which one does not hold' (Morsink, 1999: 261), something that was, of course, a present danger in Nazi Germany, as well as a special worry for minority groups all over the world. What is more, the concern about inviolability of fundamental commitments is even more explicit in the ICCPR version of Article 18: (1) 'Everyone shall have the right to freedom of thought, conscience and religion.' (2) 'No one shall be subject to coercion which would impair [one's] freedom to have or adopt a religion or belief of [one's] choice.'

The central point is that freedom as regards adherence to and avowal of fundamental commitments means protection from compulsion inflicted by the government or by non-governmental individuals or groups whose actions are ultimately the government's responsibility. It is not about how fundamental commitments are acquired, which is the preoccupation of the critics of Article 18 in their attack on the alleged Protestant bias of religious freedom language. 'Freedom to have or adopt a religion or belief of [one's] choice' defends persons against government or other outside coercive interference; it implies no opinion whatsoever about whether fundamental commitments are 'achieved' by voluntary selection or 'ascribed' by birth, by inherited rituals of bestowal, or imparted by some other quite 'unProtestant' means.

Indeed, in the light of the Nazi experience, it would have been surprising if the drafters had meant to protect only Protestant and Protestant-like fundamental commitments. The main victims under Nazi authority of the violation of the 'freedom of thought, conscience, religion, or belief,' as well as all other human rights, were the Jews, most of whom expressed their fundamental commitments in ways very different from Protestant Christians. 'Orthopraxy' rather than 'orthodoxy' is often said to characterize a key difference, and the emphasis on practice typically includes a strongly ritualistic element. Moreover, Judaism generally tilts more toward 'ascribed' than 'achieved' religion, and Judaism was a distinctly minority religion, whose unconscionable treatment provided the drafters with a special incentive to heighten the protection of minority convictions and ways of life.[29]

A similar point may be made about the allegation of the critics that the kind of commitments protected by Article 18 (in either the UDHR or the ICCPR) is limited to 'Protestant' versions, namely, those that are highly rational, doctrinal, and antiritualistic and that favor strict institutional segregation and highly individualistic ideas of conscience. To begin with, we have already seen that the fundamental commitments the drafters had in mind are not exclusively 'religious,' however the term is defined. 'Conscience' and 'belief' do not necessarily encompass religious convictions. But the idea of 'religion' in Article 18 is itself very broadly construed. According to the authoritative commentary of the Human Rights Committee, which monitors the implementation of the ICCRP, Article 18 is 'not limited … to traditional religions or to

29 It is true that, under the influence of immigrant societies like the United States and Australia, Article 27 of the UDHR, which was supposed to protect minority interests, expressed a strongly assimilationist tone. That tone was eventually modified in favor of more robust minority protection in Article 27 of the ICCPR and, even more so, in the UN Declaration on the Rights of Indigenous Peoples adopted by the UN General Assembly in 2007. See Little, 2015: 78–79.

religions and beliefs with institutional characteristics or practices analogous to those of traditional religions. The Committee therefore views with concern any tendency to discriminate against any religion or belief for any reasons, including the fact that they are newly established, or represent religious minorities that may be the subject of hostility by a predominant religious community.'[30]

In addition, Article 18 in both the UDHR and the ICCPR guarantees that the right of freedom of religion or belief may be expressed either 'individually or in community with others, and in public or private,' and to be 'manifested' 'in worship, observance, practice, and teaching.' According to the Committee, this formulation 'encompasses a broad range of acts. The concept of worship extends to ritual and ceremonial acts giving direct expression to belief, as well as various practices integral to such acts, building places of worship, the use of ritual formulae and objects, the display of symbols ... The observance and practice of religion may include ... such customs as ...dietary regulations, the wearing of distinctive clothing or head coverings, participation in rituals associated with certain stages of life.'[31]

There is no textual basis for concluding that Article 18 in either document favors a particular religious or ideological perspective. What the article does do, rather, is to offer a broadly pluralistic framework within which to understand the variety of fundamental commitments existing in different forms around the world, a variety of commitments that, in the name of human rights and the rule of law, governments are called upon to protect. If there are judicial rulings or government policies that exhibit bias, they are at variance with the authoritative interpretations of the text.

The objections to the language about freedom to change religion included in Article 18 of the UDHR, and the unfair license such language allegedly gives Christian and other missionaries to threaten communal identity and disrupt whole ways of life identified with some versions of Islam and with indigenous traditions and other 'ascribed' religions, are likewise unconvincing. They fail to take into account the underlying logic of the provisions for freedom of religion or belief in the human rights code. As indicated, the key idea is the basic conceptual divide between conviction and coercion. Thus, actions by a state itself or by other actors under the state's responsibility that use or threaten physical force and/or penal sanctions to compel religious or nonreligious people either to change, disregard, or contradict their basic convictions, or to prevent them from changing those convictions where desired, constitute an assault on the very foundations of the human rights system, whether the religion or belief in question is 'ascribed' or 'achieved.'

Significantly, representatives of religions like Islam and indigenous African traditions are themselves divided or perplexed about the freedom to change religion. In the debates over that subject in the drafting of Article 18 of the UDHR, Saudi opposition, voiced by Jamil al'Barudi, whose arguments were undoubtedly colored by the opinions of conservative Muslim clerics and jurists, was challenged by the Foreign Minister of Pakistan, Muhammed Zafrullah Khan. Khan gave expression to modernist themes 'fairly common in Indo-Pakistan Islam,' consisting of 'a critical assessment of Islamic history' and 'a fresh interpretation of the Qur'an,' that provided religious warrants for wholeheartedly supporting the language of Article 18, including the freedom to change religion (Kelsay, 1988: 47; see also Gunn, 2020). Unlike al'Barudi, who opposed recognizing the freedom to change religion based on claims that missionary activity of any sort posed a threat to the probity and stability of Muslim societies, Khan distinguished between the benefits bestowed by

30 UN Human Rights Committee, General Comment No. 22 (Art. 18), para. 2.
31 Ibid., para. 4.

honorable missionaries and the liabilities caused by those who resort to illegitimate tactics. Ever since, this intense disagreement over the right to change religion has characterized abiding and deep-seated divisions within Islam over religious freedom and the understanding of human rights.

Likewise, Makau wa Mutua, a strong defender of indigenous African religions, displays a comparable ambivalence toward the freedom to change religion. He has written eloquently of the devastating abuses inflicted on members of African indigenous religions in the process of colonialization and postcolonial settings by Christian (and Muslim) missionaries, leading him at one time to call for a total, legally enforced ban on all forms of proselytism (Mutua, 1996: 440). However, Mutua partially revised his opinion a few years later, suggesting that 'societies that prevent the entry of "foreign" values or the export of their values into other cultures deny themselves the benefits of cross-fertilization. Closing off avenues for intercultural exchanges,' he continues, 'may preserve negative aspects of tradition to the detriment of the group' (Mutua, 1999: 170). This is a striking statement since it implies that religious freedom and the possibility of change bring benefits as well as costs.

The encouraging implication of both Khan's full backing of Article 18, including language about freedom to change religion, and Mutua's revised views favoring 'the benefits of [cultural and religious] cross-fertilization' is the willingness of persons strongly sympathetic to the interests of the religious communities they identify with to stand against exclusive state support for one religion or belief, and thereby open the door to religious and cultural pluralism underwritten by the human rights code.[32]

Religious and cultural freedom, either for missionary or non-missionary religions, is not, of course, completely open-ended according to human rights standards. The possible conflict between freedom of religion or belief and other public goods is always a question. There are, in fact, provisions in 18(3) (ICCPR) permitting governments to limit religious practice, though they may not inhibit the holding or avowing of one or another belief or practice. As was said earlier, limitations may be imposed that are 'prescribed by law,' 'are necessary to protect public safety, order, health or morals or the fundamental rights and freedoms of others,' and 'must be directly related with and proportionate to the specific need on which they are predicated.'[33] Again, the essential point is that in restricting a right as fundamental as the right of freedom of religion or belief, the government bears a heavy burden of proof and is bound by the conditions of defensive force.

Assuming, then, that the opportunity to embrace, affirm, and (within limits) act upon fundamental commitments is essential to being human, protecting the right of freedom of religion or belief occupies a critical role in the defense of every self.

32 Both Article 18 of the ICCPR and Article 1 of the UN Declaration on the Elimination of All Forms of Intolerance and Discrimination Based on Religion or Belief (DEID) notably exclude reference to the freedom to change religion, reportedly as the result of increasing pressure from the forces opposed to that provision such as the representatives of Islam and indigenous African religions mentioned in the text. However, the Human Rights Committee, authorized to interpret the ICCPR, states explicitly that 'the freedom "to have or adopt" a religion or belief' language that is included in ICCPR Article 18 'necessarily entails the freedom to choose a religion or belief, including inter alia, the right to replace one's current religion or belief with another or adopt atheistic views, as well as the right to retain one's religion or belief' (General Comment No. 22, para. 5; italics added). Similarly, DEID concludes with Article 8, which in stating that 'Nothing in the present Declaration shall be construed as restricting or derogating from any right defined in the UDHR,' leaves no doubt that language ensuring the right to change religion contained in Article 18 of the UDHR still obtains (italics added).

33 Ibid., para. 8.

Conclusion

There is good reason to reject scholarly doubts about the 'organic unity' of the original human rights corpus embodied in the UDHR, the ICCPR, and the ICESCR, as well as claims about the discordant character of Article 18, the freedom of religion or belief, within that corpus. To reflect carefully on the provenance of human rights language – the urgent threat of German and other forms of fascism in the mid-twentieth century – is to apprehend the unifying moral and legal foundations of that language, including the place and purpose of the right of freedom of religion or belief.

The essence of that threat is the endangerment of the physical and intellectual or spiritual integrity of every human person by the exercise of arbitrary force, either causing death or injury or denying or neglecting the elements of basic human survival primarily for self-serving or unfounded reasons. At stake is the moral right of self-defense of every human being, both as individuals and in groups. Accordingly, that right constitutes the foundation of the organic unity of human rights, including the protection of everyone's right to embrace, affirm, and (within limits) to act upon fundamental commitments, very pluralistically understood. Because the right of self-defense, if unregulated, itself opens the door to arbitrary force, the only proper solution is the regulation of force by a government dedicated to the proposition that 'human rights should be protected by the rule of law.'

References

Alston, P., 1992. The committee on economic, social, and cultural rights. In: Alston, P., Mégret, F. (Eds.), *United Nations and Human Rights*. Oxford University Press, p. 473.

Beitz, C.R., 2009. *The Idea of Human Rights*. Oxford University Press.

Bullock, A., 1964. *Hitler: A Study in Tyranny*. Harper & Row.

Casanova, J., 2010. Remarks. *Report of the Georgetown Symposium on Proselytism and Religious Freedom in the 21st Century*. Berkley Center for Religion, Peace, and World Affairs, Georgetown University, p. 14. Available from: https://s3.amazonaws.com/berkley-center/100303ReportGeorgetownSymposiumProselytismReligiousFreedomTwentyFirstCentury.pdf>. 3 March.

Fletcher, G.P., 1988. *A Crime of Self-Defense: Bernhard Goetz and the Law on Trial*. Free Press.

Glendon, M.A., 2001. *A World Made New: Eleanor Roosevelt and the Universal Declaration of Human Rights*. Random House.

Grim, B.G., Finke, R., 2011. *The Price of Freedom Denied: Religious Persecution and Conflict in the Twenty-First Century*. Cambridge University Press.

Gunn, T.J. 2020. Do Human Rights Have a Secular, Individualistic & Anti-Islamic Bias? *Daedalus*. 149, 3, 148–69.

Hessbruegge, J.A., 2017. *Human Rights and Personal Self-Defense in International Law*. Oxford University Press.

Hurd, E.S., 2015. *Beyond Religious Freedom: The New Global Politics of Religion*. Princeton University Press.

Ignatieff, M., 2001. *Human Rights as Politics and Idolatry*. Princeton University Press.

Kelsay, J., 1988. Saudi Arabia, Pakistan, and the Universal Declaration of Human Rights. In: Little, D., Kelsay, J., Sachedina, A.A. (Eds.), *Human Rights and the Conflict of Cultures: Western and Islamic Perspectives on Religious Liberty*. University of South Carolina Press, p. 33.

Kent, G., 2005. *Freedom from Want: The Human Right to Adequate Food*. Georgetown University Press.

Lash, J.P., 1972. *Eleanor: The Years Alone*. W.W. Norton & Co.

Little, D., 2015. *Essays in Religion and Human Rights: Ground to Stand on*. Cambridge University Press.

Morsink, J., 1999. *The Universal Declaration of Human Rights: Origins, Drafting, and Intent*. University of Pennsylvania Press.

Morsink, J., 2009. *Inherent Rights: Philosophical Roots of the Universal Declaration*. University of Pennsylvania Press.

Morsink, J., 2019. *The Universal Declaration of Human Rights and the Holocaust: An Endangered Connection*. Georgetown University Press.

Moyn, S., 2010. *The Last Utopia: Human Rights in History*. Belknap Press of Harvard University Press.
Moyn, S., 2015. *Christian Human Rights*. University of Pennsylvania Press.
Mutua, M.W., 1996. Limitations on religious rights: Problematizing religious freedom in the African context. In: van der Vyver, J.D., Witte, J., Jr. (Eds.), *Religious Human Rights in Global Perspective: Legal Perspectives*. Martinus Nijhoff Publishers, p. 417.
Mutua, M.W., 1999. Returning to my roots. In: An-Na'im, A.A. (Ed.), *Proselytization and Communal Self-Determination in Africa*. Orbis Books, 169.
Paxton, R.O., 2004. *The Anatomy of Fascism*. Alfred A. Knopf.
Posner, E.A., 2014. *The Twilight of Human Rights Law*. Oxford University Press.
Schabas, W.A. (Ed.), 2013. *Universal Declaration of Human Rights: Travaux Preparatoires*. 3 Vols. Cambridge University Press.
Shklar, J.N., 1989. Liberalism of fear. In: Rosenblum, N.L. (Ed.), *Liberalism and the Moral Life*. Harvard University Press, p. 21.
Steiner, H., Alston, P. (Eds.), 2000. *International Human Rights in Context: Law, Politics, Morals*. Oxford University Press.
Sullivan, W.F., Hurd, E.S., Mahmood, S., Danchin, P.G. (Eds.), 2015. *Politics of Religious Freedom*. University of Chicago Press.
Sunstein, C.R., 2004. *The Second Bill of Rights: FDR's Unfinished Revolution and Why We Need It More Than Ever*. Basic Books.
Tyranny. 2012. *Concise Oxford English Dictionary*. Oxford University Press, p. 1552.
Ullrich, V., 2016. *Hitler: Ascent*. Alfred A. Knopf, pp. 1889–1939.

19

Dialectics of the right to freedom of religion or belief

Peter G. Danchin

> We inhabit a *nomos* – a normative universe .... [in which] law and narrative are inseparably related. Every prescription is insistent in its demand to be located in discourse – to be supplied with history and destiny, beginning and end, explanation and purpose. And every narrative is insistent in its demand for its prescriptive point, its moral (Cover, 1983: 4–5).

Introduction

In his Foreword to the 1982 Supreme Court term, Robert Cover memorably explored the reasoning of the U.S. Supreme Court in *Bob Jones University v. United States.*[1] At issue in the case was the right under the Constitution's Religion Clauses of a private university, established 'to conduct an institution of learning ... giving special emphasis to the Christian religion and the ethics revealed in the Holy Scriptures,' to deny admission to applicants engaged in an interracial marriage or known to advocate interracial marriage or dating. Prior to 1970, the Internal Revenue Service (IRS) had granted tax-exempt status to private schools without regard to their racial admissions policies. But on the basis of a 'national policy to discourage racial discrimination in education,' the IRS decided in 1970 that it could no longer justify allowing tax-exempt status to private schools that practiced racial discrimination and revoked Bob Jones University's tax-exempt status.

Delivering the opinion of the Court, Chief Justice Burger held that a compelling government interest 'in eradicating racial discrimination in education' substantially outweighed whatever burden the denial of tax benefits placed on the university's exercise of its religious beliefs. The political authority exercised by the IRS in interpreting the tax code to reflect this policy was not therefore unconstitutional.

In reaching this conclusion, the Chief Justice relied on two interrelated doctrinal propositions to reject the claim to religious liberty made by the university under the Religion Clauses of the First Amendment. The first proposition concerned the nature and scope of the right to religious liberty:

1 461 U.S. 574 (1983).

> This Court has long held the Free Exercise Clause of the First Amendment to be an absolute prohibition against governmental regulation of religious beliefs. As interpreted by this Court, moreover, the Free Exercise Clause provides substantial protection for lawful conduct grounded in religious belief.[2]

The second proposition concerned permissible grounds for limiting this right for reasons of compelling 'public policy:'

> However, '[n]ot all burdens on religion are unconstitutional .... The state may justify a limitation on religious liberty by showing that it is essential to accomplish an overriding governmental interest.' On occasion this Court has found certain governmental interests so compelling as to allow even regulations prohibiting religiously based conduct .... Denial of tax benefits will inevitably have a substantial impact on the operation of private religious schools, but will not prevent those schools from observing their religious tenets.[3]

The ambiguities internal to this dualistic structure are instantly familiar to any student of religious freedom jurisprudence, whether in national or international law. The first dilemma for the Court was how to address the constitutional relationship between the state and a *paideic* religious community (the central concern in Cover's Foreword[4]) in the case a conservative Evangelical university. This raised a host of contested questions which ultimately implicated the normative foundations of the American constitutional order itself.

In this constitutional *nomos*, the Establishment Clause stipulates the prescriptive relation between the state and 'religion.' The key concept in this political imaginary is 'religious disestablishment.' Unlike in Spain or Italy, there can be no concordat between the state and federations of religious institutions, and unlike in many Muslim majority countries there can be no recognized State or dominant religion or set of recognized minority religions. Most pertinent, and in direct contradiction to the English constitution, there can be no official or established Church.[5] Rather, religion in America must be 'free,' a matter of essentially private life and personal conviction and belief. As James Madison in 1785 memorably expressed the idea:

> [W]e hold it for a fundamental and undeniable truth, 'that Religion or the duty which we owe to our Creator and the manner of discharging it, can be directed only by reason and conviction, not by force or violence.' The Religion then of every man must be left to the conviction and conscience of every man; and it is the right of every man to exercise it as these may dictate.[6]

---

2 *Bob Jones University*, 461 U.S. 574, 603 (1983) (internal citations omitted).

3 Ibid.

4 In the 'paideic' world of the *nomos*, law is a resource in the larger effort of a community to endow life with meaning. As an ideal type, it suggests: '(1) a common body of precept and narrative, (2) a common and personal way of being educated into this corpus, and (3) a sense of direction or growth that is constituted as the individual and his community work out the implications of their law.' This is a vision of a 'strong community of common obligations' characteristic, for example, of Talmudic law and Christian conceptions of the Church where reciprocal obligations flow from commitment, not coercion, because people recognize the needs of others and respond to them (Cover, 1983).

5 American religious pluralism had its origins within the British Empire which made any notion of a common Church in the North American colonies an historical impossibility (see Haefeli, 2013).

6 J. Madison, *Memorial and Remonstrance Against Religious Assessments* (20 June 1785).

On this account, a particular conception of the true nature or 'essence' of religion is understood as *prior* to and ineluctably entangled with the right to 'free exercise' under the Constitution. This essence encompasses a notion of 'religious belief' whose location is internal to the being of a distinct religious subject: the individual for whom religion is understood on two levels simultaneously: first, theologically as 'interiorized' in terms of individual 'belief or conscience;' and second, constitutionally as 'freely chosen' in terms of the fundamental right to subjective authority.

This is a recognizably Protestant conception of religion: the idea that 'conscience was directly bound to obey and follow God and not men: a theory of the free and at the same time unfree conscience (as the "work of God," as Luther had said)' (Forst, 2014: 189). Viewing religion as *belief* or *conscience* is recognizably modern and Christian because 'it emphasizes the priority of belief as a state of mind rather than as constituting activity in the world' (Asad, 1993: 47). In this respect, the *object* of the right to religious freedom is, at its core, a conception of religion understood primarily as 'a set of beliefs in a set of propositions (about transcendence, causality, cosmology) to which an individual gives assent'.[7] In modern religious freedom jurisprudence, this is the *forum internum*: the right of the individual subject to 'have or adopt' a religion or belief that is considered to be absolutely protected from interference by the law (i.e., is nonderogable and not subject to limitation by the state).[8]

Recall again Chief Justice Burger's statement in *Bob Jones University*: 'This Court has long held the Free Exercise Clause of the First Amendment to be an *absolute prohibition* against governmental regulation of *religious beliefs*.'[9] Some version of this proposition is present in all cases arising under the Religion Clauses.[10] Strikingly similar versions appear also in the

7 Mahmood (2010: 283). See also Mahmood (2016: 15). ('The concept of religion as belief is itself part of a normative secular framework in which religion is disinvested of its materiality.')

8 The conceptual division between a *forum internum* and *externum* is present in all modern international human rights instruments: see, e.g., International Covenant on Civil and Political Rights Article 18(1), December 16, 1966, 999 U.N.T.S. 171 ('Everyone shall have the right to freedom of thought, conscience and religion. This right shall include freedom to have or to adopt a religion or belief of his choice.'); European Convention for the Protection of Human Rights and Fundamental Freedoms Article 9(1), November 4, 1950, E.T.S. No. 5, 213 U.N.T.S. 222 ('Everyone has the right to freedom of thought, conscience and religion; this right includes freedom to change his religion or belief.'); American Convention on Human Rights Article 12(1), July 18, 1978, O.A.S.T.S. No. 36, 1144 U.N.T.S. 123 ('Everyone has the right to freedom of conscience and of religion. This right includes freedom to maintain or to change one's religion or beliefs.')

9 *Bob Jones University*, 461 U.S. 574, 603 (1983) (my emphasis).

10 See, e.g., *Employment Div. v. Smith*, 494 U.S. 872, 877 (1990) (internal citations omitted) ('The free exercise of religion means, first and foremost, the right to believe and profess whatever religious doctrine one desires. Thus, the First Amendment obviously excludes all 'governmental regulation of religious beliefs as such. 'The government may not compel affirmation of religious belief, punish the expression of religious doctrines it believes to be false, impose special disabilities on the basis of religious views or religious status, or lend its power to one or the other side in controversies over religious authority or dogma.'); *Church of the Lukumi Babalu Aye v. City of Hialeah*, 508 U.S. 520, 532 (1993) ('At a minimum, the protections of the Free Exercise Clause pertain if the law at issue discriminates against some or all religious beliefs or regulates or prohibits conduct because it is undertaken for religious reasons.'); *Board of Education v. Barnette*, 319 U.S. 624, 642 ('If there is any fixed star in our constitutional constellation, it is that no official, high or petty, can prescribe what shall be orthodox in … religion, or other matters of opinion, or force citizens to confess by word or act their faith therein.')

jurisprudence of the European Court of Human Rights (ECHR) interpreting Article 9(1) of the ECHR.[11]

In the American political imaginary, this understanding of religion famously induced Tocqueville to observe that '[t]he Americans combine the notions of Christianity and of liberty so intimately in their minds, that it is impossible to make them conceive the one without the other.' The result was that 'there are things which religion prevents them from imagining and forbids them to become .... Religion, which never intervenes directly in the government of American society, should therefore be considered as the first of their political institutions.'[12]

For present purposes, the critical point is that the Establishment and Free Exercise Clauses, and two centuries of associated constitutional rights doctrine,[13] are inextricably tied to and shaped within a background Protestant discursive tradition.[14] This tradition is metaphysical in its structure and combines a complex series of not only ontological but also theological claims within a rationalist discourse built upon the two core notions of subjective right and secular reason. It is to these two complex and elusive concepts we can now turn.

The modern subject

The first core claim of religious freedom discourse is ontological in nature. Strictly speaking, the claim is not directly about religion *per se*. Rather, it concerns the *subject* whose religion it is (i.e., the individual for whom religion is an object of 'belief' or 'conscience' on the one hand, and 'free choice' on the other). The notion today that the right to religious freedom is neutral towards 'religion,' or protects 'all religions equally,' is criticized in the literature across a wide array of disciplines. Rather, it is more accurate to say that the right to religious freedom purports to treat all *rights-holders* equally.

11 See, e.g., *Kokkinakis v. Greece*, App. No. 14307/88, 260 Eur. Ct. H.R. (ser. A) § 14 (1993) (Martens J.) ('The basic principle in human rights is respect for human dignity and human freedom. Essential for that dignity and that freedom are the freedoms of thought, conscience and religion enshrined in Article 9 para. 1. Accordingly, they are absolute. The Convention leaves no room whatsoever for interference by the State. These absolute freedoms explicitly include freedom to change one's religion and beliefs. Whether or not somebody intends to change religion is no concern of the State's.'); *Leyla Şahin v. Turkey*, App. No. 44774/98, Eur. Ct. H.R., June 29, 2004, at § 104 ('The Court reiterates that, as enshrined in Article 9, freedom of thought, conscience and religion is one of the foundations of a "democratic society" within the meaning of the Convention. This freedom is, in its religious dimension, one of the most vital elements that go to make up the identity of believers and their conception of life, but it is also a precious asset for atheists, agnostics, sceptics and the unconcerned .... That freedom entails, *inter alia*, freedom to hold or not to hold religious beliefs and to practise or not to practise a religion.')

12 de Tocqueville, 1969 (1851): 292. For this reason, 'politics is free to dance lightly on the surface of life only because everything fundamental is fixed below it. The American imaginary is determined outside of politics' (Connolly, 1995: 169).

13 See, e.g., *Everson v. Board of Education*, 330 U.S. 1, 15–16 (1947) ('The "establishment of religion" clause ... means at least this: Neither a state nor the Federal Government can set up a church. Neither can pass laws which aid one religion, aid all religions, or prefer one religion over another.')

14 The notion of an historically evolving set of discourses embodied in the practices and institutions of a society and thus deeply embedded in the material life of its people is central to the conception of a discursive tradition: 'These discourses relate conceptually to a past (when the practice was instituted, and from which the knowledge of its point and proper performance has been transmitted) and a future (how the point of that practice can best be secured in the short or long term, or why it should be modified or abandoned), through a present (how it is linked to other practices, institutions, and social conditions)' (Asad, 1986: 14).

In this move, however, a seismic shift occurs in the relationship between conceptions of subjectivity, normativity (and its sources), and authority. The modern picture is ontologically grounded, not in any divine conception of heteronomous religious authority, but in a knowing moral or rational subject viewed as the self-grounding *source* of normativity itself.[15] It is now the individual who, as a matter of right, decides for herself (as a matter of authority) questions of religion, conscience, or belief (now viewed as an *object* of choice or assent).

In this series of reconfigurations, religion becomes *rationalized* in accordance with a distinctive normative model of religiosity as privatized belief in a set of creedal propositions to which an autonomous individual gives assent. This simultaneous rationalization and privatization of religion generates the distinctive and unstable co-imbrication of autonomy and belief as the 'buffered' self chooses autonomously as a matter of moral right and believes freely as a matter of theological conviction.[16]

Virtually all contemporary accounts of the right to freedom of religion or belief trace the genealogies of this modern picture to the legacies of nominalism, the collapse of medieval scholasticism, and the ensuing intellectual influence of the Protestant Reformation, humanism, and the civil and philosophical Enlightenments.[17] As Michael Allen Gillespie has powerfully argued, the origins of the modern concept of right lie most centrally in the ontological individualism proclaimed against scholasticism by the nominalist revolution at the end of the medieval period.[18] For Gillespie, the nominalist revolution on the 'problem of universals' provided a *schema* for an entirely new understanding of time and being.

Drawing upon Neoplatonic interpretations of Aristotle, what most centrally characterized the *via antiqua* of scholasticism was ontological realism: the 'belief in the extra-mental existence of universals ... [such that] species and *genera* were the ultimately real things and individual human beings were merely particular instances of these universals' (Gillespie, 2008: 20). Such universals were 'nothing other than divine reason made known to man either by illumination, as Augustine had suggested, or through the investigation of nature, as Aquinas and others had argued' (Gillespie, 2008: 20). This ontological realism had three main consequences: First, 'nature and reason reflected one another' in a rational structure. Second, while God transcended his creation, he 'was reflected in it and by analogy could be understood through it' with the result that 'logic and natural theology could supplement or, in the minds of some, even replace revelation' (with obvious implications for modern natural law theory). And third, man was a 'natural being with a natural end and was governed by the laws of nature' such that he 'did not need Scripture to inform him of his earthly moral and political duties,' although Scripture was 'necessary to understand everything that transcended nature, including man's supernatural destiny' (Gillespie, 2008: 20).

15 For Kant, enlightenment was the discovery of an exit, a 'way out,' a 'process that releases us from the status of "immaturity"' where religious authority takes the place of our conscience by a 'modification of the preexisting relation linking will, authority, and the use of reason' (Foucault, 1984: 35).

16 For discussion of the co-imbrication of autonomy and belief in religious freedom discourse, see Danchin, 2011.

17 The most prominent recent example is Taylor, 2007. See also Hunter, 2001.

18 It is for this reason that the tendency of much modern liberal rights theory to locate its origins and justification in eighteenth-century (usually Kantian) Enlightenment thought is incomplete and misleading, especially as regards its theological origins and continuing dialectic entanglements.

On the scholastic view, the ultimate source of normative order was divine and all rights, duties, and obligations of man were defined internally to this order.[19] As Alasdair MacIntyre has argued, this conception of normativity, whether placed within a classical or theistic framework, had two dominant characteristics: first, some account of the essence of man as a rational animal; and second, some account of the human *telos*. The purpose of practical reason was therefore to 'instruct us both as to what our true end is and as how to reach it.'[20]

In the history of Western legal thought, this understanding of the normative grounds for law is illustrated as much by St. Thomas Aquinas's hierarchy of eternal, natural, human, and divine positive law[21] as by modern accounts of the emergence in the mid-seventeenth century of public international law and a new system of secular sovereign states.[22]

As Gillespie suggests, the realist ontology of scholastic thought was shattered by the *via moderna* of nominalism which viewed only individual things as *real* and universals as mere fictions: 'words did not point to real universal entities but were merely signs useful for human understanding' (Gillespie, 2008: 14). Reacting against the growth of Aristotelianism, including importantly the commentaries of the Islamic philosophers Avicenna and Averroes, nominalists such as Duns Scotus and William of Ockham emphasized the divine omnipotence of God giving birth to the conception of a voluntaristic as opposed to rational God. For Ockham, faith alone confirmed that God is omnipotent with the result that 'every being exists only as a result of his willing it,' while creation is radically particular and nonteleological – 'an act of sheer grace' (Gillespie, 2008: 22). Accordingly, there is 'no immutable order of nature or reason that man can understand and no knowledge of God except through revelation.'[23]

On Gillespie's reading, the nominalist revolution had three main ontotheological effects: First, God remained a *necessary* being (all other beings being contingent creations of His will), but the nature of God was fundamentally altered. The nominalist God was 'frighteningly omnipotent, utterly beyond human ken, and a continual threat to human well-being,' thus epitomizing 'divine power and unpredictability rather than divine love and reason' (Gillespie, 2008: 15). The period of modernity arises as a complex series of attempts to find a way out of this metaphysical/theological crisis. In particular, the eighteenth-century Enlightenment

19 Koskenniemi describes the main features of international law in medieval thought as follows: '[O]rder was a natural state of affairs, existing by the force of creation and discoverable in the natural arrangement of things and men through faith or *recta ratio*. If doubt arose, it could always be dismissed by appeal to the Church's or the Emperor's authority. Behind this authority stood the Christian idea of a civitas maxima which both legitimized and constitutionalized it. Different institutions exercised powers in a system of mutual control, each submitted to legitimation proceeding "downwards" from the highest commands of divine law' (1989: 56–57).

20 MacIntrye, 1981. In the case of ethics placed within a theistic framework of divinely ordained law, whether that be Aquinas in the Christian tradition, Maimonides in the Jewish tradition, or Ibn Roschd in the Islamic tradition, the 'threefold structure of untutored human nature, human nature as it could be if it realized its telos, and the precepts of rational ethics as the means of transition from one to the other, remains central to the theistic standing of evaluative thought and judgment.'

21 St. Thomas Aquinas, 2002 (On Different Kinds of Law).

22 This historical juncture at the time of the Peace of Westphalia in 1648 is said to mark the 'great epistemological break' when religious medieval 'unity' gave way to a secular system of 'plural' territorially limited sovereign states. Between the sixteenth and eighteenth centuries, this led to the emergence of what Koskenniemi has termed the 'liberal doctrine of politics,' the driving force of which was the attempt to 'escape the anarchical conclusions to which loss of faith in an overriding theologico-moral world order otherwise seemed to lead' (1989: 52).

23 Gillespie, 2008: 22. Human beings 'thus had no natural or supernatural end or *telos*.' The result was that 'the nominalist revolution against scholasticism shattered every aspect of the medieval world' (Gillespie, 2008: 14).

philosophy of Immanuel Kant would later figure centrally in modernity's search for just such a 'way out.'[24]

Second, the two great intellectual movements that arose in response – humanism and the Reformation – agreed on the premise but differed on which of the two realms of being, man and God, was ontically primary. Humanism 'put man first and interpreted God and nature on this basis,' while the Reformation 'began with God and viewed man and nature only from this perspective' (Gillespie, 2008: 17).

And third, the radical freedom of divine will gave new importance to human will. Luther accepted the premises of ontological individualism, but rejected the problem of the impenetrability of the nominalist God. Reconfiguring the relationship of human and divine will by viewing faith alone, as opposed to philosophy, as the will to union with God, that is, right willing dependent on God, he was able to 'transform the terrifying God of nominalism into a power *within individual human beings*,' such that 'God becomes the *interior* and guiding principle of [man's] life, or what Luther calls *conscience*' (Gillespie, 2008: 33–34).

These profound effects of nominalism both underlie and ground the ontological claims of modern religious freedom discourse in making the individual the subject of the right and belief or conscience its object. For Martin Heidegger, the most decisive transformation from medieval thought to modernity is from Aristotle's *hupokeimenon* (the 'underlying thing' or substance in a thing, i.e., that which is constant and real) to the Cartesian notion of the *subjectum* as *ego*:

> According to the metaphysical tradition from Aristotle onwards, every true being is a *hupokeimenon*. This *hupokeimenon* is determined afterwards as *subjectum*. Descartes' thinking distinguishes the *subjectum* which man is to the effect that the *actualis* of this *subjectum* has its essence in the *actus* of *cogitare* (*percipere*) (Heidegger, 1939–1946: 31).

The result is that since Descartes, the human 'I' – with its new dimension of perceptive activity – has come to be the 'subject' in metaphysics. This conceptual architecture generates the familiar ontological metaphysics of rights discourse in seeking to define the *essence* of religion as such, understood as what is common to all religious subjectivity.[25] On the basis of the brief genealogy sketched out here, this essence is broadly understood today under the category of 'inner faith' or 'belief.'

Secular reason

What is striking and maddeningly elusive is how this rights-based metaphysics simultaneously enfolds within it a second, theological claim regarding not the essence, but *existence* of all beings, understood as that which is the highest or supreme, all-founding being.[26] Following Kant's use

24 *See supra* note 15 and accompanying text.

25 The ontological claim involves a search for the most general ground of beings (i.e., what all beings share in common). This 'exemplary being' is understood in terms of 'that being beneath or beyond which no more basic being can be 'discovered' or "fathomed"' (Thomson, 2000: 301–302).

26 This second claim seeks to answer the questions: '[w]hich being is the highest (or supreme) being, and in what sense is it the highest being?' The theological claim itself thus has two aspects in "striving to identify the highest or supreme being (the question of God), but [also] … to understand the being of God (that is, the sense in which God 'is', or the kind of being which God has)." The theological claim in this way "inquires into and would give an account (*logos*) of the existence of the *theion*, 'the supreme cause and the highest ground of beings'" (Thomson, 2000: 302).

of the term,[27] Heidegger argued that the entire history of Western metaphysics is 'ontotheological' in structure in the sense that it makes two ambiguous and historically intertwined foundational claims: first, in ontologically grounding an understanding of beings 'as such;' and second, in theologically legitimating our changing historical understanding of the source or 'totality' of these foundational claims (Heidegger, 1962).

Heidegger's guiding idea is that in answering the question of reality's ultimate foundation, the metaphysical tradition establishes 'both the fundamental and the ultimate conceptual parameters of intelligibility' (Thomson, 2011: 109). The result is that

> [a] series of metaphysical ontologies anchor our successive constellations of historical intelligibility, temporarily securing the intelligible order by grasping it from both ends of the conceptual scale simultaneously (as it were), both ontologically (from the inside out) and theologically (from the outside in)
>
> *(Thomson, 2011: 109).*

This second theological strand of metaphysics seeks to explain and legitimate the ultimate source or foundation of rights discourse itself and its theological structure does not disappear in modernity's self-understanding of the transition from divine to secular conceptions of reason. Despite the ontological consensus on the individual as the modern subject of the right, the ontic differences discussed above between humanist and Reformation thinkers as well as between rival religious communities and confessions played a significant role in the devastating wars of religion that completely shattered Europe in the sixteenth and seventeenth centuries. This set of theological debates was the precursor to the 'civil Enlightenment' of the early modern period in Europe which predated the philosophical *Aufklärung* of Kant by more than a century. In response to the devastating wars of religion, the civil philosophers sought to desacralize the state and this led over time to both the churches losing their civil and political authority and the gradual spiritualization of religion in the form of individual 'conscience and belief.'[28]

Importantly, however, this conception did not rest on any form of subjective right of individuals against the State. Rather, for civil philosophers such as Christian Thomasius it comprised a right of the State against intolerant religious communities.[29] The juridical construction of religious freedom in the early modern period thus sought to establish political neutrality toward ultimate theological principles as the condition of establishing parity of legal treatment for rival religions as equally valid legal associations (Hunter, 2014). This marked a shift in the understanding of religious *authority* as Erastian control of churches by the State was

27 Before Heidegger, Kant was the first to use the term 'ontotheology.' He distinguished between theology derived from reason on the one hand and revelation on the other. Within the category of the former ('reasoned theology'), he further distinguished between natural theology and transcendental theology. Natural theology was divided as between physico-theology and ethical/moral theology, while transcendental theology was divided between cosmotheology and ontotheology. For Kant, ontotheology was 'the type of transcendental theology characteristic of Anselm of Canterbury's ontological argument which believes it can know the existence of an original being [Urwesen], through mere concepts, without the help of any experience whatsoever' (Thomson, 2005: 7).

28 Hunter, 2001: 376 (arguing that in the civil tradition 'it is religion and morality that define the private domain, their inward and unenforceable character defining the kingdom of truth,' while the public sovereign domain is defined by the use of coercion to preserve social peace).

29 Negotiated and contingent relations between the state and different religious communities, groups and traditions is quite distinct from the notion of 'a right' which implies a legal/moral relation between the state and an individual subject as rights-holder, as well as a background justification not only of the right itself but its distinctive function of holding others to correlative duties.

effected to deny the coercive authority of religious institutions in enforcing the demands of conscience.[30] This was the condition of freedom in the newly emerging private sphere – a sphere defined, protected, delimited, and increasingly regulated by the State itself.

In this sequence of moves, it is important to see how, at the ontological level, normativity is now conceived in terms of radically individual beings while, at the ontic level, a radically free God retains authority in relation to such beings. Faith on this account is subjective, a matter of voluntary belief, not knowledge. This is what the 'privatization' of religion refers to, although not yet its rationalization and loss of authority to the master modern principle of autonomy.

The crucial point for present purposes is that the nominalist ontology of radical individuality lies at the origin of the modern division between knowledge and belief. It was now possible to have *true belief* about God, and God's action, on the basis of God's own self-revelation as received by faith, but it is not possible to have *knowledge* of such matters. While man and God exist independently of our thinking about them, we can only have knowledge of the former. Well before liberalism then, the category of 'conscience or belief' is contingent on the ontological individualism proclaimed by nominalism.

In contemporary theology, this thesis has been carefully expressed and elaborated in the work of John Milbank who identifies John Duns Scotus (1265–1308), and his notion of 'univocity of being,' as being the first major thinker to influence medieval thought away from Thomas Aquinas's 'analogy of being.' As Milbank argues:

> Now this [late medieval nominalist] philosophy was itself the legatee of the greatest of all disruptions carried out in the history of European thought, namely that of Duns Scotus who for the first time established a radical separation of philosophy from theology by declaring that it was possible to consider being in abstraction from the question of whether one is considering created or creating being. Eventually this generated the notion of ontology and an epistemology unconstrained by, and transcendentally prior to, theology itself (Milban et al., 1999: 23).

MacIntyre in *After Virtue* similarly observes that the Jansenist Pascal recognized that the Protestant conception of reason was at one with the conception of reason in seventeenth-century philosophy and science. Reason no longer comprehended essences or transitions from potentiality to act, such concepts belonging to the despised conceptual scheme of scholasticism. Rather, reason was calculative and could assess truths of fact and mathematical relations, but nothing more (MacIntyre, 1981).

In anticipation of Hume, Pascal thus recognized that 'a central achievement of reason is to recognize that our beliefs are ultimately founded on nature, custom and habit.' But as regards ends, 'it must be silent' (MacIntyre, 1981). In retaining the negative aspects of this conception, 'reason for Kant, as much as for Hume, discerns no essential natures and no teleological features in the objective universe available for study by physics.'[31]

---

30 Central to this strategy was the category of adiaphora: the old Stoic idea of actions that morality neither mandates nor forbids, which within Christianity was understood to refer to matters regarded as inessential to faith but nevertheless permissible for Christians or allowed in the Church. On this basis, Thomasius declared 'virtually the entirety of the visible church – all of its liturgies, sacraments and theological doctrines – to be morally indifferent with regards to salvation' while at the same time holding that "forms of worship were a matter of 'Christian freedom' to be left to the disposition of individuals or groups to the extent they posed no threat to social peace" (Hunter, 2005: 9).

31 Similarly, 'Diderot, Smith and Kierkegaard reject any teleological view of human nature, any view of man as having an essence which defines his true end' (MacIntyre, 1981).

These shifts in the conceptualization of reason have significant implications for our understanding of the contemporary nature and limits of religious freedom jurisprudence. In any legal dispute involving claims not to religious belief *per se*, but to religious *traditions* such as *halakhah* or *sharia* – discursive traditions of religious knowledge, hermeneutics, and practice – what is most at stake in such cases is ineluctably shaped by background assumptions concerning the ontology of the right itself. Does, for example, the meaning of the term 'conscience' differ if considered internally to *halakha* or *sharia*-based traditions of thought and deliberation?[32] Further, if 'religion' is the proper object of the right, how can we speak meaningfully today of entire discursive traditions encompassing their own sources, justifications, and hermeneutics and thus conceptions of religious identity, membership, and practice as being the object of such a right?

If for the scholastics God was the source of normative order and man's rights were conceived internal to that order, following the nominalist revolution either man or nature became the ontological source of secular right and God, now understood as radically free, stood in an entirely new relation to this normative order. This conceptual shift is well illustrated in Locke's empiricist epistemology which led to a conception of civil power as directed to the regulation of things that can be 'objectively known,' whereas religious belief was relegated to the status of 'subjective conviction.'[33]

By the eighteenth century, however, this early modern civil philosophy was gradually superseded by the Kantian philosophy of the Enlightenment. Locke's idea of religion as a subjective belief which is unable to be coerced because located in a private mental space marks the beginning of a new religious psychology and corresponding shift from the privatization of heteronomous religious authority to its normative interiorization and subordination to the rationalist principle of autonomy.

As Talal Asad suggests, it is the idea that the *mind* is the impregnable bastion of true religious experience that provides the modern view with its plausibility (i.e., that coercion of religious belief is irrational because impossible). Given that force can only secure an insincere profession of faith and outward conformity, true authenticity rests on the modern subject's ability to *choose* her beliefs and act on them (Asad, 2009: 44–45). This conception of belief as singular and inaccessible to other locations reinforces the idea of an autonomous 'buffered' subject able to separate itself from objects by contemplation, reasoning, and interpretation and choose from available beliefs.[34]

This intellectual disposition and sensibility prefigures the modern liberal tradition whereby the public sphere is reconceived in terms of a moral theory of justice and religious liberty grounded in a complex and unstable notion of a subjective right to freedom of thought, conscience, and belief. This conception derives most centrally from Kant's transcendental idealism which simultaneously *rationalized* religion and *sacralized* reason in a morally grounded

32 Regarding halakha, see *R (on the application of E) v. The Governing Body of JFS*, [2009] UKSC 15, [2010] 2 A.C. 728 (S.C.), discussed in Danchin and Blond, 2014; regarding sharia, see *Refah Partisi v. Turkey*, App. No. 41340/98, 37 Eur. H.R. Rep. 1 (2003), discussed in Danchin, 2011.

33 For Locke, the neutrality of civil law with respect to religion and the truth of particular religious practices was guaranteed epistemologically by relegating religious belief to the 'realm of speculation.' It was the 'discursive separation from other-worldly concerns' that therefore underpinned the capacity of civil discourse to convert incommensurable expressions of religious 'difference' into a politically indifferent 'diversity' of religious practices (McClure, 1990: 385).

34 Taylor, 2007: 35–95 (discussing the shift from the 'porous' self, vulnerable to external forces, spirits, and demons, to the new Reformed 'buffered' self, a 'disciplined and free agent living in a progressively disenchanted world').

State (see Danchin, 2011: 710–715). Consistent with the ontotheological structure of metaphysics, the former grounds the core ontological claim of modern religious freedom discourse, while the latter justifies the ultimate conceptual parameters of intelligibility in a radically new conception of secular reason.[35]

If in the early modern period God was understood as radically free, now freedom itself was reconceived as the source of normative order (autonomy in the form of the self-legislating moral law) and God became understood as an *idea* or *concept* internal to practical reason itself (pure rational faith).[36] Religion was thus now *subject* to the panoptic demands of morality and the *forum internum* was reconceived from a sphere of noninterference in freely chosen conscience to a sphere of autonomous choice of any belief at all (religious or not).

As William Connolly notes, the idea of a 'self-sufficient public realm fostering freedom and governance without recourse to a specific religious faith' encountered from the start three major dilemmas. First, the equation of religion with belief or conscience clearly derives from a Western Christian genealogy that is at odds with the core tenets of non-Western religious traditions such as Islam in which Muslims regard themselves more as claimed by a religious community they have not chosen and which foreground strongly the role of embodied practices within religious life.[37]

Second, the tendency to elide freedom of conscience with autonomy fatally undermines the normative basis for according freedom of conscience in the first place.[38] And third, the Kantian question of how to secure secular authority in the public sphere remains haunted by the twin charges of abstraction (how any conception of reason can have standing to judge the limits and competence of reason itself) and hypocrisy (the apodictic recognition of morality in virtue of a shared universal rationality being seen instead as merely a 'secondary formation reflecting the predominant Christian culture in which it is set').[39]

35 The modern drive to secure the authority of secular reason in the public sphere has both a visceral and political sense: visceral in reiterating the 'Christian and Kantian demands to occupy the authoritative place of public discourse,' and political in response to the fear that a 'non-Kantian, religiously pluralized world would fall into either disorder or religious tyranny if its participants did not endorse a single standard of rational authority, regardless of the extent to which such a standard can in fact be secured transcendentally' (Connolly, 1999: 38–39).

36 'The commanding subject is God [where] ... this commanding being is not outside man as a substance different from man.' Kant, *Opus Postum*. For Insole, this is a quasi-theological proposition: 'our giving to ourselves the moral law has the mark of divinity, such that, in a sense, we are God-like in this function. We have a sort of theosis, where human beings become transformed in the image of God; but where God disappears into the human being as this happens.' This theosis in fact 'eclipses God, rather than being an increasing participation in God' (Insole, 2013: 170).

37 As scholars such as Saba Mahmood argue, the result is that 'secular epistemologies cannot grasp the way that Islam articulates religious values, misconstruing both the Islamic subject and the public meanings of its religious practices.'

38 See Sandel, 1998: 75–84 (observing that '[t]he respect this neutrality commands is not, strictly speaking, respect for religion, but respect for the self whose religion it is, or respect for the dignity that consists in the capacity to choose one's religion freely,' with the result that '[n]ot all religious beliefs can be redescribed without loss as "the product of free and voluntary choice by the faithful"').

39 In claiming that freedom consists in the acceptance of what reason dictates as duty, Kant made three critical philosophical moves: first, he elevated a generic Christianity ('rational religion') above sectarian faith, anchoring it in a 'metaphysic of the supersensible' that binds moral agents simply in virtue of their rationality; second, in order to secure the authority of moral philosophy over theology, he reduced moral judgment to practical reason alone; and third, while he retained the 'command model of morality of Augustinian Christianity,' Kant shifted the 'proximate point of command from the Christian God to the moral subject itself' (Connolly, 1999: 31–33). See further Danchin, 2011: 683–685.

Conclusion: dialectics of the right

The genius of modern religious freedom discourse is to combine these two metaphysical strands of ontology of the modern subject and theology of secular reason within a single concept of 'right.' Accordingly, the two guiding ideas of modern doctrine are, on the one hand, religious freedom conceived as a universal human right and, on the other, the neutrality of the public sphere toward religion, with each thesis axiomatically defined in terms of the other.

The secular neutrality of the political order is thus said to be secured by the guarantee to protect the universal right to religious liberty. In this move, the disciplinary structure and secular practices of the public sphere combine to *produce* the believing subject and concomitant post-Protestant conceptions of religion (especially in relation to scripture and rituals) and religious subjectivity (especially as regards moral and ethical sensibilities). Conversely, the universality of the right is said to be secured by the neutrality of the public sphere toward religion. This requires the state ceaselessly to recognize or limit claims regarding the manifestation of religious belief and practice which in turn generates the distinctive entanglement of religion and law in different domains of the public and private spheres.

This double structure necessarily generates two interrelated paradoxes. For the reasons discussed above, by defining the secular neutrality of the public sphere in terms of the right to religious freedom, the authority of religion is privatized relative to state authority and its normativity interiorized relative to individual subjectivity. Second, and as a result, religious freedom is secured through subordination of religion to the secular power and public reason of the sovereign state. By defining the meaning and scope of freedom protected by the right in terms of secular neutrality, the claims of individuals and communities to religious liberty are in fact limited through a continuing praxis of legal recognition and regulation.[40]

We see this dialectic at work in the reasoning of Chief Justice Burger in *Bob Jones University*. Nothing permits the government to interfere with or regulate the university's 'religious beliefs,' which remain absolutely protected from state intervention in the private sphere. Consistent with the constitutional right to free exercise, the government will not restrict 'lawful conduct grounded in religious belief.' But where an 'overriding governmental interest' can be shown, the state may justify a limitation on religious liberty, including even 'regulations prohibiting religiously based conduct.'[41]

This oscillating dialectic between the neutrality of secular reason and universality of individual right defines how modern doctrine functions as a technology of secular governance and is integral to the power of the modern nation-state (Danchin, 2017). We see this in three key areas. First, in the foundational distinction between the *forum internum* on the one hand, defined as the locus of religious belief and conscience ostensibly protected absolutely by law, and the *forum externum* on the other, where the outward expression or manifestation of this belief is subject to state regulation and limitation.

Second, in debates concerning the proper subject of the right and whether this can include collective subjects and actually existing systems of religious law adhered to by both majority and

40 For a comprehensive discussion of this legal praxis, see Danchin and Blond, 2014.

41 See supra note 3 and accompanying text.

minority religions.[42] And third, in cases where conflicts of value arise between two or more claims internal to the right to religious liberty itself, where both sides to a dispute frame their arguments as a claim to religious freedom (Danchin, 2008).

Not only will the nature and scope of the *forum internum* be fiercely contested in all such cases, but so too will any restrictions on the manifestation of religion in the *forum externum* under rubrics such as 'public order' (reflecting the early modern 'civil Enlightenment' genealogy of securing social peace between rival religious factions) and the 'rights of others' (reflecting the later philosophical Enlightenment genealogy of Kantian autonomy).

What is increasingly recognized is that this double structure of the right over time generates its opposites. While the *forum internum* is purported to be sovereign and inviolable, it actually authorizes the state's continual intervention in order to determine its meaning and scope.[43] As Hussein Agrama has observed, the separation between private inner belief and public outer act or expression is in fact

> reunited through a suspicion of motives of material interest or worldly power. In the context of the freedom of religious belief, it becomes imperative to determine whether acts or expressions of belief are genuinely religiously motivated. This presumes the power to pronounce upon, and if necessary probe into, the character of one's private convictions.[44]

For this reason, 'secularism's power may lie more in the underlying question it continually provokes and obliges us to answer, than in the normativity of the categories it proposes.'[45]

Similarly, the continuing praxis in public law of recognition or limitation of religious liberty claims of individuals and communities over time privileges the values and commitments of the religious majority as the norm against which the religious practices of the minority are judged and sanctioned in the *forum externum*. The rights discourse and laws of national and international legal systems alike are thus primary sites for the construction and dissemination of particular modular conceptions of religiosity and religious subjectivity.

Importantly, this dissemination occurs not only in non-Western societies whose level of secularity is often questioned, but also those regarded as paradigmatically secular such as the United States and the states of Western Europe. For this reason, the problems of religious intolerance and discrimination cannot be understood solely as a product of cultural and social values, but must address how modern technologies of secular governance and dialectics internal to the right to religious freedom itself contribute to their ongoing vitality in modern societies.[46]

---

42 Note the latent uncertainty in *Bob Jones University* whether a private religious university, as opposed to its individual members or a 'Church', can assert a right in the *forum internum* to religious liberty. The Court states that '[w]e deal here only with religious schools – not with churches or other purely religious institutions; here, the governmental interest is in denying public support to racial discrimination in education.' This indeterminacy regarding the proper subject of the right is a recurring dilemma in Religion Clause cases. See, e.g., *Hosanna-Tabor Evangelical Lutheran Church and School v. Equal Employment Opportunity Commission*, 565 U.S. 171 (recognizing a 'ministerial exception' to antidiscrimination law in relation to religious institutions).

43 Agrama, 2015. In Religion Clause cases, the courts routinely determine whether 'religious acts or expressions are sincerely held to be essential to one's religion,' and whether 'these acts and expressions are authorized and mandated by orthodox religious texts.' Agrama, 2015 (citing Sullivan, 2005).

44 Mahmood, 2016: 3 (arguing that 'political secularism is the modern state's sovereign power to reorganize substantive features of religious life, stipulating what religion is or ought to be, assigning its proper content, and disseminating concomitant subjectivities, ethical frameworks, and quotidian practices').

45 Agrama, 2010: 500.

46 This is the argument in Mahmood and Danchin, 2014: 129 (arguing that the right to religious liberty in practice often legitimates rather than alleviates discriminatory practices of the state against religious minorities and that this paradox haunts the jurisprudence of Egyptian and other courts in postcolonial contexts as much as the European Court of Human Rights).

References

Agrama, H.A., 2010. Secularism, sovereignty, indeterminacy: Is Egypt a secular or religious state? *Comparative Studies in Society and History* 52, 495.

Agrama, H.A., 2015. Religious freedom and the bind of suspicion in contemporary secularity. In: Sullivan W.F., Hurd E.S., Mahmood S., Danchin P. (Eds.), *Politics of Religious Freedom*. The University of Chicago Press, p. 301.

Asad, T., 1986. *The Idea of an Anthropology of Islam*. Occasional Paper Series. Center for Contemporary Arab Studies.

Asad, T., 1993. *Genealogies of Religion: Discipline and Reasons of Power in Christianity and Islam*. Johns Hopkins University Press.

Asad, T., 2009. Free speech, blasphemy, and secular criticism. In: Asad T., Brown W., Butler J., Mahmood S. (Eds.), *Is Critique Secular? Blasphemy, Injury, and Free Speech*. Doreen B. Townsend Center for the Humanities, p. 20

Connolly, W., 1999. *Why I Am Not a Secularist*. University of Minnesota Press.

Connolly, W., 1995. Tocqueville, religiosity, and pluralization. In: *The Ethos of Pluralization*. University of Minnesota Press, p. 163.

Cover, R., 1983. Supreme Court, 1982 term – foreword: nomos and narrative. *Harvard Law Review*. 97, 4.

Danchin, P.G., 2008. Of prophets and proselytes: Freedom of religion and the conflict of rights in international law. *Harvard International Law Journal*. 49, 249.

Danchin, P.G., 2011. Islam in the secular *Nomos* of the European Court of Human Rights. *Michigan Journal of International Law*. 32, 663.

Danchin, P.G., 2017. Religious freedom as a technology of modern secular governance. In: Batnitsky L.F., Dagan H. (Eds.), *Institutionalizing Rights and Religion: Competing Supremacies*. Cambridge University Press, p. 184.

Danchin, P.G., Blond, L., 2014. Unlawful religion? Modern secular power and the legal reasoning in the JFS case. *Maryland Journal of International Law* 29, 414.

de Tocqueville, A., 1969 (1851). *Democracy in America*. Mayer, J.P. (Ed.) (G. Lawrence Trans.). Harper Perennial.

Forst, R., 2014. *Justification and Critique: Towards a Critical Theory of Politics*. Wiley.

Foucault, M., 1984. What is enlightenment? In: Rabinow P. (Ed.), *The Foucault Reader*. Pantheon Books, p. 32.

Gillespie, M.A., 2008. *The Theological Origins of Modernity*. University of Chicago Press.

Haefeli, E., 2013. Toleration and empire: The origins of American religious pluralism. In: Foster S. (Ed.), *British North America in the Seventeenth and Eighteenth Centuries*. Oxford University Press, p. 103.

Heidegger, M. (Ed.), 1939–1946. Metaphysics as history of being. In: *Nietzsche II*, vol. 2, p. 31.

Heidegger, M., 1962. *Being and Time*. (J. Macquarrie and E . Robinson Trans.). Blackwell.

Hunter, I., 2001. *Rival Enlightenments: Civil and Metaphysical Philosophy in Early Modern Germany*. Cambridge University Press.

Hunter, I., 2005. *Religious Offences and Liberal Politics: From the Religious Settlements to Multi-cultural Society*. University of Queensland, Cyberlibrary.

Hunter, I., 2014. Religious freedom in early modern Germany: theology, philosophy, and legal casuistry. *South Atlantic Quart*. 113, 37.

Insole, C.J., 2013. *Kant and the Creation of Freedom: A Theological Problem*. Oxford University Press.

Koskenniemi, M., 1989. *From Apology to Utopia: The Structure of International Legal Argument*. Cambridge University Press.

MacIntrye, A., 1981. Why the enlightenment project had to fail. In: MacIntyre A. (Ed.), *After Virtue: A Study in Moral Theory*. University of Notre Dame Press, p. 51.

Mahmood, S., 2010. Can secularism be other-wise? In: Warner M., Van Antwerpen J., Calhoun C.J. (Eds.), *Varieties of Secularism in a Secular Age*. Harvard University Press, p. 282.

Mahmood, S., 2016. *Religious Difference in a Secular Age: A Minority Report*. Princeton University Press.

Mahmood, S., Danchin, P.G., 2014. Immunity or regulation? Antinomies of religious freedom. *South Atlantic Quarterly*. 113, 129.

McClure, K., 1990. Difference, diversity, and the limits of toleration. *Political Theory*. 18, 361.

Milbank. J., Pickstock, C., Ward, G. (Eds.), 1999. *Radical Orthodoxy: A New Theology*. Routledge.

Sandel, M.J., 1998. Religious liberty: Freedom of choice or freedom of conscience. In: Bhargava R. (Ed.), *Secularism and Its Critics*. Oxford University Press, p. 73.

St. Thomas Aquinas, 2002. In: Baumgarth W.B., Regan R.J. (Eds.), *On Law, Morality and Politics*. (R.J. Regan Trans.). Hackett.

Sullivan, W.F., 2005. *The Impossibility of Religious Freedom*. Princeton University Press.

Taylor, C., 2007. *A Secular Age*. Harvard University Press.

Thomson, I., 2000. Ontotheology? Understanding Heidegger's Destruktion of metaphysics. *International Journal of Philosophical Studies*. 8, 297.

Thomson, I., 2005. *Heidegger on Ontotheology: Technology and the Politics of Education*. Cambridge University Press.

Thomson, T., 2011. Ontotheology. In Dahlstrom, D.O. (Ed.), *Interpreting Heidegger: Critical Essays*. Cambridge University Press, p. 109.

INDEX

For Product Safety Concerns and Information please contact our EU representative GPSR@taylorandfrancis.com
Taylor & Francis Verlag GmbH, Kaufingerstraße 24, 80331 München, Germany

www.ingramcontent.com/pod-product-compliance
Ingram Content Group UK Ltd.
Pitfield, Milton Keynes, MK11 3LW, UK
UKHW050232200926
475702UK00020B/2993
9780367634438